Connecting Social Welfare Policy to Fields of Practice

Connecting Social Welfare Policy to Fields of Practice

Edited by

Ira C. Colby
Catherine N. Dulmus
Karen M. Sowers

JOHN WILEY & SONS, INC.

Cover Photos: (clockwise from top left): © Christopher Futcher/iStockphoto; © Don Bayley/iStockphoto; © The Power of Forever Photography/iStockphoto; © Steve Cole/iStockphoto

Cover Cesign: John Wiley & Sons, Inc.

This book is printed on acid-free paper. ⊗

Published by John Wiley & Sons, Inc., Hoboken, New Jersey.
Published simultaneously in Canada.

Limit of Liability/Disclaimer of Warranty: While the publisher and author have used their best efforts in preparing this book, they make no representations or warranties with respect to the accuracy or completeness of the contents of this book and specifically disclaim any implied warranties of merchantability or fitness for a particular purpose. No warranty may be created or extended by sales representatives or written sales materials. The advice and strategies contained herein may not be suitable for your situation. You should consult with a professional where appropriate. Neither the publisher nor author shall be liable for any loss of profit or any other commercial damages, including but not limited to special, incidental, consequential, or other damages.

This publication is designed to provide accurate and authoritative information in regard to the subject matter covered. It is sold with the understanding that the publisher is not engaged in rendering professional services. If legal, accounting, medical, psychological or any other expert assistance is required, the services of a competent professional person should be sought.

Designations used by companies to distinguish their products are often claimed as trademarks. In all instances where John Wiley & Sons, Inc. is aware of a claim, the product names appear in initial capital or all capital letters. Readers, however, should contact the appropriate companies for more complete information regarding trademarks and registration.

For general information on our other products and services please contact our Customer Care Department within the United States at (800) 762-2974, outside the United States at (317) 572-3993 or fax (317) 572-4002.

Wiley publishes in a variety of print and electronic formats and by print-on-demand. Some material included with standard print versions of this book may not be included in e-books or in print-on-demand. If this book refers to media such as a CD or DVD that is not included in the version you purchased, you may download this material at http://booksupport.wiley.com. For more information about Wiley products, visit www.wiley.com.

Library of Congress Cataloging-in-Publication Data:

Colby, Ira C. (Ira Christopher)
Connecting social welfare policy to fields of practice / Ira C. Colby, Catherine N. Dulmus, Karen M. Sowers.
    p. cm.
  Includes bibliographical references and index.
  ISBN 978-1-118-17700-6 (pbk.)
  ISBN 978-1-118-43384-3 (ebk)
  ISBN 978-1-118-42096-6 (ebk)
  ISBN 978-1-118-41928-1 (ebk)
  1. Public welfare–United States. 2. United States–Social policy. 3. Public health–United States. I. Dulmus, Catherine N. II. Sowers, Karen M. (Karen Marlaine) III. Title.
  HV95.C595 2013
  361.973–dc23
                                                                                    2012027174

Printed in the United States of America

10 9 8 7 6 5 4 3 2 1

Contents

Chapter 6   **Health Care Policy: Should Change Be Small
or Large? 135**
Pamela J. Miller

Chapter 7   **Social Determinants of Health: 21st-Century Social
Work Priorities 159**
Gary Rosenberg

Chapter 8   **Property for People or the Property of People:
Urban Housing Policy and Practice in the
Developing World 175**
Sunil Kumar

Chapter 9   **Child Welfare Policy 209**

Richard J. Gelles and Carol Wilson Spigner

Preface

The provisions or benefits provided through public policies are at times somewhat difficult to understand and reconcile. This is true for liberals and conservatives alike. Conservatives typically note that welfare program benefits are too liberal and encourage dependency; liberal commenters argue that benefits are minimal at best. What is interesting to consider is when two people, looking at the exact same data or pieces of information, are drawn to different conclusions.

An interesting experiment is to take the following "facts" and survey people asking if these cash benefits are too high, just right, or too low.

In 2011:

- The maximum SNAP (Supplemental Nutritional Assistance Program) benefit for a family of three was $526 monthly or approximately $17 per day.

- The maximum SSI (Supplemental Security Insurance) benefit was $674.

- The maximum Social Security Disability payment was $2,366.

- Unemployment benefits differ by state and in Texas, state law limits unemployment benefit payments to less than $415 a week, though due to the economic recession the benefit period was increased from 26 to 93 weeks.

You might also ask if the following program policies are too limiting, appropriate, or too liberal.

In 2012:

- TANF (Temporary Assistance to Needy Families) continues to enforce a lifetime limit of 5 years for benefit eligibility.

- In most jurisdictions, runaway, throwaway, or push-out youth (e.g., homeless youth without an adult caretaker) are not allowed to stay in homeless shelters.

- In most areas, a teenager up to age 16, unless she or he has parental consent, generally is not allowed to engage in mental health counseling.

- It is common practice for "food banks" to limit the number of times an individual or family may seek assistance.

- Adults can post bail or bonds following an arrest; juveniles are not able to post bail or bond.
- In many states, pleading guilty to a crime by reason of insanity is not an option.

You will find diverse opinions from people looking at the same information. Why? The answer is very simple—people's accumulated life experiences, their personal values, and their beliefs lead them to certain conclusions.

The same holds true for elected officials, agency administrators, and individuals who sit on boards of directors in the nonprofit organizations. They create policy to address a specific problem or issue. Their assessment of the issue and how they frame a policy is based on their own experiences, personal values, and beliefs.

Social work practice is framed by these decisions. As employees in a nonprofit or in a governmental agency, practitioners simply cannot do whatever they feel is appropriate in a worker/client, agency-based situation. In effect, policies, generally crafted by others, limit the practitioners's scope of practice and the benefits/services that can be made available to the organization's clients.

The role and importance of policy in social service organizations results in two critical options or choices for social workers. First, the social worker can remain passive and follow the particular policy or policies even if the practitioner believes the policies are questionable at best. Or, second, the social worker proactively engages in *policy practice* to influence a particular policy. This text is organized in a manner that builds on the second option. In addition, it is designed as a social welfare policy practice text book for undergraduate and graduate students in social work programs. The text provides a broad overview of social policy practice in the United States and an introduction to policy practice within a global context. The book addresses policy practice with specific populations (disability, aging, persons with HIV-AIDS) and in specific practice arenas (mental health, child welfare, health care, housing). This book addresses the Council on Social Work Education (CSWE) required competencies for accreditation. Specifically, the book addresses the following required accreditation competencies:

- Educational Policy 2.1.1—Identify as a professional social worker and conduct oneself accordingly (advocate for client access to the services of social work).
- Educational Policy 2.1.4—Engage diversity and difference in practice.
- Educational Policy 2.1.5—Advance human rights and social and economic justice.
- Educational Policy 2.1.8—Engage in policy practice (analyze, formulate, and advocate for policies that advance social well-being; collaborate with colleagues and clients for effective policy action).

- Educational Policy 2.1.9—Respond to contexts that shape practice.
- Educational Policy 2.1.10—Engage, assess, intervene, and evaluate with organizations and communities.

The contributors to this text provide a variety of perspectives on different topics including mental health, persons with disabilities, health, housing, HIV/AIDS, and child welfare. Purposefully, many of the authors introduce their topical areas through global lenses to help us better understand how other nations address common issues. The authors also take clear-cut positions; they do not hide from the reader their own beliefs or perspectives.

Each chapter begins with a brief reflective overview in which the editors share their thoughts and poses general, overarching questions. The editors encourage, actually expect readers to develop their own additional questions. To be honest, the reader's individual questions are much more important and relevant to the individual. Questioning is a sound exercise that facilitates critical thinking by building different scenarios. At the end of each chapter, there is a set of suggested key words, online resources, and additional discussion questions. Again, these are simply tools to encourage you to build on the author's particular thesis: to search through various websites, do your own "data mining," open yourself to diverse opinions, form your own opinions, and propose policy solutions.

We firmly believe that social workers must be directly engaged in policy development. The social work profession can no longer afford those who do not work with individuals, families, groups, and communities to create policies. The time has arrived for the social work profession to support the crafting of just and fair public policies. Then and only then will our communities be able to grow with all people realizing their full potential. Our clients depend on the profession to fully engage in policy practice. To do otherwise will only continue to further marginalize the poor and disenfranchise certain ethnic and racial population groups.

Ira C. Colby
Catherine N. Dulmus
Karen M. Sowers

About the Editors

Ira C. Colby, **DSW**, is dean of the Graduate College of Social Work, University of Houston, in Houston, Texas. Dr. Colby has served on, chaired, or held elective positions in a number of national social work associations, including past president of the Council on Social Work Education, and serves on a number of journal editorial boards. Dr. Colby has served as principal investigator on many research projects, accumulating approximately $8 million in external funding; he has authored more than 60 publications and presented more than 70 papers at national and international forums. He has been recognized with a number of awards, including an Honorary Doctorate of Humanics from Springfield College, his baccalaureate degree institution; induction as a Fellow into the National Academies of Practice; the Distinguished Alumni Award of the Virginia Commonwealth University, and awarded Honorary Professorship, East China Technological University, Shanghai.

    Catherine N. Dulmus, **PhD**, **LCSW**, is associate professor, associate dean for research, and director of the Buffalo Center for Social Research at the University at Buffalo and research director at Hillside Family of Agencies in Rochester, New York. She received her baccalaureate degree in Social Work from Buffalo State College in 1989, a master's degree in Social Work from the University at Buffalo in 1991, and a doctoral degree in Social Welfare from the University at Buffalo in 1999. As a researcher with interests that include community-based research, child and adolescent mental health, evidence-based practice, and university–community partnerships, Dr. Dulmus has focused on fostering interdependent collaborations among practitioners, researchers, schools, and agencies critical in the advancement and dissemination of new and meaningful knowledge. She has authored or co-authored several journal articles and books and has presented her research nationally and internationally. Prior to obtaining her PhD, she acquired almost a decade of experience in the fields of mental health and school social work.

    Karen M. Sowers, **PhD**, is professor and dean of the College of Social Work at the University of Tennessee, Knoxville. She is the University of Tennessee Beaman Professor for Outstanding Research and Service. Dr. Sowers received her baccalaureate degree in Sociology from the University of Central Florida, and her master's degree and PhD degree in social work from

Florida State University. Dr. Sowers serves on several local, national, and international boards. Dr. Sowers is nationally known for her research and scholarship in the areas of international practice; juvenile justice; child welfare; cultural diversity; and culturally effective intervention strategies for social work practice, evidence-based social work practice, and social work education.

Contributors

Christopher W. Blackwell, PhD, ARNP-C
College of Nursing
University of Central Florida
Orlando, Florida

Enid Opal Cox, DSW
Graduate School of Social Work
University of Denver
Denver, Colorado

King Davis, PhD
School of Social Work
University of Texas—Austin
Austin, Texas

Elizabeth DePoy, MSW, PhD
Center for Community Inclusion
and Disability Studies
University of Maine
Orono, Maine

Sophia F. Dziegielewski, PhD, LISW
School of Social Work
University of Central Florida
Orlando, Florida

Rodney A. Ellis, PhD, CMSW
College of Social Work
University of Tennessee—Nashville
Nashville, Tennessee

Richard J. Gelles, PhD
Pennsylvania School of Social Policy
and Practice
University of Pennsylvania
Philadelphia, Pennsylvania

Stephen French Gilson, MSW, PhD
School of Social Work
University of Maine
Orono, Maine

Richard Hoefer, PhD
School of Social Work
University of Texas—Austin
Austin, Texas

Hyejin Jung, MSW
School of Social Work
University of Texas—Austin
Austin, Texas

Howard Karger, PhD
School of Social Work and
Applied Human Sciences
University of Queensland
Brisbane, Australia

Peter A. Kindle, MSW
School of Health Sciences: Social Work,
Health Affairs
University of South Dakota
Vermillion, South Dakota

Sunil Kumar, PhD
Department of Social Policy
London School of Economics and
Political Science
London, United Kingdom

Pamela J. Miller, MSW, PhD
School of Social Work
Portland State University
Portland, Oregon

Gary Rosenberg, PhD
Department of Community and
Preventative Medicine
Mount Sinai School of Medicine
New York, New York

Carol Wilson Spigner, PhD
Pennsylvania School of Social Policy and Practice
University of Pennsylvania
Philadelphia, Pennsylvania

Chapter 1
Policy Practice

Rodney A. Ellis

> How should the social work profession proceed in the political arena? Is there a way for individual social workers to engage in policy practice without condemning those with whom we might disagree? How might the profession counter the trend of social workers not running for political office?

Introduction

Policy practice is an interesting practice construct, certainly different from the more traditional micro–macro practice spheres. In this chapter policy practice is viewed as an important practice area and one that fits nicely with the social work profession. *In an ideal world policies would solve the problems they were intended to address . . . social workers are, by the nature of their profession and position, inherently involved in social policy.* Yet social workers, for the most part, tend to stay away from the policy arena. For example, in the current 112th Congress, there is a total of 435 members of the House of Representatives. These individuals report a variety of professions: 170 are lawyers, 78 are educators, 175 are in business, 15 are physicians, 5 are ordained ministers, and 4 are peace corps volunteers, plus there are 7 accountants, 6 engineers, 15 farmers, 9 ranchers, and 7 social workers (Manning, 2011). According to the National Association of Social Workers (NASW), in 2008, the last year NASW collected such data, approximately 165 individuals held elected offices at the local or state levels of government across the United States. What we can conclude is that social workers simply are not holding elective offices.

Yes, social workers are employed in key staff positions in elected officials' offices; for example, the long-term legislative director for U.S. Congressperson Luis Gutierrez (D-IL) is a social worker. Even so, social workers holding staff positions in federal, state, or local offices are not prominent. Social workers also are not commonplace in governmental relations offices, for example, lobbying firms.

What makes this confusing is that social workers, as evidenced by discussions at various state and national meetings as well as on LISTSERVs, seem to be engaged in constant "political" discussions. But for whatever reason, the discussions do not lead to the risks involved in pursuing a political career or direct engagement in political processes.

Without a doubt, social workers bring a unique, human perspective to policy discussions. Day in and day out, social workers work with people, groups, and communities around a variety of human issues in a way that is unique from other disciplines. The "practice wisdom" gleaned from such work allows social workers to put a human face on policy initiatives. We have seen the results of policies developed by and enacted by lawyers, farmers, and businesspeople. Little has changed as social issues remain fully embedded in our national human fabric. One can only wonder what would happen if there were 170 social workers in the U.S. House of Representatives rather than lawyers.

There are a variety of ways for social workers to engage in policy practice in ways other than holding an elective office. We all must understand—policy practice is not easy; it is slow, tedious, and certainly frustrating. Yet, to turn our professional collective backs on the political nature of our work is ignoring that which we know.

We also need to recognize that the social work political tent is big—social workers reflect a variety of political parties and philosophies including Democrat, Republican, Tea Party, Libertarian, Green, liberal, conservative, and radical. For every social issue you identify, social workers hold a variety of positions, often in conflict with each other. In other words, the social work profession does not nor should reflect one political ideology.

There is nothing wrong if a social worker subscribes to one particular ideology; the issue is when this same person, who believes in self-determination and individualism, penalizes others, be they students or colleagues, because they may hold a different political philosophy or argue from a different perspective. Personal ideological insecurity simply will not realize a just society.

Policy Practice

Benjamin is a BSSW-level social worker who is employed as a case manager in a mental health treatment facility. He loves his work and has an excellent record of effective practice with his clients. He is concerned, however, with one aspect of his agency's operation. He has noticed that many clients have recently discontinued their treatment despite substantial improvement in their reported issues. Curious as to why this might be occurring, Benjamin made a few phone calls to clients who had recently dropped out of treatment. He was astounded to discover that four of the five people he called had stopped attending sessions because their state-provided supplemental income benefits had been cut. These former clients reported a simple choice: They could either not pay their rent or stop attending treatment sessions. They had taken care of immediate necessities rather than their important, but less urgent, mental health needs.

Benjamin is disturbed that so many were leaving treatment, but he is even more disturbed that it was unnecessary that most of them do so. His agency had funding alternatives that would have allowed all the persons he called to remain in treatment. They had not taken advantage of those alternatives simply because they had not been aware of them. The agency had no means of assuring that the information was made available to them. Having discovered this problem, Benjamin resolves to find a way to solve it. Further, he wishes to institutionalize the solution, so that it is certain to remain in place into the foreseeable future.

Alma is the executive director of the same agency at which Benjamin is a case manager. She is unaware that her agency's clients are withdrawing from services because of the income cutbacks. She is aware, however, that the cutbacks are occurring. Alma is a part of a local coalition of social service providers that is concerned about the conditions area residents have begun to face as a result of the cuts. A community needs assessment conducted after the changes revealed that the number of persons becoming homeless had increased, the rate of the referral of children into the child welfare system had nearly doubled, and community health experts were predicting a surge in emergency room treatment and hospitalizations. Further investigation showed that all these conditions could be traced, at least in part, to the loss of income many families had experienced. Several other effects have been reported in the community including increased demand at food banks and a rising crime rate. No formal research has been conducted that could identify a link between these conditions and the cuts. There is, however, strong evidence from reports of residents that such a link exists. Further evidence is provided by the fact that these changes occurred in the wake of the cuts and have a logical relationship to them.

The coalition of agencies has been formed to study and to address the problem. Its mission is to develop and implement a plan to get the cuts reversed, and to assure a steady supply of supplemental income to the residents of its community and state. So far the coalition has met twice, collected available data about the cuts and their effects, and drafted a mission statement to guide future activities. The statement is short, simple, and to the point: "The mission of the Supplemental Income Reinstatement Coalition is to restore the level of each program recipient's supplemental income to pre-cut levels."

Both Benjamin and Alma face issues created by current social welfare policy. The problems have a common cause, the supplemental income cuts, but the manifestations of the issue and the levels at which they hope to address the issue are very different. Benjamin faces a problem at the agency level. It is a policy issue, more specifically, one caused by the absence of any effective policy to assure that an undesirable condition does not arise. He will probably find it relatively easy to identify a solution, gain access to decision makers, and persuade those decision makers to take steps to address the problem. Alma, on the other hand, faces a problem generated at a higher level, and that affects many people in a variety of ways. Although ultimately the cause of the problems they want to address is the same, the scope and goals of their efforts will differ in significant ways.

Benjamin and Alma have chosen to engage in an important social work activity: policy practice. Janssen (1999) defined policy practice as "efforts to change policies in legislative, agency, and community settings, whether by establishing new policies, improving existing ones, or defeating the policy initiatives of other people." Many social workers express little interest in policy, but their careers are intrinsically involved with social welfare policy. In fact, policy furnishes their careers. Problems are recognized by policy makers, policies written, social programs developed, and jobs created. Many are filled by social workers.

In an ideal world policies would solve the problems they were intended to address. In reality this is sometimes not the case. Take, for example, Benjamin's discovery. Policies related to mental health treatment are working well. Policies to provide alternative funding for services also exist. There is, however, a problem in agency policy. No policy has been written to assure that clients are aware of the financial supports. In this case, policies such as those providing for mental health treatment fail because of the absence of other supportive policy.

Alma's group is hoping to address policy failure at a higher and broader level. The group has only recently begun to study the issue, but it appears that this body of policy worked well at one point. Changes in the social climate or political landscape have reduced its effectiveness.

The absence of policy and changes in the social or political situation are two of the many conditions that can cause or contribute to policy failure. Among the many others are poorly conceived policies, policies that fail to consider unintended consequences, policies that fail to consider the potential for disruption at other levels, and policies that are well-conceived but are not ultimately fundable (Ellis, 2003; Janssen, 1999). Furthermore, some older social problems, such as poverty, have never been adequately addressed on a national scale, much less globally. Despite the ongoing problems faced by U.S. citizens, those problems often pale when compared to those of persons in other countries. New social problems also arise, prompted by events both national and international. The tragic events of 9/11 point to a clear need for new and innovative policies not only to prevent future terrorist tragedies, but also to provide support and assistance to their victims should the preventive policies fail. Issues related to migration and immigration, refugeeism, and human rights also cry out for solutions crafted by the hands of social workers. The new responses must be "out-of-the box" in that they must look at problems globally rather than regionally or nationally. In the modern world little happens in a national vacuum. Events in other countries and processes that cross international borders cause and exacerbate conditions within our own country. These increased pressures underscore the need for innovative solutions such as international exchange of ideas, information, and problem-solving experts. Technological developments offer methods of communication, information transfer, and exchange of ideas that might otherwise be prohibitively costly or simply impossible. Social workers are among those at the table in some of the groups planning policy-directed interventions for these international issues. More social workers and more groups are needed as global change accelerates.

It is clear from this introductory discussion that social workers are, by the nature of their profession and position, inherently involved in social policy. In addition, they may engage in policy practice at many levels, from working to add a few lines to a "Policy and Procedures Manual" to altering the laws that guide how nations interact. It is also important to recognize the unique contribution that social workers often make to policy planning. First, social workers are often in a position to be among the first to recognize social problems. Those whose lives are directly affected by the problems are typically the first to recognize their presence. However, because of the direct communication with client groups social workers such as Benjamin have with persons in the community, these direct service workers may often become aware of problems before any other group. A second reason a social work presence is important to the planning process is that it provides the opportunity to influence problem definition. Problem definition refers to the way in which policy makers interpret and explain a problem. Interpretation and explanation, in turn, influence the way a solution is formed. Consider, for example, problems experienced by persons in poverty. If, as many conservatives believe, it is possible for the impoverished to simply "pull themselves up by their boot straps," policies should be written that provide for the most cursory of interventions. The vast majority of the responsibility for change would lie with poor people and their allegorical boot straps. Social workers recognize that although a portion of the responsibility for change lies in the individual, impoverished persons face a daunting gauntlet of barriers to change. They also know how to craft and implement solutions to many of those barriers. It seems unlikely that solutions to poverty on any scale, individual or global, are likely to occur without social work participation.

Yet another important reason for social workers to engage in policy practice is the clearly defined set of ethics and values they bring to the table. Policy-related discussions often bog down because the values of the participants are not clearly expressed. This is often seen when discussions degenerate to a point that one or both sides has stalled with no more logical arguments, simply saying something like, "We must do it this way." What has often happened is that all effective arguments have been offered and countered, leaving participants with nothing more than their values as an argument. They may be unable to articulate those values because they have never sufficiently defined them. It may also be that they recognize that to speak their values clearly would actually undermine their argument by revealing less than humanitarian assumptions or motives. By clearly defining their values, social workers can verbalize much of the core motivation for their argument. Social workers also, thereby, earn the right to ask opponents to verbalize theirs. The importance of the presence of a representative of such clear values and ethics in policy-related discussion is clear. Often, its only potential source is a social worker.

It's clear that effective policy practice is important to social workers, their clients, the profession, the nation, and the world. It is also clear that any social worker may be called to engage in policy practice at any time. This chapter is about effective policy practice. Although it was written primarily with practice within the United States in mind, much of it is applicable to international practice. The chapter discusses preparation for policy practice, problem identification and definition, assembling a policy practice team, selecting an approach, conducting an analysis, developing an action plan, and evaluating the outcomes of the activities. It is intended to provide a general understanding of the processes, techniques, and strategies of policy practice, and to provide resources for gaining additional information and skill.

Preparation of the Practitioner

The process of preparing for policy practice might be conceived as a series of stages. The first involves the acquisition of a specific set of knowledge and skills needed to interact, assess, plan interventions, and evaluate within the policy arena. Practitioners who have reached this point in their training are able to perform all the basic functions necessary to engage in policy practice, and know how to acquire advanced knowledge, skills, and resources. Accredited BSSW and MSSW programs are designed to provide the basic knowledge and skills so that any graduates, however inadequate they may feel, have been taught the foundation of what they need to know. The Council on Social Work Education refers to this foundational set of knowledge and skills as "generalist" because it allows the practitioner to work across multiple settings.

Generalist knowledge refers to the theory and technique of successful professional intervention with clients and client systems. These theories and techniques are applied by practitioners as they interact with individuals, families, and groups. They include such activities as assessment, intervention planning, implementation of the selected intervention, and evaluation of the intervention's effectiveness. The theories and techniques utilize and are guided by scientifically supported principles of human behavior, including insight from social work researchers as well and from multiple disciplines, such as psychology, sociology, medicine, political science, and public administration. Interventions are also structured and guided in accordance with social work ethics, values, and emphasis on cultural competence.

Generalist knowledge and skills can be applied across a variety of professional settings. For example, social workers in a clinical setting would use assessment skills, such as active listening, identification of client strengths, and identifying and understanding client relationships. Their assessment might require knowledge of the theories of human development, psychopathology, and human motivation.

Although at first glance social workers' efforts to change the way a law is written through interactions with a state legislature might seem very different from the work of clinicians, their tasks are, on closer examination, quite similar. For instance, a social worker engaging in policy practice might use the same skills. Assessment skills such as active listening would be used as the practitioner interviewed various experts about current policy and its effects. Strengths-based assessment would be used in discussions with the population policy was being designed to benefit. Skills for analyzing interpersonal relationships would be used when assessing the relationships between stakeholders likely to support or oppose an initiative.

Policy practitioners equipped to practice at the generalist level would be able to facilitate policy change such as the one intended by Benjamin earlier with minimal support from others. A presentation of their findings to the executive committee of the agency might be all that would be required. On the other hand, a practitioner trying to produce changes in federal legislation might need to assemble a workgroup composed of persons with specialized knowledge and relationships to deal with the intricacies of practice at that level. For example, the practitioner might want to recruit a group member with knowledge and experience in utilizing a specific form of policy analysis to help lead the process. Still, the principle that generalist skills are a sufficient foundation for policy practice holds, even at the federal level. Generalist skills would be used to identify, recruit, retain, and encourage the required participation by group members.

The second stage of preparation for effective policy practice involves the development of advanced policy knowledge and skills. These are not typically available in BSSW programs (although some might be gained through unique internship experiences). They are, however, included in CSWE-accredited MSSW programs. They may also be obtained by dedicated practitioners who participate in a lifetime learning process through seminars, readings, and interaction with more experienced professionals after they have received their degrees. Further, many of these skills can be developed while the practitioner is working. For example even if Alma from the case study earlier did not have a strong working knowledge of a model of policy analysis, she could obtain books like those by DiNitto and Cummins (2006) or Ellis (2003) and follow the procedures outlined therein. Advanced policy practice includes such components as mastery of at least one model of policy analysis, the ability to develop and implement a strategic plan to change policy, and a thorough knowledge of at least one major policy area.

The third stage of preparation includes knowledge of the people, issues, history, barriers, and political environment that exist within a specific policy arena. Considering Alma once again, despite having the basic knowledge and skills required for successful policy practice and having armed herself with the materials necessary to conduct an effective analysis, she may know little about the specifics of the persons, policies, and situations that have led to the supplemental income cuts. She can develop this knowledge as she proceeds with her analysis, but would do well to bring others into the coalition who already have this knowledge to help educate coalition members about the situations they will be facing.

Some practitioners may choose to advance to the fourth stage of preparation for policy practice. In the fourth stage practitioners become adept at advanced forms of evaluation, analysis, and assessment such as cost-benefit analysis and forecasting (Ellis, 2003). Many of these tasks can be completed by specialists recruited to a team of practitioners. When funds are available external experts can be hired to perform these analyses. For example, if Alma wanted to include a retrospective evaluation of the effectiveness of the income supplement cuts in her analysis she would have several alternatives. First, she might draw on her BSSW training supplemented by books on outcome evaluation. Alternatively, she might ask a professor trained in outcome evaluation to join her team. If no one was willing to do the work on a pro bono basis, she might determine whether funds might be available to hire an expert to do the evaluation.

It is important to note that, although these four stages represent four distinct areas of competence, the lines between them are blurred. Practitioners do not necessarily obtain full proficiency at one level before progressing to the next. For example, a person with BSSW-level training might have lived and worked in a community for many years and might have obtained many of the proficiencies of level three, but might lack the formal training and resources available at level two. This practitioner might hastily seek education in these areas, or might recruit team members who could bring that level of knowledge and skill to the table. The process of building a policy practice team follows.

Assembling a Team

In a situation like that of Benjamin no team may be necessary. He may be able to assemble the necessary data and undertake the required activities without any support from anyone else. Alma, however, is clearly in a position where the support of others would be beneficial, perhaps essential.

Team members should be recruited strategically. They may bring one of three essential components to the table. These components, the same as those required for any successful task group, are influence, competence, and motivation (Ellis, Crane, Gould, & Shatila, 2006).

Influence refers to the ability to directly affect the persons and forces involved in a change. In policy practice this may mean the capacity to access important stakeholders or to influence their opinions. It might also refer to someone who has resources, such as funding or personnel, to support the effort. A policy practice workgroup may be highly skilled and very motivated, but without adequate power and resources it is unlikely to succeed.

Policy practice work groups must also contain members with competence. Competent members are those who have the essential knowledge and skills to perform the tasks required for policy analysis and planning. Persons with competence bring such abilities as team-building skills, research skills, policy analysis skills, and action planning skills, as well as the ability to write and make public presentations effectively. In policy practice that crosses cultural or international borders, team members who understand those cultures and countries will be needed.

Motivation is also critical to a policy practice work group's success. Persons with motivation bring a strong desire for change to the group. Persons with influence and competence may be very motivated, but often motivation comes from those who do not have an official role in the process. Highly motivated people might, for example, be found among the persons who are directly experiencing the policy problem.

Policy practitioners must assess their work groups to determine the degree to which these three components exist and the ways in which they can be mobilized. When components are deficient or absent, new members should be recruited who can bring them to the table. This process of assessment and recruitment should be ongoing to assure that changes in group composition or in the policy environment do not negatively impact the group's effectiveness.

Identification, Definition, and Legitimization of the Problem

Policy practice may be viewed as a series of stages. Each stage includes the gathering of information about some aspect of the policy being considered for change. Although the latter stages may build on information gathered in earlier stages, the progression need not always be an orderly progression from one step to the next. The first and foundational stage, however, involves the identification, definition, and legitimization of the problem. It is important that most of the work on this stage be completed before a great deal of effort is expended on the other stages. Identification, definition, and legitimization assure that the problem is effectively recognized, carefully articulated, and appropriately acknowledged by persons with the power to make changes.

Identification refers to recognizing the presence of a problem. At this point the practitioner may not understand much about the problem, but does recognize that people are affected by it. Benjamin reached the identification stage when he noticed an inordinate number of people who were not returning to receive services. Alma and her coalition have identified the problem of inadequate income and believe it to be the result of the income supplement cutbacks. They may, however, need some additional research to firmly establish that the cutbacks are the source of the problem.

When policy practitioners define a problem, they put it in writing. Although there is some disagreement between experts as to the exact content of the definition, four themes are commonly recognized. These themes are population, problem, perspectives, and policy (Ellis, 2003). A comprehensive problem statement, then, describes what population is affected; what its members lack and what prevents them from obtaining it (the problem); the perspectives of those who experience the problem; and the policy that addresses, causes, or should address the problem.

Legitimization occurs when some authoritative policy-making body officially says that it exists. Although thousands might become homeless and foster care numbers might skyrocket, for the purposes of policy no problem exists until persons in power acknowledge it. So, in the case of Alma, if policy makers in her state have not recognized that the problem of inadequate income is impacting persons in their communities to the degree that it is, her work group must focus on bringing it to the attention of the legislators. Armed with a well-researched, well-articulated problem statement, they can also enhance the probability that the decision makers will perceive and define the problem as they do.

It is also important to understand the degree to which policy at each level of government influences the problem. Some problems are primarily addressed at a single level. For example, Social Security provides the primary body of policy for disability insurance. Other problems, such as child abuse, neglect, and abandonment, are addressed at multiple levels: federal, state, local, and agency. In some areas of policy court decisions have also influenced the interpretation of policy, meaning that case law must also be considered to completely understand an area of policy. Practitioners must be certain they have collected and understand policy at every level to adequately formulate their definition. For example, although Alma's group appears to be dealing with a problem that has been primarily created at the state level, income maintenance policy also exists at the federal level and in some areas may be influenced locally as well. The group would need to know what responsibilities lie at which level and how the policy provisions interact between them.

Practitioners working in countries other than or in addition to the United States may find a political landscape that differs from the one described here. Levels of government that exist in the United States might not exist in many countries, for example. In other situations they might exist, but the distribution of responsibilities and power may vary. Where the structure of the government differs, practitioners should clearly identify the levels of government, assign them names, and list the responsibilities of each level in the specific area of policy being addressed. Strategies discussed in this book and in other resources can be adapted accordingly.

An additional important function of the problem statement is that it helps the group members determine whether they are all in agreement as to the nature of the problem. The problem statement will form the basis of all the rest of the work the group does. It guides the way the problem is perceived, the area of policy selected for study, and the kinds of solutions that will be proposed. Obtaining agreement between the work group members is also important to assure that they remain united during the action phase of the initiative. Unity is critical to success, and constant, effective communication and shared understanding promote unity within the team.

Although a policy definition is drafted very early in the analysis process, it should be reviewed periodically to assure that information gained during research has not changed the group's understanding. When they discover that their understanding has changed, they should adjust their definition accordingly.

Selecting an Approach

There are several approaches (often referred to as *models*) for conducting a policy analysis. Basically, the term *approach* or *model* refers to a method of collecting information about specific aspects of a body of policy. Those who analyze policy, meaning that they critically examine the aspects of the body of policy associated with their identified problem, are engaging in policy practice.

Dobelstein (1996) identified three general categories of policy analysis: *behavioral, incremental,* and *criteria-based.* Most forms of analysis fall into one of these three categories. Each has its own set of strengths and limitations, and each is, therefore, best used in different settings. Behavioral models use scientific methods and statistical analyses to identify and choose from among a group of alternatives. Incremental models identify several potential solutions, then piece portions of those solutions together to produce feasible alternatives. The final choice is made by weighing each alternative against the values of the public. This helps to determine both how useful and how acceptable each solution might be.

Approaches that are criteria-based share some of the characteristics of the behavioral and incremental models. As in the incremental model, several alternative solutions are identified as the initial steps. The solutions are then evaluated and ranked in the order of their level of acceptability to the public. Finally, the alternatives are evaluated using research methods common to behavioral models. The goal is to determine the cost, benefits, and feasibility of each alternative. A solution is then selected based on the values ranking and the research.

It is important to remember that one type of analysis may be more appropriate for one set of circumstances than for another. For example, behavioral methods are probably best suited for environments in which research reports are either already present or readily funded, and where public norms and values are unlikely to have a strong impact on a decision. Incremental methods may be best for situations in which significant compromises between competing proposals can be anticipated and public values are expected to play a major role. Criteria-based approaches are likely to be more effective when a comprehensive approach is needed to address multiple aspects of the policy environment. For example, Benjamin can probably anticipate that the values of the persons operating his agency are similar to his own and that he will not face much opposition to his initiative. A behavioral approach in which he collects and analyzes a little more data and presents his findings to the executive board will probably be adequate for his situation. Alma's group, however, is likely to need a more comprehensive approach. The group members will need to collect relevant research and supplement it with some work of their own. Research alone is likely to be inadequate, however, because of the powerful and contradictory values that affect income maintenance policy (Elwood, 1989). In this case a criteria-based method may be desirable.

Regardless of which type of analysis is selected, there are certain categories of information that must be collected and considered. These categories include: (a) information about the history and current status of the problem and the policy that has been developed to address it, (b) identification of the norms and values of the voting public, (c) recognition of the political alliances that will support or oppose the proposal, (d) review of the current system of agencies that compose the service delivery system, (e) generation of a series of alternative solutions, (f) collection or production of appropriate professional analyses, and (g) examination of potential unintended consequences. Based on the analysis of some combination of these categories of information, a decision is made as to which alternative to recommend (Ellis, 2003).

Each of the three general types of policy analysis selects from among these categories of information, using some and ignoring or minimizing others. For example, a purely behavioral approach might not require information about the norms and values of the public or about political alliances. Yet an incremental approach might consider this information vital. Each of the categories of analysis includes specific models, often named for the person who designed them. It is from these models that policy practitioners choose when they plan an analysis. Proficiency in one of them was identified as a part of the second level of preparation for policy practice identified earlier in this chapter.

Some models also include action planning for change (Ellis, 2003). Others do not include this phase. This omission reflects the diversity of roles assumed by policy practitioners in various policy initiatives. At times the practitioner might be asked to perform an analysis only, with the person or organization commissioning the analysis making the decisions as to how to proceed. At other times the practitioner and his or her team might include action plan development and implementation as a part of their analysis.

Conducting an Analysis

After a model has been selected, the practitioner or team must implement the analysis. In a team this can be accomplished by matching tasks to each member's area of proficiency. In Alma's group, for example, she may have recruited BSSWs or MSSWs who are particularly good at Internet and library research. These members might be selected for tasks such as identifying and obtaining current policies at every level. High-level agency executives with many years working in the community might be asked to identify potential friends and foes of the proposal. A university professor might be asked to develop a plan for further study.

It is important that the individual tasks and responsibilities of each step of an analysis be identified, committed to writing, and assigned to team members with specific due dates and methods of reporting the results. In the section earlier several categories of information that are used in policy analysis were identified. Practitioners must not only know what those categories are, but must know and be able to use strategies for obtaining accurate data from each.

Information About the History and Current Status of the Problem and Policy

One effective strategy for accumulating information about the history and status of a policy is online resources. In the United States and many other countries there are websites at federal, state (or territorial), and local levels from which information can be obtained. In Mexico, for example, practitioners might start at http://www.presidencia.gob.mx/ At the federal level in the United States, for example, there are sites for each branch of the federal government. A good starting point for locating these is http://www.whitehouse.gov/ Links from that site lead to the website for the executive, legislative, and judicial branches. There are also sites for obtaining the actual policy documents, such as that of the Office of the Law Revision Counsel (OLRC) (http://uscode.house.gov/search/criteria.shtml) and *THOMAS, Legislative Information* (http://thomas.loc.gov/).

State and local governments also often have websites that can be good sources for both policy and history. Most can be readily identified by using an Internet search engine with descriptor words such as the state's name and "government" or "state government." At all levels it is important to remember that policy documents may also exist within the executive branches of the respective governments. For instance, at the federal level presidential directives, executive orders, and administrative codes all contain policy.

Library research can provide useful information as well as hard copies of many policy documents. Recent documents and draft legislation may be difficult to obtain there because of the delay involved in getting the documents published and catalogued into government documents sections of local libraries. Still, for locating less recent documents and compiling information about the history of a policy area, U.S. public library government documents areas can be helpful. The availability of such library information varies between countries yet can be invaluable when it is accessed.

In many countries, including the United States, a great deal of information can be obtained from personal contact with government employees such as legislators, bureaucrats, and administrative staff. Such sources are often aware not only of the history of a policy area, but also of current trends and initiatives. Although higher-level elected officials may be difficult to access, members of their staff are often interested in providing information to those who ask. Their motivation may be varied. Some may hope that their friendly assistance will garner votes. Other may anticipate learning more about your initiative. Still others may simply wish to be helpful. Regardless of motivation, many will be willing to talk.

Other good Internet resources include the websites of special interest groups, news organizations, and other organizations that analyze or comment on social policy. Even radical or oppositional sites can be important sources of information. These sites often offer perspectives not readily available in more traditional sites and may emphasize elements neglected by those in current positions of power.

Another good source of information is textbooks and similar resources used for training in the chosen policy area. Many such documents review the history of policy and offer insight into the forces that have shaped it. Although the information may not be in depth, the texts may offer references that provide more comprehensive materials.

Identification of the Norms and Values of the Voting Public

The importance of the role of norms and values in policy making was described in earlier sections of this chapter. Proposals that run contrary to the predominant values of the voting public, or that cannot be made to appear consistent with those values, are likely to fail. Practitioners, then, must understand the values of the stakeholders (including the voting public), must be able to articulate those values, and must have the skills to be able to explain their proposals in a way that persons with a variety of values will find attractive.

There are many sources from which stakeholder values can be identified. News reports, for example, often contain statements of the motivations of legislators, the comments of other public figures, and a few reactions from members of the general public. Although media sources often have significant limitations they can provide insight into the norms and values of many different stakeholders and stakeholder groups.

Published books and articles (other than publications from media sources) are another useful resource for identifying values. In some policy areas relevant values have been carefully and accurately documented. For example, in *Poor Support: Poverty in the American Family,* Elwood (1989) identified a group of opposing values that underlie income maintenance policy in the United States. Recognizing those values is critical to understanding the historical development of policy in this area and to planning successful initiatives. Popular books, textbooks, academic journals, and popular periodicals can also help practitioners identify and articulate norms and values.

One simple way of determining the values of an individual or group is to ask them. Although some may try to mask oppositional positions with acceptable terminology, asking for a statement of position from an influential person or political group will usually provide useful information.

The statement can also be compared to the past voting records, service records, or political activities of the individual or group in question should further clarification be desired.

The values of larger groups can often be identified through focus groups or surveys. Focus groups would include experts who are likely to know the positions of experts and members of the general population. Surveys might be sent directly to citizens, and their results tabulated and summarized for the policy practice workgroup.

However information about norms and values is collected, it is important that practitioners be thorough in gathering perspectives. Thoroughness may be a particular challenge when dealing with international issues because of the diversity of groups and complexity of perspectives that may be involved. For example, a practitioner working on policy changes to benefit Kurdish immigrants to the United States might be tempted to assume that a survey within a single federal relocation area would provide a representative sampling of norms and values. However, a quick Internet search would identify 10 or more political groups currently operating within Kurdistan. Many of these groups hold very different ideals. Practitioners who wished to understand the norms and values of the Kurdish people would need to have information about all these groups, information that might or might not be available in a single relocation area.

Recognition of the Political Alliances That Will Support or Oppose the Proposal

When analyzing policy it is critical to learn what individuals and groups are likely to support or oppose a proposal. A part of understanding this political landscape is knowing about the current political parties, identifying the existing political alliances, and becoming aware of any special groups that may be interested in the initiative's outcome.

Political parties are organized groups of people who share similar values and political ideals. They unite to select candidates who then compete with persons from other political parties for offices or positions within the government. In the United States there are two primary political parties: Democrats and Republicans. Historically, Republicans have held conservative values and Democrats have held liberal values, although in recent years the differences between the two have become far less pronounced. Other parties have come and gone, and some that currently exist don't always enter a candidate in elections. The U.S. system remains predominately a two-party system.

Other countries may have only one political party, or may have a great variety of parties emphasizing an assortment of values. Regardless of the number and philosophical position of the parties, it is important to know what groups believe as well as what position they are likely to take on the proposed initiative.

The political landscape is often also filled with political alliances. These alliances may range from formal, collaborative enterprises with clear, written agreements, to informal arrangements made verbally between individuals and small groups. They may occur on either side of an issue or between political opponents. Alliances may be related to party loyalty or may have grown from an assortment of personal situations. Regardless of their nature and source, political alliances can be powerful influences in the political arena. In addition, they seem to exist in virtually every culture. Practitioners must identify them, must understand the basis for the alliances, and must plan strategies to deal with them effectively.

Review of the Current System of Agencies That Compose the Service Delivery System

Effective policy practice requires understanding the way in which the intent of a policy or body of policy is operationalized and implemented. Most often this begins with a policy-making body (such as a legislature) and extends through government agencies that either fund, provide guidance and support for, or implement (or some combination of these three) to other agencies, often private, that actually deliver the services. In the United States these other agencies are typically either not-for-profit or for-profit. In other countries they might be for-profit or nongovernmental organizations (NGOs).

When past attempts have been made to address a social problem yet the problem still exists, it is possible that something within the delivery system is either creating or contributing to the problem. In the example of Benjamin, the problem of inadequate income is not created within his agency, nor is the problem of inadequate service provision. But the failure of the agency to make its clients aware of funding alternatives does contribute to inadequate service provision.

Understanding the policy-making system allows the practitioner to determine the level at which a problem should be addressed. For example, although income maintenance policy is primarily a federal area within the United States, Alma's work group faces an unusual situation in which the state had provided a supplement, but has eliminated the supplement during budget cuts. Because the group probably has a greater probability of producing changes at a state level and because the problem was generated at a state level, the group would probably do well to address it at that level.

Generation of an Alternative Solution or Alternative Solutions

Policy practitioners must also generate alternative solutions. They may do this by devising their own solutions, or by resurrecting solutions proposed by others in the past. The solutions may be broad and comprehensive, or may offer an incremental approach, in which smaller aspects of the problem are addressed individually. Although a single solution will probably ultimately be offered, practitioners often find that generating a variety of possibilities from which they then choose is the most effective approach.

The information gathered during other portions of the analysis should be used both to inform the development of alternatives and to choose between them. The solution ultimately recommended should have a strong probability of being effective, be feasible to implement, and be desirable to a sufficient number of stakeholders to make its acceptance likely.

Collection or Production of Appropriate Professional Analyses

Many types of professional analyses are available to examine the performance of current policy and to predict how a new proposal is likely to perform. Options for professional analysis include program evaluation, needs assessment, cost-benefit analysis, forecasting, sensitivity analysis, allocation formulae, quick decision analysis, and political feasibility analysis (Ellis, 2003). A thorough discussion of these methods is beyond the scope of this chapter, and most require specialized training to conduct effectively. A careful search of available literature may yield a number of such analyses already in existence. Alternatively, policy practice work groups might hire an expert to conduct a professional analysis or recruit a group member who possesses the necessary knowledge and skill.

Examination of Potential Unintended Consequences

Whenever policy changes are enacted, there is the potential for unintended consequences to result. It seems unlikely, for instance, that the state legislators who approved the cuts in Alma's case study anticipated their devastating effects on other social service systems. A little forethought on the part of the policy makers might have prevented the current crisis.

Policy practice work groups can try to anticipate what they might not otherwise expect by using a variety of techniques. For example, they can brainstorm best- and worst-case scenarios, or research the results of similar initiatives in their chosen policy area or in similar policy areas. Alternatively, they could ask other experts in the area what they might expect, using either individual interviews or focus groups.

Selection of an Alternative or Alternatives

If the practitioner or work group develops more than a single alternative solution, most situations will require that the one perceived to be the best is selected for proposal and support. The "best" alternative will be the one that is some mixture of the most likely to succeed, the most feasible, the most acceptable, and the least likely to produce undesirable consequences.

Practitioners may make this decision through informal discussion and evaluation, or may develop a more formal method of scoring alternatives such as the marginal numerical attributions used in criteria-based methods.

It is important to remember that a solution seen as "best" for one community or geographical area may not be best for another. This is particularly true when international issues are involved. Practitioners who are considering recommendations that will impact conditions in other countries may need to remember that needs, values, support systems, and similar conditions are likely to vary between and within countries. International policy practice requires a thorough understanding of every area that will be affected.

Action Planning

In some situations practitioners may be asked only to analyze policy and provide a recommended solution or solutions. At other times they may need to develop a strategy for bringing the change to fruition. Although this might seem a daunting task, a similar process is included in any CSWE-accredited MSSW program in the form of strategic planning.

In strategic planning an overall mission statement is prepared, then goals, objectives, and tasks are identified. These goals, objectives, and tasks are, in fact, the steps that must be undertaken to accomplish the mission. When the tasks have been identified and articulated, each is assigned to an individual or a small group and a date for completion and a means of reporting the results to the overall group are specified. The results are usually recorded either in log or matrix form to allow for easy tracking.

The capacities individual members bring to a policy analysis work group should be important considerations when tasks are assigned for the action plan. Persons who bring competence in public relations, advertising, and media relations should be involved in the completion of tasks of that nature. Those who bring influence may best be involved in contact with and persuasion of decision makers. The persons who excel in motivation may be the ones with the drive and persistence to prepare and distribute brochures, make multiple phone calls, and prepare and supervise mass mailings. Some group members may want to participate in more than one type of activity, but most should be encouraged to direct their primary efforts toward those activities in which they bring the greatest capacity.

Evaluating the Outcomes

Effective social work practice requires effective evaluation. This is as true for policy practice as it is for clinical work or program development. Only when outcome measures are chosen, variables are tracked, and the results are analyzed and reported can practitioners know whether the goals they set out to meet have been accomplished.

Policy outcome evaluation uses one or more of the forms of professional analysis discussed in an earlier section. Perhaps in most cases it involves an outcome evaluation design that looks at target conditions that existed before a new policy was introduced and compares them to those conditions after the policy has gone into effect. For example, Alma's group might track income, referrals to child welfare, homelessness, and medical service utilization rates. If income increased among the target client group and referrals to child welfare, homelessness, and medical service utilization among the target client group decreased, this might be seen as evidence that the team's policy intervention was effective.

Conclusion

This chapter has identified and described the primary processes involved in policy practice. These processes include: (a) preparation of the practitioner, (b) assembling a team, (c) identification, definition, and legitimization of the problem, (d) selecting an approach for analysis, (e) conducting the analysis, and (f) evaluating the outcomes. The processes were presented primarily to address case studies based on conditions typical of the United States, but comments were included to make them more relevant to international policy practice where such comments were necessary.

Key Terms

Global	*Policy analysis*	*Social welfare*
Legislative	*Policy practice*	

Review Questions for Critical Thinking

1. Ellis writes that successful policy practice includes "putting a team together." Who would you want on your team; what kind of knowledge and experiences would you find helpful?

2. Do you think policy practice is more effective at the local, regional, state, or national level of government? Or, is policy practice equally effective?

3. Identify one social issue and develop a policy practice strategy.

4. Does it surprise you that the longest serving member in the history of the United States Senate is a social worker, Barbara Mikulski (D-MD)?

5. Do you believe that the policy practice model suggested by Ellis, as well as those models set forth by others, are systematic and logical in actual practice?

Online Resources

Center for Lobbying in the Public Interest http://clpi.org/about-us

Influencing State Policy http://www.statepolicy.org/

Lewis and Burke Associates http://lewis-burke.com/

Nancy A. Humphries Institute for Political Social Work http://www .ssw.uconn.edu/our-community/centers-institutes-projects/nancy-a-humphreys-institute-for-political-social-work

Political Action for Candidate Election http://www.socialworkers.org/pace/default.asp

References

DiNitto, D. M., & Cummins, L. K. (2006). *Social welfare: Politics and public policy* (6th ed.). New York, NY: Allyn & Bacon.

Dobelstein, A. W. (1996). *Social welfare: Policy and analysis* (2nd ed.). Chicago, IL: Nelson-Hall.

Ellis, R. A. (2003). *Impacting social policy: A practitioner's guide to analysis and action.* Pacific Grove, CA: Brooks Cole/Wadsworth.

Ellis, R. A., Crane Mallory, K., Gould, M. Y., & Shatila, S. L. (2006). *The macro practitioner's workbook: A step-by-step guide to effectiveness with organizations and communities.* Pacific Grove, CA: Brooks Cole/Wadsworth.

Elwood, D. T. (1989). *Poor support: Poverty in the American family.* New York, NY: Basic Books.

Janssen, B. S. (1999). *Becoming an effective policy advocate: From policy practice to social justice.* Pacific Grove, CA: Brooks Cole/Wadsworth.

Manning, J. E. (2011, March). *Membership of the 112th congress: A profile.* Washington, DC: Congressional Research Service.

Chapter 2
Social Welfare Policy and Politics

Richard Hoefer

As you read this chapter ask yourself if you would run for political office or consider serving as a staff person for an elected official or federal agency. Do you feel that social workers can make a difference in the political world by offering the "person perspective" and screening problems and issues through a "social justice" lens? Do you feel the social work profession can have competing political ideologies or is the profession bound to one political ideology? Is the profession stronger with one, dominant ideology or better served by embracing the range of political philosophies?

Introduction

The political world is often viewed with suspect and distrust. An April 2012 Gallup Poll found that the approval rating for the U.S. Congress was 17%, up from an all-time low of 10% in February 2012! So why would anyone want to join an organization that the general public loathes? The idea that nearly 8 out of 10 people are dissatisfied with government is discouraging, yet all levels of government are directly involved in creating public policies that social workers implement. The profession must remain vigilant and proactive in politics if we hope to craft just social policies. Social workers have long been engaged in politics: the first woman elected to Congress was social worker Jeannette Rankin in 1917, 2 years before the 19th Amendment to the U.S. Constitution was ratified today, U.S. Senator and social worker Barbara Mikulski is the longest serving women in the history of the U.S. Senate. Social workers have been elected to local school boards, city councils, and state legislatures as well as holding important staff positions in elected officials' offices and committees' staffs. Certainly social work educators and practitioners enjoy lively political discussions and debates. But social workers must move beyond the debates and become more engaged in the political arena. From electoral politics—getting the right people elected—to legislative politics—lobbying and governmental relations—social workers can strongly influence the development of fair and just public policies.

The statement "Policy affects practice and practice affects policy" helps educate and remind social workers of the dual role they play—*practitioners*, working with individuals, groups, organizations, and communities to improve currently occurring difficulties, and *advocates*, working through political means to alter or remove the causes of current problems. Working both in the present and for the future places social workers in a unique position.

Still, the connections between social policy and the political world are not always well explained or understood. This essay, after defining important terms, presents a range of political philosophies and shows how their adherents operationalize their view of the "ideal" social policy. A brief description of the process of politics and advocacy is also provided, in the context of the generalist model of social work practice. By showing the range of desired social policies, depending on the philosophy used for justification, it is hoped that readers will see more clearly the need to choose elected officials whose views are in accord with their own and the social work profession's. In this way, the political process of advocacy can be made easier. Not having to convince someone with a different view of what is good and proper in the arena of social policy means that efforts can be made to improve and expand programs rather than to defend what already exists.

Defining Social Welfare Policy

Although we might like to have one widely accepted definition of this key term, DiNitto (2007) correctly points out, "Lengthy discussions of the definition of social welfare policy are unnecessary, often futile, and even exasperating" (p. 3). Despite ambiguity, some parameters are generally accepted and are accepted here. First, social welfare policy relates to enhancing the quality of life of individuals, sometimes acting through groups or communities to do so. Second, while social welfare policy can be made by either governmental or private organizations, it is created by both action and lack of action on the part of decision makers. Finally, social welfare policy is the outcome of a process involving politics.

Defining Politics

Discussing and defining the term *politics* extends far back in time, and the term is used to denote two separate concepts. The first use of *politics* is to describe a set of beliefs, as a loose synonym for ideology. The second use describes a process of decision making.

Politics as Ideology

The question "What are your politics?" is clearly understood as a question regarding one's viewpoints, not how one believes policies should be created. It is in this sense that politics and social policy are closely intertwined—the political views controlling a decision-making body determine the social policies that emerge. Political views can be described as falling on a continuum from right (conservative) to left (socialist) and are more or less systematically set forth by political parties. These views and their implications for social policy are described later in this chapter.

Politics as Process

Describing politics as a process has a long history. Aristotle (2007), who lived in the fourth century, B.C., wrote "Man is by nature a political animal." He believed that people naturally congregate and interact with one another. This implies that processes for settling disagreements must be developed. Harold Lasswell, U.S. political scientist, defines politics as the process to decide "who gets what, when and how" (1990, p. 4). Politics, in this view, is a tool much like any tool—it can be used for creative or destructive purposes. It is therefore incumbent on social workers to understand the ins and outs of the use of this tool so that they can apply it with skill to achieve policy ends in line with their own and the profession's values.

Politics as Ideologies: Across the Spectrum of Right and Left

To show the impact of politics as ideology on social policy, this section examines a number of political philosophies and their associated political parties. Each is described and then the implications of this viewpoint for social policy are discussed.

Typically, ideology is described as moving from right to left, a by-product of French prerevolutionary governance, where supporters of the king sat on his right and those desiring change sat on his left. Several other elements besides the desire for change are embedded in the political continuum, however. Baradat (2005) notes that the desire for change helps us differentiate ideologies but that we must also examine the depth of the change desired, the speed of change desired, and the methods to be used to create the change desired to fully describe what makes one ideology different from another. In addition, it is vital to know the values and motivations behind the desire for change in order to fully describe a political view (Baradat, 2005).

The spectrum of views acceptable in a state or country varies tremendously. Some countries have the full or a nearly full spectrum represented in their political system, while other countries have an extremely truncated spectrum. What is considered far left in one country may be considered middle-of-the-road or even on the right in another country. Some countries may allow only one official political viewpoint. Even within such a uni-party system, however, different factions develop along the lines of how much (if any) change is wanted, how quickly changes should be made, and so forth.

Critics of the U.S. political system, for example, argue that there is little true difference between Democrats and Republicans, particularly in an international context. Hard-core American Republicans and Democrats, however, see large differences between (and even within) their parties. The political spectrum delimited here is purposely wider than what one finds in mainstream U.S. politics and may also be broader than found in many other countries.

Libertarians (Neoconservatism)

The key principle for Libertarians is freedom in both social and economic spheres. Libertarians thus desire considerable change from the status quo, seeking to rein in governmental excesses such as high taxes and social programs but also to keep government from interfering in personal matters such as obtaining an abortion or marrying someone of the same sex. Libertarians, by working through the electoral system, are willing to endure a slow pace of change, but the amount of change desired is considerable.

Policy Implications

"Libertarians propose to do away with large portions of government" (Murray, 1997, p. 47). This involves eliminating social programs for the poor, the aged, the ill, and almost all other groups. Because taxes would be slashed as an unjustified intrusion into people's lives and livelihoods, little money would be available to pay for social programs in any case. Still, the argument against social programs is based on principled, not pragmatic, considerations. According to this view, social problems are created or exacerbated by government subsidization and protection (Kristol, 2004; Murray, 1997). Libertarians argue that the welfare system, for example, creates problems by allowing people who make poor life choices to remain relatively unaffected by their bad decisions and thus shift costs from the individual to society. This can only be paid for by taxes taken from people who make better choices, and punishes those living "by the rules." Entitlements for benefits would be eliminated: "The general rule has to be: if it is your own behavior that could land you on welfare, then you don't get it, or you get very little of it" (Kristol, 2004, p. 148).

Because an unregulated market allows the most freedom of choice, the principle at work in social welfare policy should be: "Let people shop for what they want and pay for what they get." (Murray, 1997, p. 93). Organizations that offer education or health care would compete on both price and service, much as organizations that offer computers or other products do now.

Social problems can be reduced by decriminalizing activities such as alcohol and drug use, pornography, prostitution, and so on. People would still be required to act responsibly, and if they did not, their irresponsible crimes would be punished, but not the use of alcohol or other drugs, the viewing of pornography, or the selling of sex, in and of themselves.

Congressman Ron Paul, Republican candidate for President in 2012, consistently espouses Libertarian views. His 2012 campaign website lists his position on entitlements. It reads:

> *Honors our promise to our seniors and veterans, while allowing young workers to opt out. Block grants Medicaid and other welfare programs to allow States the flexibility and ingenuity they need to solve their own unique problems without harming those currently relying on the programs.*
>
> (RonPaul2012.com, 2012, The Issues)

Conservatism

Conservative parties exist in many countries and often have the word *conservative* in their party name (the United Kingdom, Australia, and Sweden, for example). In the United States, the Republican Party advances conservative positions. As the name implies, conservatives wish to "conserve" what they see as the best policies from the nation's traditions and to rely on a laissez-faire economy. Conservatives advocate for a limited government role in the economy (thus championing the primacy of the market in deciding the distribution of goods and income), low taxes, and little government interference in individual behavior (though some strands of conservative thought desire government action regarding issues of morality). Conservatives tend to be pessimistic regarding human nature and improvements to the social system, thus they do not expect government action to fix problems. Additional elements of conservative thought are the importance of property rights and a tendency toward elitism, where "the people" are not fully trustworthy to control the country's fate. This philosophy accepts the need for individuals to have access to social welfare services. Believing that the best government is the government that governs least, however, conservatives push for assistance to the poor to come from family members and nongovernmental organizations, particularly non-profits with a faith basis (Olasky, 2000). Decreased regulation of business and a willingness to contract with private organizations to provide services formerly provided by government agencies are additional conservative positions.

Conservative parties work through parliamentary or democratic methods. Some argue that people of conservative ideology hold the reins of power through their wealth, social connections, and control of the military-industrial complex (see, for example, Mills, 1956). Wielding power by controlling what emerges on the governmental decision-making agenda (Bachrach & Baratz, 1962), conservatives have little to fear from other philosophies, at least in the United States. Conservative forces frequently used violence and threats of violence in the past to thwart unionizing and other left-wing causes and this use of force continues in some places.

Policy Implications

Conservatives believe that . . .

> [T]he traditional values of hard work, ambition, and self-reliance will lead to individual and family well-being. . . . Their goal is equity. That is, if everyone is provided with an equal opportunity to compete, conservatives want to minimize policies that are designed to shape the final result.

> (Dolgoff & Feldstein, 2007, p. 113)

This is not to say that conservatives are all of one mind in terms of their social agenda. Some who are conservative on the economic front in terms of wanting to limit government involvement in regulating the economy are also "traditional" conservatives regarding interference with individual liberty. In other words, they do not advocate for government intervention on behalf of any religious or philosophical view to tell individuals what they can and cannot do. This type of conservative is close to being a libertarian. Others, sometimes called *cultural conservatives,* who consider themselves strictly conservative in their economic views, are eager to use government coercion to uphold their religious viewpoints regarding abortion, marriage, sex, and other issues of morality.

Some of the specific policies advocated by conservative parties include tax cuts for the wealthy, thus reducing government funds for human services; decreased government support for human service programs; and a stronger emphasis and reliance on private organizations (nonprofit and for-profit) to actually provide services to clients. Some conservatives argue for ending any right to an abortion and for maintaining or strengthening discrimination against sexual minorities.

Several Republican candidates running for President in 2012 stressed their opposition to the universal health care plan during Barack Obama's 2008–2012 presidential term. Rick Santorum, for example, running as a "true conservative," had this on his website:

> Every American should have access to high-quality, affordable health care, with health care decisions made by patients and their physicians, NOT government bureaucrats. America needs targeted, market-driven, patient-centered solutions to address the costs and underlying causes of being uninsured rather than a one-size-fits-all, government-run health care system.

> (RickSantorum.com, 2012, Healthcare)

Centrism

Centrists are generally not too upset by the status quo nor are they unwilling to see opportunities for positive change. By definition, they adopt positions that are between the more extreme views on the right (libertarian and conservative) and the left (liberal and socialist). They work within the system and tend to be pragmatic (rather than strictly ideological) in terms of proposing possible changes. Slightly adjusting policies in an incremental way to make them better achieve their goals is part of the centrist perspective. Center parties have established themselves in Nordic countries (Sweden, Finland, and Norway all have a "Center Party," for example). As an example of Center party ideas, the Swedish Center Party declares:

> Welfare payments or economic support is the public sector's ultimate economic shield. People who receive welfare often find themselves far from the labor market. In order to assist them in returning to the work force and to being self-supporting, more jobs and lower hurdles are needed as well as more assistance from unemployment and work-placement offices.
>
> (Centerpartiet, 2012, Socialbidrag [Welfare])

A U.S. example of centrism emerged in the early part of the 21st century. Noting the arrival of the Information Age, Hallstead and Lind (2001) advocate a new movement, dubbed "radical centrism." It is based on four principles:

1. Increasing the amount of choice available to individual citizens.
2. Holding citizens to a higher personal standard of self-sufficiency.
3. Providing a true safety net model of economic security for citizens.
4. Allowing federal jurisdiction to take over from state and local government when the outcome is expanding individual freedoms and choices. (pp. 19–23)

Defined by the amount of change desired and speed at which they would like to see the change occur, Hallstead and Lind (2001) do fit the idea of radical. But because they espouse ideas that tend to be between the far right and left, they are also centrists.

Policy Implications

Centrist social policy is essentially a point between trusting the common person to do the right thing, given the chance (liberalism) and not trusting the common person's integrity and desire to work (conservatism). Centrists thus believe that people want to be responsible but may need encouragement and role-modeling to know how to be self-sufficient in a market economy. Services should be available to those who are not able to work, but everyone else should be in the labor force, both for their own good and for the good of society.

Specific policies put forth by Sweden's Center Party are:

- To make it pay to move from welfare to work—this makes the individual even more motivated to look for work.
- To help the person on welfare back to self-sufficiency, through, for example, rehabilitation, education, or seeking a new job.

- To make special efforts with youth and immigrants (the most at-risk groups) so that they can go from welfare dependence to self-sufficiency. (Centerpartiet, 2007)

Hallstead and Lind (2001) argue that their four principles are more in line with the realities of the 21st-century Information Age than are other ideologies and associated political parties. They advocate the following policies:

- Mandatory private health care system for all Americans that would ensure that the poorest and least healthy are fully covered.
- Progressive privatization of Social Security, based on mandatory retirement savings for all workers.
- Broadening of the ownership of financial capital so that all Americans can benefit directly from our growing economy.

Liberalism

"Optimism about people's ability to solve their problems is the keynote of liberalism" (Baradat, 2005, p. 27). This relates to the enshrinement of human intellect that emerged during the Enlightenment. Because people are so capable, the reasoning goes, they should be able to assess problems, figure out solutions, and implement their ideas. New ideas have merit and are useful in improving the world. Liberals tend to believe in the importance of achieving equality of opportunity, as well as making strides with government policy to mitigate the excesses of the market because the free market creates high levels of inequality, discrimination, and injury to dispossessed populations.

Political parties with the name "Liberal" in them currently exist in Australia, Canada, the United Kingdom, and other countries. Classical liberals focused primarily on the importance of individual rights, particularly opposing the rights of kings to govern without input from the ruled. Thus, many liberal ideas were enshrined in the U.S. Constitution. Modern liberalism is based on dissatisfaction with the state of the world, a belief in the perfectibility of society, optimism, and a willingness to work through governmental institutions to achieve social goals. Liberals wish change to be thorough and relatively rapid, but always through a democratic process. In the U.S. system, the Democratic Party is considered the more liberal of the two major political parties.

Democrats stress the importance of equal rights for all, opportunity for "ordinary people" rather than the wealthy, health care security for all, tax cuts for middle class families, and other provisions that expand work opportunities through government programs and improve the health and safety of the public through government regulation of business. These positions show a large difference from conservative ideas that stress the role of an unfettered private enterprise system to improve people's lives.

Policy Implications

Liberal policy positions are in favor of government intervention in the market to improve society and protect human rights (as opposed to property rights), egalitarianism (as opposed to elitism), and personal liberty (as opposed to government intervention into private behavior) (Baradat, 2005).

A few examples of specific social policies supported by liberals are greater equality between racial and ethnic groups, as well as between men and women; livable minimum wage levels; provision of adequate levels of medical care, housing, and nutritious food to all; and sufficient regulation of business to ensure safety in food, medicine, and other products. Democrats believe people who are gay, lesbian, bisexual, or transgendered should have equal rights to straight people, including the right to marry.

Social Democracy and Labor Parties

Social democracy is a view espoused by political parties around the globe (for example, Australia's, New Zealand's, and the United Kingdom's Labour parties, and Germany's, Norway's, and Sweden's Social Democratic parties), although no major party in the United States fits into this category. While Social Democracy originally was a strongly socialist philosophy, now the mainstream of many Social Democratic parties has moved to the right, taking on the title of the "Third Way," a system between pure capitalism and pure socialism, although still more socialist than capitalist or conservative.

A common thread for all Social Democratic parties is repugnance concerning the excesses of capitalism, particularly inequality, poverty, oppression of various groups, and distaste for the strong individualism that negates the importance of solidarity among people and groups. According to Socialist International (SI), "Social democracy is a common denominator for those who seek progress, equality, solidarity and the affirmation of the rights of the individual and the community alike" (Socialist International, 2012).

Policy Implications

Social policy under Social Democrats follows what has been called an *institutional model* where receipt of social services is considered a normal part of life so the government provides them. Although financial realities may prevent governments from providing all services that are desired, the number and scope of services are considerable and reach from "cradle to grave."

Modern social democracy takes on a variety of positions but many national Social Democratic parties belong to the organization Socialist International (SI), which defines social democracy as an ideal form of democracy that can overcome the problems inherent in unregulated capitalism (Socialist International, 2012). Among other common policies, most Social Democrats support:

- A mixed economy rather than either a totally free market or fully planned economy.
- Extensive provisions for social security, social insurance, and income maintenance.
- Government-provided (directly or indirectly) education, health care, child care, and so on, for everyone.
- Regulations on private businesses to assure worker safety, protection, and fair competition.
- Moderate to high progressive taxes.
- Gay marriage, abortion rights, and a liberal drug policy, although this varies considerably from one country to another.

Socialism

Despite the many variations in philosophy and practice that can be found among socialists, socialism has three basic features: public ownership of production; an extensive welfare state; and the desire to create a society where material want is eliminated (the socialist intent) (Baradat, 2005).

Public ownership of production is needed because private ownership within a mixed or capitalist system assures exploitation of workers and thus must be eliminated. To make a profit, a capitalist must pay a worker less than the income that worker generates—it is the excess of income created by the worker's contribution over the costs of production (including the worker's wage) that is profit. Private owners thus always have an incentive to pay a worker as little as possible to maximize their own income. Nationalizing production or turning production over to cooperatives solves the problem of exploitation as no one individual benefits from exploiting workers.

An extensive welfare state is used by government to ensure access to the necessities of life. Universal education, health care, pensions, income maintenance, and other programs are instituted. This is in accord with the "socialist intent," the desire to reduce and then eliminate social problems. In this way, socialism is far superior to capitalism (at least in theory) because hunger, discrimination, homelessness, lack of affordable health care for all, and the other ills seen around the world in capitalist economies can be eliminated.

All socialists desire radical change in society. Different strands of socialism have varying ideas relating to the use of violence to achieve radical change. Democratic socialists eschew violence, believing in the power of democracy to bring about such a large change. Other branches of socialism, however, believe that the only true power for change comes from "the barrel of a gun."

Policy Implications

Socialist social policy results in the most far-spreading institutional system of all the philosophies described. But it is important to understand that the key element of socialism is that society is radically transformed by eliminating capitalism. The economic system is radically different than in any system where capitalism is allowed to continue, even in social democratic countries, which also have extensive social welfare programs.

Socialists have to struggle with the fact that wherever their ideas have been tried, success has been limited. Although the Soviet bloc countries may not be a true test of socialist ideas, they are an abject lesson in ways that the socialist theory can be applied with ensuing negative effects. Other experiments in socialist governance, such as the People's Republic of China and Cuba, have had both success and failures, but may not adhere closely to socialist principles at this time. Still, on a few indicators of national health, they outperform the United States (World Health Organization, 2007). Critics of socialist ideology focus on the loss of individual freedom that is demanded in return for a promised freedom from material want. The Socialist Party-USA declares its positions as the following:

> The Socialist Party strives to establish a radical democracy that places people's lives under their own control—a non-racist, classless, feminist, socialist society in which people cooperate at work, at home, and in the community.

> (Socialist Party-USA, 2012, Statement of Principles)

This survey of "politics as ideology" and the resultant social policies espoused by each political view leads to the conclusion that almost all ideologies are represented by political parties in many countries, particularly industrialized countries, around the world. Further, talk of peaceful change, even if the change desired is radical in scope and speed, is by far more common than are calls for violent revolution. The next section looks briefly at one way to approach the concept of politics as a process of advocating and achieving change in policy.

Politics as Process: How to Have an Effect on Social Policy

Jansson (2010) articulates four rationales for conducting policy advocacy:

1. To promote the values of social work.
2. To promote the well-being of clients, consumers, and citizens.
3. To create effective opposition to "bad" policies and to pressure decision makers to adopt or keep "good" policies.
4. To alter who the governmental decision makers are.

Hoefer (2012) describes advocacy practice, which he defines as a practice model to affect client outcomes in nongovernmental as well as governmental processes. He presents a series of steps that are analogous to the model of generalist practice taught in many schools of social work, thus highlighting the similarity between advocacy practice and other types of social work practice. Hoefer's model of advocacy practice is described here as a way of understanding the links between politics as a process and social policy. Knowing how to affect policy by engaging in a political process leads to empowerment on the part of social workers and their clients.

Getting Involved

The first step of the advocacy process is to "get involved," meaning to find a reason and the will to take notice of some situation that challenges one's conception of social justice. Seven variables are important in determining if one is likely to get involved or not: education (level and content), values, sense of professional responsibility, interest, participation in other organizations, skills, and time available. These variables can be altered consciously by anyone and can be shaped by the organizations that employ social workers in order to promote advocacy by employees.

Understanding the Issue

Understanding should precede action. Sometimes a strong urge to "do something" exists, but it must be resisted. The first step in understanding an issue is to agree on its definition. Advocates next determine who benefits from and who is harmed by the situation. They also assess what some of the causes (proximate and distal) of the situation are.

When this analysis is completed, advocates can move to generating possible solutions to the issue. Often, the way an issue is defined has a strong influence on what the acceptable solutions are, so it is important to try to have a neutral problem definition statement. Advocates should determine the extent to which social justice is served by any particular proposed solution. Then the proposed solutions can be rank-ordered to determine, which, if enacted, would produce the greatest improvement in social justice.

Planning Advocacy

Planning is detailing the actions needed to make the advocate's preferred solution the one that is eventually chosen by decision makers. First, one must identify what is actually wanted. The overall goal will almost always need to be broken into smaller goals, or outcomes, and the specific actions that are required to make those come true should be laid out. Second, the targets of advocacy, the people who can make the desired decision, are identified, and analysis is done to determine what would convince them to adopt the advocate's desired solution. Planning is also needed to understand how best to negotiate with or persuade the targets. The final planning step is to gather the required information (substantive and contextual) to move forward with the actual advocacy efforts.

Advocating

At this time, the previous work is put to the test as advocates meet with decision makers, make their presentations, and negotiate and persuade. Other advocates can be brought in to speak or the advocacy attempt can be an individual effort. The decision maker can be a Washington-based legislator or one's supervisor. Change processes are usually slow and advocates must understand the need for patience, as well as persistence.

Evaluating Advocacy

Advocacy is often not evaluated in any formal sense, which makes learning from past actions more difficult. Even a minimal effort at evaluation, quickly comparing the advocacy's outcomes against the desired outcomes laid out in the planning stage, yields results in showing what was accomplished, and perhaps, what techniques might work as well or better in the next advocacy effort.

Ongoing Monitoring

What was won (or lost) in the legislative branch can be reversed in the executive or judicial branches of government. Thus, advocates must monitor the actions of additional decision makers in different venues. Understanding the importance of keeping up with new developments is vital, or else gains won by social workers in one arena can be lost to advocates for other views in another.

Conclusion

This survey of social policy and politics shows the links between politics (as political ideology), politics (as a process of change), and the policies that emerge in any jurisdiction. Ruling political parties have the ability to create or destroy programs designed to improve people's lives—in other words, those in power, using their values and ideology, shape social policy to match their interests. In most democratic countries, however, individual people and groups are able to voice their opinions to have their values enacted. This chapter has also provided a brief overview of the steps that can be taken to have an impact on social policy in almost any nation where input exists. It is to be hoped that readers will understand better the range of ideas that exist to be selected from, as well as one basic approach to peaceful change—politics as advocacy.

Key Terms

Advocacy
Ideology—Liberalism,
    conservatism,
    neoconservatism,

libertarianism,
    centrism,
    and socialism
Political parties

Politics
Social welfare policy

Review Questions for Critical Thinking

1. How would you describe today's national political climate; is it any different from the political climate in your state?

2. From an advocacy perspective, should social workers align themselves with one political party or "work across the aisle" in a bipartisan effort?

3. How would you categorize the 2008 Affordable Health Care Act on the political spectrum from conservatism to socialism?

4. The United States is dominated by a two-party political system, Democratic and Republican. Do you think a third party can be a viable alternative to win the presidency of the United States?

5. Should social workers be engaged in politics, in particular run for elected office?

Online Resources

Democratic Party www.democrats.org/

Libertarian Party http://www.lp.org/

National Association of Social Workers Political Action for Candidate Election www.naswdc.org/pace/default.asp

Republican Party www.gop.org/

Tea Party www.teapartypatriots.org/

References

Aristotle. (2007). Politics. Retrieved from *The little Oxford dictionary of quotations* (2nd ed.), http://www.askoxford.com/results/?view=quot&freesearch=politics&branch=14123648&textsearchtype=exact

Bachrach, P., & Baratz, M. (1962). The second face of power. *American Political Science Review, 56*, 947–952.

Baradat, L. (2005). *Political ideologies: Their origins and impact* (9th ed.). Englewood Cliffs, NJ: Prentice Hall.

Centerpartiet (Center Party of Sweden). (2012). Socialbidrag (Welfare). Retrieved from http://www.centerpartiet.se/Centerpolitik/Politikomraden/Socialfor sakringar-och-bidrag/Politik-A—O/Socialbidrag-/ [Translated by the author].

DiNitto, D. (2007). *Social welfare: Politics and public policy* (6th ed.). Boston, MA: Allyn & Bacon.

Dolgoff, R., & Feldstein, D. 2007. *Understanding Social Welfare* (6th ed.). Boston: Allyn & Bacon.

Hallstead, T., & Lind, M. (2001). *The radical center: The future of American politics.* New York, NY: Doubleday.

Hoefer, R. (2012). *Advocacy practice for social justice* (2nd ed.). Chicago, IL: Lyceum.

Jansson, B. (2010). *Becoming an effective policy advocate* (6th ed.). Pacific Grove, CA: Brooks/Cole.

Kristol, I. (2004). The conservative welfare state. In I. Stelzer (Ed.), *The neocon reader* (pp. 145–148). New York, NY: Grove Press.

Lasswell, H. (1990). *Politics: Who gets what, when and how.* Gloucester, MA: Smith.

Mills, C. W. (1956). *The power elite.* New York, NY: Oxford University Press.

Murray, C. (1997). *What it means to be a libertarian.* New York, NY: Broadway Books.

Olasky, M. (2000). *Compassionate conservatism: What it is, what it does and how it can transform America.* New York, NY: Free Press.

RickSantorum.com. (2012). Healthcare. Retrieved from http://www.ricksantorum.com/healthcare

RonPaul2012.com. (2012). The Issues: Entitlements. Retrieved from http://www.ronpaul2012.com/the-issues/ron-paul-plan-to-restore-america/

Socialist International. (2012). About us. Retrieved from http://www.socialistinternational.org/about.cfm

Socialist Party-USA. (2012). Statement of principles. Retrieved from http://socialistparty-usa.org/principles.html

World Health Organization (WHO). (2007). Core health indicators. Retrieved from www3.who.int/whosis/core/core_select_process.cfm

Chapter 3
New Federalism, New Freedom, and States' Rights

The Uncertain and Fragmented Direction of Public Mental Health Policy in the United States

King Davis and Hyejin Jung

> In the year 2050 how do think mental services will change; will they be organized around an open, public framework or will programs be private in nature? Will mental illness continue to be stigmatized or in 2050 will the public embrace a proactive social justice perspective that neither judges nor categorizes persons? Will mental health receive full and equitable parity with physical health issues? Given that the social work profession is the primary provider of mental services, what then are the profession's obligations and responsibilities to assume leadership in the mental health arena?

Introduction

Social workers provide the majority of mental health services in the United States—more than psychologists, psychiatrists, or any other specific mental health discipline. For this one fact, social workers and the profession should be profoundly aware of and involved in the development of mental health policies, programs, and services. The costs to our communities both in terms of actual dollars and human capital are staggering. To do nothing or, at best, provide minimal interventions only results in a downward economic spiral. The treatment of persons with mental health issues has changed dramatically: The 18th-century approach was to put those with mental illness in jails or almshouses, often chained to restrict their actions; the 19th century saw a virtual explosion of the so-called insane asylum; and the 20th century brought about psychoanalysis, electroshock treatment, and psychotropic drugs. Through "evidence-based practice" social workers can make a significant difference in the provision of mental health services. Similarly, today's researchers must move to "translational research," that is, interpreting research findings to direct practice.

The Epidemiology and Burden of Mental Illness

Interest in the epidemiology, causation, and cost of mental illness is evident in numerous academic studies and government reports published in the United States for more than a century. Although data and conclusions from many earlier studies were severely limited by subjective bias, they were used to formulate a narrow conceptual basis for mental health policy, planning, financing, control, and practice in the United States. State governments drafted mental health policies that resulted in long-term institutionalization, social control, segregation by race and disability, criminalization of the mentally ill, involuntary admissions, and the abrogation of constitutional rights (Babcock, 1895; Blanton, 1931; Carothers, 1940; Cartwright, 1851; Evarts, 1914; Faris & Dunham, 1939; Fischer, 1969; Gould, 1981; Grossack, 1963; Herrnstein & Murray, 1994; Hurd et al., 1916; Jackson, 1960; Jarvis, 1842, 1844; Keeler & Vitols, 1963; Kleiner & Parker, 1959; Kramer, Von Korff, & Kessler, 1980; Lidz & Lidz, 1949; Malzberg, 1940, 1953; McCandless, 1996; O'Malley, 1914; Pasamanick, 1959; Scott, 1997; Witmer, 1891). The federal government maintained a minimalist role in ameliorating these mental health concerns until the beginning of the 20th century (Burnim, 2006; Mechanic, 1989; Rothman, 1970; U.S. Congress, 1946, 1980).

Over the past two decades, however, a series of more contemporary epidemiological studies and reports introduced alternative hypotheses and findings about the probable causes, distribution, treatment, burden, disparities, and costs of mental and physical illness in the United States and worldwide (Adebimpe, 1994; Andreasen, 1997; Chandra & Skinner, 2003; Epstein & Ayanian, 2001; Institute of Medicine, 2005; Jackson et al., 1996; Keppel, Pearcy, & Wagener, 2002; Kessler et al., 2005; Neighbors & Lumpkin, 1990; Plepys & Klein, 1995; Regier et al., 1993; Robins & Regier, 1991; Takeuchi & Cheung, 1998; U.S. Department of Health and Human Services, 1999, 2001; World Health Organization [WHO], 2001). In addition, more contemporary studies measure the financial resources invested in the system (sources, savings, distribution) and the economic losses from untreated mental illness (Altman & Levitt, 2002; Congressional Budget Office, 1999; Frank, 2006; Heldring, 2003; Institute of Medicine, 2005; Manderscheid & Henderson, 2001; Moscarelli, Rupp, & Sartorious, 1996; Mulligan, 2003; National Mental Health Association, 2001; Rice & Miller, 1996; Substance Abuse and Mental Health Services Administration [SAMHSA], 2010a, 2011; Unutzer, Schoenbaum, & Druss, 2006; WHO, 2001). Other studies and reports have focused more closely on assessing the functioning of the systems of services provided by state governments (National Alliance on Mental Illness, 2009).

A report by the World Health Organization shows that the total number of adults affected worldwide was close to 450 million persons and that approximately 20% to 25% of the world's population of adults has a diagnosable mental illness during their lifetimes (WHO, 2001). The 2010 National Survey on Drug Use and Health (NSDUH) reported that approximately 45.9 million adults (20% of the U.S. adult population) and

11.4 million adults (5% of the U.S. adult population) suffered from any mental illness (AMI) and serious mental illness (SMI) in the past year, respectively. Among young children, 1.9 million youths, or 8% of children aged 12 to 17, suffered from major depressive episode (MDE) and 1.3 million youths (5.6%) from MDE with severe impairment (SAMHSA, 2012). *Mental Health, United States, 2008* (SAMHSA, 2010a) suggested that 5% of children aged 4 to 17 had severe emotional and behavioral difficulties and 15.5% had minor difficulties. The National Health Interview Survey showed that in 2005 to 2006, parents of close to 8.3 million children, or 14.5% of U.S. children aged 4 to 17, had sought a health care provider or school staff about their child's emotional or behavioral difficulties. Among those with emotional and behavioral difficulties, 5.1% were prescribed medication and another 5.3% of the children received other treatment (or both), such as behavioral therapy, family therapy, or alternative therapy (Simpson, Cohen, Pastor, & Reuben, 2008). Of those adults affected by mental disorders, about 6% to 8% has a diagnosis of severe illness (schizophrenia, depression, or bipolar disorder) while close to 5% of children have a serious emotional disorder (National Institute of Mental Health, 2006). Mental disorders occur at different rates in the population but with minimal variation by country of origin. For example, only 1.5% to 3% of the world's population develops schizophrenia, although the overall burden of this illness is extreme. Close to 16% of the world's population develops clinical depression and 7% develops bipolar disorder. Anxiety (13%) is the most frequently occurring disorder in children and substance abuse disorders (2%) the least frequent (U.S. Department of Health and Human Services, 1999). In 2004, worldwide, there were 151.2 million persons with unipolar depressive disorders, 29.5 million with bipolar affective disorder, 26.3 million with schizophrenia and 125 million with alcohol use disorders (WHO, 2008). Recent replication studies in the United States support these data.

Kessler et al. (2005) sought to identify lifetime prevalence rates and age of onset in their U.S. replication study. Using the sample generated from the National Comorbidity Survey, Kessler notes that the lifetime prevalence of all disorders (not including schizophrenia) in the United States is close to 46%. The highest overall prevalence per disorder was for major depressive disorder at 17% while alcoholism occurred at a rate of 13% and phobic disorder at 12.5%. When examined by class of disorders, anxiety ranked first at 29% with substance abuse disorder at 25% and mood disorders at 21% in the U.S. population. The most surprising finding reported by Kessler was the age of onset. Anxiety disorders occur at a medium age of 11 while substance abuse tends to occur at a medium age of 20 and mood disorders at age 30. Kessler also reported that women had higher risks of developing both anxiety and mood disorders. African Americans and Hispanics were at lower risk for anxiety, mood, and substance abuse disorders while all lower educated populations, regardless of race, were at greater risk for substance abuse.

Wang et al. (2005) examined the use of mental health services in the same nationally representative sample of 9,282 North Americans over a

12-month period. The researchers were interested in the extent to which the sample was differentiated by such factors as receipt of services by sector (general medicine, specialty care, and alternative medicine), number of visits during the year, and quality of treatment. In addition, the research explored the relationship between the use of services and race, gender, and income.

Overall Wang et al. (2005) found that the majority of North Americans with mental disorders (60%) do not obtain services. In addition, the services they receive are often of poor quality (68%) and are not consistent with evidence-based practices. The median number of visits during the 12-month study period was only 3.0 per person. Compared to earlier studies, the researchers found that 41% of the sample obtained services during the year whereas in 1990 only 25% of the sample obtained care and 19% received care in a prior study in 1980. The chance of obtaining care increased based on the person being below age 60, "female, non-Hispanic white, and previously married; not having a low average family income; and not living in a rural area" (p. 632). Sociodemographic variables place limits on access to quality services, but do not appear to increase substantially the rates of occurrence (U.S. Department of Health and Human Services, 2001; Wang et al., 2005).

Similarly, the 2010 NSDUH reported that of those suffering from AMI or SMI, 39.2% and 60.8%, respectively, used mental health services in the past year. More females (17.7%) and white groups (16.2%) than males (9.5%) and other ethnic groups (5.3% Asians, 13.5% American Indians/Alaska Natives, 7.9% Hispanics, and 8.8% Blacks) utilized mental health services. However, contrary to the study by Wang et al. (2005), mental health service utilization in the age group 18 to 25 was lower than that of their older counterparts. Among youths, of those with MDE or MDE with severe impairment, 37.8% and 41.2%, respectively, received mental health treatment (SAMHSA, 2012).

Recent reports from WHO show the extent to which mental disorders contribute to a variety of major problems (described as burdens) for the individual, family, community, employer, and society in general (WHO, 2000, 2001, 2004, 2008). Some of the problems that accompany mental disorders include:

- **Long-term disability:** The WHO reports document that mental disorders are among the major sources of disability throughout the world. In 2004, among the 20 leading causes of disability, six of them were mental disorders—depression (3rd leading cause), alcohol dependence and problem use (7th), bipolar disorder (12th), schizophrenia (14th), panic disorder (17th), and drug dependence and problem use (20th) (WHO, 2008). Unlike other chronic diseases that generally cause disability among older people, mental disorders lead to disability among younger age groups, 0 to 59 years (New Freedom Commission on Mental Health, 2003b; WHO, 2008). In addition, unipolar depressive disorder was the third leading cause of burden of disease and was projected to be the leading cause of burden of disease in 2030. However, when reviewed by region, unipolar depressive disorder was the most leading cause of burden of disease in the United States and Canada (WHO, 2008).

- **Productivity losses:** Part of the burden of mental disorders is the loss of wages and productivity. The National Mental Health Association (2001) found two major effects of mental disorders. In 1997, the National Mental Health Association (NMHA) reported there was a loss of more than $100 billion in productivity associated with mental illness. NMHA measured productivity losses through the annual number of days of lost employment. In 1997, the workforce in the United States lost more than 1 billion days of work (National Mental Health Association, 2001) while in 2000, losses from a single disorder (depression) accounted for 200 million lost days. Hertz and Baker (2002) reported a total of 217 million lost days of work due to behavioral health disorders. Among the disorders, major depression cost a total of 136.9 million days of work loss (Hertz & Baker, 2002). Kessler et al. (2008) examined loss of wages by analyzing the National Comorbidity Survey Replication (NCS-R). The study measured loss of wages by comparing earnings in the past 12 months of people with and without mental illness. As a result, they estimated that in 2002, a loss of $193.2 billion in the total U.S. population was attributable to serious mental illness (Kessler et al., 2008). When loss of earnings was added to health care expenditures and disability benefits (SSI and SSDI), a total of $317.6 billion was the least economic cost of serious mental illness, since this estimation did not include other indirect costs, such as incarceration, homelessness, and burden of family members (Insel, 2008). Other job-related effects include a higher frequency of job termination either through resignations or firing (*Houston Chronicle,* 2006). A key policy dilemma for persons with mental disabilities is the potential loss of coverage under the Americans with Disabilities Act once they begin treatment. The U.S. Supreme Court decided that whether a finding of disability is warranted is dependent on the effects of treatment or medication (U.S. Supreme Court, 2006a, 2006b, 2006d).

- **High unemployment rates:** Various studies report that compared to their counterparts, people with mental illness have a higher unemployment rate (National Alliance on Mental Illness [NAMI], 2010; New Freedom Commission on Mental Health, 2003b). Some indicate that 60% to 80% of people with mental illness suffer from unemployment (NAMI, 2010). Others indicate that the unemployment rate can reach up to 90% or more for those with severe mental illness (New Freedom Commission on Mental Health, 2003b).

- **High suicide rates:** In 2007, suicide ranks as the 10th highest cause of death for all ages and the fourth highest for adults aged 18 to 65 in the United States (National Institute of Mental Health, 2007).

Suicides took 34,598 lives at a rate of 11.3 per 100,000. Although suicides account for less than 2% of all deaths, the overall number is two times greater than the number of deaths from homicides. Of those persons who commit suicide, the greatest majority (90%) have a diagnosis of depression (National Institute of Mental Health, 2006). There are marked differences in rates of suicide according to such factors as gender, age, and race. Men are more successful in carrying out suicides although women make more attempts. Whites and American Indians and Alaska Natives generally commit suicides at significantly greater rates than other racial and ethnic groups. Suicide was the third highest cause of death for young adults and adolescents in 2007. Advanced age is also a risk factor for suicide, with older adults committing suicide at rates that are disproportionately higher than their numbers in the general population (National Institute of Mental Health [NIMH], 2007).

Epidemiological data from several contemporary studies offer a fundamentally different conceptual basis for future mental health policy, planning, and practice in the United States. More of these contemporary studies and reports support insurance, community-based care, culturally specific services, earlier intervention, evidence-based practices, integrating care across health and mental health sectors, utilization review, continued investment in research, use of technology, and increased involvement of consumers and families. However, over several decades, national concerns about lower quality of care, lack of human rights, unnecessary admissions, discrimination, high rates of deaths, and slow rates of innovation have increased frustration with the pace of change and the degree of involvement by the federal government in state mental health affairs. Unfortunately, unresolved differences over federalism, remnants of states' rights philosophy, and inconsistent federal encroachment in state affairs have had the impact of introducing and maintaining high levels of uncertainty and destructive fragmentation in mental health policy, planning, and service implementation in the United States (New Freedom Commission on Mental Health, 2003b). Unresolved differences between state and federal governments limit the ready adoption of newer epidemiological findings, conceptualizations, and evidence-based methods for managing mental disorders and their socio-economic side effects.

In this chapter, the focus is on identifying and understanding the uncertain direction and fragmentation of mental health care policy in the United States. The chapter also identifies and discusses four processes utilized by the federal government to encroach on decisions heretofore under the aegis of state governments. The chapter concludes with a recommendation for state and federal governments to share the responsibility for mental health care as the basis for promoting a clear future public policy in the United States. Such a plan would decrease the role of the states while substantially increasing the involvement of the federal government beyond its current fiscal support role.

Unresolved Federalism in Mental Health Policy

The history and climate of public mental health policy generally in the United States reflects long-term tension between the federal and state governments over the extent of power (federalism) each can exercise over specific areas of policy as well as the policy making process (Drake, 1999; Pinkney, 1818). These tense differences of opinion are seen currently in the debates over the Affordable Care Act and the efforts by 26 states to have the Supreme Court reverse the act. Federalism is defined as the actual "sharing of power between the states and the national government" (Close Up Foundation, 2006). Other authors describe federalism as the most "striking aspect of the American Constitution" (Pinkmonkey, 2006), albeit unclear as to power sharing is decided, maintained, or evaluated. Descriptions of federalism underscore the importance of determining who makes policy and the various interests that propel the policy direction selected. State government interests determined the direction of public mental health policy from the colonial period to the 21st century.

The U.S. Constitution is the primary source document for defining the respective powers of the states and the federal government. Although the Constitution is explicit about the enumerated powers of the federal government vis-à-vis the states, it does not adequately address the extent to which the federal government has implied power (Street Law, 2006). Nor is it clear from the Constitution the extent of powers reserved to the states. Chief Justice Marshall in *McCulloch v. Maryland* (1819) sought to clarify the multiple questions about enumerated powers as well as the implied powers of the federal government in his 1819 majority decision (Pinkney, 1818). In his opinion, Marshall reached the conclusion that not all powers of the federal government can be specified in the Constitution. The court concluded that an absence of specificity does not preclude, however, the Congress from creating legislation; that is, by implication, congruent with the interests of the nation as a whole. In addition, Marshall's majority opinion gave supreme power to the federal government and Congress where disputes arise over federalism (Marshall, 2006).

The vague distribution of power between the federal and state governments continues to require Supreme Court interventions and reflect deep divisions over what constitutes an acceptable balance of power held by various levels of government (Drake, 1999; Hernandez & Pear, 2006). Although the *McCulloch v. Maryland* (1819) case focused on the ability of the federal government to establish a banking institution not subject to state tariffs, a variety of issues have fueled the long-term debate over federalism: slavery, voting rights by race and gender, school integration, death penalty, right to life, use of stem cells, equal protection, assisted suicide, gay marriage, eminent domain, and more recently mandated coverage under the Affordable Care Act.

Most efforts to resolve these disputes over federalism refer to the 10th Amendment to the Constitution and to precedents established by the McCulloch case (Pinkney, 1818). Based on interpretations of this amendment, states concluded that they have all those powers specifically guaranteed to them under the Constitution as well as those that are not specifically denied them (U.S. Congress, 1787). To some extent, states attempt to use the same theory of implied powers put forth by the Supreme Court in *McCulloch*. States also propose that they and not federal authorities govern the creation of public policy and determine what federal policies are binding on them.

Several alternative conceptualizations of federalism have evolved over the years. Boyd (2006) provides definitions of various forms of federalism as well as the periods in which a particular form emerged. In Table 3.1, Boyd's four chronological periods of federalism are expanded in this chapter to include key mental health issues, policy responses, and social justice issues associated with each different form of federalism.

Boyd defines the period 1700 to 1788 as *prefederalism*. During the prefederalism period, the loose federation of states promulgated the Articles of Confederation to define its relationships and the distribution of authority, power, and decision making. When Boyd's conceptualization of federalism is placed in the context of mental health policy, two categories of interest emerge (each of these categories are applied for each type of federalism). First, the major mental health policy problem during the period of prefederalism was the extent of untreated mental illness in the colonial population—irrespective of race, gender, legal status, and class. Second, the policy response to this issue was twofold. Colonies, starting with Virginia, imported the hospital-oriented policies and structures that were current in Europe. These formal policies and structures emerged to displace the more informal mechanisms of family caregiving and local community care that were prominent prior to 1750. During the prefederalism period, there were also a number of important social justice issues on the horizon. These included issues of citizenship, slavery, women's suffrage, poverty, securing the rights of Native Americans, and unemployment. In response to these issues the federal government passed a series of naturalization acts (Davis & Iron Cloud Two-Dogs, 2004; U.S. Congress, 1790) designed to specify who within the population qualified for citizenship, holding public office, and participation in voting. Local communities were expected to manage poverty and idleness in the population (Pumphrey & Pumphrey, 1961).

Boyd's second period extended from 1789 to 1901. He sees this as the first example of dual federalism. In dual federalism, there is extremely limited sharing or collaboration between the federal and state governments. Each form of government establishes its own power base and seeks to disempower the other. The key mental health issue during the first portion of this period (1789–1865) was the increased demand for hospital-based services. Many states had developed state hospitals but these had quickly become overcrowded, eliminating almost all possibilities of effective treatment (Dain, 1964). The policy response was an effort by the states to build additional facilities, expand existing ones, and increase the number of admissions to the breaking point. Appeal by the states for federal assistance to acquire land to build additional hospitals was throttled when

Table 3.1 **Mental Health and Changes in Federalism, 1700–2006**

Period	Key MH Issue	Level of Federalism (Boyd, 2006)	Policy Response	Social Justice Issues
1700–1788	Untreated mental illness	Prefederalism	State hospitals Family caregiving Local responsibility Church involvement Almshouses	Slavery Citizenship Women's suffrage Poverty Native American rights
1789–1865 1865–1901	Increased demand for services	Dual Federalism	Increased number of facilities; increased admissions; segregation by race and class; state responsibility; Pierce Veto	Reconstruction Voting rights Education Equal protection Employment Economic equality Segregation
1901–1960	Custodial care Access Readiness	Cooperative Federalism	NIMH; state MH departments; National study Psychological readiness for war; postwar mental health services	Migration Racial violence School integration Civil rights Voting rights World wars Poverty
1961–1968	Deinstitutionalization	Creative Federalism	Community mental health; Medicaid; Medicare; CRIPA; Head Start; war on poverty	Human rights Civil rights Poverty Homelessness Health disparities Vietnam War
1968–2006	Community mental health expansion; Fragmentation	Contemporary Federalism; New Federalism	HMO Act; Omnibus Reconciliation Act; block grants; parity; managed care; transformation	Integrated care Human rights Access to services Evidence-base Cultural competence Consumer involvement

[1]Based on *American Federalism, 1776 to 1997*, by E. Boyd, 2006, retrieved from http://usa.usembassy.de/etexts/gov/federal.htm

President Pierce vetoed the congressional legislation supporting the measure (Pierce, 1854). The key social justice issues during this period were the federal efforts to reconstruct the south following the end of the civil war and the decision to override state interests by extending the right of citizenship and voting to African males (Davis & Iron Cloud Two-Dogs, 2004). In the second portion of the first dual federalism period, the major issues centered on such social justice concerns as equal protection under the law; voting rights for women; economic equality; out-migration of Native American populations; immigration of Chinese men; and the rapid rise in hostility, discrimination, and segregation of former slaves.

Boyd describes the period from 1901 to 1960 as the first example of cooperative federalism. He defines this as a period in which there is a marked level of cooperation between the respective levels of government. Overt hostilities are lessened in favor of measures that increase the chances that both levels of government will achieve their aims. Boyd identified Roosevelt's "New Nationalism," Wilson's "New Freedom Program," the 16th Amendment that allowed income taxes, and the New Deal as examples of this expanded cooperation between the federal and state governments. Boyd interpreted this as a period in which the states and the federal government came to an agreement on the balance between civil rights for African Americans and the remnants of states' rights. During the period of cooperative federalism, a prime issue in mental health was the high proportion of Americans who failed to enter the military because of lowered intelligence scores and the high rate of postwar psychiatric casualties (Berlien & Waggoner, 1966; Brill & Kupper, 1966). A secondary issue was the heightened awareness that care in state hospitals was increasingly custodial.

Caplan (1961) was instrumental in identifying the value of providing prevention, early intervention, and emergency services as a precursor to the development of community mental health. During the cooperative federalism period, Congress passed legislation creating the first national mental health study commission (U.S. Congress, 1946). Its report focused on the conditions within state hospitals that violated human rights and acceptable psychiatric care. In response to these mental health concerns, NIMH was developed and most states created state departments of mental health.

A number of important social justice issues were evident during the period of cooperative federalism. Chief among these were school integration, immigration, migration of low-income Blacks from southern states, voting rights issues, access to Social Security, segregation in the military, and the continued presence of poverty and discrimination against women. Change in these social justice issues required considerable involvement by the federal courts combined with civil rights demonstrations and advocacy by Lyndon Johnson and key congressional supporters (U.S. Congress, 1964). Many of these issues were conceptualized as having important mental health implications (Allport, 1954; Arnoff, 1975; Biegel, Milligan, Putnam, & Song, 1994; Brody, 1966; Byrd & Clayton, 2002; Cannon & Locke, 1977; Chandra & Skinner, 2003; Cross, Bazron, Dennis, & Isaacs, 1989; Grossack, 1963; Hansen, 1959; Neighbors, Jackson, Campbell, & Williams, 1989; Snowden, 2000; U.S. Department of Health and Human Services, 2001; Zane, Takeuchi, & Young, 1994).

The shortest period of federalism took place from 1961 to 1968. Boyd describes this period as creative federalism. Boyd sees Lyndon B. Johnson as the architect of creative federalism, as reflected in his great society programs (Boyd, 2006). Johnson made a concerted effort to obtain legislation that would eliminate poverty. In addition, it was during his administration that Medicaid and Medicare were passed. Johnson also signed amendments to extend community mental health centers legislation. During the Johnson years, the key mental health policy issue was deinstitutionalization of residents from state mental hospitals. Community mental health legislation and the introduction of new medications were seen as the twin factors that would make deinstitutionalization occur, if not succeed. The long-term implications of deinstitutionalization for creating a national dilemma of homeless mentally ill were not projected in either analysis for forecasting. The disproportionate implications of deinstitutionalization by race were not foreseen at the federal or state level. Johnson also used the power of his presidency to introduce federal legislation to break down barriers that remained at the state level (U.S. Congress, 1960, 1964, 1965c, 1965d, 1968). Johnson sought to resolve numerous social justice issues during the period. These included voting rights, homeless mentally ill, racial discrimination, unemployment, health disparities, and access to equal protection.

Boyd's final period of federalism occurs from 1968 through 2006. Boyd describes this as the period of contemporary federalism. What distinguished this period were the multiple changes that occurred in relations between the two branches of government. The impetus for contemporary federalism is the vast change in philosophical orientation and values between the individuals who acquired the presidency. From 1968 to 2005, Johnson, Nixon, Ford, Carter, Reagan, Bush, and Clinton occupied the Oval Office. There were numerous differences in perceptions of federalism within this group. Johnson and Carter were similar in their orientation while Nixon, Ford, Reagan, and Bush sought to empower the states and weaken the federal hold on power. In this period, Jimmy Carter sought to return to an expanded role of the federal government similar to LBJ. However, when Carter lost the presidency, Ronald Reagan promptly curtailed his federal expansion plans. The most prominent mental health issue during this period was the continued fragmentation of vision, planning, and financing of care. Carter's commission documented these gaps at the beginning of the period and Bush's commission reaffirmed their presence in almost exact terms. Throughout the period, the federal government took numerous positions on federalism and the mental health system. It was during this period that HMO legislation was passed with support and leadership from Nixon and Ted Kennedy (Ambrose, 1985; Nixon, 1972). Reagan empowered the states through the Omnibus Reconciliation Act and his block grant program (Boyd, 2006; Thomas, 2006). Clinton assisted in the development of managed health care and parity, while Bush ushered in transformation of mental health care at the state level.

Although Boyd's conceptualization ends in 2006, some of the most intense debates over federalism have occurred in the first 3 years of the Obama Administration, 2008 to 2011. The current debates focus on differences in the overall role of the federal government vis-à-vis the states, particularly the southern states. Conservative proponents allege that the current administration is attempting to expand the role of the federal government through such new laws as the Affordable Care Act. The inclusion of a mandate to purchase health insurance coverage is portrayed as a clear indication that the federal government will control all aspects of health care, thus reducing freedom of choice. Throughout this debate mental health issues of importance are the implementation of integrated health care that combines primary care, mental healthcare and substance use treatment; closure of state mental hospitals due to the pressure of reduced state budgets; and homeless mentally ill. The key social justice issues during this period are protecting the voting rights of minority populations and efforts to limit the access of U.S. women to health care, abortions, and contraception.

The vast differences in priorities, values, and goals of these administrations resulted in a constant pattern of expansion and contraction, uncertainty, and fragmentation in mental health policy at the state level. States, community mental health centers, state hospitals, and insurers could not be certain about the direction that federal policy in mental health would take from one presidential administration to the next. No federal policy direction seemed permanent and no funding assured for the long term. States may have found their value on states' rights and maintenance of state hospitals a source of security and certainty that was lacking in the numerous changes in federal perspective. The least amount of federal involvement and control of mental health may have been preferred at the state level (Breeden, 1976; Drake, 1999).

States' Rights and Control of Mental Health Policy

As early as 1765, state and local (colonial) governments developed a myriad of public policies and residential services for responding to and managing persons with mental illness (Baseler, 1998; Deutsch, 1949; Foucault, 1965; Grob, 1973; McCandless, 1996; Rothman, 1970). These initial state/local policies were designed to quell the intense fear of the mentally ill within the colonies, offer respite to distressed family and religious caregivers, and reduce the terse news editorials that charged inaction and disinterest by colonial governments (Davis, 1998). An increasingly large segment of the public wanted immediate protection from a recent series of violent acts by men living in the community considered mentally ill and dangerous to others. In response to these publicized fears, the Virginia House of Burgesses passed legislation in 1763 to build the Public Hospital for Persons of Insane and Disordered Minds to treat mental illness in free white persons (Colonial Williamsburg, 2006; Dain, 1964, 1968). Simultaneously, the Virginia legislature empowered local governments to use coercive powers to force individuals into state institutions.

Passage of this hospital-oriented mental health policy, albeit a first in the United States, was not without considerable international precedent. Several European countries had relied on similar policies to segregate people with tuberculosis, leprosy, and other communicable diseases from the general population. Virginia's colonial government assumed that a similar segregationist policy would prove successful in managing persons with mental illness and restoring the fragile integrity of colonial society (Deutsch,

1949; Grob, 1994; Rothman, 1970). However, U.S. asylums segregated persons with mental illness from the general population, their families, and communities for lengthy periods, sometimes for life. Such lengthy periods of segregation may have contributed to the development of stigma, disability, and difficulty integrating persons with mental illness back into their communities. Successful challenge of the long-term segregation of the mentally disabled did not occur until passage of the Americans with Disabilities Act in 1990 (U.S. Congress, 2005; U.S. Supreme Court, 2006c).

Other colonial governments quickly replicated the hospital-oriented policies crafted in Virginia. In less than 50 years, almost all state governments developed uncontested monopolies over the multiple domains of mental health care: policy development, inpatient services, management and oversight, and financial support. Prior to state monopolies in mental health, families provided the majority of long-term support for the mentally ill (Belknap, 1956; Deutsch, 1949; Hatfield, 1987).

State control of mental health policy resulted in the development, maintenance, and expansion of hundreds of fledgling mental hospitals that provided economic, employment, and emotional security to the small agrarian communities in which they were located. Although these mental institutions were unable to cure or arrest mental illness, the economic and employment advantages of long lengths of stay and consistent rates of admissions brought major increases in state general fund dollars, staffing, authority, power, and influence well into the 20th century. Institutionalized segregation of the mentally disabled became the de facto national policy in the United States for close to 200 years.

Until 1945, most mental hospital directors or superintendents reported directly to the governors of their states and had direct access to the "money" committees in the state legislature (Poen, 1979). In addition, state hospitals developed powerful lay boards of directors who petitioned state government on their behalf and on behalf of their employees. State facilities created jobs, sales, wealth, and votes at the local level. The federal government's direct involvement in state mental health policy came first in 1865 with passage of legislation creating the Freedman's Bureau and the requirement that states provide mental health treatment for former slaves (Department of Mental Hygiene and Hospitals, 1960). However, federal intervention terminated quickly. Federal intervention in the mid-1800s resulted in the creation of state mental institutions segregated by race as well as disability.

In addition to passage of hospital-oriented mental health policies, colonial governments passed a series of related public policies to address poverty, communicable diseases, mental retardation, unemployment, crime, abandoned children, and dependent elderly (Rothman, 1970). Here too colonial governments relied increasingly on the building of isolated institutions that segregated afflicted persons from the community as a means of protection and social control. If needed, colonial governments could justify their control of public mental health and related problem areas through an interpretation of the 10th Amendment to the U.S. Constitution that gave them all of the rights explicitly articulated as well as those not specifically denied them (states' rights) in this historic document (U.S. Congress, 1787). States deftly used these interpretations to maintain almost total control of the public policy making apparatus in mental health and related areas for over 200 years (Davis & Iron Cloud Two-Dogs, 2004). However, there were few efforts by the federal government to alter the course of mental health care or policy at the state level until near the end of the 19th century.

To the contrary, the federal government maintained a minimalist role in each of the domains of mental health, but particularly in the constructing of public policies and financing of hospital construction and staffing costs. The federal government conveniently saw the states as financially and programmatically responsible for the care of the mentally ill. The federal position was made clearly as early as 1854, when President Pierce (1854) vetoed a Senate bill aimed at providing federal lands to the states to construct mental institutions. Pierce expressed concern that approval of the bill would soon extend federal support to the states for support of similar services and other indigent populations. Pierce believed that extending this level of support to the states violated the U.S. Constitution. Specifically, the basis of the veto was Pierce's concern that the tenuous balance of power (federalism) between the federal and state governments was at risk.

However, after congressional and presidential action in 1945, the federal government became increasingly involved in creating national policy that focused specifically on harmful conditions in state hospitals. Until development of the community mental health centers program in 1963 (PL 88–164), the federal government did not provide direct funding for mental health care at the state or local level. State general funds were the primary source of operating dollars for state hospitals and for support of some aftercare services from 1765 to 1965. Public Law 88–164 was unprecedented in that it authorized federal resources to support new outpatient and five essential inpatient mental health services by local nonprofit organizations (community mental health centers) that bypassed the state. Federal plans were to develop close to 2,500 community mental health centers that would eventually displace aging and overcrowded state mental hospitals. However, it was unclear what would happen to the economies in local communities once the state hospitals closed. Additionally, it was not clear what would happen to the 550,000 persons who were in state institutions up through 1963 when the deinstitutionalization plans were implemented.

When Reagan and not Carter was elected president in 1980, federal plans to empower community mental health centers ended with less than 700 centers completed (Manderscheid & Henderson, 2001). Federal support of community mental health centers ended although the centers that received construction grants had a legal obligation to continue providing services for no less than 20 years. The community mental health centers policy established a federal precedent for involvement in the design, delivery, and evaluation of mental health services at the state and local level. Later policies in Medicaid, Medicare, and constitutional standards of care (human rights) would permanently change the balance of power between the federal and state governments in mental health.

Part of the impetus for the minimalist position of the federal government in mental health was the unacceptable risk that states would rely on the federal treasury to provide unlimited financial support for state hospitals and other institutions. The risk for the states was the potential that acceptance of federal dollars would be followed by federal encroachment in what was interpreted as the sovereign right of each state to develop their unique policies in mental health, health, education, voting, and public accommodations (NAACP Legal Defense Fund & Marshall, 1954). The federal government was concerned that their involvement in the creation of state mental health policies and services would eventually result in these becoming fixed federal tax obligations. In addition to costs, the continued federal focus on conditions in state hospitals was a clear message that the federal government saw these facilities as ineffective and their harmful practices as eventually the basis for congressional action. However, it was unclear what constitutional basis the federal government would exercise to enable increased involvement in policy matters considered reserved to the states.

States' rights was a key southern political strategy from the 1840s through the 1950s that sought to maintain the idea that the federal government could not interfere with decisions made by the states (Drake, 1999). Southern strategists (strict constructionists) saw states' rights as a legitimate philosophical basis for raising a number of questions about shared political powers. These questions include determining the appropriate distribution of decision-making power; the taxing power of each branch of government; whether slavery would continue in the southern states, and if not, would there be compensation for the immediate and long-term financial loss for slave owners (Althouse, 2001; Baker & Young, 2001; Drake, 1999; Lincoln, 1862). The more successfully the states' rights idea could be sold and adopted, the less power would have been held by the federal government to intervene in key areas of civil rights, ostensibly protected under the Constitution of the United States. The essence of the states' rights strategy was the intent by the Southern states to control the legal distribution of access to all social institutions.

It was in part the failure of the Southern states to demonstrate an ability or willingness to abide by the constitutional provisions of equal protection under the law (in racial and disability areas) that stimulated the federal government to encroach on responsibilities formerly monopolized by the state (Ennis & Siegel, 1973; U.S. Congress, 1980). In effect, states' rights was a seriously flawed strategy based primarily on an abrogation of constitutional rights of individuals and groups by race, social class, residency, income, and disability (Breeden, 1976; Drake, 1999; U.S. Congress, 2005). The long-term purported failure of the states to meet constitutional requirements in mental health raises the critical question of what if any constitutional authority the federal government holds in matters of mental or physical health services. Are these health matters the sole prerogative of the states? Does the federal government have the constitutional authority to become involved in how the states provide mental health care to its residents? Have the repeated violations alleged to have taken place under the aegis of the state risen to such an egregious level that federal intervention is warranted?

Federal Encroachment in State Mental Health Policy and Services

Increased federal involvement in multiple domains of mental health is the most critical variable in determining the current status and future direction of public mental health care in the United States. Although the federal government avoided substantive financial, policy, and programmatic responsibility for state mental health systems for almost two centuries, the degree of federal involvement in mental health has expanded in direct response to the level of federalism espoused by the President and Congress since 1945. The monopoly formerly exercised by state mental health authorities, governors, and legislative bodies over mental health policy direction became diluted as the power of the federal government increased. From 1945 to 1980, federal power increased steadily as state control over mental health waned. Is this expansion in power over mental health a reflection of the implied powers of Congress and in concert with the Constitution (Marshall, 2006)? Once the state fails to carry out constitutional guarantees over a protracted period, is there an obligation on the part of the federal government to protect citizens against the state in matters of mental health as in other areas (NAACP Legal Defense Fund & Marshall, 1954; Reno, 1999)? Does the finding that long-term institutionalization of the mentally disabled constitutes segregation obligate the federal government to take corrective action? Have the states failed in their constitutional obligation to provide safe mental health care to all citizens?

In response to persistent mental health problems (particularly harmful conditions in state hospitals), the federal government used four connected strategies (Table 3.2) to increase its enumerated power vis-à-vis the states: passage of a host of national mental health acts (public laws), application of findings from presidential commissions, new requirements based on financing and reimbursement policies, and federal lawsuits and court decisions.

National Mental Health Acts/Public Laws

From 1869 to 2003, the U.S. Congress passed numerous public laws aimed at correcting a wide variety of problems in public mental health care. Ten of these public laws are included in Table 3.2. President Pierce reinforced the minimalist federal role in mental health policy development in 1854. At that time, Pierce issued his now famous veto that prevented the federal government from donating land to states on which to build state mental hospitals. Pierce based his veto on the risk that federal support of state

Table 3.2 Federal Strategies, Actions, and Outcomes

Federal Strategy	Specific Action	Outcomes
Mental Health Acts/ Public Laws	Pierce Veto of 1854	Precluded federal land for state hospitals
	Freedman's Act 1865	Required state hospital care for former slaves and Native Americans
	MH Act 1946 [PL 79–487]	Created NIMH and single state mental health agency; subcommittee on race
	MH Act 1955 [PL 84–142]	Created Joint Commission on Mental Health to Study Conditions in Mental Hospitals
	MH Act 1963 [PL 88–164]	Created community mental health centers financed by federal revenue
	MH Act 1965 [PL 89–105]	Extended prior legislation Allowed federal government to sue states to protect civil rights
	MH Act 1980 [PL 96–416]	Rescinded community mental health centers; established block grants
	MH Act 1981 [PL 97–35]	Protection and advocacy for the mentally ill; established human rights
	MH Act 1987 [PL 99–319]	Housing assistance for homeless persons with mental illness
	ADA 1990 [PL 101–336]	Sought parity between health and mental health coverage in insurance
	MH Act 1998 [PL 100–77]	Targeted barriers to the disabled; saw long-term hospitalization as segregation and discrimination
	Paul Wellstone and Pete Domenici Mental Health Parity and Addiction Equity Act of 2008 [PL 110–343]	
Presidential Commissions and Executive Orders	Carter Commission	New legislation to expand federal support of mental health centers
	Bush Commission	Recommended transformation of mental health systems
Financing	PL 88–164 Medicaid Medicare Omnibus Reconciliation Act [PL 97–35]	Monies for construction and staffing in community mental health centers Amended Social Security Act to provide federal payments to the states for medical and psychiatric care Provided monies to the states in "block grant" format
Judicial Decisions/Public Laws and Class Action Suits	*Wyatt v. Stickney*, 1972	Established standards for services; rejected cost arguments of the states
	PL 96–416, 1980	Allowed federal government to sue states for conditions in institutions that violate the Constitution
	Olmstead v. L.C., 1999	Reinforced the right to life in the community for the mentally disabled

mental hospitals would be followed quickly by similar requests to support other services heretofore supported by state general funds. Substantive federal involvement in state matters of mental health came initially through the Bureau of Refugees, Freedmen, and Abandoned Lands in 1865. The U.S. Congress, fearing a postslavery increase in mental illness, required southern states to establish mental institutions for former slaves. Soon after passage of this act, the state of Virginia passed legislation creating the first state mental hospital (Central Lunatic Asylum for the Colored Insane) exclusively for Africans in America (Brown, 1887; Denton, 1960; Department of Mental Hygiene and Hospitals, 1960; Drewry, 1916). Within a few years, all of the southern and border states established mental hospitals that were segregated by race—as were many other public facilities up to 1968.

The National Mental Health Act of 1946 was passed during the Truman Administration following widespread national concerns about psychiatric disorders and preparedness for war (Berlien & Waggoner, 1966; Brill & Kupper, 1966). In this act, the federal government used its resources to encourage states to establish single departments of mental health. Prior to this act, state hospitals reported directly to the governor of each state. The Mental Health Act of 1946 also created the National Institute of Mental Health and charged it with improving the mental health of the nation. Improvement was defined as increases in resources for research, training, enhanced diagnosis and treatment, and monetary assistance to the states. Part of the impetus for both actions was the research and eventual publication by Deutsch (Deutsch, 1948) on the horrid conditions in state mental hospitals.

The Mental Health Study Act of 1955 (U.S. Congress, 1955) established the Joint Commission on Mental Health. The Joint Commission's major strategy was to study and evaluate the condition of state mental institutions and make recommendations to the president and Congress at its conclusion. Deutsch's 1948 publication provided the benchmark for a critical study of state hospital conditions. At the time the Joint Commission began its work in 1955, more than 550,000 persons were warehoused in state mental institutions. The majority of these individuals would spend their lives in state institutions with limited opportunity for recovery, return to the community, or gainful employment. The stark and inhumane conditions exposed by the Joint Commission's report sparked national interest in deinstitutionalization and closure of state institutions (Joint Commission on Mental Illness and Health, 1961; Sharfstein, 2000; U.S. Congress, 1955). The effort to close state mental hospitals has increased in intensity since the beginning of the recession in 2006 as a cost-cutting measure by the states (SAMHSA, 2011).

This Joint Commission's report chronicled the squalid and unsafe conditions in state hospitals throughout the United States and the absence of quality health or mental health care. These conditions were not unlike those found in community care earlier by Dorthea Dix (Gollaher, 1995) and thought to be ameliorated with the development of "humane" state hospitals. The Joint Commission found high rates of death in state institutions that lacked rudimentary medical care. However, the major impetus for deinstitutionalization was the need to find a more permanent means to limit the growth in expenditures of state general funds. The Joint Commission's findings and recommendations did not result in actual federal policy until 8 years later during the Kennedy Administration. PL 99–164 (Community Mental Health and Mental Retardation Construction Act), contained many of the recommendations from the Joint Commission (U.S. Congress, 1955, 1963, 1965c). This public law energized the effort to develop community mental health centers but did not alter state operation of mental institutions or the concentration of power in state legislatures.

Public Law 88–164 provided federal funding for the construction of buildings to house community mental health and mental retardation functions. Kennedy's novel approach to community mental health followed the recommendations of the Joint Commission's report as well as psychiatric experiences in World War II (Berlien & Waggoner, 1966; Brill & Kupper, 1966). In addition, community mental health practice was supported by new research on the benefits of newly discovered psychotropic drugs (Healy, 2002). Sharfstein (2000) points out that community mental health "emphasizes better access to high-quality care" based on the philosophical tenets of the movement in 1963. The federal government followed the construction grants with funding for staffing grants in 1967 (U.S. Congress, 1967). These staffing grants required community mental health centers to offer five essential services (outpatient, inpatient, consultation and education, day care, and emergency services) to a defined catchment area not to exceed 250,000 individuals. The construction and staffing grants also had the impact of shifting the locus of inpatient and outpatient care from state institutions to the nonprofit sector of the community. By the time the community mental health program officially ended in 1981, centers were to offer 15 services and be fiscally self-sustaining. The greater the number of discreet services provided, the greater the chances of providing quality treatment and prevention was assumed.

In its effort to improve quality of care at the community level, community mental health center legislation essentially bypassed states' rights tradition and the maintenance of state hospitals, and created a totally new nonprofit infrastructure, only minimally under the direction of state governments. States could not supplant federal funding or discontinue their own existing fiscal commitments. Community mental health centers were an indirect federal effort to circumvent state control of mental health services and quality without the federal government assuming clinical responsibility for direct care for thousands of low-income chronically ill individuals.

The public laws passed by Congress from 1945 to 1980 had an impact on the power of states in three areas. Federal mental health laws established standards of care that seek to hold states legally accountable. The federal government used these laws to establish alternative service structures financed by the federal treasury that had the potential effect of reducing utilization of state hospitals. Public laws passed over the past 50 years established clear guidelines to ensure that states did not violate or ignore constitutional or human rights of persons with mental disabilities. Where states were in violation of these laws, the federal government could sue the states and force compliance.

Increases in Federal Financing

Historically, states have exercised a monopoly, albeit burdensome, over the mental health system through their control of mental health episodes and the general funds that support state hospitals. State control of inpatient services, where the majority of mental health episodes took place, gave states the maximum opportunity to determine the direction of mental health care and policy in the United States. As recently as 1969, the majority (80%) of mental health episodes took place in state and county mental hospital facilities, justifying the continued investment of scarce state general funds (Manderscheid & Henderson, 2001). States also contributed close to 85% of all the funding during this period. State funds provided direct support to state hospitals but more importantly were the major source of employment for those communities in which state hospitals were located. However, federal funding and reimbursement policies precipitated major changes in utilization of inpatient care and associated costs from 1969 to 2012. For example, in 1990, there were close to 750 state mental hospitals that consumed 40% of all mental health expenditures (SAMHSA, 2006b). However, by 2008, the number of state mental hospitals had declined to 216 and accounted for 28% of all state mental health agencies -controlled expenditures (SAMHSA, 2011).

Historically, the federal government would not provide financial resources or reimburse states under Medicaid to offset the cost of operating state hospitals or free standing private psychiatric inpatient for services to persons between the ages of 21 to 64 (U.S. Congress, 1965c). The original Medicaid policy, as well as its numerous amendments, treats institutions for mental diseases (IMD) differently from general hospitals with psychiatric units. Federal funding for persons with psychiatric disorders is available to support services for children (under age 21) in state mental institutions, for adults over age 65, and for adults 21 to 64 served in general hospital psychiatric units. Federal regulations governing reimbursements under Medicaid have helped shift an increasingly larger share of psychiatric episodes away from state mental institutions toward general hospitals with psychiatric units (Manderscheid & Henderson, 2001).

From 1986 to 2005, expenditures for mental health and substance abuse services increased from approximately $41 billion to $135 billion (SAMHSA, 2010b). Of the total, mental health expenditures alone grew from $32 billion in 1986 to $113 billion by 2005. Expenditures for mental health grew at a slower rate per annum (6.9%) between 1986 and 2005 than all health spending (7.9.%). When controlled for inflation, national expenditures for mental health grew at 4.3% per annum versus 5.3% for overall health care (SAMHSA, 2010b).

Between 1986 and 2005, the pattern of expenditures by state and federal governments moved in opposite directions. Overall, expenditures by states declined as a percentage of total national expenditures while the federal share of overall expenditures for mental health grew substantially (Mark, Coffey, Vandivort-Warren, Harwood, & King, 2005; SAMHSA, 2010b). In 1986, state and local governments accounted for 35% of all mental health expenditures while the federal government accounted for 23%. By 2005, the state local share had declined to 30% while the federal share had ballooned to 28% of all mental health expenditures (SAMHSA, 2010b).

The growth in federal expenditures has principally been restricted to offsetting the cost of medication and outpatient services—thus continuing the trend toward community services established by Kennedy and Carter. Payments to specialty inpatient facilities declined significantly over the period, paralleling the decline in number of inpatient beds, psychiatric episodes, and number of state hospitals (Manderscheid & Henderson, 2001; Mark et al., 2005; SAMHSA, 2006b; Wang et al., 2006).

Mark et al. (2005) examined the changes in federal financial participation in the funding of mental health care from 1991 to 2001. Of the $104 billion expended, close to 82% was spent for mental health care alone and only 7.6% for substance abuse care. When compared to total health care spending in the United States, behavioral health accounted for only 7.6% of the total. Of interest was the difference between the amounts of funding paid for by governmental agencies and that paid from private sources (insurance and out of pocket). The governmental share of total behavioral health care spending was approximately 65% versus 35% from these private sources. Of the federal share of behavioral health funding, close to 26% came through Medicaid (PL 88–197). Interestingly, state governments paid out an amount in behavioral health care (26%) that was roughly equal to that of the federal government. When total behavioral costs are calculated, however, close to 37% is paid for by the states.

Several policy conclusions can be reached through examination of these decennial expenditures. First, what is clear here is that behavioral health care remains a policy (and service) responsibility of the federal and state governments and less of a responsibility in the private sector. For example, the overall share of total costs assumed by the government increased from 58% in 1986 to 62% by 2005 (SAMHSA, 2010b). Beyond this conclusion, behavioral health care costs are borne by the government principally for low-income populations through Medicaid expenditures shared between the federal and state governments. However, when all expenditures are included, mental health and substance abuse service remains a primary responsibility of state governments increasingly dependent on federal funds.

What is equally clear is that the federal government establishes its policy agenda through the budget. Recent efforts by the federal government to reduce Medicaid funding for disabled populations appears to undercut the emphasis on recovery. A second conclusion is that government is increasingly supporting nonhospital services for persons with behavioral health problems. Between 1986 and 2005, hospital care for behavioral health declined from 45% of total expenditures to 26% (SAMHSA, 2010b). In contrast, expenditures for community mental health care have increased. During 1981 to 2007, while experiencing reduced expenditures for hospital care, state mental health agencies expenditures for community-based mental health services increased from 33% to 71% (SAMHSA, 2011). A third major policy conclusion that can be drawn is that behavioral health care is increasingly being addressed through medication or prescription drugs, which accounted for the majority of cost increases over the decade. It is these marked changes in the actual amount of federal funding, combined with new regulations, that has allowed the federal government to exercise greater control of the state mental health infrastructure.

Presidential Commissions and Involvement in Mental Health Policy in the United States

In April 2002, President George Bush appointed a 15-member commission to "conduct a comprehensive study" of the mental health system in the United States (Bush, 2002; New Freedom Commission on Mental Health, 2006). Bush's executive order establishing the charge to the commission was similar in language and content to the first presidential mental health commission appointed by Jimmy Carter in 1978 (Bush, 2002; Grob, 2005). On the surface, each president sought to catalog the extent of problems in the existing system, improve the quality of mental health care, propose new policies, and offer solutions for controlling the escalating cost of care. The focus of this investigatory work by both presidential commissions was public mental health systems (facilities, centers, and clinics) historically managed by state mental health authorities. Carter expected his commission to offer a variety of recommendations for meeting the needs of the underserved mentally ill through expanded federal support of non-profit community mental health centers (Grob, 2005) while Bush wanted his commission to focus on newer concepts of transformation, rehabilitation, and recovery and their ties to employment. Bush's commission also sought to enlist the participation of families and consumers, state agencies, and federal organizations under the direction of the federal government (New Freedom Commission on Mental Health, 2003b). The activist role of the federal government proposed by the Bush commission's report was similar to that proposed by Carter but at clear political odds with Reagan's concept of "New Federalism" (Boyd, 2006; Stoesz & Karger, 1993). Under "New Federalism," Reagan wanted states to regain greater control of resources, decisions, and policy making as the federal government's authority receded. To Reagan, Carter's policies inappropriately enhanced federal power and control at the expense of the southern states' rights agenda.

Beneath the surface, however, Carter and Bush, both former southern governors, understood the complex labyrinth of state mental health could not change without effective new medications, fully funded community services, improved care in state hospitals, increased insurance coverage, and affordable housing for persons with mental illness. Kennedy came closer to public recognition of these dilemmas when he sought to increase the investments by the federal government following completion of the Joint Commission's Report (Joint Commission on Mental Illness and Health, 1961; Kennedy, 2006b). What further distinguished Carter and Bush's historic commissions was the different mental health policy context that birthed them. Carter's commission was established at a time when there was substantive support for expanding the number and financing of federal community mental health centers. At its conclusion, Carter's commission recommended new legislation to drive its findings and polices. However, President Reagan rescinded Carter's Mental Health Centers Act within the first few weeks of his administration. Reagan interpreted Carter's policies as increasing federal power over the states and increasing the financial burden on government and business (Thomas, 2006).

Bush appointed his commission at a time when such values as increased privatization, recovery, disease management, religious involvement, evidence-based practice, and family participation were at their zenith. These values coincided with Bush's intent (New Freedom Commission on Mental Health, 2003a) to "promote increased access to educational and employment opportunities for people with disabilities" (p. 1). Following completion of his commission, however, Bush did not actively press for new legislation or issue executive orders to implement its major findings or recommendations. Surprisingly, the Bush Administration sought to reduce support from Medicaid, Medicare, housing, and health care for the mentally disabled. Consumer advocates found Bush's willingness to reduce existing Medicaid benefits and housing contrary to the recommendations of his commission and inimical to recovery.

One year after President Bush appointed his New Freedom Commission it issued an extensive final report of its findings and recommendations (New Freedom Commission on Mental Health, 2003b). Not surprisingly, the Bush commission reported that mental health services in the United States were characterized by the following problems/obstacles:

- Fragmentation in services for children and adults and the aged
- Stigma that surrounds mental illnesses
- Unfair treatment and financial requirements placed on benefits in private insurance
- Numerous barriers that impede care
- High rates of unemployment and disability
- Disparities by race and class
- Limited access to treatment
- Discrepancies between evidence-based treatments and services available
- A mental health workforce that lags behind need
- Excessive rates of suicide and limited suicide prevention
- Limited goals

These findings were not unlike those articulated by Carter's commission 24 years before (Carter, 2006; Grob, 2005), or the Joint Commission on Mental Health established by Congress in 1955 during the Eisenhower Administration (Joint Commission on Mental Illness and Health, 1961). It is important to identify and understand the factors that reinforce delay of new policy directions and maintain such uncertainty 50 years after the first comprehensive study of mental health care. Such an understanding may be valuable in helping drive the multiple recommendations in the Bush commission's report towards implementation (National Technical Assistance Center [NTAC], 2004; SAMHSA, 2005).

The Bush commission reviewed the previous literature of studies, reports, and findings on mental health care (U.S. Department of Health and Human Services, 1999, 2001) and concluded that the answer to the long-term problems of fragmentation and poor quality of care required transformation of public and to some extent private mental health systems. Initially, it was unclear how the Bush Administration and its commission defined transformation operationally. The Bush commission defined transformation as a vision, a process, and an outcome (Anderson, 1994). However, the administration found Cebowski's definition more acceptable: Transformation is a highly complex and continuous process that seeks to create or anticipate the future (Power, 2004). Furthermore, Cebowski indicated that transformation might entail creating new principles, sources of power, and structure, culture, policy, and programs.

To achieve its transformation goal, the federal government needed to provide incentives to overcome the inertia and resistance of the states. The federal government issued an RFP that provided $15 million over 5 years to each of seven states to support their transformation efforts (SAMHSA, 2006a). The amount provided per state represented a small percentage of the annual budgets of these agencies and seemed insufficient to bring about transformation. In addition to funding, the seven states obtained federal technical assistance in how to develop and implement comprehensive transformation plans. At the end of the first year of funding, the federal government suddenly directed that any future transformation efforts in other states would require funding via a state's existing block grant program. To reach this conceptual goal, the Bush commission identified and defined a complex series of specific concepts, goals, targets, strategies, analyses, forums, plans, and processes that would take place at the federal, state, and local level to achieve transformation (SAMHSA, 2005).

The Bush mental health commission report was the first since the Carter commission in 1981 and only the fifth effort by a U.S. president (Truman, Eisenhower, Kennedy, and Carter) to make major policy recommendations to improve the quality of mental health care as a national priority. Each president sought substantive changes in the power relationship between the federal and state governments. Kennedy outlined critical questions about these relationships and the implications for the mentally disabled if they were left unresolved (Kennedy, 2006a, 2006b, 2006c).

The practical value of Truman's, Eisenhower's, Kennedy's, Carter's, and Bush's recommendations for changes in public mental health was severely limited by the continued presence of two unresolved/historical public policy dilemmas. First, there is no agreement between the states and the national government on the acceptable level of federalism in mental health policy and related services. For almost two centuries, state governments controlled the mental health policy process and the delivery of services. The federal government was essentially kept at bay in a dual federalism position described by Boyd (2006). It was this power imbalance in mental health that the Kennedy Administration questioned and identified as an impediment to developing new financial and services arrangements consistent with the recommendations of the Joint Commission on Mental Health. It was Kennedy's belief that improved quality at the state (hospital) level required increased federal pressure, legislation, and finances (Kennedy, 2006b, 2006c). Truman, Kennedy, Johnson, and Carter proposed an increase in the power of the federal government but the nature of the power relationships between the state and federal government remained unclear (Kennedy, 2006b).

The historical tension between the two levels of government remains significant and exacerbated by the frequent expansions and contractions and directional changes in federal and state policy.

Second, the states implemented their long-term monopoly of mental health by investing the majority of their energy and resources in the construction, staffing, and maintenance of state mental hospitals. The shift toward community mental health services resulted from critical federal reports (Joint Commission on Mental Illness and Health, 1961), and human rights litigation (U.S. Congress, 1980), followed by legislative support of nonprofit organizations. Federal community mental health policy essentially bypassed the traditional state authority (U.S. Congress, 1963). Did the federal government have the authority to provide federal revenues to support alternative mental health services in the states but outside the aegis of state government? The Supreme Court's decision in *McCulloch* (Marshall, 2006; Pinkney, 1818) supports the idea that federal intervention in mental health at the state level is consistent with the theory of implied power.

The New Freedom Commission Report is similar in breath and quality to the Joint Commission's and the Carter Commission's Reports. The New Freedom Commission Report was completed in 2003; however, all of its subreports have yet to be issued publicly. In addition, the implementation guidelines were issued in July 2005; however, no executive orders or legislation have followed. The New Freedom Commission Report seems to be following a similar pattern to that of previous commissions and their findings in which policy action lags behind incisive analysis.

The New Freedom Commission Report and President Bush's major goals are at best a set of indirect federal recommendations to state governors and legislators. However, these federally generated goals do not carry the strength of public law, executive order, and have no immediate enforcement powers. By conceptualizing the report and President Bush's goals as recommendations to the states, the federal government has to identify multiple incentives or sanctions to get states to share or exchange their long-term control of the mental health policy process and adopt new federal standards for practice. Neither of these tasks can be achieved without the expenditure of significant political and economic capital, both of which were in shorter supply following 2 years of a weakened incumbent administration, where reelection was no longer a lever to entice compliance. What power does the federal government have that would be instrumental in increasing the chances that state governments will voluntarily adopt federal recommendations?

Federal Lawsuits and Judicial Cases Against the States

Two federal court cases (*Wyatt v. Stickney*; *Olmstead v. L.C.*) and two public laws (PL 96–416 Civil Rights of Institutionalized Persons Act; PL 100–336 Americans with Disabilities Act) established similar federal quality standards for state mental health systems. These two judicial cases and two public laws also created a legal foundation for federal intervention and penalties when states fail to meet federal standards. Prior to these judicial and public law interventions, the federal government did not seek to force states to comply with any set of national standards of treatment or service.

However, *Wyatt v. Stickney* (Johnson, 1972) stands as one of the most important federal judicial decisions in the history of U.S. mental health law. Wyatt was a psychiatric patient in Bryce State Hospital in Alabama and Stickney was the commissioner of mental health for the state. When Alabama sought to reduce its operating costs, it planned to decrease the number of staff and the overall staff to patient ratio. However, Wyatt, through his guardian, objected to this change by the state and argued that his constitutional right to effective treatment would be compromised if the ratio were changed. Furthermore, Wyatt argued that the long-term nature of his hospitalization amounted to involuntary confinement with very limited chance of his ever returning to the community. The reduction in staffing would therefore further decrease his chances of release from confinement.

The federal court agreed with Wyatt's argument and used his pleadings to build a consent decree that outlined the quality treatment standards the state of Alabama had to adopt. The list of requisite changes became the Wyatt standards and established a precedent for other state mental health systems.

Arguments between the federal government and the state in the Wyatt case took place over a 30-year period. The case was finally closed in 1993 when the courts agreed that Alabama reached a reasonable degree of compliance with the agreed-on standards of care. The Wyatt case was significant in the ongoing struggle between the federal and state government because it forced the state to adopt and meet specified standards. In addition, Wyatt's case successfully countermanded the state's claim that a lack of funding was sufficient justification to maintain a status quo that violated human rights and constitutional guarantees.

The Civil Rights of Institutionalized Persons Act (CRIPA; U.S. Congress, 1980) (PL 96–416) gave the U.S. Department of Justice the power to bring suit against the states for constitutional violations that took place in state facilities. The legal basis of PL 96–416 parallels the arguments made successfully in *Wyatt v Stickney* in 1972. CRIPA concluded that residents of state (public) institutions maintain their constitutional rights while confined, and the act prevents states from ignoring these rights. The rights identified in the act include a right to treatment, a right to periodic evaluations, protection from abuse and harmful treatment, a right to medical care, and a right to return to the community. Where a state institution violates these rights, the Justice Department has the authority to conduct on-site evaluations and seek voluntary compliance with its findings and recommended changes. Where states are unwilling to abide by the findings, the Justice Department files charges and institutes court proceedings.

From 1980 to 2000, the U.S. Justice Department successfully sued 28 states for violations of CRIPA. The U.S. Congress passed the Civil Rights of Institutionalized Persons Act in 1980. This act allowed federal intervention in protecting the constitutional rights of persons in prisons. However, the federal government expanded the purview of the act to encompass the rights of persons with mental illness who were residents of state mental institutions. Recently, the act was expanded to include an unprecedented community remedy. In Hawaii, the Department of Justice required the state mental health system to develop and implement a community services plan that would provide services outside the state hospital (Adult Mental Health Division, 2005; Chang, 2006; Creamer, 2001; Gorman, 2006; Hanson-Mayer, 2006; Kobayashi, 2006; Minkoff, 2006).

The Americans with Disabilities Act focuses on eliminating all barriers to persons with disabilities—mental as well as physical. The ADA concluded that confining "persons with disabilities in institutions constitutes unnecessary and illegal segregation" (U.S. Congress, 2005). To eliminate this segregation, the ADA required states, local governments, and employers to remove all barriers—behavioral and physical. Specifically, the ADA concluded that individuals with disabilities had a right to life in the community.

The second legal case of importance in mental health was *Olmstead v. L.C.,* filed in 1999. This case was heard in Georgia and was brought by two plaintiffs who were confined in the Georgia Regional Hospital Center. The plaintiffs alleged that they were being held in the state facilities in violation of the ADA and prior judgments in other cases. Furthermore, the plaintiffs claimed that the state had consistently failed to place them in a less restrictive community setting although they were found clinically eligible.

In response to the plaintiff's arguments, the state of Georgia sought to defend its actions based on funding shortages and potential harm to the states programs or systems. In essence, the state sought to base its claim on the proposal that the accommodations sought by the plaintiffs were too costly. On appeal, the state's cost base defense was deemed worthy of examination and the case was remanded back to the district court for review. The case was eventually heard by the U.S. Supreme Court.

The Declining Financial Health of State Governments: Implications for the Future of State Mental Health Policy

The severe recession that occurred in the United States in 2007 has had the most devastating effects in history on revenue and expenditures at the state level (McNichol, Oliff, & Johnson, 2012). "As of the third quarter of 2011, State revenues remained 7% below pre-recession levels" (McNichol et al., 2012, p. 1). Only six states (Alaska, Arkansas, Montana, North Dakota, West Virginia, and Wyoming) reported that they were not experiencing deficits this fiscal year (Combs, 2012; McNichol et al., 2012). Each of the other states reported deficits that ranged from 2% of their total spending from the 2011 fiscal year (Indiana) to 45% (Nevada) (McNichol et al., 2012). The extent of the states' future fiscal crisis and the tepid growth in revenue does not allow the states to meet their current obligations or offset anticipated continued growth and service demand in their largest programs such as education, Medicaid, and human services. The downturn in the economy actually creates a circular demand for some human services at a time when the states have decreased capacity to raise revenue. As the state economy weakens, unemployment increases, new housing starts decline, and consumers have considerably less discretionary income to make purchases and pay sales taxes. It is these sales taxes that undergird the local and state ability to provide various services. Under the new Affordable Care Act, states are anticipating a major increase in their financial obligations under Medicaid as the number of eligible citizens is enrolled.

The states have put in place multiple strategies to reduce the $530 billion deficit they encountered from 2009 to 2012. The four strategies applied by the states include using their reserves or rainy day funds, special appropriations from the federal government through either increased Medicaid or stimulus funding, increased revenues through taxes, and targeted spending cuts. Although the federal financial stimulus gave temporary respite to the states, more recent reductions in federal support, forced by Congress, have increased the dire financial circumstances at the state level. Short-term federal funding was instrumental in helping the states to avoid massive layoffs of state workers and termination of programs that help with recovery from the recession. As federal funding support declines, the states experience even deeper recessionary pressure. The projected condition of state budgets over the next decade could be considered more fragile and unpredictable than at the federal level since 49 out of 50 states are obligated to balance their budgets at the end of each fiscal year and states have less flexibility to borrow funds at favorable rates of interest (McNichol et al., 2012). Collectively, the budget deficit for the states for the upcoming fiscal year exceeds $112 billion with minimal opportunity or legislative enthusiasm to raise taxes. The elimination of three of the four options available to the states means that to prevent insolvency, there will be major reductions in staffing and programs.

The current and anticipated budget shortfall is a major factor in a range of policy debates and decisions that have been made and are under consideration by governors and legislators. To balance their budgets and move toward recovery, some states are considering—and others have implemented—unprecedented reductions in education, Medicaid, preventive health care services for low-income women, and other related social service programs (Combs, 2012). These reductions in spending are based principally on reductions in the level of state employment. Unless state revenues increase in the next fiscal year beyond the 8.3% seen in 2011, further reductions in human service programs are predicted. Although state revenues have increased 8.3% over the past year this rate of growth is unlikely to be sufficient in the short run to offset the impact of the deficits and limited tax revenue. It has been estimated that even with an 8.3% annual growth it will take states close to 7 years to recover from the recession (McNichol et al., 2012). During the ensuing years, the states are likely to make additional major reductions in human services.

The states face numerous obstacles to achieving recovery or restoring programs and services that were eliminated or severely reduced. One option for the states has been increased revenue from the federal government over the past several years. That route for supplemental funding is closed. Because mental health policy is a primary product of state governments, the current and projected fiscal crisis may force states to restrict funding and services to the mentally disabled. One potential option for states is to explore ways to nationalize their financial responsibility for mental health care so that the federal government assumes a larger long-term role. States would substantially increase their revenues if they were able to bill the federal government for services in their state hospitals. The current state fiscal crisis, however, may be an opportunity to reconsider the role of state governments in establishing mental health policy, maintaining state institutions, and supporting the single emphasis mental health centers, as well as an opportunity to address the long-term fragmentation, inequity, and inequality that have been documented in numerous reports since the 1940s.

The multiple reports, studies, and congressional commissions completed over the past several decades reached similar pessimistic conclusions about the status of state-financed mental health care in the United States. Overall, there seem to be minimal differences between the range of widespread problems noted in the 1946 report completed for President Truman, the Joint Commission Report in 1955, the Carter Commission in 1980, and those noted in the 2003 report from the Bush Administration. The preponderance of the long-term epidemiological, economic, and services evidence confirms that the mental health system at the state level remains in substantial crisis, even financial failure. The laissez-faire U.S. mental health policy of state-run systems, supported with inconsistent federal funding, has been far less than successful. Although some progress is evident in mental health care from one decade to another (Frank & Glied, 2006), few national models of effectiveness have been identified for widespread adoption. The recent easing of restrictions on the reimbursement of stand-alone psychiatric hospitals (Institutions for Mental Disease) is a promising change in policy (Rosenbaum, Teitelbaum, & Mauery, 2002). However, over-all progress in mental health, as noted by Kessler et al. (2005), Frank and Glied (2006) and Wang et al. (2006), has been slow, uneven, and met with limited enthusiasm (Frank & Morlock, 1997). Frank and Glied (2006) con-clude that the traditional state mental health authority model of care is wan-ing in strength, influence, and control, albeit at a slow pace. They base their conclusions on the significant reduction in state general funds and the shift-ing to federal funds that support services at the state and local level. The current recession and the slow recovery are likely to reduce state financed mental health care at a faster pace than in the previous decade. As federal funding approximates 75% of state mental health support, does the federal government have a responsibility for policy direction or control of services?

As noted, in the past 5 years, state general funds have reached their lowest levels in recent memory (McNichol et al., 2012). And, close to 75% of the states have seen a major reduction in funding during the current recession. As a result of their declining revenues, states have identified a number of mental health programs and services to close or reduce. One of the primary targets for closure is state mental institutions. Although such facilities are a primary source of employment and revenue for local com-munities and businesses, state legislators are using the current budget crisis as the rationale for adopting a closure policy. In Alabama, the legislature reduced the state mental health budget by 25% for fiscal year 2013 (Stovell, 2012). Soon after the legislature's decision the state mental health author-ity indicated plans to close four out of six state mental hospitals. Are these reductions that target human services a true fiscal necessity or an oppor-tunity by more conservative legislatures to eliminate programs viewed as contributing to individual dependency?

The Center in Budget and Policy Priorities published figures to show the extent of deficits in the states by total amount but also as a percentage of expenditures in the prior fiscal year (Combs, 2012). Only the top 10 states are included in Table 3.3.

As recently as 2003, the New Freedom Commission on Mental Health (2003b) documented the continued depth of fragmentation, uncertainty, disarray, and barriers to effective and cost-efficient services. The long-term reoccurring nature of these problems undoubtedly influenced the commission's critical recommendation to "transform" the entire system of care. Although stated more subtly in its report, the New Freedom Commission's recommendation for transformation aims principally at changing antiquated state (public) mental health systems—hospitals, community mental health programs, and their policies (*Medical News Today*, 2006).

Table 3.3 **Top 10 States Ranked by 2012 Deficit**

State	2012 Deficit (Millions)	Deficit as % of 2011 Spending	Rank by Percent
Nevada	1.5 billion	45.20	1
New Jersey	10.5 billion	37.40	2
Texas	13.4 billion	31.50	3
California	25.5 billion	29.30	4
Oregon	1.8 billion	25.00	5
Minnesota	3.8 billion	23.60	6
Louisiana	1.6 billion	20.70	7
New York	10 billion	18.70	8
Connecticut	3.2 billion	18.00	9
South Carolina	877 million	17.40	10

The oblique focus on state mental health systems in the Commission's recommendation is apparent in that the only decisive action taken by the Bush Administration, following the report, was the issuance of state transformation grants (SAMHSA, 2006a). Each of these grants went to individual states to the exclusion of either local governments or the private sector. Clearly, transformation is perceived by the federal government as an issue for state governments and seems to raise dormant questions about federalism, states' rights, constitutionality, finances, and future direction of public mental health policy in the United States. However, the level of funding to achieve transformation is inadequate. The current state fiscal crisis does afford the federal government an opportunity to implement many of the goals included in the New Freedom Commission's report.

The New Freedom Commission's transformation recommendation raises three substantial questions about the depth of the state mental health crisis and the potential role of the federal government in managing such a change. First, has the quality of functioning of the U.S. mental health system reached a point where the nation's productivity and stability are at risk? Affirmative responses to societal concern about these issues led to the establishment of state mental hospitals in the 18th century. Second, does the level of risk, human rights violations, or slow rate of change in state mental health services rise to the level that direct federal intervention is required? Third, does the federal government have constitutional authority, if any, to intervene in mental health matters of state governments? Each of these questions has been answered affirmatively for decades.

Kessler's replication study found the lifetime rate of incidence of mental disorder in the U.S. population to be 45% (Kessler et al., 2005). His findings are buttressed by findings from Wang et al. (2005) that 68% of those persons who need mental health services in the United States are not obtaining them, and that when they do access services, there is a discrepancy between what is provided and the standard evidence-based practices in the field. The recent study by the National Alliance on Mental Illness found that the key variable in risk and cost is the extent to which depression is treated (*Houston Chronicle,* 2006). Where treatment is either unavailable or provided poorly, cost of medical care increases substantially. In an earlier study (National Mental Health Association, 2001), the NMHA estimated that untreated and poorly treated mental disorders cost the United States in excess of $100 billion a year in lost productivity. The functioning of state mental health systems is related to the national risk of lowered productivity and economic instability. The United States expends close to $320 billion annually for mental health. Of this amount close to $200 billion represents lost wages. Other published works (Ettner, Frank, & Kessler, 1997; Stoudemire, Frank, & Hedemark, 1986; Timbe, Horvitz-Lennon, Frank, & Normand, 2006) show various linkages between economic, labor force, and psychiatric variables. Further evidence of the potential impact on the national economy is shown in the following long-term problems:

- Fragmentation in funding and policy direction
- Difficulty accessing service
- Disparities by race and class
- Lag in the application of innovation
- Low quality of services
- Failure to use evidence-based methodologies
- Most persons in need do not seek services
- Increased suicide rates
- High rates of comorbid conditions
- Inadequate number in the workforce
- Conflict within levels of government
- Excessive cost
- Lowered productivity

Mental health care is a major financial and policy responsibility of state governments, albeit underfinanced in almost all states. Although the day-to-day operations are under the aegis of state commissioners or directors, policy change rests with governors and legislators who appoint them and oversee the budgets of state mental health agencies. State mental health agencies cannot pursue a policy direction unless it is supported by or is consistent with that the state administration. Because of the highly politicized environment in which they operate, mental health systems are greatly constrained and have been slow to make rapid or substantive change that will reduce local employment levels. However, with the current recession, governors and legislators seem more willing to reduce the number of state mental institutions and justify a major reduction in the state employment level. To install quality and transformation seems to dictate an alternative strategy to that used to initiate community mental health. Without the political cover provided by the recession, states seem unable to sustain reform despite continued scandals, deaths, injuries, and federal intervention (Chang, 2006; Minkoff, 2006). Heretofore, states have not been able to provide consistent policy direction to solve the long-term crisis in mental health. The New Freedom Commission's Report seems to affirm that solving the mental health crisis in the United States requires strategic federal intervention, long-term financial support, and technical assistance (New Freedom Commission on Mental Health, 2003b; NTAC, 2004; Power, 2006; Unutzer et al., 2006).

Nationalization of the financing of state mental health systems through the Affordable Care Act (ACA) seems to offer such a strategy. Nationalization is a voluntary policy agreement between the federal and state governments in which control of the existing state system and its infrastructure transfer to the U.S. government as the ACA is implemented. As part of the voluntary agreement, states would be required to maintain their current level of expenditures matched by an equal amount of federal funding. Federal funding and policy direction would require states to merge behavioral health with the establishment of health care exchanges that would manage all aspects of the existing system including all facilities, community centers, and central offices. Day-to-day management of the system would be through the state health care exchanges. Policy and planning would be congruent with the provisions of the Affordable Care Act with an expectation that such planning would aim at total transformation of the existing system of care. Nationalization of state mental health systems is proposed as a short-term (5- to 10-year) strategy for helping to resolve the political risks incurred by state-level actors and as a means of installing transformation.

The federal government could enter into a contractual relationship with the states to assist in transforming their mental health systems, create a collective future vision, develop statewide plans, and implement those plans through the exchanges. Nationalization would involve cost sharing by all levels of government and would allow the federal government to plan for the integration of health and mental health services. As part of nationalization, the federal government could develop, with the states, a planned closure of state facilities and the transfer of their responsibilities to the primary care sector. Transferring current inpatient services to the primary care sector would eliminate the fiscal constraints on institutions for mental disease and would immediately increase the potential quality of health care for persons with mental or addictive illnesses.

Over the past 45 years, there has been a gradual shift toward national control of public mental health systems. The shifts have come about through increases in federal funding, lawsuits against the states, expanded federal laws, and the introduction of new services concepts from federal reports and commissions. Clearly, the shift in responsibility and control has been to such an extent that public mental health systems are experiencing a decline in their authority and control. Nationalization/federalization is an unspoken reality. There is value in completing the federalization/nationalization of public mental health systems as a means of transforming mental health care in the United States as proposed in the New Freedom Commission Report (New Freedom Commission on Mental Health, 2003b).

Any proposal to increase federal authority over traditional state functions raises numerous concerns and questions. Obviously, such a proposal raises questions about appropriate levels of federalism, old issues that remain unresolved. States, too, will see such a proposal as an infringement or encroachment on their sovereign rights to make policy decisions. Others will question whether there is a constitutional basis for such federal action, although couched here in terms of voluntary agreement. Nationalization of public mental health care seems to be a necessary and vital policy strategy for the United States. The lifetime prevalence of mental disorders, escalating costs, and an annual loss of billions of dollars in productivity offer a compelling case that mental health care in the United States is in serious crisis, if not an epidemic. Equally compelling is the conclusion that state governments alone cannot resolve the crisis and thus reduce the human and economic losses. The economic, political, and employment value of maintaining state hospitals in small communities precludes an easy solution to the crisis. The current fiscal crisis at the state level appears to be of such proportions and historical precedent that federal action is needed to redirect public policy towards the elusive goal of transformation.

Key Terms

Federal encroachment   Mental health policy   States' rights
Federalism   New Freedom

Review Questions for Critical Thinking

1. From 1945 to 1980, federal power increased steadily as state control over mental health waned. Is this expansion in power over mental health a reflection of the implied powers of Congress and in concert with the Constitution?

2. How does the 1854 Pierce Veto reconcile or reflect the U.S. Supreme Court's 1819 decision, *McCulloch v. Maryland*?

3. To what extent does the 21st-century mental health system reinforce health disparities in the United States?

4. Why do most Americans with mental health disorders not seek treatment? To what extent does the "system" create barriers and/or disincentive to seeking help?

5. There is a long history of tension between the states and federal government regarding responsibilities, funding, and mandates around mental health services. To what extent do you see these tensions being resolved, or do you feel they will continue and result in a fragmented, dysfunctional system of care?

Online Resources

National Alliance on Mental Illness http://nami.org/

National Comorbidity Survey http://www.hcp.med.harvard.edu/ncs/

National Mental Health Association http://www.thenationalcouncil.org/

Substance Abuse and Mental Health Services Administration http://www.samhsa.gov/

World Health Organization http://www.who.int/en/

References

Adebimpe, V. R. (1994). Race, racism and epidemiological surveys. Hospital and community psychiatry, *45*, 27–31.

Adult Mental Health Division. (2005). Statewide comprehensive integrated service plan. Honolulu: State of Hawaii, Department of Health.

Allport, G. W. (1954). The nature of prejudice. Cambridge, MA: Addison-Wesley.

Althouse, A. (2001). Why talking about "states' rights" cannot avoid the need for normative federalism analysis. *Duke Law Journal*, *51*, 363–376.

Altman, D. E., & Levitt, L. (2002). The sad history of health care cost containment as told in one chart. Health Affairs. [web exclusives] doi: 10.1377/hlthaff.w2.83.

Ambrose, S. E. (1985). *Nixon: The triumph of a politician: 1962–1972* (Vol. 2). New York, NY: Simon & Schuster.

Anderson, C. (1994). *Black labor, white wealth: The search for power and economic justice.* Edgewood, MD: Duncan and Duncan.

Andreasen, N. C. (1997). Linking mind and brain in the study of mental illnesses: A project for a scientific psychopathology. *Science, 275,* 1586–1593.

Arnoff, F. (1975). Social consequences of policy toward mental illness. *Science, 188,* 1277–1281.

Babcock, J. W. (1895). The colored insane. In *National Conference of Charities and Corrections* (Ed.), (pp. 184–186). Boston, MA: National Conference of Charities and Corrections.

Baker, L. A., & Young, E. A. (2001). Federalism and the double standard of judicial review. *Duke Law Journal, 51,* 143–149.

Baseler, M. C. (1998). *Asylum for mankind: America, 1607–1800.* Ithaca, NY: Cornell University Press.

Belknap, I. (1956). *Human problems of a state mental hospital.* New York, NY: Blakiston Division, McGraw-Hill.

Berlien, I. C., & Waggoner, R. W. (1966). Selection and induction. In R. S. Anderson, A. L. Glass, R. J. Bernucci, J. B. Coates, & L. Ahnfeldt (Eds.), *Neuropsychiatry in World War II* (pp. 153–188). Washington, DC: Office of the Surgeon General, Department of the Army.

Biegel, D. E., Milligan, S. E., Putnam, P. L., & Song, L. Y. (1994). Predictors of burden among lower socioeconomnic status caregivers with chronic mental illness. *Community Mental Health Journal, 30,* 473–494.

Blanton, W. B. (1931). *Medicine in Virginia in the eighteenth century.* Richmond, VA: Garett and Massie.

Boyd, E. (2006). *American federalism,1776 to 1997: Significant events.* U.S. Government [Online]. Available at http://usinfo.state.gov.usa/infousa/politics/states/federal.htm

Breeden, J. O. (1976). States rights medicine in the old south. *Journal of Southern History, XXV*, 53–72.

Brill, N. Q., & Kupper, H. I. (1966). The psychiatric patient after discharge. In R. S. Anderson, A. J. Glass, R. J. Bernucci, J. B. Coates, & L. Ahnfeldt (Eds.), *Neuropsychiatry in world war II* (pp. 735–759). Washington, DC: Office of the Surgeon General, Department of the Army.

Brody, E. B. (1966). *Psychiatry and prejudice.* S. Arieti. [3]. New York, NY: Basic Books. American Handbook of Psychiatry.

Brown, G. O. (8-9-1887). Original request to rent (Bacon Tate's) land for Central State Hospital. 1. Richmond, Virginia, Freedmen's Bureau.

Burnim, I. A. (2006). The ADA's "integration mandate" should promote community services. Bazelon Center [Online]. Available at http://www.bazelon.org/issues/disabilityrights/incourt/olmstead/ibtest.html

Bush, G. W. (2002). New freedom commission executive order. Federal Register Vol. 67, No. 86. Friday, May 3, 2002. Available at http://www.gpo.gov/fdsys/pkg/FR-2002-05-03/pdf/02-11166.pdf

Byrd, W. M., & Clayton, L. A. (2002). *An American health dilemma: Race, medicine, and health care in the United States 1900–2000* (Vol. II). New York, NY: Routledge.

Cannon, M. S., & Locke, B. Z. (1977). Being black is detriment to one's mental health: Myth or reality. *Phylon, 38,* 408–428.

Caplan, G. (1961). *An approach to community mental health.* New York, NY: Gruene and Stratton.

Carothers, J. C. (1940). Some speculations on insanity in Africans and in general. *East African Medical Journal, 17,* 90–105.

Carter, J. (2006). Presidents Carter's commission on mental health. The American Presidency Project [Online]. Available at http://www.presidency.ucsb.edu/ws/print.php?pid=6643

Cartwright, S. (1851). Report on the diseases and physical peculiarities of the negro race. *New Orleans Medical Surgical Journal, 7,* 692–705.

Chandra, A., & Skinner, J. (2003). *Geography and racial health disparities.* Cambridge, MA: National Bureau of Economic Research.

Chang, K. (2006). *Twelfth report and recommendation to the U.S. district court of Hawaii* (Rep. No. Civil 91-00137). Honolulu: U.S. District Court.

Close Up Foundation. (2006). Federalism. Close Up Foundation [Online]. Available at www.closeup.org

Colonial Williamsburg. (2006). Public hospital at colonial Williamsburg. Colonial Williamsburg Foundation [Online]. Available at http://www.history.org/Almanack/places/hb/hbhos.cfm

Combs, D. (2012). State budget gaps: How does your state rank. Pew Charitable Trust [Online]. Available at http://www.stateline.org/live/ViewPage.action?siteNodeId=136&languageId=1&contentId=15158

Congressional Budget Office. (1999). *Economic and budget outlook: Fiscal years 2000–2009.* Washington, DC: Author.

Creamer, B. (2001). Federal court puts state hospital under the gun. *Honolulu Advertiser* [Online]. Available at http://www.honoluluadvertiser.com

Cross, T. L., Bazron, B., Dennis, K., & Isaacs, M. (1989). *Toward a culturally competent system of care.* Washington, DC: Georgetown University Child Development Center.

Dain, N. (1964). *Concepts of insanity in the United States 1789–1865.* New Brunswick, NJ: Rutgers University Press.

Dain, N. (1968). *History of Eastern State Hospital.* Williamsburg, VA: Colonial Williamsburg Foundation.

Davis, K. (1998). Race, health status and managed health care. In F. L. Brisbane (Ed.), *Special collaborative edition CSAP cultural competence series* (pp. 145–163). Rockville, MD: Bureau of Primary Care, Center for Substance Abuse Prevention.

Davis, K., & Iron Cloud Two-Dogs, E. (2004). The color of social policy: Oppression of indigenous tribal populations and Africans in America. In K. Davis & T. Bent-Goodley (Eds.), *The color of social policy* (pp. 3–20). Alexandria, VA: Council on Social Work Education.

Denton, T. G. (1960). *Central State Hospital 1865–1960.* Richmond, VA: Department of Mental Hygiene and Hospitals.

Department of Mental Hygiene and Hospitals. (1960). *Central state hospital, 1865–1960.* Richmond, VA: Department of Mental Hygiene and Hospitals.

Deutsch, A. (1948). *The shame of the states.* New York, NY: Harcourt Brace.

Deutsch, A. (1949). *The mentally ill in America: A history of their care and treatment from colonial times* (2nd ed.) New York, NY: Columbia University.

Drake, F. D. (1999). *States' rights and American federalism: A documentary history.* Westport, CT: Greenwood Press.

Drewry, W. F. (1916). *Central state hospital* (Vol. III). Baltimore, MD: Johns Hopkins Press.

Ennis, B. J., & Siegel, L. (1973). *The rights of mental patients.* New York, NY: Baron.

Epstein, A. M., & Ayanian, J. Z. (2001). Racial disparities in medical care. *New England Journal of Medicine, 344,* 1471–1473.

Ettner, S. L., Frank, R. G., & Kessler, R. C. (1997). The impact of psychiatric disorder on labor market outcomes. *Industrial and Labor Relations Review, 51,* 64–81.

Evarts, A. B. (1914). Dementia praecox in the colored race. *Psychoanalytic Review, 1,* 388–403.

Faris, R., & Dunham, H. W. (1939). *Mental disorders in urban areas.* Chicago, IL: University of Chicago Press.

Fischer, J. (1969). Negroes, whites and rates of mental illness: Reconsideration of a myth. *Psychiatry, 32,* 438–446.

Foucault, M. (1965). *Madness and civilization: A history of insanity in the age of reason.* New York, NY: Random House.

Frank, R. (2006, February 2). *Mental health care: Gains and gaps.* Unpublished presentation to Grantmakers in Health Summit, San Francisco.

Frank, R. G., & Glied, S. (2006). *Better but not well.* Baltimore, MD: Johns Hopkins Press.

Frank, R. G., & Morlock, L. L. (1997). *Managing fragmented public mental health services.* New York, NY: Milbank Memorial Fund.

Gollaher, D. (1995). *Voice for the made: The life of Dorothea Dix.* New York, NY: Free Press.

Gorman, P. G. (2006). *Final evaluation of the adult mental health division* (Rep. No. 7). Lebanon, NH: U.S. District Court.

Gould, S. J. (1981). *The mismeasure of man.* New York, NY: Norton.

Grob, G. (1973). *Mental institutions in America: Social policy to 1875.* New York, NY: Free Press.

Grob, G. N. (1994). *The mad among us: A history of the care of America's mentally ill.* Cambridge, MA: Harvard University Press.

Grob, G. N. (2005). Public policy and mental illnesses: Jimmy Carter's presidential commission on mental health. *Milbank Quarterly, 83,* 425–456.

Grossack, M. M. (1963). *Mental health and segregation.* New York, NY: Springer.

Hansen, C. F. (1959). Mental health aspects of desegregation. *Journal of the National Medical Association, 51,* 450–456.

Hanson-Mayer, G. (2006). *Final evaluation of the adult mental health division* (Rep. No. 12). Lexington, MA: U.S. District Court.

Hatfield, A. B. (1987). Families as caregivers: A historical perspective. In A. B. Hatfield & H. P. Lefley (Eds.), *Families of the mentally ill: Coping and adaptation* (pp. 3–29). New York, NY: Guilford Press.

Healy, D. (2002). *The creation of psychopharmacology.* Cambridge, MA: Harvard University Press.

Heldring, M. (2003, April 7). Mental health funding is part of cost effect reform—Health care reform. *Seattle Times.*

Hernandez, R., & Pear, R. (2006, July 12). Once an enemy, health industry warms to Clinton. *New York Times.*

Herrnstein, R. J., & Murray, C. (1994). *The bell curve: Intelligence and class structure in American life.* New York, NY: Free Press.

Hertz, R. P. & Baker, C. L. (2002). *The impact of mental disorders on work* (Publication No. P0002981). Pfizer Outcomes Research: Pfizer Pharmaceuticals Group. Retrieved from http://www.hawaii.edu/hivandaids/The%20Impact%20of%20Mental%20Disorders%20on%20Work.pdf

Houston Chronicle. (2006). National survey finds depression costs nearly tripled for individuals with limited access to care. *Houston Chronicle* [Online]. Available at http://www.chron.com/cs/CDA/printstory.mpl/conws/4038661

Hurd, H. M., Drewry, W. F., Dewey, R., Ilgrim, C. W., Lumer, G. A., & Urgess, T. J. W. (1916). *The institutional care of the insane in the United States and Canada.* H. M. Hurd. [III]. Baltimore, MD: Johns Hopkins Press.

Insel, T. R. (2008). Assessing the economic costs of serious mental illness. *American Journal of Psychiatry, 165* (6), 663–665.

Institute of Medicine. (2005). *Crossing the quality chasm—Adaptation for mental health and addictive disorders.* Washington, DC: Institute of Medicine.

Jackson, D. D. (1960). *The etiology of schizophrenia.* New York, NY: Basic Books.

Jackson, J. S., Brown, T., Wiliams, D. W., Torres, M., Sellers, S., & Brown, K. (1996). Perceptions and experiences of racism and the physical and mental health status of African Americans: A thirteen-year national panel study. *Ethnicity and Disease, 6,* 132–147.

Jarvis, E. (1842). Statistics on insanity in the United States. *Boston Medicine and Surgery Journal, 27,* 116–121.

Jarvis, E. (1844). Insanity among the colored population of the free states. *American Journal of the Medical Sciences, 7,* 71–83.

Johnson, M. (1972). *Wyatt v. Stickney.* Wyatt. [344 F. Supp. 373]. Alabama Court of Appeals. 1974.

Joint Commission on Mental Illness and Health. (1961). *Action for mental health.* New York, NY: Science Editons.

Keeler, M. H., & Vitols, M. M. (1963). Migration and schizophrenia in North Carolina negroes. *American Journal of Orthopsychiatry, 33,* 557.

Kennedy, J. F. (2006a). Kennedy's remarks on proposed measures to combat mental illness and mental retardation. The American Presidency Project [Online]. Available at http://www.presidency.ucsb.edu/ws/pring.php?pid=9547

Kennedy, J. F. (2006b). Letter to secretary Ribicoff concerning the role of the federal government in the field of mental health. The American Presidency Project [Online]. Available at http://www.presidency.ucsb.edu/ws/print.php?pid=8469

Kennedy, J. F. (2006c). Letter to the board of commissioners of the District of Columbia. The American Presidency Project [Online]. Available at http://www.presidency.ucsb.edu/ws/print.php?pid=9563

Keppel, K. G., Pearcy, J. N., & Wagener, D. K. (2002). *Trends in racial and ethnic-specific rates for the health status indicators: United States, 1990–98* (Rep. No. 23). Hyattsville, MD: Centers for Disease Control and Prevention/National Center for Health Statistics.

Kessler, R. C., Berglund, P., Demler, O., Jin, R., Merikangas, L. R., & Walters, E. E. (2005). Lifetime prevalence and age-of-onset distributions of dsm iv disorders in the national comorbidity survey replication. *Archives of General Psychiatry, 62,* 593–602.

Kessler, R. C., Heeringa, S., Lakoma, M. D., Petukhova, M., Rupp, A. E., Schoenbaum, M., Wang, P. S., & Zaslavsky, A. M. (2008). Individual and societal effects of mental disorders on earnings in the United States: Results from the National Comorbidity Survey Replication. *American Journal of Psychiatry, 165,* 703–711.

Kleiner, R. J., & Parker, S. (1959). Migration and mental illness: A new look. *American Sociological Review, 24,* 687–690.

Kobayashi, K. (2006). State still lagging in mental health services. *Honolulu Advertiser* [Online]. Available at http://www.honoluluadvertiser.com

Kramer, M., Von Korff, M., & Kessler, L. (1980). The lifetime prevalence of mental disorders: Estimation, uses and limitations. *Psychological Medicine, 10,* 429–436.

Lidz, R. W., & Lidz, T. (1949). The family environment of schizophrenic patients. *American Journal of Psychiatry, 106,* 332.

Lincoln, A. (9–22–1862). *Preliminary emancipation proclamation.*

Malzberg, B. (1940). *Social and biological aspects of mental disease.* New York, NY: State Hospital Press.

Malzberg, B. (1953). Mental diseases among negroes in New York state, 1939–41. *Mental Hygiene, 37,* 450–476.

Manderscheid, R. W., & Henderson, M. J. (2001). *Mental health, United States, 2000.* Washington, DC: Center for Mental Health Services.

Mark, T. L., Coffey, R. M., Vandivort-Warren, R., Harwood, H. J., & King, E. C. (2005). U.S. spending for mental health and substance abuse treatment, 1991–2001. *Health Affairs,* 133–142.

Marshall, J. (2006). The Marshall cases: McCulloch v. Maryland (1819). Groninger University [Online]. Available at http://www.let.rug.nl/~usa/D/1801–1825/marshallcases/mar05.htm

McCandless, P. (1996). *Moonlight, magnolias, & madness: Insanity in South Carolina from the colonia period to the progressive era.* Chapel Hill: University of North Carolina Press.

McNichol, E., Oliff, P., & Johnson, N. (2012). States continue to feel recession's impact. Center for Budget and Policy Priorities [Online]. Available at http://www.cbpp.org/cms/?fa=view&id=711

Mechanic, D. (1989). *Mental health and social policy* (3rd ed.) Englewood Cliffs, NJ: Prentice-Hall.

Medical News Today. (2006). 92 million dollars allocated for transformation grants. [Online]. Available at http://www.medicalnewstoday.com/medicalnews.php?newsid=31366

Minkoff, K. (2006). *Twelfth team evaluation of the Hawaii adult mental health division.* Acton, MA: U.S. Federal District Court.

Moscarelli, M., Rupp, A., & Sartorious, N. (1996). *Handbook of mental health economics and health policy.* New York, NY: Wiley.

Mulligan, K. (2003, January 3). Mental health system reform must start with funding. *Psychiatric News, 38,* 9.

NAACP Legal Defense Fund & Marshall, T. (5–17–1954). *Brown et al. v. Board of Education of Topeka et al. Brown v. Topeka Board of Education.*

National Alliance on Mental Illness. (2009). *Grading the states: A report on America's health care system for serious mental illness.* Alexandria, VA: Author.

National Alliance on Mental Illness. (2010). *The high costs of cutting mental health: Unemployment.* Arlington, VA: Author.

National Institute of Mental Health. (2006). In harm's way: Suicide in America. NIH [Online]. Available at http://www.nimh.nih.gov/publicat/harmsway.cfm

National Institute of Mental Health (2007). *Suicide in the U.S.: Statistics and prevention.* (NIH Publication No. 06–4594). Retrieved from http://www.nimh.nih.gov/health/publications/suicide-in-the-us-statistics-and-prevention/index.shtml#factors

National Mental Health Association. (2001). *Labor Day 2001 report: Untreated and mistreated mental illness and substance abuse costs U.S. $113 billion a year.* Alexandria, VA: National Mental Health Association.

Neighbors, H. W., Jackson, J., Campbell, L., & Williams, D. (1989). The influence of racial factors on psychiatric diagnosis: A review and suggestions for research. *Community Mental Health Journal, 25,* 301–311.

Neighbors, H. W., & Lumpkin, S. (1990). The epidemiology of mental disorder in the black population. In D. S. Ruiz & J. P. Comer (Eds.), *Handbook of mental health and mental disorder among black Americans* (pp. 55–70). New York, NY: Greenwood Press.

New Freedom Commission on Mental Health. (2003a). *Achieving the promise: Transforming mental health care in America—Executive summary of final report* (Rep. No. DMS-03–3831). Rockville, MD: DHHS.

New Freedom Commission on Mental Health. (2003b). *Achieving the promise: Transforming mental health care in America. Final report* (Rep. No. SMA-03–3832). Rockville, MD: DHHS.

New Freedom Commission on Mental Health. (2006). New freedom commission members. *New Freedom Commission* [Online]. Available at http://www.mental healthcommission.gov/minutes/Hune02.htm

Nixon, R. M. (3–2-1972). Health care: Request for action on 3 programs: Message to Congress on health care, Public Law 93–222. Committee on Labor and Public Welfare.

National Technical Assistance Center. (2004). Answering the challenge: Responses to the president's new freedom commission final report. Network, 8.

O'Malley, M. (1914). Insanity in the colored race. *Journal of Insanity, 71,* 309–336.

Pasamanick, B. A. (1959). *The epidemiology of mental disorder.* Washington DC: American Association for the Advancement of Science.

Pierce, F. (1854). Franklin Pierce's 1854 veto. Disability Museum [Online]. Available at http://www.disabilitymuseum.org/lib/docs/682.htm?page=print

Pinkmonkey. (2006). *Federalism.* Pinkmonkey [Online]. Available at http://www.pinkmonkey.com/studyguides/subjects/am_gov/chap2/a0200001.asp

John James McCulloch v. The State of Maryland. McCulloch v. Maryland. [17 U.S. 316 (1819)]. U.S. Supreme. 2–6-1819.

Plepys, C., & Klein, R. (1995). *Health status indicators: Differentials by race and hispanic origin* (Rep. No. 10). Hyattsville, MD: Centers for Disease Control and Prevention/National Center for Health Statistics.

Poen, M. M. (1979). *Harry S. Truman versus the medical lobby: The genesis of medicare.* Columbia: University of Missouri Press.

Power, A. K. (2004). *Mental health system transformation bridging science and service.* Bethesda, MD: NIMH.

Power, A. K. (11–13–2006). *Letter re strategies for the financing and organization of mental health services.* Harbin, H., Edwards, B. C., Goldman, H., Koyanagi, C., Pires, S., Rosenberg, L., and Schwalbe, L. 11–13–2006.

Pumphrey, R. E., & Pumphrey, M. W. (1961). *Heritage of American social work.* New York, NY: Columbia University Press.

Regier, D. A., Farmer, M. E., Rae, D. S., Meyers, J. K., Kramer, M., Robins, L. N.,... Locke, B. Z. (1993). One-month prevalence of mental disorders in the United States and sociodemographic characteristics: The Epidemiologic Catchment Area study. *Acta Psychiatrica Scandinavica, 88,* 35–47.

Reno, J. (1999). *United States v. Antonio J. Morrison et al. U.S. v. Morrison.* [529 U.S. 598]. U.S. Supreme. 5–15–2000.

Rice, D. P., & Miller, L. S. (1996). The economic burden of schizophrenia: Conceptual and methodological issues, and cost estimates. In M. Moscarelli, A. Rupp, & N. Sartorious (Eds.), *Handbook of mental health economics and health policy* (pp. 321–324). New York, NY: Wiley.

Robins, L. N., & Regier, D. A. (1991). *Psychiatric disorders in America: The epidemiological catchment area study.* New York, NY: Free Press.

Rosenbaum, S., Teitelbaum, J., & Mauery, R. (2002). *An analysis of the medicaid IMD exclusion. Center for Health Services Research* [Online]. Available at http://www.gwumc.edu/sphhs/departments/healthpolicy/CHPR/downloads/behavioral_health/reports/IMD%20Report%201202.pdf

Rothman, D. (1970). *The discovery of the asylum.* Boston, MA: Little, Brown.

Scott, D. M. (1997). *Social policy and the image of the damaged black psyche 1880–1996.* Chapel Hill: University of North Carolina Press.

Sharfstein, S. S. (2000). Whatever happened to community mental health? *Psychiatric Services, 51,* 61–620.

Simpson, G. A., Cohen, R. A., Pastor, P. N., & Reuben, C. A. (2008). *Use of mental health services in the past 12 months by children aged 4–17 years: United States, 2005–2006.* (NCHS data Brief, No. 8). Hyattsville, MD: National Center for Health Statistics.

Snowden, L. R. (2000). Inpatient mental health use by members of ethnic minority groups. In J. M. Herrera, W. B. Lawson, & J. J. Smerck (Eds.), *Cross cultural psychiatry.* Chichester, United Kingdom: Wiley.

Stoesz, D., & Karger, H. J. (1993). Deconstructuring welfare: The Reagan legacy and the welfare state. *Social Work, 38,* 619–628.

Stoudemire, A., Frank, R. G., & Hedemark, N. (1986). The economic burden of depression. *General Hospital Psychiatry, 8,* 387–394.

Stovell, K. (2012). Alabama to close state hospitals in move to transform MH system. *Mental Health Weekly, 33,* 1–8.

Street Law. (2006). Powers of the federal government. Street law and the Supreme Court historical society [Online]. Available at www.landmarkcases.org

Substance Abuse and Mental Health Services Administration. (2005). *Transforming mental health care in America: The federal action agenda: First steps* (Rep. No. SMA-05-4060). Rockville, MD: SAMHSA U.S. Department of Health and Human Services.

Substance Abuse and Mental Health Services Administration. (2006a). Mental health transformation state incentives grant program. SAMHSA [Online]. Available at http://www.samhsa.gov/matrix/mhst_ta.aspx

Substance Abuse and Mental Health Services Administration. (2006b). National expenditures for mental health services and substance abuse treatment 1991–2001. SAMHSA [Online]. Available at: http://www.samhsa.gov/spending estimates/chapter 4.aspx

Substance Abuse and Mental Health Services Administration (2010a). *Mental Health, United States, 2008.* (HHS Publication No. (SMA) 10–4590). Rockville, MD: Center for Mental Health Services, Substance Abuse and Mental Health Services Administration.

Substance Abuse and Mental Health Services Administration (2010b). *National expenditures for mental health services and substance abuse treatment, 1986–2005.* (DHHS Publication No. (SMA) 10–4612). Rockville, MD: Center for Mental Health Services and Center for Substance Abuse Treatment, Substance Abuse and Mental Health Services Administration.

Substance Abuse and Mental Health Services Administration. (2011). *Funding and characteristics of state mental health agencies, 2009.* (HHS Publication No. (SMA) 11–4655). Rockville, MD: Author.

Substance Abuse and Mental Health Services Administration. (2012). *Results from the 2010 National Survey on Drug Use and Health: Mental Health Findings* (Office of Applied Studies, NSDUH Series H-42, HHS Publication No. SMA 11–4667). Rockville, MD: Author.

Takeuchi, D. T., & Cheung, M. K. (1998). Coercive and voluntary referrals: How ethnic minority adults get into mental health treatment. *Ethnicity and Health, 3,* 149–158.

Thomas, A. R. (2006). Ronald Reagan and the commitment of the mentally ill: Capital, interest groups, and the eclipse of social policy. *Electronic Journal of Sociology 1998* [Online]. Available at http://www.sociolkogy.org/content/vol003 .004/thomas.html

Timbe, J. W., Horvitz-Lennon, M., Frank, R. G., & Normand, S. L. T. (2006). A meta-analysis of labor supply effects of interventions for major depressive disorder. *Psychiatric Services, 57,* 212–218.

Unutzer, J., Schoenbaum, M., & Druss, B. (2006). Transforming mental health care at the interface with general medicine: Report for the president's new freedom commission for mental health. *Psychiatric Services, 57,* 37–47.

U.S. Congress. (9–17–1787). *Constitution of the United States.* 10th Amendment.

U.S. Congress. (3–24–1790). The Naturalization Act of 1790. 1 Stat. 103–104.

U.S. Congress. (1946). National Mental Health Act, Public Law 79–487.

U.S. Congress. (1955). Mental Health Study Act of 1955, Public Law 487.

U.S. Congress. (1955). Mental Health Study Act of 1955. Public Law 94–182.

U.S. Congress. (1960). Civil rights act of 1960.

U.S. Congress. (1963). Mental Retardation Facilities and Community Mental Health Centers Construction Act of 1963. Public Law 88–164.

U.S. Congress. (1964). Civil Rights Act of 1964.

U.S. Congress. (1965a). Civil Rights Act of 1965, The Voting Rights Act of 1965.

U.S. Congress. (1965b). Hart-Celler Act (Immigation and Naturalization Act of 1965).

U.S. Congress. (1965c). Medicaid–Institutions for mental diseases, Public Law 89–97. 42 CFR 441. Original Legislation establishing Medicaid Provisions.

U.S. Congress. (1965d). Mental retardation facilities and community mental health centers construction act amendments of 1965, Public Law 89–105.

U.S. Congress. (1967). Mental health amendments of 1967, Public Law 90–31.

U.S. Congress. (1968). Civil rights act of 1968: Fair housing act of 1968.

U.S. Congress. (1980). Civil Rights of Institutionalized Persons Act.

U.S. Congress. (2005). Americans with Disabilities Act.

U.S. Department of Health and Human Services. (1999). *Mental health: A report of the surgeon general.* Rockville, MD: U.S. Department of Health and Human Services, SAMHSA, and NIMH.

U.S. Department of Health and Human Services. (2001). *Mental health: Culture, race, and ethnicity: A supplement to mental health: A report of the surgeon general.* Rockville, MD: U.S. Department of Health and Human Services, Substance Abuse and Mental Health Services Administration, Center for Mental Health Services.

U.S. Supreme Court. (2006a). Albertsons, Inc. v. Kirkingburg. Bazelon Center [Online]. Available at http://www.bazelon.org/issues/disabilityrights/resources/99scotus.htm

U.S. Supreme Court. (2006b). Murphy v. United Parcel Services. Bazelon Center [Online]. Available at http://www.bazelon.org/issues/disabilityrights/resources/99scotus.htm

U.S. Supreme Court. (2006c). Olmstead, Commissioner, Georgia Department of Human Resources, et al. v. L. C., by Zimring, Guardian. Cornell University Law School [Online]. Available at http://supct.law.cornell.edu/supct/html/98-536.ZS.html

U.S. Supreme Court. (2006d). Sutton v. United Airlines, Inc. Bazelon Center [Online]. Available at http://www.bazelon.org/issues/disabilityrights/resources/99scotus.htm

Wang, P. S., Demler, O., Olfson, M., Pincus, H. A., Wells, K. B., & Kessler, R. C. (2006). Changing profiles of service sectors used for mental health care in the United States. *American Journal of Psychiatry, 163,* 1187–1198.

Wang, P. S., Lane, M., Olfson, M., Pincus, H. A., Wells, K. B., & Kessler, R. C. (2005). Twelve-month use of mental health services in the United States. *Archives of General Psychiatry, 62,* 629–640.

Witmer, A. H. (1891). Insanity in the colored race in the United States. *Alienist and Neurologist, 12,* 19–30.

World Health Organization. (2000). *The world health report 2000—Health systems: Improving performance.* Geneva, Switzerland: Author.

World Health Organization. (2001). *The world health report 2001: Mental health: New understanding, new hope.* Geneva, Switzerland: Author.

World Health Organization. (2004). *The world health report 2002: Changing history Geneva,* Switzerland: Author.

World Health Organization (2008). *The global burden of disease: 2004 update.* Geneva, Switzerland: Author.

Zane, N. W. S., Takeuchi, D. T., & Young, K. N. J. (1994). *Confronting critical health issues of Asian and Pacific Islander Americans.* Thousand Oaks, CA: Sage.

Chapter 4
Aging in the United States

Challenges to Social Policy and Policy Practice

Enid Opal Cox

> Given the complexities of aging in a global society, from living longer productive years to the continued discrimination and abuses faced by older persons, what then should the public policy response be? How do we solve the problems faced by elders without jeopardizing their status? At the same time, is it possible to find solutions short of asking the common question, should we be investing more of our scarce resources into seniors or into children?

Introduction

According to the Pew Research Center, on January 1, 2001, the first wave of the so-called Baby Boomers celebrated their 65th birthday. Pew went on to report that on that day, today, and for every day for the next 19 years, 10,000 baby boomers will reach age 65. Not surprisingly, the Pew Research Center concludes that the aging of this cohort of Americans, roughly 26% of the total U.S. population, will dramatically change the composition of the country. The 2008 economic global recession has forced nations to reexamine how and to what extent governments will support seniors in their retirement years. In the United States, spending is much higher during the last year of life for Medicare beneficiaries. During most of Medicare's history, the figure has been in the 25% range. As more and more people are living longer, the associated costs for health care will continue to increase. Similarly, Social Security's future is bleak—while there is currently a $2.5 trillion reserve fund invested in government bonds, with the impact of the 2008 recession, less money is coming into the trust fund and, as a result, the fund is drawing on reserves. The result: The Congressional Budget Office estimates that the reserve fund and payroll taxes will cover full payment of benefits up to the year 2043. What then is the future for older Americans? The current health care insurance system is far from adequate and the same can be said for the nation's public retirement program. The data is clear, but the political will to make difficult decisions is nothing short of fear.

For decades, gerontologists in the United States, Europe, Japan, and in other economically advantaged capitalist and socialist countries—as well as gerontologists who were working with nongovernmental organizations, such as Help Age International (Tout, 1989) and governmental organizations serving India, China, and other developing countries—have advocated for attention to the increasing numbers of older persons. These advocacy efforts have focused on both the needs of older adults as well as issues related to their societal roles. At the turn of the 21st century, the dramatic increase in the number of older adults in countries around the world, the increasing percentage of national populations represented by those 65 and older, increased longevity, concerns about the dependency ratio, and to a lesser extent, growing diversity within this older population—both worldwide and within national jurisdictions—have generated attention (Takamura, 2001; Wells & Taylor, 2001). Questions are being asked with greater frequency in the political arena concerning the potential social, economic, and political impact of these demographic changes.

In the United States, a recent profile of statistics regarding adults over 65 provides the following data:

- In 2010, there were 40.4 million adults 65 and over in the United States (13.1% of the total population); in 2030, there will be an estimated 71.5 million (approximately 20% of the total population) (Administration on Aging [AOA], 2012).
- The 85-plus population is expected to rise from 5.5 million in 2010 to 7.3 million in 2020 (AOA, 2006; AOA, 2012).
- In 2010, there were 53,364 seniors over age 100, a 53% increase since 1990 (AOA, 2012).
- In 2004, 18.1% of those 65-plus were members of ethnic minority populations. Of these, 8.2% were African Americans; 6.0%, persons of Hispanic origin; approximately 2.9%, Asian or Pacific Islanders; and less than 1%, American Indians or Native Alaskans (AOA, 2006).
- Projections for 2050 suggest that, of a total population of 65-plus (80.1 million), 65 million will be white (non-Hispanic), 12.5% Hispanic, 8.4% African American, and 6.7% other ethnic populations (Hooyman & Kiyak, 2005).

The aging of the United States and countries around the world is a mark of success and a challenge. "For most of recorded history, average life expectancy at birth was less than 30 years. By 1900, average life expectancy in the United States had reached nearly age 50, and by 2000 it had reached age 74 for men and 80 for women. These vast improvements can be traced to a wide array of nutritional and environmental factors as well as advances in medicine. Recent advances in medical care, particularly surrounding the detection and treatment of heart disease, have led to marked increases in life expectancy after 65 (Friedland & Summer, 2005). On the one hand, we can expect increased longevity with better health; on the other hand, long life has meant increased years of disability and need for care for some elders, especially those over the age of 85.

Unfortunately, the political discourse is currently characterizing the aging population dynamic as a "crisis" around the world, often requiring the preferred neoliberal solution of social welfare cuts. Fears in the United States regarding public expenditures that support older Americans have been widely expressed, as resources directed to war and other economic conditions lead to increased national deficits.

In response to this crisis imagery, Friedland and Summer (2005) caution that society's future is not determined solely by demographic changes. In their analysis, the role of economic productivity, changes in health status and behaviors, changes in workforce participation of older adults, and related public policy decisions are identified as key determinants of the impact of aging on societies. Focus on these factors as well as population growth is important to advocates for policy that addresses aging societies.

The purpose of this chapter is to provide an overview of the nature and content of social policy and social services targeting older Americans, with attention to implications for social workers engaged in policy practice. The larger political/moral economy will be briefly introduced as critical to the understanding of aging issues and policy in the United States. In addition, key content of policy and social/moral debate in the United States that has direct impact on policy development will be explored. The specific policy overview and discussion section will be limited to key policies and policy trends in selected areas of special concern to older adults, such as income, employment, health care, housing, transportation, and the resulting network of health and social services.

The Political/Moral Economy Context of Aging Societies

Any exploration of the aging of societies and social policy and programs developed in response to needs and/or strengths of older adults requires recognition of the larger political/moral/economic context (Cox & Pawar, 2006). McMichael (2000) notes, "We can no longer understand changes in our society without situating them globally" (p. xxxvii). The resources, technology, policies, and interventions designed to meet human need will be increasingly related to international impact on national political economies. The relative power of internationalization on policy decisions will be related to the depth of integration of economies through the globalization movement. Gerber (1999) offers the following definition of shallow and deep integration that suggests the potential power of this movement:

> *Shallow integration is the elimination or reduction of tariffs, quotas, and other border-related barriers, such as customer procedures that restrict the flow of goods across borders. Deep integration is the elimination, reduction, or alteration of domestic polices when they have the unintended consequences of acting as trade*

barriers. Major examples include labor and environmental standards, investment regulation, the rules of fair competition between firms, and allowable forms of government support for private industry. (p. 9)

The trend toward deep integration is evident in the regulations of such institutions as the International Monetary Fund and the World Bank, coupled with regional trade alliances. Rapid development in technology, with respect to communication and other devices that facilitate international production systems, internationalization of the labor market, and intelligence, provide strong support for deep integration (Friedman, 2005).

Proponents of the rapid advance of globalization of a laissez-faire market system tout the ability of this process to raise the standard of living of countries within less-developed economies and suggest that this process is an inevitable change (Macarov, 2003). However, opponents warn of the current and future potential of this form of globalization of markets to increase poverty around the world in both industrialized/ postindustrial nations and economically less-developed countries (Macarov, 2003).

Often using the rational of international economic development, the United States, Europe, and Japan have adopted the politics of neoliberalism. This shift in philosophy, which promotes less government, less skepticism of business, cooperation with the needs of a global laissez-faire market system, and a higher degree of individual responsibility for meeting human need (especially in the United States), provided the framework for social welfare change during the 1980s and 1990s. During the second Bush Administration, the United States has shifted into a framework of neoconservatism and cultural conservatism that promotes radical privatization of social welfare and stronger government regulation of social/moral values and issues, such as attacking the separation of government and religion in the United States (Hart, 2006). These shifts, coupled with government deficits (related to changing economic factors and military expenditures), have strong implications for present and future aging policy in the United States (Estes, 2001a; Gilbert & van Voorhis, 2003; Karger & Stoesz, 2005; Leonard, 1997).

In summary, the changes we see in social welfare programs in the United States and elsewhere are a product of the current process of internationalization of economies plus national political, social, and economic factors. Together, these elements are producing or promoting:

- Deep cuts in social welfare programs;
- Devolution (shifting responsibility to lower levels of government);
- Privatization of social programs (shifting responsibility to private for-profit and not-for-profit firms and organizations);
- Shifting of responsibility to individuals and families;
- Deregulation.

Social policy targeting older adults in the United States is being developed and modified in the context of these trends as well as other factors unique to the United States. The social construction of aging in the United

States has taken directions that define the particular policy and service approaches that exist. Ongoing changes in the discourse concerning older adults will continue to have an important role in future policy. The following section provides a discussion of the political/moral economy of aging in the United States and other related social processes that provide the specific framework for aging policy.

Changing Social Perceptions, Expectations, and Policies

Inherent in the social change process are both the social construction of issues and related discourses (Leonard, 1997). Robertson (1999) stresses that the concept of moral economy is broader than the concepts of rights and needs in that it "is as much about our obligations to one another as it is about the claims we are entitled to make against each other" (p. 81). This section briefly reviews a few prevalent historical perceptions regarding the status of older adults. It also discusses selected dimensions of the current discourse regarding perceptions of older adults, including their social roles and issues related to resource allocation in an aging society. Other key factors, reflecting issues that have been raised regarding future policy targeting older adults, are also noted, including ageism and age discrimination, diversity within the aging population, and the potential of technological development. These factors provide the context for a number of specific policy areas affecting older adults in the United States and are strongly influenced by overall factors in the political economy described above.

Medicalization of aging, other political/moral perceptions regarding the nature and appropriateness of roles of older adults, and perceptions of fair entitlement of older adults to public resources are particularly relevant to understanding the moral economy of aging in the United States. Rapid change in the political economy, coupled with the ongoing concern about population increase, have spurred an escalated attention to these aspects of aging. In turn, the social/moral context of aging has had strong impact on past policy in aging and will have important influence on future policy.

Medicalization of Aging

Perhaps the most powerful stranglehold on aging policy, the meaning of aging, and the status of older persons in the United States has been and continues to be the widely accepted social construction of aging as a medical problem. This view of aging brings with it the need for medical solutions to the issue of aging. Estes, Wallace, Linkins, and Binney (2001) note that "the biomedical model emphasizes the etiology, clinical treatment and management of disease of the elderly as defined and treated by medical practitioners while giving marginal attention to the social and behavioral process and problems" (p. 46).

The power of the medical industrial complex has not only guided social policy discourse and mobilized large percentages of government and private resources targeting older adults into the provision of health-care services and health-related research; it has also assured the dominance of the medical model in service provision. The medical model is essentially characterized by diagnosis and focus on illness of the problem, the expectancy that professionals will cure the problem, and compliance expectations by medical professionals (Ambrosino, Hefferman, Shuttlesworth & Ambrosino, 2005; Atchley & Barusch, 2004; Manning, 1998). This model has dominated the scope of sanctioned social work services and the nature of social work interventions available to older adults in an ever-expanding arena of settings. Its impact is further addressed in the discussion below regarding social services and social work policy practice.

Estes et al. (2001) provide critical understanding of the role of commodification of health care as another contextuating factor contributing to the medical impact on aging policy. They define commodification as "the process of taking a good or service that has been produced and used, but not bought or sold, and turning it into an item that is exchanged for money" (p. 49). This process includes the shift of health care from the arena of social needs and rights to a source of private profit. Related to the issue of health care and profit is the complication of the increasing tendency to associate older adults with the overall problems of health-care costs in the United States. Specifically, political commentary often blames older Americans for the high health-care expenditures of the public sector, without taking into consideration private sector factors involved in high costs of health care.

Older Adults, Status, Roles, and Resources

Historical reviews present a complex picture of the status of older adults over time in the United States. Status changes, in general, are primarily related to the labor market or economic productivity capacity of older persons within the context of overall changes associated with modernization, including factors such as (a) size of the labor pool; (b) physical demands of available work; (c) importance of experience as a factor in worker productivity; and (d) ability to adapt to new technology and work place structures, such as larger bureaucracies (Barusch, 2006). It is important to note that social policy initiated on behalf of the elderly has often been in response to needs of the economy rather that the elders. For example, the Social Security Act (1935; passed into law, 1936) was initiated in large part to shrink the labor market in a time of great unemployment.

Fostered by industrial revolution, many European countries had begun to institutionalize retirement through government pensions, with the United States following with the introduction of Social Security in 1935 (Moody, 2006). Many sociologists and historians have argued that, between 1950 and 1970, retirement was increasingly considered a widely accepted social process. Retirement became popularly viewed as a "natural" process, representing a reward for long periods of economic contribution or payment of deferred wages. Other observers have contended that retirement's strong development was due to its usefulness as a tool for business to control its labor pool. Retirement was also widely associated with the idea that ability to continue working was diminished for older workers (Moody, 2006; Phillipson, 1999).

Another area of the historical political/moral economy, strongly relevant to the elderly and social policy in the United States, has been the status of older Americans with respect to public assistance. Over time, older adults have enjoyed a position of lesser stigma with respect to need for and use of public resources. Poor elderly were among the "worthy poor," as documented by historical accounts of social welfare in England and the United States (Axinn & Stern, 2005; Day, 2003). However, this status did not guarantee adequate governmental support, as evidenced by consistently low levels of assistance, placement in poor houses, and consistently high levels of poverty among older people in the United States, which persisted through the 1950s (Applebaum & Payne, 2005; Day, 2003; Hudson, 2005).

Advocates for older adults in the 1930s were able to use this "worthy poor" status in addition to labor issues to facilitate the Social Security Act, passed into law in 1936, and the passage of several policy initiatives during the 1960s and 1970s. Among these policy initiatives were Medicare and Medicaid (1964) and the Older Americans Act (1965). Additionally, other resources, including income, health and social services, employment, housing, and a wide variety of senior discounts were initiated at all levels of government and by nongovernmental not-for-profits (Binstock, 2004).

In the late 1970s the political tide had turned to neoliberal perspectives, and both the economic and health status of older adult showed improvement. Consequently, the long-accepted tenet of age as a key criterion for eligibility for social welfare began to come under scrutiny (Hudson, 1997).

Questions concerning both "need" and "worthiness" of older Americans became part of political discourse, and a number of political and academic knowledge-based movements or agendas were initiated during the 1980s and 1990s that challenged the social construction of aging and older adults. These activities generated important challenges that continue to linger in current political debate, specific to older adults. Such challenges were fueled by the "crisis" concept of population aging in the United States, economic stagnation, war-related deficits, and popular acceptance of the assumption of powerlessness of national governments to make decisions that were not controlled by the dictates of competition in a global economy. Thus issues regarding the status of older adults, with respect to (a) social welfare entitlements and other benefits, (b) changing role expectations of older Americans, (c) attention to diversity in the aging population, (d) identifying the nature of ageism in the United States, and (e) attention to the potential role of technology, were added to the political arena.

Changing Perceptions of Older Adults and Social Welfare

The need to quell the popularity of age-based programs fit both neoliberal and neoconservative agendas. An overall concern with increasing numbers of older adults (the aging of "baby boomers), together with decreased public resources and increasing concern about Social Security and Medicare/Medicaid costs, have provided a supportive environment for challenging the social construction of older Americans as a worthy group for collective support.

Social Welfare Worthiness of the Elderly

In the 1980s, a well-financed campaign was launched that sought to frame social welfare issues as a contest between the elderly and the young (Atchley & Barusch, 2004; Cox & Parsons, 1994). Popular media began to support a shift of perceptions of older adults from a "needy/worthy population" to a "greedy population." Stories of extravagant recreational pursuits of retired persons and cartoons flooded the popular press. One cartoon, for example, depicted elderly individuals traveling with bumper stickers that stated, "We are spending our children's inheritance." "Wealth and waste" was the essence of the message concerning the status and morality of older adults (Stoller & Gibson, 2000).

A political movement supporting this perspective, the Intergenerational Equity Movement initiated in the mid-1980s, gave organized political and policy articulation to creating "old versus young debate" surrounding public-policy support for older adults. Social Security and Medicare were obvious targets for this perspective. The older population was portrayed as taking too much from existing public resources and being the cause of the poverty of children in the United States (Minkler, 2006).

Overall, these efforts challenged both the need premise for public support of older adults and their assumed moral worthiness, which had been based primarily on economic and social contribution though life-long work. The extent to which these efforts increased intergenerational conflict requires further investigation. However, the failure of neoconservative efforts to severely cut Social Security and Medicare to this point in time, the great amount of long-term care assistance provided by families to their elderly members, and the addition of drug benefits to Medicare represent circumstances that raise issue about the effectiveness of this movement. Hudson (2005) states that "although there remained no evidence that generational tensions had permeated the thinking of the general public, it became common if not accepted knowledge in policy circles that ageing benefits had to be reined in" (p. 322). Additionally, little data has been gathered regarding the impact this propaganda has had on state and local and not-for-profit resource decisions. In many arenas this issue may not be as dead as it is assumed to be by some gerontologists.

The effort to change the general image of older persons from a worthy population to a greedy population that represents a burden to children, was in part responsible for efforts to counter this imagery. Two such efforts, largely initiated in academic circles, were the "successful aging" and the "productive aging" movements.

Successful Aging   Gerontologists, interested primarily in challenging negative or false perceptions of older adults and increasing the role potential in
late life, worked to advance more positive images of this older group based
on their research and advocacy interests. One such effort was the concept
of *successful aging.* Successful aging was defined in a MacArthur Foundation study as a combination of (a) good physical heath, (b) high cognitive
functioning, and (c) continuing participation in social activity at a high
level (Rowe & Kahn, 1997). Whereas this image of optimum success for
older adults drew considerable support, especially from the medical profession, critiques of this vision were quick to follow. Such appraisals included
the challenge that achievement of these criteria was based on middle-class
values, including staying young and related structural opportunities. Class,
cultural differences, and conditions over one's lifetime had not been considered in the definition of successful aging (Hooyman & Kiyak, 2005; Rowe
& Kahn, 1997).

Productive Aging   The concept of *productive aging* was advanced in a similar attempt to focus attention on the fact that most elderly people are
productive, society must provide structural access to valuable roles for older
adults, and the opportunity to participate in valued roles enhances health
and mental health (Caro, Bass, & Chen, 2006; Morrow-Howell, 2006). Caro
et al. (2006) put forth their definition of productive aging as follows: "Productive aging is any activity by an older individual that produces goods
or services or develops the capacity to produce them, whether they are
to be paid for or not" (p. 247). These scholars acknowledge that their
definition differs from other definitions that have included activities of personal enrichment. Holstein (1999) calls attention to a fourth dimension
of the productive aging discussion. Based on her analysis, the focus on
productive aging as a movement "affirms a cultural ideal: It is good and
desirable for U.S. culture to evaluate productivity as a ruling metaphor for
a 'good' old age" (p. 359). This aspect of the productive-aging emphasis
has resulted in critiques similar to those of successful aging, especially
regarding the way in which the advancement of this concept as a goal
for late life relates to minority ethnic populations, women, and those with
less economic resources and life-long, limited access to labor-market-related
productivity (Holstein, 1999; Hooyman & Kiyak, 2005).

In the long run, even with many attempts to make productivity an
inclusive term, the historical linkage of this term to market productivity
is likely to prevail. The important goal of promoting productive aging, as
an effort to increase knowledge about the contributions of older adults to
society and the need to remove barriers to these contributions, may be
offset by a politically inspired dictate to older adults that they must be
engaged in productive market-related labor as their primary, socially acceptable role. This perception also justifies cuts in aging-related social welfare
programs.

Challenge to the Social-Institution Status of Retirement

Closely related to efforts to characterize older adults as healthy and able is the political-social movement to delegitimitize the institution of retirement. Retirement, as discussed earlier, enjoyed increasing status as a social institution around the world during the 1950s through the 1980s, especially in economically developed societies. In the United States, for example, acceptance of retirement is indicated by a substantial change in the 65-plus, employed population, from 54.7% in 1950 (Moody, 2006) to 14.4% in 2004 (AOA, 2006). Even though there was a push for early retirement during the 1980s and somewhat during the 1990s, concurrently there was a growing concern about the economic feasibility of retirement. During the first decade of the 21st century, we are witnessing a challenge to the acceptability of retirement as a social institution. This challenge is based on the assumed better health and economic status and ability to work of older adults, fears about the ability of governments to continue their current levels of support regarding income and health care for older adults, and questions about the potential need for older adults in the labor force (Atchley & Barusch, 2004; Ghilarducci, 2006; Hudson, 1997; Moody, 2006).

Ageism and Age Discrimination

The nature and depth of ageism and age discrimination in the United States requires further study, but significant evidence exists to suggest the strong prevalence of many different forms and settings related to these two concepts (Atchley & Barusch, 2004; Butler, 2006; Cohen, 2001; Palmore, 2005). Studies also affirm that numerous older adults have internalized many of the cultural stereotypes held by other age groups. Historically, discrimination in employment has been the primary academic focus regarding age discrimination. The powerful imagery of "aging as progressive decline" provided support in addition to economic factors for the development of mandatory retirement, beginning in the 1920s, and has continued to be a factor in other decisions negatively impacting older workers (Butler, 2006; Novak, 2006).

A comprehensive report conducted in 2006 under the direction of Robert Butler has identified many forms of age discrimination in key areas of concern to older adults. The following examples of these findings illustrate their potential significance to aging-related policy:

- One to 3 million Americans aged 65 and older, have been abused by someone they depend on for care, and more than 5 million are estimated to be victims of financial exploitation each year;
- Nine out of 10 nursing homes are inadequately staffed;
- Of workers 65 and over, 16.9% perceive that they experienced work-related discrimination in 2002;
- Only 10% of people aged 65 and over receive appropriate screening tests for bone density, colorectal and prostate cancer, and glaucoma,

despite increased susceptibility to these conditions by older adults (Butler, 2006).

These examples represent only a few of those identified in the report and do not include the elaborate array of prejudicial attitudes (ageism), including (a) treatment in daily life of older adults as mentally disabled (e.g., asking younger individuals instead of older customers what they want), (b) negative media portrayal, (c) the ignoring of ideas presented by older adults, and (d) forced societal disengagement (Atchley & Barusch, 2004). The increasing awareness of the comprehensiveness and complexity of age discrimination in the United States brings challenge to both issues related to the work/retirement agenda and efforts to provide older adults access to a range of meaningful roles in the postmodern social structure.

Other Forms of Elder Abuse

State and local elder protective service agencies report a variety of types of abuse. More commonly known are physical and psychological abuse, though as Dolgoff and Feldstein note, there are other forms of abuse, which include neglect, abandonment, financial or material exploitation, and self-neglect (Dolgoff & Feldstein, 2013, pp. 361–362). Sadly, seniors also face substandard housing, suffer from inadequate nutrition, and live in dangerous environments.

Recognition of Diversity in the Aging Population

Perhaps the most significant dimension of aging in the United States beyond demographic aging is the increasing diversity among older adults in the aging population and its implications for public policy. The multiple facets of diversity within the older adult population, including class, age, sex, ethnicity, and health status, have become more widely recognized as a critical factor in today's policy arenas (Dressel, Minkler, & Yen, 1999; Hudson, 1997; Torres-Gil, 2001). Age-based policy development during the 1960s and 1970s has primarily utilized chronological age, usually 55, 60, 62, or 65, as the basis for eligibility for public resources. This universal approach was supplemented by a number of selective or means-based programs, such as Supplemental Security Insurance (SSI) and Medicaid.

As attention is called to strengths and needs of different groups within the aging population, profound differences in the ability to meet basic needs will be identified. Estes (2001b) notes that, from a political economy perspective, "social policy for the aged mirrors the structural arrangements in the U.S. society and the distribution of material, political, and symbolic resources within it" (p. 13). Advocates for older adults face an intensifying challenge to preserve universal programs, while at the same time meeting social justice mandates to assure that basic needs are met for all older adults. Questions regarding adequacy, appropriateness, and accessibility of social welfare provisions must be continually evaluated and addressed. In sum, it is evident that diversity within the aging population, as in society as a whole, will have significant impact on social policy, especially within the confines of increasing globalization and neoconservative and/or neoliberal political approaches.

Potential Role of Technology

The future role of technology in the lives of older Americans has generated the interest of both the public and private for-profit sector. The primary focus of development of technology for older adults has targeted issues of disability and frailty as well as assisting caregivers (Charness, 2005; Setting Priorities for Retirement Years, SPRY, Foundation, 2005; Takamura, 2001). Technology assistance for caregivers includes, for example, a wide range of monitoring devices, technological setups to allow "virtual house calls," electronically linked systems for contact with emergency services, systems to allow more intense interaction with care providers (including a variety of over-the-phone medication monitoring); and services that assist with a patient's physical self-care, such as advanced-capacity wheel chairs. The primary aim has been to facilitate institutional activities of daily living.

Some advocates of the potential role of technology in an aging society suggest a much greater potential for technology in other aspects of older Americans' lives. Most importantly, they identify the need to enhance knowledge and skills of older adults with respect to use of technology. In 2010, approximately 40% of adults over age 50 reported being extremely or very comfortable using the Internet (Koppen, 2010); this was a marked increase from 2002 when only 17% of adults over age 50 reported using the Internet (Center for Research and Education on Aging and Technology Enhancement, 2002). Education of older adults, access to computers, and making computers more user-friendly represent significant challenges. However, the quest for independence in late life will continue to be strongly related to older adults' ability to access and use computers and other technological devices.

Coughlin and Lau (2006a) suggest an integrated approach to technological development targeting older adults, including the following areas of development: (a) health, (b) safety, (c) connectivity, (d) contribution, and (e) legacy. Health and safety interventions include those suggested earlier, whereas connectivity technology would encompass communications with a broader range of purposes, such as entertainment, transportation, and development of livable communities. Contribution and legacy technological development refer to education-, workplace-, and cognitive-enhancement technologies, as well as cross-generational learning enhancement.

The challenge to independence and privacy that may well come with increased surveillance is an issue that has been raised by many older adults as well as gerontologists. Surveillance capacity has greatly increased and can monitor almost every movement and activity in one's home or in an institution. Coughlin and Lau (2006b) state the issue as follows:

> *Although the potential benefits of these technology applications are many, the important question of privacy remains. How we can maintain independent lives*

while preserving our health and safety as we age is the essential tension in intro-ducing and financing many innovations. Who decides: How is the data managed, to whom is it reported, and under what conditions? These are just a few of the questions raised by existing and emerging technologies in some homes today and in all our lives tomorrow. (p. 3)

These questions will have ongoing impact on policy decisions in many arenas of aging policy. The following sections provide a brief overview of issues and policy trends in selected areas of aging policy and an overview and analysis of issues in health and social services in aging. The social issues and changes described are important factors in social policy, specific to the needs of older adults.

Overview of Selected Policy and Services

From a political economy perspective, the interconnectedness of interna-tional, national, and local policy is evident. Indeed, an attempt to distin-guish aging policy from general political/economic or social welfare policy requires constant awareness of this background. In addition, any overview of aging-related policy exposes an array of policy arenas too comprehen-sive for the boundaries of this chapter. The following is a discussion of selected policy areas that addresses specific common needs of older adults and selected key policies related to these areas. The policy areas selected include income, employment, health, housing, and transportation, as well as an overview of other supportive/social services, including the contribu-tion of the Older Americans Act.

Current issues in aging policy in the United States reflect the trends, discussed earlier, of privatization, social welfare cuts, devolution, and deregulation. In addition, historical characteristics of U.S. social welfare provisions, including "shared responsibility" among the federal govern-ment, state government, and private sector (for-profit and not-for-profit) as well as individual and/or family responsibility (emphasized to an ever-greater degree) have been made increasingly complex by these larger trends. This is discussed further in the overview of health and social services outlined later in this section.

Income Issues in Late Life and Related Policies

Most older Americans are concerned about adequate income in late life. In fact, according to Ekerdt (2004), adults of all ages are becoming increas-ingly aware of the need to save for "retirement," even to the detriment of other needs. Retirement income for older adults most frequently comes from four sources: Social Security, work, pensions, and savings, supplemented by means-tested programs, such as Supplemental Security Insurance (SSI) for individuals with very low income and resources.

The relationship of these sources of income to need is complex. Income policy provides an example of Estes' (2001b) contention, noted earlier, that policy tends to reinforce lifelong inequities. Higher income and social status throughout one's life span allow for higher accumulation of Social Security income, higher savings rates, and better employment opportunities before and after retirement age. Sources of income reported by older persons in 2009 include Social Security (87%), income from assets (53%), private pensions (28%), government employee pensions (14%), and earnings (26%). Of these sources, Social Security benefits accounted for 38% of the aggregate income of the older population; and for 35% of these older adults, Social Security accounted for 90% or more of their income (AOA, 2012). According to an earlier Social Security Administration study, earnings accounted for 25% of this population's income; asset income, 14%; and pensions, 19%. Access to these sources of income is strongly influenced by class, sex, educational, and ethnic status (Social Security Administration, 2004).

A critical look at statistics regarding income and need, especially cost of living, is required to guide future policy advocacy. Specific to those 65 and over, the 2011 federal poverty line is $10,788 for individuals and $13,596 for couples (United States Census Bureau, 2012). In 2009, 8.9% of this older population was reported at or below the poverty line and another 5.4% at or below 125% of the poverty line. In 2011, the median income for household headed by an older person was $34,354 (DeNevas, Proctor, & Smith, 2010, p. 5). These income amounts have little meaning separated from the costs of basic need (housing, utilities, food, and medical expense not covered by other funds). Some estimates suggest that as many as one third of U.S. families have difficulty meeting daily needs. See, for example, Ehrenreich's (2002) publication regarding everyday needs.

Furthermore, there is great diversity with respect to the gravity of poverty and which population groups among adults 65-plus are represented in poverty. For example, 5.8% of individuals over 65 have less than $5,000, 49.4% have less than $14,999, and more than 30% of households headed by these older Americans have annual incomes less than $24,999. Ethnic diversity in income distribution, related to elders having income below the poverty line, includes, for example, 7.5% of Whites (non-Hispanic) compared to 23.9% of African Americans, 18.7% of Hispanic Americans, and 13.1% of Asians Americans over 65 (AOA, 2005). These statistics indicate that a large percentage of older persons have cause for serious concern about the adequacy of their late-life income. Need and income is also complicated by extremely high medical costs that can quickly decimate wealth.

Advocates for older adults facing income deficiencies have begun to engage more aggressively in comparisons of the U.S. poverty line to cost of living in regions throughout the United States. Future policy related to poverty among older adults will no doubt focus on this discrepancy and the need to advocate for acceptance of a livable poverty guideline.

Specific current debates surrounding income policy target Social Security reform, the changing nature of pension systems and pension stability, and concerns about a variety of issues related to employment. The specific policy debates related to these issues are strongly influenced by the neoliberal-neoconservative political perspectives described earlier.

Social Security Issues

Social Security is currently a primary target for reform, based on these competing political perspectives. Social Security was created in the vortex of the depression of the 1930s, among many conflicting political agendas, including the need to remove older adults from the labor market and the desperate poverty of a "deserving population." Today, this perspective has been challenged, as noted earlier, by such factors as changing images of older adults, their increasing numbers, and better health and economic status. Social Security has been a primary factor in this improved economic status.

The status of Social Security has currently been presented in the political arena as being in crisis, framing the issue as an intergenerational equity debate rather than reflecting intergenerational interdependence and current economic circumstances, including the increasing government deficit—largely a result of the war in Iraq. Fueled by a neoconservative political perspective, opponents of Social Security in its present form have initiated proposals based on various degrees of privatization of social security. Schieber (1997), for example, suggests a strategy that would allow a portion of Social Security taxes to be placed in individual investment accounts, while preserving a basic flat rate benefit ($410, in 1996-adjusted dollars), to be earned with 10 years of covered earnings. Politically, many supporters are concerned that this quasi-privatization approach will eradicate the social principles of government responsibility as well as a sense of mutual support inherent in the current system.

Opponents of basic changes in Social Security disagree with drastic predictions of the oncoming fiscal crisis in Social Security and suggest a number of moderate reforms. Reforms include such strategies as increasing the age of eligibility for full entitlement, basing the amount of entitlement on 38 years rather than 35 years of contribution, making small increases in the payroll taxes, and increasing the percentage of Social Security benefits that are taxed (see, for example, Bush, 2005; Herd, 2005; Schultz, 2001).

It is also important to note that this current policy debate regarding Social Security has taken focus away from the issue of basic adequacy of the program for meeting the income needs of older adults—a guiding emphasis in the Social Security reforms of the 1970s and early 1980s. Increasing diversity among older adults will require that the policy be modified to better meet the needs of diverse populations (e.g., women and populations with lower life expectancy) and the increasing progressive redistribution for low-income populations.

Supplemental Security Insurance (SSI), a public assistance program, was initiated in 1974 to provide a minimal income for the elderly, blind, and disabled persons with very limited income and assets ($2,000 for individuals and $3,000 for couples in 2012). The 2012 income levels for eligibility are $698 for individuals and $1,048 for an eligible individual with an eligible spouse (Social Security Administration, 2012). Approximately 20% of SSI payments go to older adults (Applebaum & Payne, 2005). Cost containment, adequacy, changes in eligibility requirements to exclude individuals with alcohol or drug disability, and ongoing immigrant status issues, as well as very uncoordinated administration, are the primary policy issues surrounding this program.

Private Pension Issues

In response to current economic changes, many private pension plans are facing challenges. For example, workers from several major corporations who had pension plans based on profit-sharing have seen their pensions devastated by stock devaluations, mergers, and other changes. Workers owning 401(k) and similar plans have also seen pension losses due to stock downturns. These problems have raised serious concerns among many older adults and occur at a time when public and private pension systems are changing from *defined benefit plans*, usually backed by the Pension Benefit Guaranty Corporation, to *defined contributions plans*, which increase personal risk for employees and pensioners. Defined benefit plans promise a specific amount of income at retirement, usually dependent on salary and years of service. Defined contribution plans consist of individual accounts composed of contributions from either the worker or the employer or both. The employee is then responsible for the outcomes of investment of these funds.

Public policy issues related to the government's role in monitoring these plans include, for example, placing limits on profit-sharing systems, the high risk placed on employees, and protections against fraud or other illegal practices. Other related issues concern ever-changing government tax policy regarding pre- versus post-tax saving opportunities for 401(k)-type pension funds and Individual Retirement Accounts (IRAs); taxing of pensions; and concerns about portability, inflation protection, and coverage of dependents.

Employment Issues

To address income issues of older adults, a wide range of employment issues must be addressed, such as age-based layoffs and age-based discrimination in training opportunities, promotion, and hiring. Among ways to remove the barriers to employment of older workers are the following two strategies: (1) provision of adequate research and administrative support to improve implementation of the Age Discrimination and Employment Act (ADEA) objectives, and (2) resources to initiate innovative ways to retain older workers, such as the development of flexible and/or reduced-hour systems, appropriate technology training, and continued support of current federal and state older-workers' programs (Barnett, 2005; Butler, 2006; Hooyman & Kiyak, 2005).

Health Policy Issues

Health care is a primary concern of older Americans. Medicare, initiated in 1965 as a federal health care insurance program for adults 65 and over, as well as some younger disabled persons, currently provides core coverage of hospital care; short-term rehabilitative nursing-home care; home-health and hospice care (Part A); and supplemental medical insurance, a voluntary component (Part B) of physicians' care.

Despite this important program, most poor and middle-income older adults in the United States are deeply concerned about either ongoing uncovered costs of late-life health care or the potential cost of long-term institutional care in nursing homes or intensive in-home care services. In 2004, the cost for nursing home care averaged $70,080 according to Elderlaw Answers (Elderlaw, n.d.). A 2011 study by MetLife found that average cost per year had increased to $87,235 while assisted living averaged $41,724 (MetLife, 2011).

Key areas of health policy of special concern to older adults include limitations and changes in Medicare, Medicaid, and long-term-care resources and services. Policy debates in these arenas have overlapping, complementary, and different issues related to health care and older adults. Both Medicare and Medicaid provide some resources for long-term care. Medicaid costs for nursing-home care are of great concern.

Medicare Issues

Medicare policy concerns have historically included the fit between the chronic illnesses that are common among older adults and an acute medical-model care system that is oriented toward curing acute illnesses, hospitalization, emergency care, surgical care, treatment through drugs, short-term intervention in physicians' offices, and so on. A number of changes have occurred, aimed at this mismatch, including expansion of the program to include increased home health care (Hooyman & Kiyak, 2005). However, from a social work perspective, these changes fall far short of financial support for a social model of care. In addition, severe limitations on Medicare-funded home care continue to inhibit adequate psychosocial community services. Examples of such limitations include the requirement that eligible recipients of care be strictly "homebound" and that specific nursing, physical therapy, and/or occupational therapy care be required to allow the continuation of any social services.

In addition to this ongoing core issue, there are an increasing number of policy issues surrounding Medicare. Salient issues include (a) political concerns about the increasing costs of the overall program; (b) increased pressure for privatization of the program as a whole and in part; (c) ever-increasing premiums, deductibles, and cuts in coverage (as cost-saving strategies); (d) mental health parity; (e) a variety of issues concerning access and quality related to the contracting of health maintenance organizations; (f) early discharge from hospitals related to prospective cost-containment strategies; (g) lack of coverage for dental and eye care; and (h) issues regarding structure, access, and adequacy of the 2003 Medical Prescription and Drug Act.

Medicaid Issues

Medicaid was initiated in 1965 to provide health care for low-income Americans and is funded by a combination of federal and state monies. States have a range of authority over program access and included services. Policy issues include (a) political concerns about rising costs (especially nursing-home costs for older adults who either were initially eligible for Medicaid or spend down to eligibility, often due to loss of resources, mostly through nursing-home costs); (b) cuts in eligibility of special populations, such as elderly immigrants and individual with alcohol and/or drug addictions; and (c) concerns related to limited coverage and quality, similar to issues facing Medicare.

Long-Term-Care Policy Issues

Issues surrounding long-term-care (LTC) policy encompass both long-term institutional care in nursing homes and intensive in-home care services that involve community-based long-term care. LTC issues include (a) lack of a national policy that provides financial support for older adults requiring nursing-home care and/or community-based care; (b) the ongoing struggle for resources between institutional and community-based long-term care; (c) the extremely high cost of care; (d) the critical shortage of care providers; (e) competency, training, and supervision of care providers; (f) the need to expand support for family/personal caregivers; (g) the need to support a wide range of institutional-care supports, including the ongoing struggle between patients rights and institutional monitoring functions; (h) the need to expand prevention and health-promotion interventions as well as other social and community interventions; and (i) the high cost and scant coverage of existing private, long-term-care insurance policies (Hooyman & Kiyak, 2005).

Housing Policy Issues

Lisbon (2006) states that "a crisis exists for older Americans who need affordable housing and the crisis is getting worse" (p. 9). Among the challenging housing policy issues for older adults are (a) ongoing cuts in federal support for building affordable housing, (b) limited affordable housing vouchers and other forms of rental supplements since the 1980s, (c) the difficulty of relying on state and local affordable housing development, (d) increasing costs of rentals (including loss of existing affordable housing through mortgage maturation of federally financed building projects and related changes), and (e) lack of resources to sustain and renovate existing housing (Lisbon, 2006).

Clearly, the cost of housing is a significant challenge for many older Americans. According to the AOA (2005), "Of the 21.6 million households headed by older persons in 2003, the following situations existed: (a) 80% were owners and 20% renters, (b) median year of construction of the housing was 1965, (c) almost 73% of older homeowners owned their homes free and clear, and (d) the median values of this housing was $122,790" (p. 11). In light of these statistics, issues surrounding maintenance and repair have become critical, in addition to those related to availability of appropriate housing and the cost of purchase or rental. Other salient issues pertaining to housing are associated with the linkage to potential health and social services, and neighborhood/location considerations, such as transportation availability, safety for walking and shopping, nearness of supportive relationships, and lack of unsympathetic or hostile neighbors.

A wide range of "senior housing" units have been developed by private and governmental resources during the past 25 years, leading to the development of an array of supportive services, both in housing settings and the community (e.g., food services, personal care, medication assistance, and housekeeping services) (Wilson, 2005–2006). This expansion of senior-specific housing has also raised policy issues concerning age-segregated versus intergenerational housing settings, affordability, and level of monitoring (especially as health-related services become involved).

Transportation Issues

Policy makers do not consistently give great attention to transportation issues of older adults; however, this issue ranked third among concerns of delegates attending the most recent White House Conference on Aging in 2005. The next Conference is set for 2015 (Hudson, 2006). Transportation policy issues range from concerns about the abilities of older drivers and lack of public transportation (especially in suburban areas) to availability of special transportation programs to meet health and shopping needs. Again the mix between public- and private-sector roles is central to many policy arguments as regards increasing costs, safety concerns, liability as a barrier to volunteer services, and the possible future role of technology.

Common Policy Directions

This brief look at selected policy issues affecting older adults demonstrates the interrelatedness of these policy areas and illustrates common trends. Such trends include (a) the predominant concern with cost, (b) cuts in programs or failure to keep up with increasing needs, (c) the need for attention to diverse circumstances of older adults, and (d) overall dominance of the medical model in resource allocation. These trends continue to have strong impact on income, housing, transportation, medical benefits, and other resources allocated to older adults in the United States.

Neoconservative solutions are proposed across policy areas, and realities of "need" and lack of attention to special populations are not well-articulated on current politically accepted policy agendas. Policy that strongly supports older adults' strengths and targets ageism (including age discrimination) is not emphasized. Leaders in the gerontological community note the decline in effective advocacy for older adults' issues and strongly support the need to re-create effective advocacy approaches to assure quality of life for older adults in the United States (Rother, 2004; Stone, 2004).

Older Americans Act

The Older Americans Act (OAA) was passed in 1965. It established the following national objectives for all older Americans:

- An adequate income in retirement.
- The best possible physical and mental health.
- Suitable housing.
- Full restorative services for those needing institutional care.
- A broad range of community-based services.
- Employment opportunities without discrimination.
- Retirement in health and dignity, after years of contribution to the economy.
- Access to participation in civic, cultural, educational, and training opportunities.
- Access to a range of community-based supportive services.
- Freedom, independence, and free exercise of individual initiative in planning and managing their own lives.
- Participation in decision making regarding services.
- Immediate benefit of aging-related research. (OAA, 1965)

These objectives have provided substantial support to advocacy efforts in ensuing decades.

Through grants to states and community programs, the OAA provides for the establishment and funding of a wide range of home- and community-based services under Title III. Multipurpose senior centers, congregate and home-delivered meals, case management, protective services, telephone reassurance, and caregiver support are among many more programs and services that have been funded. Title VII of this act provides for state-administered ombudsman programs to assure residents' rights in nursing homes, assisted living facilities and boarding homes (with some limitations depending on the state), and elder abuse programs. Other titles of the act fund separate programs for Native-American reservations, employment programs, and research and training projects.

In addition, the Older Americans Act (OAA) also provided for the establishment of the Administration on Aging (AOA), currently located in the Department of Health and Human Services. The AOA was charged with the responsibility of carrying out the core responsibilities of planning, advocacy, and mobilization of priority and innovative programs and services for older Americans related to these objectives. Furthermore, the AOA established an aging network, consisting of state offices on aging and, in most states, a number of regional agencies on aging (National Association of Area Agencies on Aging, 2006).

Choices for Independence is an AOA-sponsored initiative that was included in the 2006 OAA reauthorization proposal. This initiative provides strong support and financial resources to states for expansion of consumer-directed care approaches to community-based, long-term care. Choices for Independence provides an example of the AOA approach to influencing health and social services and could provide opportunities for social work practitioners who are committed to empowerment and strengths practice models (Kunkel & Nelson, 2005).

It is important to note that AOA programs were never designed or funded at a level to meet the needs of all older adults, but rather to act as catalyst for state and local development in addressing these needs. Great diversity exists in the programs that are available at local levels. Since initiated, AOA services have retained universal eligibility for programs; however, in recent decades, services have begun to target those most in need (income-based). Furthermore, in recent years, more focus has been given to medically related services. Overall, OAA represents a powerful tool in maintaining focus on the special needs and contributions of older adults. The leadership provided through the aging network has expanded and maintained this focus throughout the country during radically changing political eras.

Title XX Services

In the late 1950s and the 1960s, social workers working in county departments of public assistance were able to provide a broad range of social services, including protective services and casework (case management) services regarding long-term, care-related issues that encompassed advocacy, education, finding resources, and work with elders and their families. However, since the mid-1970s, as noted earlier, aging services have primarily focused on medical approaches, funded through Medicare and Medicaid. Currently, Title XX of the Social Security Act provides a number of community-based social service programs. However, this program has lost funding over the years, and especially services for the elderly have been cut. Presently, most county departments of social service provide case management (often contracted to private providers), adult protective services, and a few other services to older adults with very limited income.

Characteristics of the Health and Social Service Delivery Systems

These overall policies and diverse programs for older adults have resulted in a service delivery system with the following characteristics:

- Change from entitlements to charity approaches or work requirements.
- Predominance of medical-model programs and services.
- Services provided by one level of joint efforts or two or more levels of government, with increasing eligibility requirements and cuts in provisions.
- Services provided by for-profit and not-for-profit organizations (funded by a variety of foundations and other charitable efforts,

government contracts, and fees for service), with little coordination and many resulting gaps in service.

- Categorical assistance that restricts access, as opposed to universal programs.
- Complex and changing eligibility requirements designed to limit access.
- Strong political focus on privatization strategies and cuts in social welfare.
- Diversity in programs available, depending on geographical location.
- Lack of attention to special needs and strengths of ethnic/cultural minorities, older women, those with least resources, and other diverse populations, as well as to the development of cultural competence in program planning and among providers.

A comprehensive review of service delivery issues is not possible in the scope of this chapter to address the many issues facing health and social service design and implementation, or areas of concern such as rural versus urban issues, the breadth of caregiver/care-receiver concerns, and other critical issues. However, the overall reinforcement of class differences and increasing bipolarization of income and opportunity noted by Estes (2001b); the ongoing processes, noted earlier, relative to globalization of the economy; and U.S. economic circumstances all suggest that turbulent times are ahead. New ways of meeting needs, forms of intervention, and refocusing on issues of social justice are among the goals we must pursue.

Implications for Social Work Policy Practitioners

The dynamic interface of international and national political/moral economies, the aging of societies around the world, and the ongoing struggle to address human need and social justice raise many challenges and opportunities for social workers engaged in policy practice. The struggle to secure resources, protect the environment, and develop the necessary political power to achieve these goals will require new knowledge, skills, and strong commitment. History and current status suggest that special focus will be required to assure equity of older adults as this process evolves.

The social work profession has placed little emphasis on the older population during most of its history (Rosen & Zlotnik, 2001; Takamura, 2001). Recent efforts sponsored by the John A. Hartford Foundation and other contributors have resulted in increased attention to aging in social work education, faculty development, and research (Rosen & Zlotnik, 2001). However, a significant emphasis of this movement supports health- and mental health–related development. The potential for social work to assume leadership and expand interventions necessary to more fully address the many issues facing older adults will require expansion of these boundaries.

Several definitions can be found for social-work-related policy practice. Jansson (1999) defines policy practice as "efforts to change polices in legislative, agency and community settings whether by establishing new polices, improving existing ones, or defeating the policy initiatives of other people" (p. 10). Barusch (2006) emphasizes a wide variety of strategies that focus on assessment, analysis, and empowerment, such as advocacy, negotiation, compromise, coalition building/maintaining, and persuasive strategies. A challenge not fully addressed in most reviews of policy practice is the need for more knowledge about both micro- and macroeconomics. The policy practice suggestions presented later are compatible with this broader range of activities and are inclusive of Jansson's arenas of focus, cited earlier, as well as use of an international perspective and facilitation of opportunity for social work opportunities.

Key Directions for a Policy Practice Agenda

Although numerous gerontological policy practice issues that require attention have been identified, only the following eight overall recommendations for a social work policy practice agenda are presented here:

1. Expand the political economy perspective of policy analysis and development of social welfare approaches and advocacy to include an international context.
2. Work with coalitions to maintain and improve existing benefits for older adults, such as Social Security, Medicare, Medicaid, and Older Americans Act benefits.
3. Work with members of oppressed populations within the older adult population to define strengths and needs, and acquire culturally acceptable policy, including adequate resources.
4. Develop a strong role in framing the debates concerning older adult policy.
5. Create partnerships with older adults, their advocates, and mass-based organizations serving older adult agendas.
6. Provide policy support to establish social work practice in critical arenas beyond medical/mental-health model settings.
7. Provide policy support for new models of practice and innovative interventions in all arenas of gerontological practice.
8. Focus on adequate training and resources to apply state-of-the-art technology to policy practice efforts.

International Focus

Knowledge about national and international political-economy issues is increasingly becoming related directly to social welfare issues at the national and local level. Social workers need to be not only aware of current trends in the internationalization of economies and apparent outcomes, but also well informed about alternative visions and critiques of these directions. In order to provide leadership with respect to addressing rationales for social welfare cuts, labor market changes, and other economic factors, social workers must be confident of their knowledge of economic issues and the range of alternatives. Moreover, gaining a comprehensive knowledge of social welfare policies and program strategies around the world, especially in aging-related areas, will become ever more important as various countries find creative ways to address long-term-care needs and better integrate older adults into society.

Maintaining Existing Entitlements and Addressing Issues of Diversity

The future presents challenging agendas for advocates supporting the needs of older adults. In the context of increasing demand and diminishing resources, the struggle to maintain existing entitlements and other key programs, as well as identify and find ways to meet the needs of populations not adequately served by these programs, will encourage old and new debates regarding universal versus selective government provision. Long-time inequities will have to be addressed, and social justice strategies may be politically placed in competition with preservation of middle-class older adults. Leadership in policy action will require strong commitment and skills (Binstock, 2004).

Framing Debates Concerning Older Adult Policy

Selected current issues in aging-related policy, and the surrounding debates and assumptions concerning the nature of older adults and the political economy, have been discussed above. Active assertions and remnants of these moral economy discourses, such as (a) the struggle to present a balanced perspective of older adults that includes strengths, contributions, and needs through the active/productive aging movements; (b) focus on older adults as the cause of high medical costs; (c) focus on intergenerational inequities rather than interdependence; and (d) the medicalization of aging, all continue to provide parameters of the discussion concerning aging in society and strongly affect policy issues and advocacy efforts.

Observing the changing political paradigms in the United States, Lakoff (2004) raises the issue of the critical need for reframing and proactive framing of current discourse to develop more progressive politics. He urges an aggressive participation in framing policy debate and suggests one example of a progressive think tank—Rock Ridge Institute—that is at work in this process. (Please refer to Rock Ridge Institute, 2006.)

Leonard (1997) provides comprehensive examples of the power of popular discourse in impacting and supporting social welfare and social policy in postmodern times. He recommends widespread efforts to develop a critical consciousness and multiple coalitions supporting an emancipatory project that promotes social justice as well as a political economy supportive of human need. Social work policy practitioners will need ever-increasing knowledge and skills in communication strategies and related technology as well as organizing and coalition-building skills to be effective participants in such a task.

Partnering With Older Adults, Other Advocates, and Mass-Based Organizations

Social work policy practitioners have knowledge and skills for organizing and/or developing partnerships with elderly and intergenerational constituencies to participate in the policy process. Additionally, partnerships can be developed with a wide range of existing membership-based senior organizations and related intergenerational groups, including organized associations representing ethnic minority elders, older women, and large membership organizations, such as the American Association of Retired Persons (AARP), Generations United, Health U.S.A., and the Alliance for Retired Americans (ARA). These organizations, in addition to the many special interest groups addressing income, housing, and medical issues of older adults (e.g., the American Association of Homes and Services for the Aging, AHSA), have well-funded research and policy advocacy components (Stone, 2004).

Social workers in policy practice must increase representation both in professional positions within these organizations and as members of boards and committees that govern policy activity. Such exposure will benefit the leadership capacity of the social work profession in gerontology.

Expanding Arenas of Social Work Practice in Gerontology

Policy practice targeting governmental, private-foundation, and organizational/agency policies can be a major contributor to the development of opportunities for expansion of social work interventions in a wide variety of new settings or in settings in which social work is poorly represented. In addition to the development of more diverse settings, opportunities for implementation of new models of practice and practice approaches that are not often supported in existing settings must be supported in both new and existing social work settings. For example, promoting a better balance between medical and social services in nursing homes, hospitals, in-home care, and assisted-living facilities requires legislative support.

Today, aging newsletters are raising questions about older adults' willingness to be "cases" or "managed." A number of current practice models emphasize the strengths and resiliency of older adults, as well as acknowledge their capacity and current efforts as they continue to contribute to society (Cox & Chapin, 2001; Greene & Cohen, 2005; Silverstone, 2005). These models often suggest the necessity of forming professional relationships that represent consultative partnerships in addressing late-life issues.

The development of settings that promote efficacy-building and partnership approaches to intervention can greatly enhance the partnerships with older adults critical to social action and policy change. Of particular note are (a) empowerment-oriented models that facilitate social action as an integral part of intervention outcomes—even those targeting elderly who require significant care to meet daily needs (Cox & Parsons, 1994; Gutierrez, Parsons, & Cox, 1998) and (b) community development interventions (Austin, Camp, Flux, McClelland, & Sieppert, 2005; Rosalynn Carter Institute for Caregiving, 2006). Policy and programs that focus on consumer-directed care (AOA, 2005), care-net development, self-care, naturally occurring retirement communities (NORCs), health promotion, and a wide variety of senior volunteer programs also present opportunity for expansion of linkages and partnerships with older adults who can provide support for policy issues and efforts to frame policy discourse.

Key Terms

Ageism

Old Age, Survivors, Disability Insurance (OASDI)

Older Americans Act of 1965

Political/moral economy

Title XX services

Review Questions for Critical Thinking

1. Should the retirement age be increased beyond age 70? Why or why not?

2. Do you believe that the Social Security Retirement Program will be solvent in 25 years?

3. To what extent should the federal government be responsible for health care for older Americans?

4. Compare and contrast the Canadian health care system with the U.S. health care program. Which seems to be more comprehensive and why?

5. How does the Affordable Care Act of 2010 impact health care for older Americans?

Online Resources

Alliance for Aging Research http://www.agingresearch.org/

American Association of Retired Persons (former name, now referred to as AARP) www.aarp.org

Medicare Information Center www.medicare.gov

National Council on Aging www.ncoa.org

National Senior Citizen Law Center http://www.nsclc.org/

U.S. Administration on Aging www.aoa.gov

References

Administration on Aging. (2005). *A profile of older Americans: 2005.* Washington, DC: U.S. Department of Health and Human Services. Retrieved from http://www.aoa.gov/prof/Statistics/profile/profiles.asp

Administration on Aging. (2006). *2006 HHS poverty guidelines*. Retrieved from http://www.aoa.gov/prof/poverty_guidelines/poverty_guidelines.asp

Administration on Aging. (2012). *A profile of older Americans: 2011.* Washington, DC: U.S. Department of Health and Human Services. Retrieved from http://www.aoa.gov/aoaroot/aging_statistics/Profile/2011/docs/2011profile.pdf

Ambrosino, R., Heffernan, J., Shuttlesworth, G., & Ambrosino, R. (Eds.). (2005). *Social work & social welfare: An introduction* (5th ed.). Southbank, Australia: Brooks-Cole/Thompson.

Applebaum, R., & Payne, M. (2005, Spring). How supplemental security income works. *Generations: Journal of the American Society on Aging, 29*(1), 27–29.

Atchley, R. C., & Barusch, A. S. (2004). *Social forces and aging: An introduction to social gerontology* (10th ed.). Belmont, CA: Wadsworth/Thompson.

Austin, C. D., Camp, E. D., Flux, D., McClelland, R. W., & Sieppert, J. (2005). Community development with older adults in their neighborhoods: The Elder-Friendly Communities Program. *Families in Society: The Journal of Contemporary Social Services, 86*(3), 401–409.

Axinn, J., & Stern, M. J. (2005). *Social welfare: A history of the American response to need* (6th ed.). Boston, MA: Allyn & Bacon/Pearson.

Barnett, R. C. (2005). Ageism and sexism in the workplace. *Generations: Journal of the American Society on Aging, 29*(3), 25–30.

Barusch, A. S. (2006). *Foundations of social policy: Social justice in human perspective* (2nd ed.). Belmont, CA: Brooks-Cole/Thompson.

Binstock, R. H. (2004, Spring). Advocacy in an era of neoconservatism: Responses of natural aging organizations. *Generations, 28*(1), 49–57.

Bush, G. (2005). *Strengthening Social Security for future generations.* Retrieved from http://www.whitehouse.gov/infocus/social-security/

Butler, R. N. (2006). *Ageism in America: The status reports.* New York, NY: Open Society Institute.

Caro, F. G., Bass, S. A., & Chen, Y.-P. (2006). Achieving a productive aging society. In H. R. Moody (Ed.), *Aging concepts and controversies* (5th ed.). Thousand Oaks, CA: Sage/Pine Forge Press.

Center for Research and Education on Aging and Technology Enhancement. (2002). *Aging, information technology and the new millennium.* Ithaca, NY: Edward R. Roybal Centers for Research on Applied Gerontology.

Charness, N. (2005, Fall). Age, technology, and culture: Gerontopia or dystopia? *Public Policy & Aging Report, 15*(4), 20–23.

Cohen, E. S. (2001). The complex nature of ageism: What is it? Who does it? Who perceives it? *Gerontologist, 41*(5), 576–577.

Coughlin, J. F., & Lau, J. (2006a, Winter). Cathedral builders wanted: Constructing a new vision of technology for old age. *Public Policy & Aging Report, 16*(1), 4–8.

Coughlin, J. F., & Lau, J. (2006b, March–April). Invention vs. innovation: Technology and the future of aging. *Aging Today, 27*(2), 3–4.

Cox, E. O., & Chapin, R. (2001). Changing the paradigm: Strengths-based and empowerment-oriented social work with frail elders (pp. 165–179). In E. O.

Cox, E. S. Kelchner, & R. Chapin (Eds.), *Gerontological social work practice: Issues, challenges, and potential.* New York, NY: Hawthorne Press.

Cox, E. O., & Parsons, R. (1994). *Empowerment-oriented social work practice with the elderly.* Pacific Grove, CA: Brooks/Cole.

Cox, D., & Pawar, M. (2006). *International social work: Issues, strategies, and programs.* Thousand Oaks, CA: Sage.

Day, P. J. (2003). *A new history of social welfare* (4th ed.). Boston, MA: Allyn & Bacon/ Pearson.

DeNevas, C., Proctor, B., & Smith, J. (2010). *Income, poverty, and health insurance coverage in the United States, 2009.* Washington, DC: U.S. Census Bureau.

Dolgoff, R., & Feldstein, D. (2013). *Understanding social welfare* (9th ed.). Pearson.

Dressel, P., Minkler, M., & Yen, I. (1999). Gender, race, class, and aging: Advances and opportunities. In M. Minkler & C. L. Estes (Eds.), *Critical gerontology: Perspectives from political and moral economy* (pp. 275–294). Amityville, NY: Baywood.

Ekerdt, D. J. (2004). Born to retire: The foreshortened life course. *Gerontologist, 44*(1), 3–9.

Ehrenreich, B. (2002, June/July). Everyday needs consume energy, wages. *Habitat world: The publication of habitat for humanity international.* Retrieved from http://www.habitat.org/hw/june-july02/feature5.html

Elderlaw Answers. (n.d.). Average costs of nursing home room tops $70,000 a year. Retrieved from http://www.elderlawanswers.com/resources/article.asp?id=3417&section=4

Estes, C. (2001a). *Crisis, the welfare state and aging.* In C. Estes (Ed.), *Social policy and aging: A critical perspective* (pp. 95–117). Thousand Oaks, CA: Sage.

Estes, C. (2001b). *Social policy and aging: A critical perspective.* Thousand Oaks, CA: Sage.

Estes, C. L., Wallace, S. P., Linkins, K. W., & Binney, E. A. (2001). The medicalization and commodification of aging and the privatization and rationalization of old age policy. In C. L. Estes (Ed.), *Social policy and aging: A critical perspective* (pp. 45–60). Thousand Oaks, CA: Sage.

Friedland, R. B., & Summer, L. (2005, March). *Demography is not destiny, revisited.* Washington, DC: Center on an Aging Society, Georgetown University. Retrieved from http://www.cmwf.org/usr_doc/789_friedland_demographynotdestinyII.pdf

Friedman, T. L. (2005). *The world is flat: A brief history of the twenty-first century* (1st ed.). New York, NY: Farrar, Straus, & Giroux.

Gerber, J. (1999). *International economics.* Menlo Park: CA: Addison-Wesley.

Ghilarducci, T. (2006, May). The end of retirement. *Monthly Review, 58*(1), 12–27.

Gilbert, N., & Voorhis, R., van (Eds.). (2003). *Changing patterns of social protection.* New Brunswick, NJ: Transaction.

Greene, R. R., & Cohen, H. L. (2005). Social work with older adults and their families: Changing practice paradigms. *Families in Society: The Journal of Contemporary Social Services, 86*(3), 367–373.

Gutierrez, L. M., Parsons, R., & Cox, E. O. (Eds.). (1998). *Empowerment in social work practice: A sourcebook.* Pacific Grove, CA: Brooks-Cole/Thompson.

Hart, G. (2006). *God and Caesar in America.* Golden, CO: Fulcrum.

Herd, P. (2005). Universalism without targeting: Privatizing the old-age welfare state. *Gerontologist, 45*(3), 292–298.

Holstein, M. (1999). Women and productive aging: Troubling implications. In M. Minkler & C. L. Estes (Eds.), *Critical gerontology: Perspectives from political and moral economy* (pp. 359–373). Amityville, NY: Baywood.

Hooyman, N. R., & Kiyak, H. A. (2005). *Social gerontology: A multidisciplinary perspective* (7th ed.). Boston, MA: Allyn & Bacon/Pearson.

Hudson, R. B. (1997). The history and place of age-based public policy? In R. B. Hudson (Ed.), *The future of age-based public policy* (pp. 1–22). Baltimore, MD: Johns Hopkins University Press.

Hudson, R. B. (2005). The new political environment in aging: Challenges to policy and practice. *Families in Society: The Journal of Contemporary Social Services, 86* (3), 321–327.

Hudson, R. B. (2006, Winter). The white house conference on aging: No time for seniors. *Public Policy and Aging Report, 16* (1), 1–3.

Jansson, B. (1999). *Becoming an effective policy advocate: From policy practice to social justice.* Pacific Grove, CA: Brooks/Cole.

Karger, H. J., & Stoesz, D. (2005). *American social welfare policy: A pluralist approach.* Boston, MA: Allyn & Bacon/Pearson Education.

Koppen, J. (June 2010, June). Social media and technology use among adults 50 + . Washington, DC: AARP. Retrieved from http://assets.aarp.org/rgcenter/general/socmedia.pdf.

Kunkel, S., & Nelson, I. (2005, Fall). Consumer direction: Changing the landscape of long-term care. *Public Policy and Aging Report, 15* (4), 13–16.

Lakoff, G. (2004). *Don't think of an elephant! Know your values and frame the debate.* White River Junction, VT: Chelsea Green.

Leonard, P. (1997). *Postmodern welfare: Reconstructing an emancipatory project.* Thousand Oaks, CA: Sage.

Lisbon, N. (2006). The sad state of affordable housing for older people. *Generations: Journal of the American Society on Aging, 29* (4), 9–15.

Macarov, D. (2003). *What the market does to people: Privatization, globalization and poverty.* Atlanta, GA: Clarity Press.

Manning, S. S. (1998). Empowerment in mental health programs: Focusing on fields. In L. M. Gutierrez, R. Parsons, & E. O. Cox (Eds.), *Empowerment in social work practice: A sourcebook* (pp. 89–107). Pacific Grove, CA: Brooks-Cole/Thompson.

McMichael, P. (2000). *Development and social change: A global perspective* (2nd ed.). Thousand Oaks, CA: Pine Forge Press.

MetLife. (2011, October). *MetLife market survey of long-term costs.* Retrieved from http://www.metlife.com/assets/cao/mmi/publications/studies/2011/mmi-market-survey-nursing-home-assisted-living-adult-day-services-costs.pdf

Minkler, M. (2006). "Generational equity" and victim blaming. In H. R. Moody (Ed.), *Aging: Concepts and controversies* (5th ed., pp. 181–190). Thousand Oaks, CA: Pine Forge Press.

Moody, H. R. (2006). *Aging: Concepts and controversies* (5th ed.). Thousand Oaks, CA: Pine Forge Press.

Morrow-Howell, N. (2006, Winter). Civic engagement at the 2005 white house conference on aging. *Public Policy and Aging Report, 16* (1), 13–17.

National Association of Area Agencies on Aging. (2006). Retrieved from http://www.n4a.org

Novak, M. (2006). *Issues in aging.* Boston, MA: Pearson.

Older Americans Act of 1965, 42 U.S.C. § 35–1–3001. [Congressional declaration of objectives]. Retrieved from http://www.law.cornell.edu/uscode/uscode42/usc_sup_01_42_10_35.html

Palmore, E. (2005, Fall). Three decades of research on ageism. *Generations, 29*(3), 87–90.

Phillipson, C. (1999). The social construction of retirement: Perspectives from critical theory and political economy. In M. Minkler & C. Estes (Eds.), *Critical gerontology: Perspectives from political and moral economy* (pp. 315–327). Amityville, NY: Baywood.

Robertson, A. (1999). Beyond apocalyptic demography: Toward a moral economy of interdependence. In M. Minkler & C. Estes (Eds.), *Critical gerontology: Perspectives from political and moral economy.* Amityville, NY: Baywood.

Rock Ridge Institute. (2006). Retrieved from http://www.rockridgeinstitute.org

Rosalynn Carter Institute for Caregiving. (2004). *Caregivers together. Establishing your own care-net: The community caregivers network* [Manual]. Americus: GA: Southwestern State University.

Rosen, A. L., & Zlotnik, J. L. (2001). Demographics and reality: The "disconnect" in social work education. In E. O. Cox, E. S. Kelchner, & R. Chapin (Eds.), *Gerontological social work practice: Issues, challenges and potential* (pp. 81–97). New York, NY: Haworth Press.

Rother, J. (2004). Why haven't we been more successful advocates of elders? *Generations, 28*(1), 55–58.

Rowe, J., & Kahn, K. (1997). *Successful aging.* New York, NY: Pantheon.

Schieber, S. J. (1997). A new vision for social security: Personal security accounts as an element of social security reform. In R. B. Hudson (Ed.), *The future of age-based public policy* (pp. 134–143). Baltimore, MD: Johns Hopkins University Press.

Schultz, J. H. (2001). *The economics of aging* (7th ed.). Westport, CT: Auburn House.

Setting Priorities for Retirement Years (SPRY) Foundation. (2005). *Computer-based technology and caregiving of older adults: What's new, what's next?* Washington, DC: Author.

Silverstone, B. (2005). Social work with the older people of tomorrow: Restoring the person-in-situation. *Families in Society: The Journal of Contemporary Social Services, 86*(3), 309–319.

Social Security Administration. (2004). Income sources of aged units: Percentage with income from specified source, by marital status, sex of non-married persons, and age, 2004. Retrieved from http://www.ssa.gov/policy/docs/statcomps/income_pop55/2004/sect01.pdf

Social Security Administration. (2012). OASDI & SSI program rates limits, 2012. Retrieved from http://www.ssa.gov/policy/docs/quickfacts/prog_highlights/index.html

Stoller, E. P., & Gibson, R. C. (2000). *Worlds of difference: Inequality in the aging experience.* Thousand Oaks, CA: Pine Forge Press.

Stone, R. (2004). Where have all the advocates gone? *Generations, 28*(1), 59–64.

Takamura, J. (2001). Towards a new era in aging and social work. In E. O. Cox, E. S. Kelchner, & R. Chapin (Eds.), *Gerontological social work practice: Issues, challenges and potential* (pp. 1–11). New York, NY: Haworth Press.

Torres-Gil, F. (2001). Multiculturalism, social policy and the new aging. In E. O. Cox, E. S. Kelchner, & R. Chapin (Eds.), *Gerontological social work practice: Issues, challenges and potential* (pp. 13–32). New York, NY: Haworth Press.

Tout, K. (1989). *Ageing in developing countries.* New York, NY: Oxford University Press.

United States Census Bureau (2012). Retrieved from http://www.census.gov/hhes/www/poverty/data/threshld/index.html.

Wells, L. M., & Taylor, L. E. (2001). Gerontological social work practice: A Canadian perspective. In E. O. Cox , E. S. Kelchner, & R. Chapin (Eds.), *Gerontological social work practice: Issues, challenges, and potential.* New York, NY: Hawthorne Press.

Wilson, K. B. (2005–2006, Winter). Introduction: Where older people live, how needed care is provided. *Generations: Journal of the American Society on Aging, 29* (4), 5–8.

Chapter 5
Explanatory Legitimacy and Disjuncture

A Multidimensional Model for Disability Policy Development and Analysis

Stephen French Gilson and Elizabeth DePoy

There are financial costs for structural and time accommodations, for example, extra time set aside for work and tasks to be completed. Would you consider such interventions as basic, core activities rooted in a John Rawl's social justice philosophy? Or, would you see this as the "Nanny State" gone wild? How would you frame social policies that create an opening environment for all people, or do you see this goal as impossible to achieve?

Introduction

The Americans with Disability Act (ADA), enacted in 1990 and amended in 2008, is a basic, fundamental civil rights law that ensures rights and privileges are extended to people with physical and mental disabilities. Without a doubt, this was a commonsense law based on the fundamental principles of justice. Yet, there were groups and associations who opposed the ADA. Some religious groups worked to defeat the proposal because the law included religious institutions as "public" and because, as a result, they would have to make structural changes to accommodate all people. Business groups, such as the Chamber of Commerce, argued that the costs to small business to provide accommodations would result in higher costs for services/products. Even Greyhound Lines argued that the proposed ADA would deprive services to many inner-city and rural people. Disability, or "ability" policy, remains controversial and is a focal point for those who believe the government is overintrusive in the day-to-day lives of Americans.

In this chapter we discuss and analyze contemporary disability policy in the United States, with a specific focus on several seminal federal policies. We conclude with a "full meal" for thought and nourishment of policy action. To set the context for our analysis, we begin by providing a conceptual framework, Explanatory Legitimacy, through which to examine and analyze disability policy as an axiological process that locates humans within categories that then beget group-specific responses based on worth. Within this framework, we propose disjuncture, an explanatory theory of disability itself, as the foundation for thinking about disability as a complex phenomenon requiring policy that moves beyond simplistic rhetoric to the depth necessary for profound and meaningful thought and action. We then take a brief look back in history to set the context for contemporary disability policy. This glance is a reminder that disability itself is a variable, context-bound, construct and thus definitions have reciprocal relationships with policy. That is to say, disability definitions shape policy and conversely, policy molds conceptualizations of disability. Before our concluding commentary, we proceed with the application of the analytic model to disability policy exemplars.

For clarity, we begin our discussion with three definitions.

1. **Policy.** There are numerous definitions of policy, many of which guide the discussions in each of the chapters of this book. Policy definitions range from informal rules that govern conduct and access to resources at multiple system levels, to formal legislation advanced by government bodies. In this chapter, we define policy as the set of explicit formal statements that guide legitimate status, and responses to members in the form of resource access, allocation, and other action responses. Although we do not limit policy definitions to federal legislation, in this chapter we focus our analysis on specific federally legislated policy exemplars.

2. **Disability.** As we discuss in detail later, we define disability as a contextually embedded dynamic grand category that challenges the boundaries of acceptable humanness, is complex, and is located within the interstices between corpus and surrounding.

3. **Disability policy.** We define disability policy as the set of statements that legitimize membership criteria in the disability category and guide responses to legitimate category members.

Explanatory Legitimacy Theory

Explanatory Legitimacy Theory (DePoy & Gilson, 2011, 2012) builds on historical and current diversity analyses and debates. Different from locating disability in a singular domain of the body or the environment, explanatory legitimacy analyzes the construct of disability as a contextually embedded, dynamic grand category of human diversity, and most often a condition that challenges the boundaries of acceptable citizenship and even humanness. Thus, who belongs and what policy responses are afforded to category members are based on differential, changing, and sometimes conflicting judgments about the value of explanations for diverse atypical human phenomena. Explanatory legitimacy considers the influence of multiple factors (including but not limited to natural, chronological, spiritual, and intellectual trends) on value judgments as the key to understanding categorization, the legitimacy of individuals and groups who fit within a category, and the policy responses that are deemed legitimate for members.

Explanatory Legitimacy Theory makes the distinctions among descriptive, explanatory, and the axiological or the legitimacy dimensions of the categorization of human diversity, and identifies the relationships among these elements. Thus, similar to legitimacy-based analyses of other areas of humanity (Coicaud, 2002; Rossanvallon, 2011), disability, defined and analyzed through the lens of explanatory legitimacy, is comprised of the three interactive elements: description, explanation, and legitimacy. This tripartite analytic framework provides a potent platform through which to examine policy responses to members of categorical groups (DePoy & Gilson, 2009). Let us look at each element now.

Description

Description encompasses the full range of human activity (what people do and do not do, and how they do what they do), appearance, and experience. Of particular importance to an understanding of disability definitions and policy responses is the statistical concept of the *norm*. Because the understanding and naming of what is normal and thus in contrast not normal are value-based, use of terms such as *normal* and *abnormal* do not provide the conceptual clarity sufficient for distinguishing description from axiology. Thus, in applying explanatory legitimacy to disability policy, we use the terms typical and atypical to depict frequently and infrequently occurring human description respectively. Disability is located in the realm of the atypical.

Explanation

The second element of Explanatory Legitimacy Theory is explanation. Applied to disability, explanation is the set of reasons for the atypical. What is important to highlight with regard to the link between description and explanation is that explanation is always an inference. Because of the interpretative nature of explanation, this definitional element lends itself to debate, differential value judgment, and diverse policy responses. As we discuss further, the current explanatory debate between two explanatory genres (medical-embodied and distal causes of disability) is a heated one and has great relevance for policy. Medical-embodied causes attribute atypical phenomena to a diagnostic condition of long-term or permanent duration (Smart, 2008), while the distal lens identifies an unwelcoming and even discriminatory environment as causal of disability, in which the descriptors are met with barriers and exclusion. As we discuss later in the chapter, we propose a third explanation, Disjuncture Theory, which analyzes disability as a dynamic poor fit between embodied and distal conditions (DePoy & Gilson, 2008, 2011).

Legitimacy

The third and most important definitional element of Explanatory Legitimacy Theory is legitimacy, which is comprised of two subelements: judgment and response. Judgment refers to value assessments of competing groups on whether what one does throughout life (and thus what one does not do), how one looks, and the degree to which one's experiences fit within what is typical, have valid and acceptable explanations consistent with both explicit and implicit value sets. Category membership in this case is a value-encased determination about the extent to which the posited explanation for the atypical renders individuals and groups eligible for disability category membership and to an extent for membership as citizens and even as acceptable humans.

Responses are the actions (both negative and positive) that are deemed appropriate by those rendering the value judgments about explanations for membership. Consider this example. Two individuals have a similar atypical gait, one explained by an accident while driving under the influence of alcohol, and the other explained by an injury in active military duty. Each has an identical embodied condition (description), but the explanation for the descriptive element differs as does the response to each with regard to benefits. Through a legitimacy lens, disability policy, which codifies explanatory value, lies in the response element of explanatory legitimacy, occurring throughout multiple points in time. Policy begins with the decision to consider the need for a category specific approach, proceeds to the promulgation of the actual policy, continues with who is legitimately eligible for consideration under the policy, and finally culminates with the response to legitimate category members guided by the content and nature of the policy. Thus teasing apart description, explanation, and values provides the opportunity for understanding and analyzing policy formulation and enactment from a complex, context-embedded perspective (DePoy & Gilson, 2004, 2011).

Disjuncture Theory

As introduced earlier, we propose that although there are many explanatory theories of disability, for us the construct is best characterized by Disjuncture Theory. Theorizing is not simply an academic exercise, but rather provides a conceptual scaffold to frame a useful understanding necessary for meaningful and sustained policy that addresses rather than circumvents social problems. We come back to this point later in the chapter.

The word *disjuncture* is defined as a disconnected relationship between at least two entities. Conversely, *juncture* refers to a relationship of connection and goodness-of-fit. Applied to disability, Disjuncture Theory transcends the explanatory debate, which places disability into one of two opposing camps, embodied or distal, and rather looks to the nonexistent or limited fit of humans and multiple environments as explanatory of disability. Thus, unlike the binary debate about the correctness of disability as either embodied or distal, Disjuncture Theory holds neither element as solely responsible but rather highlights the relationship between the two as the explanatory locus. This relational gaze not only halts the ongoing argument about the "true" nature of disability, but furthers the pluralistic opportunity for dialog, cooperative thinking, and policy that is effective in resolving the social problems for which policy is promulgated. Considering disability as a dynamic relationship between corpus and distal surrounding provides a multidimensional universe through which to examine, analyze, and revise policy to confer full citizenship, participation, and access for those who currently are denied equity and distributive rights (DePoy & Gilson, 2011).

Looking Back

Before proceeding further, we briefly look back in history to inform the chronological foundation on which the policy arenas of the 21st century are built. History provides intellectual and axiological continuity, reminding us that policy does not spring up without the beauty as well as the baggage of yesteryear.

As early as ancient civilizations (Chahira, 2006), there is documentation of a range of responses to "the atypical human" from fascination to revulsion (Nakuamura, 2006; Olyan, 2008; Rispler-Chiam, 2007). This history creates an opaque but important window on how civilizations responded to embodied difference. Unfortunately, in this short space, we cannot do justice to the richness of this history, but we can discuss some critical turnings and trends necessary to inform current debates and understand contextual policy responses to atypical humans in contemporary times. Although a range of thinking about and approaches to atypical bodies has occurred, the following four commonalities can be seen across chronology and geographies:

1. What is atypical differs according to context.
2. In each context there have been several potential assumed and accepted explanations for a single atypical human characteristic.
3. These explanations form the basis for legitimate placement and subsequent response to category members.
4. The responses proffered provide an analytic window on the beliefs, values, politics, economics, intellectual trends, and level of technological development of the contexts, as well as a reflective platform

on how current definitions of disability influence how we interpret history (Rose, 2003) and the membership in the category of humanity.

We enter our history through a language portal, as this symbolic element of social and cultural groups is critical in revealing contextual meaning (Baudrillard, 1995; Belsey, 2002). (Note that, as discussed earlier, we use the terms *typical* and *atypical* to denote a full range of frequency from most to least respectively.)

The English term *disability* has only recently become a signifier for the grand category of atypical bodies. Early Islamic, Hebrew, and Shinto literature does not contain a single term for embodied conditions, but rather tethers what today would be considered as disabled to blemished lives and families, defect, and illness of the body and heart (Nakuamura, 2006; Olyan, 2008; Rispler-Chiam, 2007). Interestingly, many languages still do not have a single equivalent for the term *disability*.

The lexical predecessor to disability, *handicap*, was alleged to have emerged from 16th-century England during the reign of Henry VII. Recognizing the plight of injured soldiers, he was fabled to have formally allowed worthy citizens to beg in the streets as a means to their own subsistence, ergo the phrase "cap in hand" to denote begging was allegedly shortened to name a category of "unfortunates" (Ciota & Hoveb, 2010).

In the early part of the 20th century, the term *handicap* was ascribed to individuals with skill or bodily differences that ostensibly placed them at a disadvantage, and ultimately the word *handicap* in this sense came to mean a specific embodied condition such as a "physical or mental handicap." Given the stigmatized and devalued notion of bodily inferiority, it is no surprise that a euphemistic term to replace *handicap* was sought to describe bodies that did not conform to the *typical*. It is curious that the term *disability* was selected given that the prefix "dis" emerged from DIS, the name given by ancient civilizations to the ruler of Hades, or the underworld (DePoy & Gilson, 2011; Rose, 2003). Current translations include *inkompetenz* in German and *discapacidad* in Spanish (Ciota & Hoveb, 2010).

Looking back to the Middle Ages, Latin words such as *imbecillis, deformans,* and *defectus* were used to describe embodied phenomena (Metzler, 2006; Yong, 2007). Curiously, because of their association with extreme poverty, these conditions and others such as blindness or lameness were typical and thus were not necessarily considered as unusual, aberrant, or unacceptable (DePoy & Gilson, 2011; Green, 2006). Of particular note was the growth of institutional and charity approaches to individuals who were atypical, particularly for those who were not embedded within strong kinship systems of their own (Farmer, 2002; Green, 2006). The seeds of faith-based hospitals were sewn in the Middle Ages, as it was not unusual to find members of the clergy in the Christian religions, Islamic societies (Rispler-Chiam, 2007), and Buddhist Monks in the Far East (Nakuamura, 2006) providing medical treatment to those who were considered ill. Charity in the form of service and almsgiving exonerated the giver in the eyes of

God, once again providing a purposive explanation for the extremes of human difference.

Moving forward in chronology, as the complexity and differences around the globe became known to civilizations, history outgrew the boundaries of a single narrative of one's own people. Of particular importance to understanding contemporary disability policy responses were the abstract creations of Quetelet, who invented the mathematical constructs of the normal or bell-shaped curve and measures of central tendency. These two ideas form the foundation of contemporary empirical knowledge and fabricated the dissection of humanity into the two categories of "normal" and "abnormal" (DePoy & Gilson, 2007). Applying the bell-shaped curve to human variation, Quetelet extrapolated the concept of "the normal man," who was considered to be both physically and morally normal. Synthesizing probability theory with the "normal man" construct, normal was not only interpreted as the most frequently occurring phenomenon but became a standard for what "should be." Observation therefore turned to prescription, and anyone with observed phenomena on the tail ends of the curve was categorized as "abnormal," or pushing the boundaries of acceptable humanness. With the emergence of the Industrial Era, the concept of normal became an even more important disability policy driver, as mass production, mechanization, and production standards were based on statistical projections of what an average worker should "normally" accomplish within a given set of parameters (Axinn & Stern, 2004; Stone, 1986). Anyone who fell short of average productivity was considered deficient.

It is curious to note that the definition of disability in the early 20th century did not include medical diagnostic conditions, as revealed in the 1906 edition of the Standard Dictionary of the English Language (Funk & Wagnalls, 1906) that proffered:

- Lack of ability of some sort.
- Impotence.
- The state of being disabled.
- A crippled condition.
- Lack of competent means.
- Inability as the disabilities of poverty.
- Legal incapacity or the inability to act, as the disability of lunatics and infants.

Note that these definitions are both expansive and progressive in that they do not limit disability to specific diagnostic conditions or exclusively embodied phenomena but rather approach disability from a broad descriptive stance not entwined with medical explanation. Moreover, the fundamentals of what is referred to as the social model in contemporary disability-studies literature, while gaining prominence in the late 20th century, were actually well documented in Victorian Europe, in which communities defined disability as those conditions for which European cultures were unprepared (Holmes, 2004).

In colonial America, several trends specific to the "New World" emerged that provided the foundation for the emergence of contemporary disability definitions and U.S. policy responses. First was the growth of the U.S. economy. In part, because of roots in the uninvited procurement of land on which indigenous populations lived and in the importation of involuntary labor from other countries (Axinn & Stern, 2004), the existing policies guiding poor relief in colonial America that were based in homogenous communal values and shared beliefs were ultimately challenged by the geographic proximity of diverse peoples. Thus, economic advantage became coupled with social upheaval (Davis, 1995, 2010; Goldberg, 1994) and set the stage for categories of worth that shaped policy responses to people who demonstrated atypical characteristics (DePoy & Gilson, 2004, 2011). Second, along with the realization of diverse inherent human characteristics such as race and ethnicity, explanations for what people did and did not do, how people looked, and what they experienced expanded as well with the burgeoning field of medicine (DePoy & Gilson, 2004, 2011). Despite the appearance of medicine on the explanatory scene, however, morality and social circumstance remained dominant explanations for the atypical for as long as religion was the most prominent explanatory factor in American communities. Moreover, with the vast resources available to "everyman" in the New World, tolerance for poverty (and thus acceptance of poverty as a legitimate explanation for the atypical) waned in an environment that allegedly provided golden opportunity for anyone who was willing to exert some elbow grease, so to speak (Axinn & Stern, 2004). In response to the increasing social costs and disapproval of poverty, towns and cities began to develop policies that supported segregation of the unproductive, with the result of the remanding of "undesirables" to poorhouses (DePoy & Gilson, 2004, 2011).

During this time, in large part due to the associational link between diverse populations resulting from immigration and urbanization, observable diversity—including race, ethnicity, and other atypical intrinsic humandifferences, or "bodies and background" difference (DePoy & Gilson, 2011)—erroneously bagan to supplant poverty as a major explanatory factor for struggle. This error in deductive logic, in which association is misinterpreted as causation, ascribed poverty to all members of a marginalized group, without support for the membership criterion as the cause. That is to say, the atypical body, while frequenting the roles of poverty, did not create it. Yet, many entitlement and safety-net resource policies continue to focus on group membership (e.g., disability, race and ethnicity, gender) rather than level of poverty, as the basis for eligibility for fiscal resource support, thereby derailing direct policy response to poverty and redistribution (Michaels, 2006). We are not suggesting that those with embodied limitations are not disproportionally overrepresented within the group of people considered poor. However, through the lens of explanatory legitimacy, we can analyze the value-based misinterpretation of association as causation. This insight thus illuminates the misplacement and evisceration of entitlement and benefits policy rhetorically passed to reduce and eliminate disparity (Ford, 2011). Moreover, if category membership is addressed as a proxy for poverty, direct dialog and action to revise resource distribution does not have to occur.

During the 20th century, as the medical industry grew in power, medical explanations for the atypical became synonyms for disability types and the primary focus of disability policy responses. Literature now parses disability into subgroups such as "intellectual disability," "psychiatric disability," "physical disability," and "autism spectrum disorders" (May & Raske, 2004), with medical explanatory sets for each subgroup. What each has in common with the other is assumed permanent or long-term limitation in functioning in a particular area, primarily explained by an intrinsic medical condition. The permanency of the "functional deficit" led to early-20th-century policy supporting institutionalization and thus segregation of those individuals and groups that were unable to "function" in environments designed for the "normal" person.

Policy supporting institutionalization proliferated for several reasons. As we noted earlier, diagnostic explanations made the prediction of life-long "abnormality" possible and in need of "treatment." Second, as women entered the workplace, they were no longer able to be the primary supports for atypical family and community members. However, according to Gill's classic work (1992), the most important reason for institutional policy responses was the burgeoning "care" industry through which many professional stakeholders gained significant economic benefit from their work with institutionalized atypical individuals and institutional systems.

Remember the notion of the atypical being placed on the earth to engender charitable responses from laypersons? We see its continuation in the charitable model of disability policy and practice response operationalized as not-for-profit organizations, which provided fundraising and services for worthy individuals whose atypical characteristics had acceptable medical explanations for disability determination and response.

However, parallel to charity policies was the development of public policy support for a particular disability group, individuals who had to leave the work world because of injury sustained on the job. Clearly, U.S. values on work and productivity were reflected in workers' compensation law as early as 1902 (Maryland State Archive, 2005). And thus the importance of economic productivity in shaping policy responses was clearly observed by the turn of the 20th century. Further illustrating this hegemonous U.S. value on work was the passage of the vocational rehabilitation law in 1920 for veterans of World War I, designed to return men to the workplace whose atypical characteristics were explained by injury in service to their country (DePoy & Gilson, 2004).

It is important to note that in contemporary times up through the middle and even latter parts of the 20th century, regardless of the nature of the atypical, explanations were primarily medical. It followed that policies focused on supporting care or cure responses to help atypical individuals heal and not place undue financial burden on their families and communities (DePoy & Gilson, 2004).

Twentieth and 21st-century trends of medical hegemony, technology, and an expanding global market economy have coalesced to locate disability within the corpus as a condition to be changed, eliminated, attenuated, or, in some cases, legally extinguished, as exemplified by policies such as wrongful life and assisted suicide. Although embodied explanations remain primary in defining disability even now, the history of disability took an important turn in the latter half of the 20th century that is critical for understanding contemporary rights policies. Disability-rights scholars and activists claimed the "social model" as their original insight, eschewing the deficit medical model. Thus disability-studies activists and scholars apprehended Victorian thinking to advance a policy agenda focusing on social justice, equality of opportunity, and specialized rights for those who were members of the disability group (DePoy & Gilson, 2011; Nussbaum, 2006; Stein, 2006). Rather than accepting themselves as the "work" for the disability industry, disabled scholars followed the Victorians in looking external to the body to explain disability and thus to shape disability policy responses. Early scholars such as Oliver (1996) and Linton (1998, 2006) and those who furthered this general viewpoint (Nussbaum, 2006; Stein, 2006) proposed a model of disability in which the disabling factors are the intolerance and rigidity of social and built institutions rather than embodied medical conditions. Words such as *inclusion, participation,* and *nondiscrimination* were introduced into the disability vernacular reflecting the notions that people who did not fit within the central tendencies of Quetelet's (1969) "normal curve" were disabled by stigma, prejudice, marginalization, segregation, and exclusion, not by their bodies. The view of disability (rather than caused by a medical condition) theoretically expands needed responses beyond rehabilitation and individual accommodation to the larger policy arenas of the built, natural, virtual, social, and conceptual environments. Still, professions, policies, and theory, despite their assertions to look beyond the corpus, explicitly or implicitly situate disability within the organic human domain, as evidenced by reference to embodied conditions even for local, national, and global human rights and antidiscrimination legislation, and further exposed by persons-first language (persons with physical, intellectual, learning, mental, etc., disabilities). Because deficient bodies are the object of disability-rights discourses and policy responses, this conceptual quagmire reveals the inherent hegemony of internal "abnormality" in explaining the atypical and locating disability within the body regardless of the degree to which narrative indicts systems of oppression and environmental barriers as disabling factors.

To briefly summarize, disability has a rich and diverse history. Understandings of disability are embedded in and reflective of their axiological contexts, and thus shape thinking and action responses to the atypical. These factors have intersected to produce two overarching and hotly debated views of disability in the current literature: embodied medical and distal (DePoy & Gilson, 2011). Embodied medical definitions locate the causes of the atypical within humans and explain disability as an anomalous medical condition of long-term or permanent duration. Thus, within this conceptualization, the domain of disability definition and response remains within the medical and professional communities. Group-specific policy focusing on special services and resources for disability category members logically follows from corporeal medical-diagnostic definitions of disability.

In opposition, however, to what was perceived as a pejorative, the distal view of disability indicts social, cultural, and other environmental influences as disabling factors regardless of one's body. Policies that focus on equality of opportunity through environmental change should follow logically from this explanatory approach. Both explanatory genres provide a forum for rich policy debate and response. Yet, as we propose in our conclusions, we would suggest that neither by itself is sufficient for resolving the complex social problems of the 21st century.

But for now, let us move on to the analysis of exemplars of contemporary disability policy, with our thinking and analysis guided by explanatory legitimacy. We save disjunctured explanations for our look to the future.

Explanatory Legitimacy Theory Analysis of Policy Exemplars

Typically, disability policy has been categorized into two areas: policies that guide the provisions of specialized services and resources, such as Social Security Disability Insurance (SSDI) (established by the Social Security Amendments of 1956; Berkowitz, 1989), for legitimately disabled populations, and more recently those policies, such as the Americans with Disabilities Act (ADA) (1990) and the ADA Amendments Act (ADAAA) (2008) that rhetorically prohibit discrimination and thus purport to protect and advance the civil rights of legitimately disabled populations. However, through the lens of Explanatory Legitimacy Theory, and in the context of the 21st century, we suggest a different taxonomy, depicted in Table 5.1. Note that we locate disability policy within a larger axiological context in which the extent of deviance from typical and the acceptability of explanations for such phenomena to a large extent are proxies for defining the acceptable limits of humanness.

Let us examine this table in more detail.

The horizontal axis consists of three divisions of policy on the basis of both content and explicitly intended outcome. As illustrated by our exemplars, these categories are not mutually exclusive.

Within the category of legitimacy for material benefits, policies for nonworkers guide the provision of income and related benefits for the disproportionately high number of legitimately disabled individuals who are not working or underemployed (and to some extent their family members). Policies that guide the provision of benefits to advance employability direct

Table 5.1 A New Taxonomy

	Legitimacy as Worthy of Human Life	Legitimacy as Citizens of Disabled Individuals and Groups	Legitimacy for Material Benefits		
			Safety-Net Benefits for Nonworkers	Benefits to Advance Employability	Generalized Benefits and Privileges
Corporeal Explanations	Right to die; Abortion rights; Genetic manipulation; Wrongful life; Wrongful birth	Vocational Rehabilitation Act of 1954; Rehabilitation Act of 1973; ADA and ADAAA	SSDI; SSI	Vocational Rehabilitation Act of 1954; Rehabilitation Act of 1973 IDEA	ADA and ADAAA; Access Pass (free entrance into National Parks); IDEA
Distal Explanations		Vocational Rehabilitation Act of 1954; Rehabilitation Act of 1973; ADA and ADAAA		Ticket to Work and Work Incentives Improvement Act of 1999	ADA and ADAAA

the provision of training and retraining for disabled individuals, with the explicit intended outcome of entry and/or reentry into the workforce.

Policy governing the legitimacy of disabled individuals and groups as citizens contains specialized legislation that asserts group specific protections from discrimination of disabled populations and individuals. Finally, policies that govern legitimacy as worthy of human life govern the nature and even existence of bodies and the boundaries beyond which bodies are no longer acceptable as humans. The policies that we chose as exemplars are not exhaustive by any means but they offer a range of diverse approaches to disability policy in the United States.

The vertical axis of Table 5.1 contains two divisions, corporeal and distally focused policy, each responding to its particular explanatory approach to disability. From a simple and linear standpoint, we would expect that the policies that fall under the division of "embodied" should guide treatment or responses to bona fide category members. Similarly, distal policies accept nonembodied explanations as legitimate and would be expected to address the barriers that exclude disabled groups from participation and human rights. However, the divisions are not as simple as they might appear to be.

To understand Table 5.1, we now look at the policy exemplars through the lens of explanatory legitimacy. We suggest that different from analyzing disability policy through its explicit content and intended outcomes, policy is much more complex than its verbiage. Using the framework of explanatory legitimacy, disability policy is understood as a value-based response to purported explanations of atypical human characteristics. Policy therefore

Table 5.2 Heuristics

1. Value, context, and veiled interest mediate logic and thus disability policy is not logical.
2. All policies, even if guiding distal action, emerge from an embodied causal explanation of disability, even if the cause is not accurate.
3. Disability policy is organized along a value hierarchy of medical explanations and not all explanations are acceptable for benefits and protection or even for life.
4. Disability policy is based on nomothetic assumptions about a group that does not necessarily share commonalities.
5. Disability policy has an economic foundation although it is often obfuscated.
6. Disability policy, while producing some advances in access and participation, has long-term consequences of segregation and inequality.
7. Antidiscrimination policies are insufficient to resolve profound social problems such as disparities in civic participation, employment, and even the right to exist.

can be characterized and revised by laying bare its value stance and under-lying prescriptions of acceptable human characteristics. Moreover, there are commonalities that unite disability policy that we present in Table 5.2.

As we see by the heuristics and consistent with classic nonrational models of policy analysis (Stone, 2011), explanatory legitimacy suggests that because values and context mediate logic, disability policy is not lin-ear and cannot be understood through rational policy analysis approaches (see DePoy & Gilson, 2009, 2010, for further detail and discussion). Second, although some policies as shown in Table 5.1 are ostensibly targeted at pre-scribing environmental standards for universal participation, legitimacy for coverage under these policies is restricted only to a small subset of corporeal explanations of disability. This disjuncture becomes problematic if we try to understand the link between the articulated social problem that the pol-icy is ostensibly designed to remediate and the causal assumption. Third, atypical embodied characteristics that are observable and assumed to be caused by conditions beyond the control of the individual are more legit-imate for disability category membership than those that are not directly ascertainable and/or considered to be caused by factors over which indi-viduals have control. And even more profound are the boundaries beyond which judgments about humanness and thus worthiness for life are made (Carollo, 2012). Fourth, disability theory and policies are frequently based on assumptions about the commonalities of a group, which may or may not be accurate. Fifth, in a global economic context, disability policy, similar to all federal policy, directly or indirectly addresses resources. Finally, we discuss the last heuristics, Number 6 and Number 7, toward the conclusion of the chapter.

Let us examine several of our policy exemplars to illustrate.

Social Security Disability Insurance (SSDI)

If we analyze Social Security Disability Insurance (SSDI) (Berkowitz, 1989), we see that ostensibly it is intended to provide income and benefit support for individuals who, because of a long-term or permanent medical explanation, are unable to work. Yet, to legitimately qualify, an individual not only must meet the internally located definition of disability advanced by the Social Security Administration, but also must have previously contributed to Social Security, which one cannot do without working.

Because disability status and response under SSDI are internally situated, the process for legitimacy under SSDI places a medical or human service professional in the gatekeeping role. To be deemed legitimately disabled, one must be determined by a physician (or other specified professional, depending on the explanatory diagnosis for not working) to fit with the legitimacy criteria. To qualify for benefits, an individual must prove disability legitimacy, which is not assured even if one meets the descriptive eligibility criteria. Explanations such as alcohol dependence, obesity, and chemical sensitivity, which may be associated with poverty and need for resources, and which in other policy arenas are explained as medical but often considered to be under one's personal control, personally excessive, or even hypochondriacal, are not acceptable explanations for legitimate disability status or benefits under SSDI policy even though these explanatory conditions may be consistent with the descriptive outcome of long-term or permanent impairment advanced under the policy guidelines. We have referred to this hierarchy of acceptable conditions as disability pedigree to illustrate ranking of worth (DePoy & Gilson, 2004, 2011).

A careful examination of acceptable and unacceptable pedigree reveals SSDI policy values rooted in notions of personal responsibility, previous economic contribution, and charity. That is to say, an individual is legitimate only if he or she is not responsible for his or her inability to contribute to the economy regardless of financial need. The meager income benefits hearken back to the charity model of disability in which historically, disabled individuals were pitied enough for some altruism, but not sufficiently valued for support necessary to fully participate in their communities.

While supported on SSDI, individuals can receive Medicaid (U.S. Department of Health and Human Services, CMS: Centers for Medicare & Medicaid Services, 2012a), and in some cases Medicare (U.S. Department of Health and Human Services. CMS: Centers for Medicare & Medicaid Services, 2012b), the health insurance programs for those in poverty and for elders respectively. However, until the passage of the Ticket to Work and Work Incentives Improvement Act in 1999 (Public Law 106–170; TWWIIA) (Employment Support Institute, 2012; Wehman, 2000), an individual who returned to work would lose all benefits including health insurance. With this newly crafted legislation, health benefits and some income can continue as people attempt to return to work. Nevertheless, if an individual is supported on Social Security, it is likely that he or she will be poor, the very condition that the policy purports to mediate.

And we also draw your attention to another issue related to health and income support benefits. Although these are most important for recipients of service, don't forget that health insurance pays providers for their work and the processes through which disabled individuals are qualified as legitimate and then afforded services under SSDI policy comprise a large segment of the labor industry in the United States. Thus, SSDI policy, while benefiting legitimate individuals who do not earn, are valued payment systems for those who do. The economic value not only for direct policy beneficiaries but also for the labor market is a critically important element to consider in policy analysis and change (DePoy & Gilson, 2010). The TWWIIA policy illustrates this point.

Before its passage, SSDI provided a disincentive for its beneficiaries to work because, as we mentioned earlier, returning to work, often in low-paying positions, eliminated health insurance and income benefits that often exceeded what a former SSDI recipient earned in the job market. Thus, rather than enabling individuals to move away from public support, SSDI maintained recipients in the category of public welfare consumer. TWWIIA Act was one of several federal policies enacted to remediate this institutional mistake that rendered SSDI in conflict with its articulated value base of economic self-sufficiency and personal responsibility. Yet, empirical evidence demonstrates that TWWIIA policy has not met its explicit aim of increasingly long-term employment and self-sufficiency for eligible recipients. Rather, studies show an unimpressive employment outcome, other than for those individuals who would have worked without such benefits (Livermore & Roche, 2011).

SSDI provides an important exemplar of benefits to nonworkers. We contend that policies that establish and support job training and even specialized education fit under the second content subcategory of advancing employability. Several of these policies such as the Education for All Children Act of 1975, Individuals with Disabilities Education Act (IDEA) of 1990, IDEA Regulations of 1999, and the IDEA of 2004 (Disability Rights Education & Defense Fund, 2006; Lipton, 1999; Pelka, 1997) and the Rehabilitation Act of 1973 also fit under the category of material benefits in that they provide specialized accommodations and resources on the basis of legitimate disability membership regardless of the accessibility of the employment or educational arena. These policies, based on nomothetic principles of group commonality and association between embodied atypical characteristics and poverty, rather than causal relationships, while beneficial to some who might have benefited without such support, do not take into account that all category members may not want or need the resources provided to individuals on the basis of category membership alone. Part of the quagmire in policies that address population categories is that rather than responding to the descriptive need of poverty, category membership is the mediator and the locus for policy.

Now consider the Access Pass (National Parks Service, U.S. Department of the Interior, 2011) policy that allows disabled individuals to access national parks without paying. The policy, which assumes financial need on the basis of disability membership, is targeted at the broad category of disability. Thus, whether category members are financially needy, they obtain the privilege of free entrance, unlike individuals who have financial need but who are not legitimate members of the disability group. IDEA and job training policies are similar in that they posit legitimacy for benefits on the basis of assumed need because an individual is legitimately qualified in a category, not because need for the resources and services under these policies is verified. On the other hand, given that specialized education and job training resources are not equivalent to those afforded to the typical population, the paradox of too many and too few resources under categorical policies, such as disability policy based on nomothetic assumptions, continues.

We now move to policies that are designed to assert and advance citizenship. Consistent with civil rights policy for other disenfranchised groups, this genre of legislation fits under the category of protective or antidiscrimination policy. As we address in Heuristics Number 6 and Number 7, protective disability policy such as the ADA and ADAAA, while creating some changes in access for delimited groups with acceptable embodied explanations, in the 21st century are limited in promoting long-term equality of opportunity. Let us look to the ADA and ADAAA as examples.

The ADA and ADAAA

The Americans with Disabilities Act of 1990 and ADAAA of 2008 are protective policies that apply to disabled individuals. Similar to other protective legislation, these policies prohibit discrimination on the basis of disability and assert the guarantee of equal opportunity for individuals with disabilities in public accommodations, employment, transportation, state and local government services, and telecommunications. Note that we locate the ADA and ADAAA in the embodied medical explanations category of disability policy. Similar to policies that we have discussed earlier, although the locus of the problem and its resolution is planned as modifications to distal environment attributes, eligibility for protection under the ADA and ADAAA is determined by the pedigree of embodied explanations for atypical characteristics. Look at the definition of who qualifies as legitimately disabled under the ADA:

> [A]n individual who has physical or mental impairment that substantially limits one or more major life activities, and the individual has a record of such an impairment, or is regarded as having such an impairment.
>
> Americans with Disabilities Act [ADA], 1990

Because of its perceived potential not only to provide opportunity where it did not exist, but also to support accommodations and thus special treatment, many groups with embodied explanations for atypical function have attempted to seek coverage under the ADA. The court cases and decisions, although decreased by the 2008 ADA Amendments Act, are the evidence of what we refer to as pedigree wars, as groups of individuals seek legitimate disability status in order to obtain "rights" that they may feel that they are otherwise denied. Moreover, note that we also locate the ADA and ADAAA under the policy genre of benefits for this reason.

As we have introduced earlier, while protective and nondiscrimination policy was the avenue taken to advance inclusion and civil rights, its use as a long-term solution is problematic.

We acknowledge that many individuals with atypical characteristics, particularly those that are observable, have experienced overt and covert discrimination and oppression. As a policy response, the ADA and ADAAA have made changes in access to the physical environment, the workplace, the communications and transportation systems, and the educational arena for people who without these policies may not be able to participate in those domains of daily life. Yet, as a permanent solution, protective policies, which on the surface appear sound, are riddled with value and social action conflicts (DePoy & Gilson, 2011). First, rather than assuring that policy for all citizens governs the rights of disability category members, the presence of the ADA and ADAAA implies that disabled individuals need specialized legislation layered on the policy that should already protect their rights. Second, the ADA and ADAAA stipulate that discriminatory practices such as environmental and telecommunication barriers need to be replaced with accessible structures in instances where cost would not be prohibitive. Thus, we see that the legitimate policy responses to discrimination are mediated by cost considerations that diminish civil rights and equality of opportunity of the very group that the policy is ostensibly designed to protect. Third, exactly who fits under ADA policy, even with the ADA Amendments Act of 2008, which was designed to expand coverage, and what protections are afforded are not clear, and interpretation is thus subject to differential and context embedded cultural, social, political, and economic value.

And finally, as eloquently discussed by Ford (2011), discrimination may be only one barrier to participation. Ford suggests that protections from discrimination, while proposing moral positions, do not take into account the complexity of the meaning of justice.

> *Civil rights are remarkably effective against overt prejudice perpetrated by identifiable bigots. But they have proven impotent against today's most severe social injustices.*
>
> (Ford, 2011, pp. 242–243)

Rather, we agree with Ford in suggesting that complexity of injustices needs to be met with complexity of thinking and response. In our conclusions, we suggest that Disjuncture Theory provides the explanatory theoretical container to provoke productive, logical, and effectual policy.

Our final horizontal category—legitimacy as worthy of human life—requires a full encyclopedia on its own. We include and only briefly discuss this category, however, to illustrate how policy reflects value. The policies that are contained in this category allow significant embodied revision, change, and even elimination for corporeal conditions and experiences that exceed acceptable humanness. We place then in the vertical category of corporeal explanations. The complexity of issues and values within these policies requires careful analysis, parsing, and clearly identifying the multiple purposes of the policy. As example, abortion rights speak to family choice, which we support. However, who is considered to be a viable fetus is another issue and reveals the value-based policy direction of homogenization. Synthesized with wrongful life and wrongful birth policies, valued and devalued bodies are lined up from acceptable to in need of revision to fodder for elimination. We leave this topic for another time and set of works (DePoy & Gilson, in press).

Conclusions

As we leave specific exemplars to move to general conclusions, we ask you to revisit the historical snippets to set the context for this last part of our discussion on disability policy. If we gaze back in chronological time, we see the roots of contemporary disability policy in the United States in values, context, economy, and intellectual trends.

Our first comment refers to the reciprocal relationship between disability theory and policy. As we discussed earlier, two competing theories of disability—embodied-medical and distal—argue with one another about which is most accurate. Clearly, we see that despite rights policies claiming to address distal issues, they remain entwined with embodied diagnosis as the value-based, explanatory qualifier for coverage. We would suggest that this conceptual morass can be logically and precisely clarified by understanding disability through the lens of Disjuncture Theory, where bodies and distal conditions interact in a dynamic continuum from full-fit to ill-fit, and, at worst, no-fit. As an example, policy to provide distal features to eliminate barriers (e.g., ramped entrances and automatic doors for public buildings) creates access for mobility impaired individuals despite its more expansive benefit. Thus, the targeted population is delimited by corpus despite the targeted policy action occurring distal to the body. Yet, the antidiscrimination policy rhetoric does not extend to all who are disability category members, given that only certain embodied conditions are considered for eligibility. Moreover, as analyzed by Ford (2011), repairing barriers through assuming that discrimination is the sole cause and thus needs to be eliminated, fails to capture the complexity of political, economic, technological barriers to equality of participation in public spaces. Viewing disability as disjuncture looks at fit between body and usability of space, regardless of the nature of the category membership. Analyzing disability as a multidimensional kaleidoscope of social problems to be solved, shapes and colors 21st century responses that can address, rotate, and innovate, by linking injustice fragments into a dynamic whole.

Rather than framing disability policy in the United States from a population subcategory specific approach that assumes nomothetic causal need from mere association, Disjuncture Theory within the broader framework of Explanatory Legitimacy Theory provides the thinking tools to understand and revise value-based policies that do not achieve their articulated aims. As we move into the 21st century, we face the challenges and opportunities of an expansive global and virtual environment. We are presented with the juxtaposition of diverse worldviews and experiences, while gifted with the thinking and action tools to operationalize the values of tolerance and symmetry of opportunity (DePoy & Gilson, 2011, 2012). Informing and rethinking disability policy through contemporary theory can move us toward policy that analyzes the meaning of "rights," resources, privileges, and humanness such that innovative and effectual policies logically and directly resolve complex problems on the basis of human description and need rather than on tacit and nomothetic assumptions about individual embodied worth for benefits and even life. Our charge is to analyze, rethink and implement policies that shape our world as one that is welcoming of all.

Key Terms

Disability policy   *Embodied*   *Population category*
Disjuncture Theory   *Explanatory legitimacy*   *membership*

Review Questions for Critical Thinking

1. How has the definition of *disability* changed over time?

2. To what extent does the 2010 Affordable Care Act enhance or diminish the 1990 American with Disabilities Act and the 2008 ADA Amendments Act?

3. What are three main challenges faced within the global and virtual environments for persons with disabilities?

4. To what extent is the federal government's Social Security Disability Insurance (SSDI) successful in maximizing the rights of persons with disabilities?

5. How do Explanatory Legitimacy Theory and Disjuncture Theory differ? Which theory do you believe is reflected through 21st-century public policy as it impacts persons with disabilities?

Online Resources

Americans with Disabilities Department of Justice www.ada.gov/

Center for Community Inclusion and Disability Studies www.ccids .umaine.edu/

Center for Medicaid and Medicare Services www.cms.gov

Center for Universal Design www.ncsu.edu/www/ncsu/design/ sod5/cud/

Disability Rights Education Defense Fund www.dredf.org

References

Americans with Disabilities Act (ADA) of 1990, Public Law 101–336, 104 Stat. 327 (1990).

Americans with Disabilities Act Amendments Act (ADAAA) of 2008, Public Law 110–325, 122 Stat. 3553 (2008).

Axinn, J., & Stern, M. J. (2004). *Social welfare: A history of the American response to need* (5th ed). Boston, MA: Allyn & Bacon.

Baudrillard, J. (1995). *Simulacra and simulation: The body in theory: Histories of cultural materialism.* (S. F. Glaser, Trans.). Ann Arbor, MI: University of Michigan Press.

Belsey, C. (2002). *Post-Structuralism: A very short introduction.* New York, NY: Oxford University Press.

Berkowitz, E. D. (1989). *Disabled policy: America's programs for the handicapped: A twentieth century fund report.* Cambridge, United Kingdom: Cambridge University Press.

Carollo, K. (2012, March 2). Couple sues over Down Syndrome misdiagnosis. *Medical Unit. ABC News.* Retrieved from http://abcnews.go.com/blogs/health/2012/ 03/02/couple-sues-over-down-syndrome-misdiagnosis/#.

Chahira, K. (2006). Dwarfs in ancient Egypt. *American Journal of Medical Genetics, 140*(4), 303–311.

Ciota, M. G., & Hoveb, G. V. (2010). Romanian approach to media portrayals of disability. *Disability and Society, 25*(5), 525–538.

Coicaud, J. M. (2002). *Legitimacy and politics: A contribution to the study of political right and political responsibility* (D. A. Curtis, Ed. and Trans.). New York, NY: Cambridge University Press.

Davis, L. J. (1995). *Enforcing normalcy: Disability, deafness, and the body.* New York, NY: Verso.

Davis, L. (2010). *The disability studies reader* (3rd ed.). New York, NY: Routledge.

DePoy, E., & Gilson, S. F. (2004). *Rethinking disability: Principles for professional and social change.* Belmont, CA: Wadsworth.

DePoy, E., & Gilson, S. (2007). The bell-shaped curve: Alive, well and living in diversity rhetoric. *International Journal of Diversity in Organisations, Communities and Nations, 7*(3), 253–260. Retrieved from http://ijd.cgpublisher .com/product/pub.29/prod.514

DePoy, E., & Gilson, S. F. (2008). Disability studies: Origins, current conflict, and resolution. *Review of Disability Studies: An International Journal, 4*(4), 33–42.

DePoy, E., & Gilson, S. F. (2009). Policy legitimacy: A model for disability policy analysis and change. *Review of Disability Studies: An International Journal, 5*(4), 37–48.

DePoy, E., & Gilson, S. F. (2010). Disability design and branding: Rethinking disability within the 21st century. *Disability Studies Quarterly, 30*(2). Retrieved from http://www.dsq-sds.org/article/view/1247/1274

DePoy, E., & Gilson, S. F. (2011). *Studying disability: Multiple theories and responses.* Thousand Oaks, CA: Sage.

DePoy, E., & Gilson, S. F. (2012). *Human behavior theory and applications: A critical thinking approach.* Thousand Oaks, CA: Sage.

DePoy, E., & Gilson, S. F. (in press). *Branding and designing disability.* Abingdon, United Kingdom: Routledge.

Disability Rights Education & Defense Fund. (2006). *Individuals with Disabilities Education Act.* Berkeley, CA: Disability Rights Education and Defense Fund. Retrieved from http://www.dredf.org/idea/index.shtml

Education for All Children Act of 1975, Public Law 94–142, U.S.C. § 1400 et seq. (1975).

Employment Support Institute. School of Business. Virginia Commonwealth University. (2012). *Ticket to work and work incentives improvement act of 1999.* Retrieved from http://www.workworld.org/wwwebhelp/ticket_to_work_and _work_incentives_improvement_act_of_1999.htm

Farmer, S. (2002). *Surviving poverty in medieval Paris: Gender, ideology, and the daily lives of the poor.* Ithaca, NY: Cornell University Press.

Ford, R. T. (2011). *Rights gone wrong.* New York, NY: Farrar, Straus & Giroux.

Gill, C. (1992, November). Who gets the profits? Workplace oppression devalues the disability experience. *Mainstream, 12*, 14–17.

Goldberg, D. T. (1994). *Multiculturalism: A critical reader.* Oxford, United Kingdom: Blackwell.

Green, M. H. (2006). (Review of the book *Disability in medieval Europe: Physical impairment in the high Middle Ages, c. 1100–c. 1400*). *Social History of Medicine, 19*(3), 539–540.

Holmes, M. S. (2004). *Fictions of affliction.* Ann Arbor: University of Michigan Press.

Individuals with Disabilities Education Act of 2004, Public Law 108–446, 104 Stat. 1142. (2004).

Linton, S. (1998). *Claiming disability: Knowledge and identity.* New York, NY: New York University Press.

Linton, S. (2006). *My body politic: A memoir.* Ann Arbor: University of Michigan Press.

Lipton, J. (1999). *Individuals with disabilities education act amendments of 1997 and IDEA Regulations of 1999: Summary of changes (with emphasis on IEPs and discipline).* Berkeley, CA: Disability Rights Education and Defense Fund. Retrieved from http://www.dredf.org/idea10.html

Livermore, G., & Roche, A. (2011). Longitudinal outcomes of an early cohort of ticket to work participants. Retrieved from http://www.ssa.gov/policy/docs/ssb/ v71n3/v71n3p105.html

Maryland State Archive. (2005, July 22). *State workers' compensation commission origin & functions.* Retrieved from http://www.mdarchives.state.md.us/msa/ mdmanual/25ind/html/80workf.html

May, G., & Raske, M. (2004). *Ending disability discrimination: Strategies for social workers.* Saddle River, NJ: Allyn & Bacon.

Metzler, I. (2006). *Disability in medieval Europe: Physical impairment in the high Middle Ages, c. 1100–c. 1400.* New York, NY: Routledge.

Michaels, W. B. (2006). *The trouble with diversity.* New York, NY: Metropolitan Press.

Nakuamura, K. (2006). *Deaf in Japan.* Ithaca, NY: Cornell University Press.

National Park Service. (2011). *American the beautiful: The national parks and federal recreation lands pass series.* Retrieved from http://www.nps.gov/findapark/passes.htm

Nussbaum, M. (2006). *Frontiers of justice: Disability, nationality, species membership.* Cambridge, MA: Belnap Press.

Oliver, M. (1996). Defining impairment and disability: Issues at stake. In G. Barnes & G. Mercer (Eds.), *Exploring the divide: Illness and disability* (pp. 39–54). Leeds, United Kingdom: Disability Press.

Olyan, M. (2008). *Disability in the Hebrew Bible: Interpreting mental and physical differences.* New York, NY: Cambridge University Press.

Pelka, F. (1997). *ABC-CLIO companion to the disability rights movement.* Santa Barbara, CA: ABC-CLIO.

Quetelet, A. (1969). *A treatise on man and the development of his faculties: A fascism reproduction of the English translation of 1842.* Gainesville, FL: Scholars' Facsimiles & Reprints.

Rehabilitation Act of 1973, Public Law 93–112, 87 Stat. 355. (1973).

Rispler-Chiam, V. (2007). *Disability in Islamic Law.* AA Dordrecht, The Netherlands: Springer.

Rose, M. L. (2003). *The staff of Oedipus: Transforming disability in Ancient Greece [Corporealities: Discourses of Disability].* Ann Arbor: University of Michigan Press.

Rossanvallon, J. (2011). *Democratic legitimacy: Impartiality, reflexivity, proximity.* Princeton, NJ: Princeton University Press.

Smart, J. (2008). *Disability, society, and the individual* (2nd ed.). Austin, TX: Pro-Ed.

Standard Dictionary of the English Language (1906). Funk & Wagnalls.

Stein, M. (2006). *Distributive justice and disability: Utilitarianism against egalitarianism.* New Haven, CT: Yale University Press.

Stone, D. A. (2011). *Policy paradox: The art of political decision making* (3rd. ed.). New York, NY: Norton.

Stone, D. A. (1986). *The disabled state.* Philadelphia, PA: Temple University Press.

Ticket to Work and Work Incentives Improvement Act of 1999, Public Law 106–170. (1999).

U.S. Department of Health and Human Services. CMS: Centers for Medicare & Medicaid Services. (2012a, March 6). *Disabilities.* Retrieved from http://www.medicaid.gov/Medicaid-CHIP-Program-Information/By-Population/People-with-Disabilities/Individuals-with-Disabilities.html

U.S. Department of Health and Human Services. CMS: Centers for Medicare & Medicaid Services. (2012b, March 6). *Medicare.* Retrieved from http://www.cms.gov/home/medicare.asp

Vocational Rehabilitation Amendments of 1954, Public Law 83–565. (1954).

Wehman, P. (2000). Strategies for funding supported employment: A review of federal programs. *Journal of Vocational Rehabilitation, 14*, 179–182.

Yong, A. (2007). *Theology and down syndrome.* Waco, TX: Baylor University Press.

Chapter 6
Health Care Policy

Should Change Be Small or Large?

Pamela J. Miller

> Health care is one of the more galvanizing political firestorms of the 21st century. Should we focus on health care prevention or medical attention? How should end-of-life health services be addressed, in particular with terminally ill persons? Is health care a right or privilege? Shouldn't individuals be responsible for deciding if they purchase health insurance? Is universal health care affordable for the United States? Should euthanasia or assisted suicide be available options for a terminally ill person?

Introduction

Depending on who you believe, the studies you read, or your personal experiences, the health care system in the United States is in disrepair and dysfunctional; or, health care is without a doubt the best in the world; or, you may possibly characterize U.S. health care being somewhere in the middle of these contradictory positions.

In late March 2012, the U.S. Supreme Court heard the arguments for and against the law though the results of their decision—to uphold the law in its entirety, to overturn the entire law, or to strike some provisions while maintaining others—were not known at the time of this writing. The results and impact of the U.S. Supreme Court's decision are well known by the time you read this chapter.

The 2010 health care law, derogatorily called *Obamacare* by its critics, was basically health insurance reform, which sought to expand insurance coverage. The bill's implementation began in 2010 with various changes occurring annually and the overall implementation to be enacted in 2018. The Act includes many reforms, far too many to list. Some of the key provisions, however, included the elimination of limits on lifetime coverage, that young adults (up to age 26) could remain on their caretaker's policy, that people could not be turned down due to preexisting conditions, that small business owners received tax credits for providing employee health insurance, and that most people (by 2014) would be required to obtain health insurance.

Health insurance is critical. Without insurance, access to care is unavailable unless a person (a) pays for the service directly out of pocket or (b) the individual goes to a hospital's emergency room for noncritical care. Nationally, the uninsured rate has been increasing since 2008, climbing to 17.1% in 2011 (Mendes, 2012). Just as, if not more, disturbingly there are 8 million uninsured children in the United States (Children's Defense Fund); most disturbing are the health disparities that show a disproportionality when race and ethnicity are considered—1 in 14 White children is uninsured, the statistic jumps to nearly 1 in 9 for Black children and 1 in 5 for Latino children.

Although the Act tackles insurance coverage, there were no reforms to the health care system including the costs for services.

But is reform needed? The data is not compelling one way or the other; in fact, reports suggest that gains have been made in some areas while not in others. Consider the following data from the Centers for Disease Control and Prevention report *Health, United States, 2010* (2011).

- In 2007, 25% of all deaths were from heart disease, and 23% were from cancer.
- Between 1997 and 2007, the heart disease death rate for adults 65 years of age and over—the leading cause of death in this age group—decreased 26%.
- The birth rate among teenagers 15 to 19 years of age fell 2% in 2008.
- In 2009, the percentage of sexually active high school students who reported using a condom the most recent time they had sexual intercourse was 61%, up from 46% in 1991.
- Between 1988–1994 and 2007–2008, the prevalence of obesity among preschool-age children 2 to 5 years of age increased from 7% to 10%.
- In 2005–2008, the percentage of adults with diabetes increased with age from 4% of persons 20 to 44 years of age to 27% of adults 65 years of age and over.
- In 2009, 21% of adults 18 years of age and over had at least one emergency department visit in the past year, and 8% had two or more visits.
- The percentage of the population with at least one prescription drug during the previous month increased from 38% in 1988–1994 to 48% in 2005–2008.
- Between 1997 and 2009, among adults 18 to 64 years of age, the percentage who reported not receiving, or delaying, needed medical care in the past 12 months due to cost increased from 11% to 15%.
- In 2009, 37% of adults 18 to 64 years of age who were uninsured did not receive, or delayed, needed medical care in the past 12 months due to cost, compared with 9% of adults with private coverage and 14% of adults with Medicaid.

Obesity has been gaining significant attention in the news as well as with federal programs, such as the Centers for Disease Control and Prevention. The Health United States 2010 report (Centers for Disease Control and Prevention) found that from 1988–1994 to 2007–2008, the percentage of adults 20 years of age and over who were obese increased from 22% to 34%. A May 2012 HBO documentary *Weight of the Nation* found that $73.1 billion is the lost labor force revenue due to obesity, while obesity-related health care costs $150 billion each year (Weight of the Nation, 2012).

In 2008, the United States spent approximately 16% of the Gross Domestic Product (GDP) on health care (Henry J. Kaiser Family Foundation, 2010). The United States per capita health care expenditure of $7,538 was $2,535, or 51%, higher than Norway, the next largest per capita spender, and more than double the expenditures of Germany, France, and Sweden among other western nations. Interestingly, the United States spent $3,409, or 64%, more per person compared to Canada, whose universal health care system is criticized by conservative commentators as being too costly as well as ineffective. Yet, the following outcomes suggest that the U.S. health care system is far less successful.

- The United States leads the world in obesity, teenage pregnancy, and mortality of young people.
- Twenty-three nations have a greater life-expectancy compared to the United States.
- The United States is 29th in the world in the prevalence of diabetes.
- The United States ranks 27th in the world in opiate drug consumption.
- The United States ranks 14th in the world in global well-being. (Countries Rank, 2012)

Prior to the full implementation of the Patient Protection and Affordable Care Act, the United States continues to spend more on health care compared to other nations around the world, yet fewer Americans have health insurance. Health outcomes are poor with the United States often leading in the wrong categories while lagging behind in most areas. Is so-called "Obamacare" the panacea for the issues that plague the U.S. health care system? Clearly the answer is no, but we should recognize that the Act was at least a step in the right direction. No matter what the U.S. Supreme Court's 2012 decision, access to health care, steps to strengthen health care services, and cost containment must be fully addressed. To do otherwise only jeopardizes the future of this country.

How does one explain current health care policies? For educators, students, and practitioners alike, policies that are currently in place in the United States to offer health services are complex, underfunded, disparate, inconsistent, state of the art, miraculous, successful, unjust, illogical, and so on. There are too many adjectives, positive, negative, and somewhere in between, that can describe the U.S. approach to health care. This range of successes and failures is described by Enthoven and Kronick (1989) as a paradox of excess and deprivation. Our country has state-of-the-art technology, yet at times many citizens go without health or medical care. Students often feel completely overwhelmed by health policies, particularly those concerning insurance coverage, unfunded care, and the many different programs embedded in the private and public sector. Students also need help to remember that policy drives practice. What happens in health systems and what social workers are able to do in their day-to-day work environment are directly linked to the policies that are a part of the institution, the state and federal governments, and the private insurance industry.

Although it can be difficult, if not impossible, to understand all of the policies that have an impact on health care, this chapter chooses a select group of policies that are relevant in today's practice context. Not all of them might be considered mainstream policies, for example the Radiation Exposure Compensation Act (RECA), or Oregon's Death with Dignity Act. These are offered along with better known policies, for example, the Medicare Hospice Benefit, Medicare Part D, the Patient Self-Determination Act (PSDA), the End-Stage Renal Disease Program (ESRD), and policies specific to women's reproductive health. These are policies, however, that social workers should know about, that have a huge impact on clients and systems, and most importantly, need to be changed, updated, rewritten, and potentially discarded through advocacy on the part of our profession. Although an examination of these policies within a historical and political framework may not help the practitioner or student feel comfortable with the constraints imposed by current policies, at least some understanding of how the policy developed and how the policy is placed into action may be of benefit. Students and practitioners may have the "ah-ha" experience when they come to understand the background and political context in which policies evolved. Knowledge is needed for change, and the true motive behind exploration of these policies is to both frighten and inspire students. By examination of multiple health policies, the hope is that just one will spark the student or practitioner to get involved in the change process.

Needed Background

Before launching into each selected policy, two major points must be covered: (1) the uninsured and underinsured in this country; and (2) health disparities. Both of these are threads that run through every one of the policies that are explained in more detail later. Underinsurance and health disparities have overarching and far-reaching implications on every facet of the individual policies that will follow and for all health policies in general in the United States.

The Uninsured/Underinsured

The health care crisis that President Clinton identified in the 1990s is still with us. Our leaders may not be talking about it or working on it, but for those who are in the field and for many of our citizens, the crisis has intensified. The United States is among the few industrialized countries in the world that does not provide health care to all citizens. On the other hand, medical technology is superior and highly utilized by those who can pay for it. The United States also spends 13% of its gross domestic product on health as well as $4,631 per capita, the highest in the world. All of this money spent, however, does not provide the best measures of health status. Starfield (2000) compared the United States with 13 other countries and found that the United States ranked on average at number 12 across several health indicators. The two most important signals of the health of a country are life expectancy and infant mortality. For infant mortality, the United States had the highest rate, and for life expectancy for females, the United States ranked 11th and for males, 12th out of 13.

Despite our medical miracles and fascination with technology, it is estimated that 18,000 deaths occur in the United States each year due to persons having no insurance or being underinsured (Institute of Medicine [IOM], 2004). With about 15% of the population uninsured, these deaths are a part of the legacy of the U.S. health care system. The Institute of Medicine's Committee on the Consequences of Uninsurance has published six in-depth reports that cover in great detail the impact of lack of health insurance in this country (IOM, 2004). The Institute's overall conclusion is that a lack of health insurance for such a large part of our population "is a critical problem . . . that can and should be eliminated. The Committee believes that leaving 43 million Americans uninsured is costly to the country and should no longer be tolerated" (p. 18). The Institute, part of the National Academy of Sciences, believes that the President and Congress should work to insure all Americans by 2010. They acknowledge the incremental policy changes over the years, yet as a developed country, the United States has a major percentage of uninsured citizens, much like Mexico and Turkey. This group strongly supports an approach that eliminates the $85 billion of uncovered care that happens each year, 85% of which is covered by tax dollars.

There certainly has not been a lack of attempts at health care for all citizens in this country over the past 100 years. The Progressives made an attempt in the early part of the last century, and after women were granted the right to vote, the Sheppard-Towner Act provided tax supported care to infants and mothers (Seifert, 1983). The New Deal legislation did not cover health care, despite numerous attempts after 1935 to do so. In the Great Society years, two groups of people were given health coverage through the Social Security Act: the poor through Medicaid (Title 19) and the old through Medicare (Title 18). This fit with the War on Poverty and the grassroots efforts by the elderly for relief from medical costs (Katz, 1986). The last attempt for a national health program during the Clinton years was dismantled just like the previous attempts by insurance companies, organized medicine, pharmaceutical corporations, patriotic and special interest groups, elections, ideological passions, a reluctance to pay for it by the U.S. public, and many other diversions (Bodenheimer & Grumbach, 2005).

Health insurance coverage in the United States is tied to work, not citizenship. Again, this grew out of our political history as our country grew and developed. Political stability was not as much of a challenge here as it was in Europe in the 1800s where socialism emerged as a political force. In this country, as labor unions grew, they did not align themselves with the socialist party, so there was not a powerful working class support for social insurance (Starr, 1982). Labor unions demanded health insurance from employers, not from the government. This helps explain why 55% of the population has health insurance through employment-based, private means. There are many Americans who work and do not have health insurance, either because it is not offered or it is not affordable. Almost 80% of those without health insurance in the United States work at least part time or have someone in the household who works at least part time (Bodenheimer & Grumbach, 2005). Tying health insurance to employment is not working as it was once envisioned to work.

States have also made attempts to cover the uninsured. Oregon blazed this trail in 1994 with the Oregon Health Plan (OHP), spearheaded by John Kitzhaber, a state legislator and governor. This policy was developed to offer health insurance to *all* poor Oregonians, not just those in the federally defined categories for Medicaid. The plan had three parts: health insurance for all Oregonians with incomes below the poverty level, employer mandates, and the development of an insurance pool for those who could not purchase insurance. The plan was controversial and defined politically by some as rationing. The plan was in a sense illegal and had to be given special consideration by the federal government to be enacted. In fact, the Bush Administration would not approve the waiver needed to allow the plan to go forward. The Clinton Administration did approve the Section 1115 waiver in 1993 after Kitzhaber, a Democrat, assisted Clinton in winning Oregon in the 1992 presidential election (Lunch, 2005). In the initial stages, the plan worked well, covering many more Oregonians than typical Medicaid (the uninsured rate fell from 18% to 11%) and reducing charity care at hospitals across the state (Bodenheimer, 1997). Unfortunately, as the state's economy faltered in the recent past, OHP had to drop many of those who were recently added and now Medicaid in the state looks much like it did 15 years ago.

Massachusetts' governor signed into law legislation aimed at providing health insurance to most of the state's citizens (Commonwealth of Massachusetts, 2006). This plan requires citizens with incomes above 300% of federal poverty level to purchase health insurance from private companies at reduced rates. Employers, particularly small businesses, will be strongly encouraged to make a contribution toward health insurance premiums as well. The state is making efforts to find and sign up those who are eligible for Medicaid. In the next phase of the legislation, an insurance pool was developed for the working poor and those citizens who were not employed. In 2011, Massachusetts' uninsured rate was approximately 5.3%, the lowest of all states. It will be interesting to see if the market-based reform plan continues to work and how former Massahcusetts Governor and 2012

Republican presidential nominee Romney use his Massachusetts experiences during the 2012 presidntal election (Gallup). Other states, such as Utah, have tried to resolve or at least ameliorate the crushing financial and political issue of the uninsured and most have floundered or failed. Clearly, the tie to political aspirations has not worked well, and, with many states plagued by current insured rates of 15% to 25%, it would seem unlikely that states can do this alone.

Health Disparities

Often health disparities are defined in terms of race. However, gender can also be a barrier when health outcomes are evaluated. Obstetrical and gynecological policies are discussed later. However, women are less likely to receive heart surgeries and kidney transplants and more women donate kidneys as live donors (Kayler et al., 2002). African-American women also receive treatment in the later stages of breast cancer and so are more likely to die of the disease than white women. In a study on race *and* gender, findings suggested that both influenced how physicians treat chest pain, with African-American women getting the least intervention (Schulman et al., 1999). There was quite a reaction when this article was published and the American Medical Association wanted to be clear that doctors were not racists. In the true sense of the word, this may be mostly the case. However, there are clear differences in access to health care, use of resources, and outcomes for our citizens of color. The institutionalization of racism may be more subtle and individuals within health systems may not consciously make racist decisions; however, the effects of disparate treatment are well-documented.

African Americans have far worse health than white Americans. African Americans have lower life expectancy; double the infant mortality rate of Whites; and higher mortality rates for cancer, strokes, and heart disease. Native Americans also have poor health outcomes. Other racial groups in the United States have varied health outcomes and some groups have lower mortality rates than Whites (Bodenheimer & Grumbach, 2005). Immigrants may be healthier than U.S. citizens in the early years of living in the United States, but acculturation may have a negative impact on health over time (Abraido-Lanza & Dohrenwend, 1999). Health disparities also follow people into the aging process through disparate care in nursing homes (Mor, Zinn, Angelelli, Teno, & Miller, 2005).

In 2002, the Institute of Medicine released a report entitled Unequal Treatment (IOM, 2003). One of the tenets of the report is that even when insurance status, income, age, and medical conditions are similar, racial and ethnic minorities tend to receive less quality care than Whites. Many examples are given. Citizens of color are less likely to receive kidney dialysis or transplants, cancer screening, and up-to-date treatments for HIV/AIDS, and are more likely to receive amputations. The report is clear that disparities do exist and that there are many reasons for the disparities, and it also offers ways to reduce disparities. The report puts forth the notion that most health care providers are not racist. However, due to time pressure, the complexities of the clinical encounter, combined with previously learned ideas about people of color, stereotyping does occur. These stereotypes then lead to inferior and unequal care.

Policy Topics

There are numerous exisiting health policies and issues that are worth exploring as we consider the future of health care. This section briefly examines exisiting policies, some more known then others, as well as key health problem areas.

Radiation Exposure Compensation Act

This federal policy is one that most students have little or no knowledge about yet find quite interesting from a historical and political perspective. Congress passed this legislation in 1990 to compensate citizens who may have contracted particular cancers from exposure to nuclear weapons testing that occurred in the 1940s and later. Three groups are eligible to make claims: those who worked at the test sites, those who lived downwind from the test sites, and those who worked in uranium mines. For the downwinders in particular, the compensation is $50,000 for people who have developed 19 kinds of cancer and who live in 21 counties in Utah, Arizona, and Nevada.

The Institute for Energy and Environmental Research (IEER) analyzed data from a Congressionally mandated study conducted by the Department of Health and Human Services, the Centers for Disease Control and Prevention, and the National Cancer Institute. IEER estimates that 80,000 people who lived in or were born in the United States between 1951 and 2000 will get cancer as a result of fallout from nuclear testing and that at least 15,000 of those cancer cases will be fatal (IEER, 2002).

The Health Resources and Services Administration (HRSA), who operates the Radiation Exposure Screening and Education Program (RESEP) for RECA, asked the National Academy of Sciences (NAS) to study and make recommendations on three areas of the program: (1) how to improve accessibility to the program and boost the quality of education and screening; (2) whether more recent scientific data could shed light on radiation exposure; and (3) whether more people or more locations in the United States should be added to the list of eligibility. During this time, IEER sent a letter to the NAS Chair of the Committee to Assess the Scientific Information for the Radiation Exposure Screening and Education Program, Dr. Julian Preston (Makhijani & Ledwidge, 2004).

The letter states that the United States is a leader in the compensation of those made ill by nuclear tests. The letter asks that NAS consider: (a) that persons who live in other parts of the nation should be informed of their potential risk because of exposure; (b) that medical professionals should be educated about the risks and diseases related to fallout; (c) that the definition of downwinder should be expanded to include other locations; (d) that the benefit of the doubt should be given to those exposed, not to the U.S. government because it caused the harm, particularly because the milk supply appeared to be one of the primary methods for exposure; (e) that many Americans do not have health insurance and some of them are ill because of exposure, including those who were infants or in utero during the 1950s and 1960s; and (f) that the large amount of thyroid cancer and thyroid disease in the United States may be attributable to radiation fallout.

When the Committee released its report in April 2005 (NAS, 2005), they did recommend that RECA eligibility should not be limited to the boundaries that were implemented in the original legislation of 1990. The Committee recommended that coverage should be extended to the continental United States, Hawaii, and other U.S. territories. Although the Committee did not add to the list of diseases, they did advise that Congress set new eligibility criteria and requested that the screening criteria be made more efficient and inclusive. The Committee also recommended more outreach and education about exposure from fallout through education and communication.

Local or regional communities may also have downwinders, for example, the Hanford downwinders in Washington, Idaho, Montana, and Oregon. This group of concerned citizens maintains that many people have been exposed and made ill by radiation through food, air, and water from the Hanford site, located in Washington, that manufactured plutonium for nuclear weapons. There has been ongoing litigation since 1990 with DuPont and General Electric, who operated the facility at different times for the U.S government between 1946 and 1965 (www.downwinders.com). This example and the RECA program highlight the need for policies that attempt to ameliorate problems caused by government. Social workers can be involved in advocacy and analysis to improve and develop programs that help with health problems caused by our country's war and nuclear efforts. There is much work to be done here.

Medicare Part D

Many elderly people in the United States worry about how to pay for drugs and how to pay for long-term care in their own home or in an institution. The Medicare Prescription Drug, Improvement, and Modernization Act passed through Congress in 2003 and added drug coverage for the nation's elderly and disabled. This was the largest change in the Medicare program since it was first enacted by Congress in 1965. There is a long political and social justice history behind why it took so long to offer this benefit (Larkin, 2004; Oliver, Lee, & Lipton, 2004). There are also politics involved in the passage of the bill in December 2003.

There is certainly no doubt that Medicare beneficiaries needed assistance with drug coverage, and from a political perspective, there were many obstacles, particularly from powerful interest groups. However, according to Weissert (2003), six reasons for its passage came together late in 2003 that allowed for passage of the bill: (1) both political parties needed a drug benefit because their constituents wanted one; (2) the President's poll performance was dropping; (3) there were problems with the war in Iraq; (4) the economy was sluggish; (5) the President had problems with staff leaks that hurt him politically; and (6) Florida would continue to be a key Republican state for the next Presidential election in 2004, it would be politically prudent to pass such a bill. Also, it was difficult to oppose the bill because it included increased payments to physicians. So, both parties would benefit from passage. There was an "extraordinary political window of opportunity in 2003," (Oliver et al., 2004, p. 289).

Medicare Part D is complex and remains controversial. All individuals who have Medicare or Medicaid must receive their drug coverage through Medicare. So the poor elderly who normally received drugs through their state Medicaid programs would now receive them from Medicare as would other poor elderly at or below 135% of poverty level (Families USA, 2004). Otherwise, the drug benefit is administered through private firms on a regional basis. The elderly person chooses a plan and then pays a monthly premium and co-payments for each prescription. If an individual had not signed up for the program by May15 in 2006, extra charges would be imposed if the person decided to sign up at a later date.

It is interesting to note that the drug industry actually supported this bill in the later stages of its development and movement through Congress. Why is it that the drug industry opposed any and all bills related to government involvement before this? The answer is easy. Drug corporations got a huge piece of business from a group of people who buy lots of drugs; the bill actually prohibits cost control; the government will not be involved in direct administration of the program (that happens in the private- and mostly for-profit sector); and the law does not allow the legalization of importing drugs. Just a couple of years earlier, both Maine and Oregon had decided to try and control drug costs in their own states and the pharmaceutical industry was opposed to these programs (Palfreman, 2003). So, this was a nice package for the drug industry in many different ways. Tucker (as cited in Oliver et al., 2004) states, "The bill pays private insurance companies to take elderly patients. You know how one of the tenets of conservative philosophy is that private companies can always deliver a product better and cheaper? So why does the Medicare bill offer billions in subsidies to private insurers to induce them into the market? That's not competition, that's corporate welfare" (p. 319).

This legislation also fueled reelection campaigns in 2004. The President delivered a campaign promise and some Democrats who voted for the bill received negative feedback from constituents who saw its passage as major victory for President Bush (Mapes, 2003). The American Association of Retired Persons (AARP) supported the bill through newspaper and television and this prompted 60,000 members who disagreed with this decision to either resign from the organization or refuse to renew membership

(Pear & Toner, 2003). There certainly was much to consider and maybe it was better to have drug coverage for the elderly and disabled now rather than wait several more years for another political point in time to pass such a complex piece of policy. In any case, the price tag for drug coverage under Medicare was estimated at $400 billion and this would cover about one fifth of the estimated $1.85 trillion that Medicare beneficiaries will spend in the next 10 years (Oliver et al., 2004). However, the true price tag may have been withheld as a person in the Medicare administration was ordered to withhold cost estimates during the bill's hearings (Pear, 2004).

Social workers are already involved in helping Medicare beneficiaries sift through the options available through Plan D. It could prove to be unfortunate that the program is basically run through private insurance providers and that the drugs are purchased with no cost controls. The price tag may prove to be unbearable but who knows? Once again our leaders have enacted a policy that helped some elected officials in the short term yet may have put citizens at risk for little or no benefit. There is much work to be done here.

Patient Self-Determination Act and the Medicare Hospice Benefit

Although these two policies are different pieces of legislation, they are related in the sense that they are tied to end of life. Certainly both are tied to the right-to-die movement that was gaining momentum in the 1970s and 1980s and it was in 1990 that the Patient Self-Determination Act (PSDA) was passed in Congress. The Medicare Hospice Benefit became law in 1982 and hospices began their certification process for the program as soon as the rules were written. Both of these federal policies have had successes, setbacks, and failures. As before, both pieces of legislation have interesting political histories.

The Patient Self-Determination Act was passed, in part, by the uproar over the Cruzan case. This young woman was injured in a car accident, and although her family believed she would not want to live in a persistent vegetative state, they did not have any of her wishes in writing. This case went to the U.S. Supreme Court and then back to local courts, and so the family requested that the feeding tube be removed (Colby, 2002). Senator John Danforth lived in Missouri, the same state as the Cruzan family, and he was worried about many other families that were affected by the same dilemmas as the Cruzans. He proposed and pushed the PSDA as a way for citizens to write down their requests for end-of-life treatment in hopes that situations like the Cruzans could be avoided (Glick, 1992). The law requires that all health agencies that receive federal funds must inform patients about their organizations' polices, states' laws, and rights within the PSDA. Each state has different forms and procedures that meet this requirement. There was hope that all Americans would write down their requests but unfortunately, this has not been the case. Except for a wave of activity after the Schiavo case in 2005 (in which government at many levels became very involved), the rate of implementation of advance directives has remained low, somewhere around 18% of the population (Fagerlin & Schneider, 2004).

The Medicare Hospice Benefit became law in 1982 as part of the Tax Equity and Fiscal Responsibility Act. This was the only social program passed during this session of Congress under the Reagan Administration. The bill might not have passed if the results of the National Hospice Study had been completed before Congress voted, as it found that hospice care really did not save money, despite how it was pitched to the House and Senate. The hospice benefit is an incremental policy change in that it builds on the home care program already well-established in the Medicare program. One major change was the coverage of drugs for the terminal illness. This was viewed as quite a landmark at the time. The payment method of hospice was prospective, rather than fee-for service, in anticipation of Diagnostic Related Groups (DRGs) that began under the Medicare program in 1983 (Miller & Mike, 1995).

Now the terminally ill in our country had the right to state what they wanted, or more importantly at times, what they did not want at the end-of-life. And now a program under Medicare was available to take care of beneficiaries when life was projected to last 6 months or less. As with PSDA, the hospice benefit is underutilized and for many, not used at all. The median length of stay in a hospice program nationwide remains at 22 days with 35% of patients dying in 7 days or less after admission (National Hospice and Palliative Care Organization, 2006). There are many reasons given for this problem: denial of death, overtreatment, doctors unwilling to suggest hospice, patients wanting to continue treatment, the inability to predict the time of life left, the complexities of switching into the Medicare benefit, financial concerns, and so on. Many who are chronically ill could benefit from hospice-like services but are not eligible despite a trajectory toward death. Our policies that define life and death, who can receive services and when, and what will be covered by insurance are cutting out a large group of the seriously and chronically ill who become terminal too late to take advantage of the hospice benefit (Abraham, 1993; Bern-Klug, 2004). There is much work to be done here.

Oregon's Death with Dignity Act

Oregon's Death with Dignity Act (ODWDA) was approved by voters in 1994 and was also rejected as a repeal ballot measure in 1997. Under 8 years of the law, 246 people have used the law to end their lives with a lethal dose of medication (Oregon Department of Human Services, Health Services, 2006). The amount of federal involvement in this case is quite compelling. Congress tried to intervene, and John Ashcroft, Attorney General in the first Bush administration tried to stop the law through stating that it violated the Controlled Substances Act (Miller & Werth, 2005). The U.S. Supreme Court ruled in January 2006 that this was not the case. In 1997, the federal government enacted the Assisted Suicide Funding Restriction Act that states that federal monies may not be used for a hastened death. This essentially acts like the Hyde amendment for abortion (Miller, 2000). Oregon is the only state that has a law that legalizes a physician to prescribe a lethal dose of medication to end life. Other states may follow but it is hard to know (Miller & Hedlund, 2005). At least six other states have some kind of legislation similar to Oregon's that is either pending or in committee (Miller, Hedlund, & Soule, in press). In 2009, the state of Washington also impmeneted a "death with dignity" protocol following a state-wide referendum in 2008. In general, however, the so-called red and blue states, through their legislatures, have yet to show clear support for such laws as resistence remains well entrenched in all regions of the country.

Because so many who have used the law have been hospice patients, social workers have been involved with many patients and families who have considered the law and/or used it to end their lives. From a policy perspective, this has been an interesting time to observe how policy drives practice and how the guidelines for the law were developed and implemented. All professionals were surprised when the law passed and most were unprepared for how to deal with the option that now appeared to be legal. Leadership emerged at Oregon's Health and Science University and many end-of-life practitioners came together, despite their own personal beliefs, and worked to craft guidelines for practice within the law. The policies that were written have changed and modified over time and represent the best practices available to those who choose to use the law and those who work within the Act (Task Force to Improve the Care of Terminally-Ill Oregonians, 2006). There is much work to be done here.

Women's Reproductive Health

This topic also brings us to the right to choose and the controversy about life and death. This includes policies about abortion and contraception for all women, young women, poor women, and also whether states require insurance coverage of contraception, as well as the availability of emergency contraception. There is much written on this subject from many vantage points and women's reproductive rights have been a battle for social workers and the American Medical Association for more than a century (Haslett, 1997; Wolinsky & Brune, 1994). Feldt (2004) describes the battle over abortion as a War on Choice and she believes that women's health around the world is in jeopardy as the right to choose is not available or is taken away. Ipas, an international organization for women's reproductive health, estimates that 70,000 women die each year from unsafe abortions, almost half of those in Asia (Ipas, 2006).

The *Roe v. Wade* Supreme Court case established the right for abortion in the United States but this did not necessarily guarantee access. The first major legislation to limit access after this famous court case was the Hyde amendment in 1976. This federal law prevents Medicaid funds from being used for poor women's abortions and quickly several states decided to enforce this funding restriction. The Supreme Court even had to rule that the Hyde amendment was constitutional before it took effect in 1980.

Since then, numerous states do not fund abortions for poor women, except in cases of rape, incest, or endangerment of health. Some states will pay for the procedure with out-of-state funds (for a current list of those states, see Guttmacher Institute, 2006).

A study by Jones, Darroch, and Henshaw (2002) looks at the trends and patterns for abortion in the United States. The authors state that the abortion rate fell by 11% between 1994 and 2000. This decline was most notable in young women ages 15 to 17, those in higher socioeconomic groups, and women with college degrees. The rate actually went up for poor women and for poor teenagers. This means that the rates went up for women of color as they are disproportionately poor. Health disparities hit here also. The article emphasizes that all women need access to ways to prevent unwanted pregnancies and that poor women may find it difficult to obtain and use contraception. The authors tie the increase in the abortion rate for poor women to welfare reform at this time. This reform had an impact on Medicaid coverage coupled with the general increase of women with no health insurance coverage. The authors are clear that there is a "clear association between poverty status and abortion, the abortion rate being higher among poor and low-income women than among those with incomes greater than 200% of poverty" (p. 234).

The state of South Dakota recently passed a ban on all abortions, even those for rape or incest, and the only abortions allowed would be when the woman's life, not health, was in danger. Doctors would be fined $5,000 and put in prison for 5 years for violating this law. This would be the most restrictive state measure to date if put into motion. South Dakota already has restrictive policies for abortion and has one clinic that performs abortions by physicians flown in from Minnesota as no doctors who reside in the state will do abortions (Nieves, 2006). Those opposed to choice want the law to be taken to the U.S. Supreme Court with the hope that the current Court will overturn *Roe v. Wade.* No court appeals have been filed. However, citizens in the state gathered signatures for a petition requesting that this law not be put into effect until citizens of the state could vote on it. At least 10 other states have attempted to challenge *Roe v. Wade* by banning all abortions but none, besides South Dakota, have passed such legislation. Many other states have attempted to reduce access in various ways (Guttmacher Institute, 2006).

Year in and year out, states continue to seek new ways to challenge women's health rights. For example, in 2012, 20 states had enacted laws that would limit or eliminate abortion if Rov v. Wade is completely overturned (FactCheck.org). Similarly, in 2011, the federal government looked to reduce Planned Parenthood's subsidy by $363 million; 90% of Planned Parenthood programs are for preventive services (Dwyer, 2011). The attacks on Planned Parenthood continued in 2012 with the U.S. House of Representatives' Labor Health and Human Services appropriations committee eliminating support for basic programs such as lifesaving cancer screenings, STD testing and treatment, Pap tests, and birth control (Planned Parenthood, 2012).

Access to abortions for teens is also under great scrutiny, controversy, and change. Parental involvement is required for teens who seek an abortion in 34 states. This could mean parental notification or parental permission. Some states require one parent to be involved and others may require both parents, and sometimes both biological parents, to be involved. In January 2006, the Supreme Court ruled that states can require parental involvement in abortion decisions for minors (Ipas, 2006). There is quite a bit of state legislative action on the rights of minors around sexual health, most to restrict rights. Many states have laws about access for birth control and emergency contraception for teens (Guttmacher Institute, 2006).

The American Academy of Pediatrics released an update on current trends in adolescent pregnancy (Klein & the Committee on Adolescence, 2005). The authors note that high pregnancy rates for teens in the 1950s and 1960s dropped after abortion became legal until 1986, then the rates went up, and now the rates have gone down again since 1991. However, at least 4 out of 10 women have been pregnant once before the age of 20. The United States also has the highest adolescent birth rate of all industrialized countries, even when compared with countries where sexual activity is higher. The Committee on Adolescence has many clinical considerations that have an impact on policy. The overarching theme is the need to educate young people about sex and parenting, but also to have contraception, including emergency contraception, available as part of good medical care (Klein & the Committee on Adolescence, 2005, p. 284).

Emergency contraception policies are quite complex and differ all over the country. The medication, a high dose of a drug contained in birth control pills, taken within 72 hours after unprotected sex, can prevent a pregnancy up to almost 89% of the time. Some view this as equivalent to an abortion and have many of the same arguments against the use of what has become known as Plan B. At the federal level, the Food and Drug Administration's (FDA) scientific advisors supported the sale of the drug over the counter in December 2003. In an unusual move in August 2005, the Commissioner of the FDA, Lester Crawford, stated that Plan B would not be available over the counter until more research could be obtained about the use of the drug in young teens. The director of the FDA's Office of Women's Health resigned soon after this decision was made and Davidoff (2006) believes that sex, politics, and morality collided in this debate.

When Barr Laboratories agreed to have it available to only women 17 and older, the FDA still said no, despite the data that shows that half of all unwanted pregnancies (3 million each year in the United States, and 800,000 of those teens), could be cut down by 50% (Advocates for Youth, 2006). There are many state policies about emergency contraception that apply to hospital emergency rooms, selling the drug over the counter, not forcing pharmacists to fill it (as is allowed for contraceptives as well), whether to cover this drug through Medicaid, and so on (Guttmacher Institute, 2006). Even campus health centers have wrestled with whether this drug should be available to college students (August, 2003).

Behind the abortion debate and the ongoing controversy about teens' rights to health care, the coverage of contraceptives by health insurance also rages on. Many private health insurance plans cover prescription drugs, but some do not cover contraception and medical services for such. Take Oregon, for example. There is not a law or mandate or policy that requires private health plans to cover contraception (Guttmacher Institute, 2006). State employees, through policy, do have coverage. There has been an attempt in Oregon, as well as at the federal level, to mandate health insurance for contraception. In 2004, a Catholic social service agency in California was told by the state's Supreme Court that they must provide birth control in its health plan for employees, despite the church's opposition to contraception (California Catholic Conference, 2006). The questions are: Should women who work for religious organizations have the right to coverage of contraception? Or are women who work for religious organizations to be held to the moral beliefs of the employer?

When discussing women's health, disparities emerge as a problem for access and treatment across many health indicators. Women of color are less likely to receive adequate care for their reproductive health and therefore have higher rates of infant and maternal mortality, late screening for breast and cervical cancer, and higher incidences of HIV/AIDS and other sexually transmitted diseases. Language and cultural barriers may contribute to these problems. More than 16 million women are uninsured and even when insured, some reproductive services are not covered (National Association of Social Workers [NASW], 2004). It seems like women are caught in a loop—the President of the United States wants to reduce the number of abortions yet access to birth control is limited. As Davidoff (2006) states,

> Like all powerful forces-terrorism, hurricanes, pandemics—the power of sex can seem appalling, terrifying, something that must be controlled at all costs. And since men exert most organized social control, the control over sexuality is asserted primarily by controlling the sexual and reproductive lives of women. (p. 25)

There is much work to be done here.

End-Stage Renal Disease Program (ESRD)

President Richard Nixon signed the ESRD program into law in October 1972. This program was instituted partly because the technology was available at the time for dialysis, the cleansing of the blood, or kidney transplantation. This program covers the expenses of those with kidney failure that would die without dialysis or transplant through the Medicare program. There is an interesting history behind this federal program and so it is included in this chapter for that reason.

In 1962, *Life* magazine published an article entitled, "They Decide Who Lives, Who Dies," by Shana Alexander. The story is about a group of seven people who meet a few times a year to decide who can receive dialysis. They were selected as volunteers from the community to serve on this committee at the Swedish Hospital in Seattle. The patients served by this program were in an experiment of sorts to determine if the dialysis treatment, then costing about $15,000 per year, was feasible for the entire country. This group did not make medical decisions, they decided, based on some criteria, who merited the treatment and who did not. Those rejected from the program died.

The article goes on in great detail about the meetings of the committee and the process by which they made decisions over time. There are also quotes from the committee members identified only through their profession; their names are not used. They did not know the names of the patients until this article was published. The criteria used to consider those who would receive dialysis were (p. 105): the patient's age and sex (those over 45 and children were not considered as a rule), marital status, number of children, income, net worth, emotional stability, educational background, occupation, future potential, and names of references. The Committee wrestled with the situation of a woman with two children who would have to move to Seattle but did not have the funds and a man with six children who had a good job. Both needed the treatment and would die if not chosen. One of the members spoke to the problem of remarriage of the surviving spouse of the one not chosen, and what would be the burden to society of a particular person's death? This was truly difficult work and we can look back on it now and see the snapshot of the social and cultural norms of that time.

Dialysis and transplantation did become more available over time and were seen as ways to save lives and keep people in the workforce. There was still hope that universal health insurance might be a possibility in the near future, particularly since in 1965, coverage for the elderly and poor had been established. Medicare coverage for the disabled was also passed into law in 1972. Congress believed that kidney dialysis and transplantation clearly saved lives and deserved Medicare coverage. Wilbur Mills, a Democrat from Arkansas, actually proposed the idea of the ESRD program and arranged for a patient to be dialyzed at a House Ways and Means Committee meeting in late 1971 (Iglehart, 1993). When the program passed both the House and Senate in the fall of 1972, there was little discussion about the bill and it seemed that Congress "implied that the value of life is beyond price," (p. 367).

The ESRD program provides Medicare coverage for kidney failure to those eligible by disease and by work covered by Social Security. Even children can be covered because their parents have worked enough and contributed to Social Security. The United States has a higher treatment rate than other countries because the criteria used to select those eligible are fairly broad. This also means that survival rates for the United States are lower as well (Iglehart, 1993). The intricacies and complexities of this program are enormous. Social workers are mandated to work with patients who come to dialysis centers. The interesting point about dialysis is that almost all of it is carried out in the for-profit sector. The program has also gotten more expensive over the years as more and more people begin dialysis or get a transplant when an organ is available. Although the program is only one half percent of those on Medicare, it uses 6.7% of the Medicare budget. Another way to understand this is that the average Medicare patient uses $6,100/year and in the ESRD program, $41,700/year (United States Renal Data System, 2005). Those who voted on this so quickly in 1972 truly believed the program would continue to be available to those who had no other health complications and that dialysis would help them get back to work, in effect a budget-neutral program.

Students often scratch their heads and wonder why the Medicare system covers only one disease when so many other diseases go uninsured. The politics of the times and the history of the ESRD program offer a policy that began as way to save lives based on up-to-the moment technology and then turned into a program that its founders probably did not expect. Iglehart (1993) sums this up well, "The End Stage Renal Disease Program demonstrates the humane impulse that strikes Americans periodically to act on behalf of a vulnerable population. The legislative history of the program suggests that this impulse is driven more by emotions, timing, and the political need to expand benefits than by rational planning" (p. 371). There is much work to be done here.

Policies/Programs Worth Exploring

The National Commission on Prevention Priorities (NCPP) released a study about cost-effective preventative services. The impetus for this research rests with the knowledge that our health system emphasizes cure and treatment of disease rather than working to stop problems before they begin, e.g. prevention. Couple this with the aging baby boomers and the continued advancement of technology, health care spending may grow significantly in the next decade (National Commission on Prevention Priorities [NCPP], 2006). The study ranked preventative services based on a score of what service produced the most health benefit added to a score on cost effectiveness. Twenty-five evidence-based clinical preventative services were ranked.

Three services received a perfect score of 10: discussing daily aspirin use with high-risk adults, immunizing children, and tobacco-use screening and treatment. Eight services received a score of 7 or higher: adult vaccines for influenza and pneumonia, screening for cancer of the cervix and the colon, vision screening for those over 65 years of age, and screening for hypertension, cholesterol and alcohol intake. Nussbaum (2006) explains that,

> [I]f colorectal cancer screening were offered at recommended intervals to all people 50 aged years and older, 18,000 deaths could be prevented each year . . . colorectal cancer screening costs less than $13,000 per year of life saved, demonstrating its value as a high-impact, cost-effective preventive service. Yet, less than half of the target population uses this service. (p. 1)

People are dying because they do not receive preventative services in a country with some of the most advanced technology in the world. The problem comes back again to lack of health insurance and health disparities and our continued focus on services after disease has taken hold. The finding that screening and treatment for tobacco and alcohol would be beneficial and cost-effective is also quite interesting. The use of these two substances, in the author's opinion, are often overlooked, denied, ignored, diminished, distorted, dismissed, and so on, by health care professionals. It is so easy to get caught up in the heat of the medical problem at hand and not look at the other factors that are brought into the medical situation. Social workers in health systems must be aware of the need for these screenings and advocate for them with their patients. If our health systems are to survive, prevention must take a lead in how citizens are served in this country. Social workers are trained and educated well to offer some of these services. The problem is there are no mechanisms for payment and that is why they are not a priority.

The federal government, through the U.S. Department of Health and Human Services, launched Healthy People 2010 with two main goals: to increase quality and years of health life, and to eliminate health disparities. There are 28 identified focus areas and 10 Leading Health Indicators that are identified as the major health concerns: physical activity, overweight/obesity, tobacco use, substance abuse, responsible sexual behavior, mental health, injury and violence, environmental quality, immunization, and access to health care. This project is currently undergoing public comment (Healthy People 2010). There are numerous coalitions, businesses, and communities involved in trying to work on the goals and the focus areas. The goals are big yet very critical.

I end the chapter with sharing a movement that is small but growing in the state of Oregon. It is called the Archimedes Movement and was started in January 2006 by former Governor John Kitzhaber (www.archimedes movement.org). He believes that tension must be created and leadership must emerge to create change in our health care system. The movement is also based on the ideas that the health programs we have now (in particular Medicare and Medicaid) cannot be updated or upgraded through incremental change and that politics and politicians will not help resolve the health crisis. Communities and coalitions must work together on common goals and values around health care and push our legislators to either defend the current system (which is hard to do) or to push them to work on new alternatives and structures for the health care system. Kitzhaber says so eloquently, "The Archimedes Movement seeks to position Oregon, and hopefully several other states, to request a broad range of waivers (both statutory and administrative) that will force Congress to compare the current system to a comprehensive vision of how we should be providing health care to our people—a vision rooted in traditional and pragmatic values of fairness, inclusion, and quality [that] promotes health as the fundamental cornerstone of upward mobility in a democratic society."

Concluding Remarks and Future Directions

The above policies are all a part of the health policy course that I currently teach to graduate students. Other important policies and policy topics, of which there is not enough room to cover in this chapter are: the Americans with Disabilities Act, transplantation, blood supply, egg donation, funding for and research on stem cells, human subjects research, procedure d and x preparation for psychological and behavioral consequences of bioterrorism, AIDS, the Ricky Ray Hemophilia Relief Fund, long-term care, the Ryan White Act, the effect of the Tuskegee study on African Americans and research, and RU-486. The list of topics and the political and social history behind each one is rich with background and the politics of the time. Students must understand these histories to be better prepared to focus on the next steps for policy development in health care. Otherwise, we will make the same mistakes and lose the strength and power of what has come before. As stated after each policy topic, there is much to do.

I believe the student/practitioner/reader of this chapter has to decide both professionally and personally what matters . . . should the focus be on something small, like revamping a state's Medicaid policy, or large, like redesigning the entire way health care is delivered? Should we continue the path of market reform of the identified problems or create new ways, outside of the private, for profit sector, to handle our health crisis? There is certainly much political wrangling, both throughout history and today, about how changes should be made and how votes might be garnered by particular stances or ideas. I maintain, somewhat softly, that we appear to have enough data to show that the health system is failing and needs life support of its own. As seen from the policies presented above, many experts, professional groups, scientific organizations, and government agencies have sounded the alarm with solid data about the extreme problems of health care delivery in our country. We certainly had less hard data before beginning a war on terror. I advocate for a war on uninsured Americans. How do we make this a priority? One small path is to educate about the political past to plan for a better future.

Policy drives practice and all of the clinical training in the world cannot change this fact. The lesson plan in my health policy class is to discuss and explore a wide variety of policies in the hope that students will find one tiny policy that will pull them in and get them excited about how to be involved . . . the frightened and then inspired plan for action! Issues of social justice are in every single policy presented here. When students can understand how a policy works, where it came from, who it concerns, what politics are involved, and so on, they can then begin to work for change. The change may come in day-to-day practice awareness or in community involvement for new programs, or logging on to a website and getting involved in the creation of a new structure for how health care is delivered, or taking leadership around election platforms. The possibilities and strategies are plentiful (Jansson, 2004). The reasons for change are clear: too many die due to lack of health coverage and disparities. If we heard about these needless deaths as much as the lives lost in terrorist attacks or hurricanes, maybe some attention to the problem could take hold. We have a natural disaster unfolding every day in the United States through a lack of insurance and disparities. As we say, sometimes in jest and sometimes with great seriousness... what is wrong with this picture? Why are our political leaders not paying attention?

Key Terms

HMO, PPO, POS *Preexisting condition* *Uninsured*
  HDHP/Sos *Privilege and right* *Universal*

Review Questions for Critical Thinking

1. What effects do you expect to see as a result of the *Patient Protection and Affordable Care Act* in your community?

2. Is health care a universal right or a privilege?

3. Should the United States be bound by health-related conventions of the United Nations, such as those identified in the United Nation's 2015 Millennium Goals?

4. Should a person be able to legally elect euthanasia or physician-assisted suicide as an end-of-life option?

5. Should restructuring of the U.S. health care system continue with market-driven reforms of the identified problems or should the transformation of the health care system rely on the government?

Online Resources

Centers for Disease Control www.cdc.gov

Healthy People 2020 www.healthypeople.gov

National Hospice and Palliative Care Organization www.nhpco.org

Partnership for Prevention http://www.prevent.org/

World Health Organization www.who.int

References

Abraham, L. K. (1993). *Mama might be better off dead.* Chicago, IL: University of Chicago Press.

Abraido-Lanza, A. F., & Dohrenwend, B. P. (1999). The Latino mortality paradox: A test of the "salmon bias" and healthy migrant hypothesis. *American Journal of Public Health, 89* (10), 1543–1548.

Advocates for Youth. (2006). *Emergency contraception.* Retrieved from www .advocatesforyouth.org

August, M. (2003, June 2). A battle over the morning-after pill. *Time, 8.*

Bern-Klug, M. (2004). The ambiguous dying syndrome. *Health & Social Work, 29* (1), 55–65.

Bodenheimer, T. (1997). The Oregon health plan—Lessons for the nation. *New England Journal of Medicine, 337* (9), 651–723.

Bodenheimer, T. S., & Grumbach, K. (2005) *Understanding health policy.* New York, NY: McGraw-Hill.

California Catholic Conference. (2006). *California Supreme Court rules against Catholic Charities.* Retrieved from www.cacatholic.org/courtdecision.html

Children's Defense Fund. (n.d.). Uninsured children. Retrieved from http://www .childrensdefense.org/policy-priorities/childrens-health/uninsured-children/

Colby, W. H. (2002). *Long goodbye: The deaths of Nancy Cruzan.* Carlsbad, CA: Hay House.

Commonwealth of Massachusetts. (2006). Romney launches healthcare reform in Massachusetts. Retrieved from www.mass.gov

Countries Rank, 2012. (2012). Retrieved from http://www.photius.com/rankings

Davidoff, F. (2006). Sex, politics, and morality at the FDA: Reflections on the plan B decision. *Hastings Center Report, 36* (2), 20–25.

Dwyer, D. (April 8, 2011). Planned Parenthood at Center of Budget Shutdown Threat. Retreived from http://abcnews.go.com/Politics/planned-parenthood-center-budget-shutdown-threat/story?id=13328750

Enthoven, A., & Kronick, R. (1989). A consumer-choice health plan for the 1990s. *New England Journal of Medicine, 320* (1), 29–37.

FactCheck.org. Effect of Overturning *Roe v. Wade*. Retrieved from http://www .factcheck.org/2008/04/effect-of-overturning-roe-v-wade/

Fagerlin, A., & Schneider, C. E. (2004). Enough: The failure of the living will. *Hastings Center Report, 34* (2), 30–42.

Families USA: The Voice for Health Care Consumers. (2004). Gearing up: States face the new Medicare law; is your state ready for 2006? An introduction to what the new Medicare part D prescription drug benefit means for Medicaid. Retrieved from www.familiesusa.org/site/DocServer?docID=4401

Feldt, G. (2004). *The war on choice.* New York, NY: Bantam Books.

Gallup (2011). Texas and Mass. Still at Health Coverage Extremes in U.S. Retrieved from http://www.gallup.com/poll/149321/Texas-Mass-Health-Coverage-Extremes.aspx

Glick, H. R. (1992). *The right to die: Policy innovation and its consequences.* New York, NY: Columbia University Press.

Guttmacher Institute. (2006). State facts on about abortion, emergency contraception, and insurance coverage for contraceptives. Retrieved www.guttmacher.org

Haslett, D. C. (1997). Hull House and the birth control movement: An untold story. *Affilia, 12* (3), 261–277.

Healthy People 2010. What is healthy people 2010? Retrieved from www.healthy people.gov

Health, United States, *2010* (2011). Retrieved from http://www.cdc.gov/nchs/hus .htm

Henry J. Kaiser Family Foundation. (2010, April). *Health care spending in the United States and selected OECD countries April 2011.* Retrieved from http:// www.kff.org/insurance/snapshot/oecd042111.cfm

Iglehart, J. K. (1993). The end stage renal disease program. *New England Journal of Medicine, 328* (5), 366–371.

Institute for Energy and Environmental Research. (2002). About eighty thousand cancers in the United States, more than 15,000 of them fatal, attributable to fallout from worldwide atmospheric nuclear testing. Retrieved from www.ieer .org/comments/fallout/pr0202.html

Institute of Medicine. (2003). *Unequal treatment: Confronting racial and ethnic disparities in health care.* Washington, DC: National Academies Press.

Institute of Medicine. (2004). *Insuring America's health: Principles and recommendations.* Washington, DC: National Academies Press.

Ipas. (2006). The global problem of unsafe abortion. Retrieved from www.ipas .org

Jansson, B. S. (2004). *Becoming an effective policy advocate: From policy practice to social justice.* Pacific Grove, CA: Brooks/Cole.

Jones, R. K., Darroch, J. E., & Henshaw, S. K. (2002). Patterns in the socioeconomic characteristics of women obtaining abortions in 2000–2001. *Perspectives on Sexual and Reproductive Health, 34* (5), 226–235.

Katz, M. B. (1986). *In the shadow of the poorhouse.* New York, NY: Basic Books.

Kayler, L. K., Meier-Kriesche, H., Punch, J. D., Campbell, D. A., Leichtman, A. G., Magee, J. C.,... Merion, R. M. (2002). Gender imbalance in living donor renal transplantation. *Transplantation, 73* (2), 248–252.

Klein, J. D., & The Committee on Adolescence. (2005). Adolescent pregnancy: Current Trends and issues. *Pediatrics, 116* (1), 281–286.

Larkin, H. (2004). Justice implications of a proposed Medicare prescription drug policy. *Social Work, 49* (3), 406–414.

Lunch, W. (2005). Health policy. In R. A. Claus, M. Henkels, & B. S. Steel (Eds.), *Oregon politics and government.* Lincoln: University of Nebraska Press.

Makhijani, A., & Ledwidge, L. (2004, September 2). IEER letter to National Academy of Sciences committee that is assessing the radiation exposure screening and education program. Archived at www.ieer.org/comments/fallout/nasltr0904html

Mapes, J. (2003, December 5). Wyden, Wu test waters among constituents on Medicare bill. Oregonian, pp. A1, A15.

Mendes, E. (2012, January 24). More Americans uninsured in 2011. Retrieved from http://www.gallup.com/poll/152162/americans-uninsured-2011.aspx

Miller, P. J. (2000). Life after death with dignity: The Oregon experience. *Social Work, 45* (3), 263–271.

Miller, P. J., & Hedlund, S. C. (2005). "We just happen to live here": Two social workers share their stories about Oregon's death with dignity law. *Journal of Social Work in End-of-Life & Palliative Care, 1* (1), 71–86.

Miller, P. J., Hedlund, S. C., & Soule, A. (in press). Conversations at the end-of-life: The challenge to support patients who consider death with dignity in Oregon. *Journal of Social Work in End-of-Life & Palliative Care.*

Miller, P. J., & Mike, P. B. (1995). The Medicare hospice benefit: Ten years of federal policy for the terminally ill. *Death Studies, 19*, 531–542.

Miller, P. J., & Werth, J. L. (2005). Amicus curiae brief for the United States Supreme Court on mental health, terminal illness, and assisted death. *Journal of Social Work in End-of-Life & Palliative Care, 1* (4), 7–33.

Mor, V., Zinn, J., Angelelli, J., Teno, J. M., & Miller, S. C. (2005). Driven to tiers: Socio-economic and racial disparities in the quality of nursing home care. *Milbank Quarterly, 82* (2). Retrieved from www.milbank.org/quarterly/8202feat .html

National Academy of Sciences. (2005). *Assessment of the scientific information for the radiation exposure screening and education program.* Washington, DC: National Academies Press.

National Association of Social Workers. (2004). *Reproductive health disparities for women of color.* Retrieved from www.naswdc.org

National Commission on Prevention Priorities. (2006). *Priorities for America's health: Capitalizing on life-saving, cost-effective preventive services.* Retrieved from www.prevent.org/ncpp

National Hospice and Palliative Care Organization. (2006). *Hospice facts and figures.* Retrieved from www.nhpco.org

Nieves, E. (2006, February 23). S. D. abortion bill takes aim at "Roe." *Washington Post,* p. A01.

Nussbaum, S. R. (2006). Prevention: The cornerstone of quality care. *American Journal of Preventive Medicine.* Available at www.prevent.org/content/view/50/101

Oliver, T. R., Lee, P. R., & Lipton, H. L. (2004). A political history of Medicare and prescription drug coverage. *Milbank Quarterly, 82*(2), 283–354.

Oregon Department of Human Services, Health Services. (2006). *Eighth Annual Report On Oregon's Death with Dignity Act.* Portland, OR: Author. Retrieved from http://egov.oregon.gov/DHS/ph/pas/docs/year8/pdf

Palfreman, J. (Producer). (2003). *The other drug war* [Frontline]. Arlington, VA: PBS.

Pear, R. (2004, May 4). Agency sees withholding of Medicare data from Congress as illegal. *New York Times,* p. A17.

Pear, R., & Toner, R. (2003, November 18). Medicare plan covering drugs backed by AARP. *New York Times,* p. A1.

Planned Parenthood (n.d.). Planned Parenthood Condemns Unprecedented Suite of Attacks on Women's Health. Retrieved from http://www.plannedparenthood.org/about-us/newsroom/press-releases/planned-parenthood-condemns-unprecedented-suite-attacks-womens-health-39918.htm.

Schulman, K. A., Berlin, J. A., Harless, W., Kerner, J. F., Sistrunk, S., Gersh, B. J.,...Escarce, J. J. (1999). The effect of race and sex on physicians' recommendations for cardiac catheterization. *New England Journal of Medicine, 340*(8), 618–626.

Seifert, K. (1983). An exemplar of primary prevention in social work: The Sheppard-Towner Act of 1921. *Social Work in Health Care, 9*(1), 87–101.

Starfield, B. (2000). Is U. S. health really the best in the world? *Journal of the American Medical Association, 284*(4), 483–485.

Starr, P. (1982). *The social transformation of American medicine.* New York, NY: Basic Books.

Task Force to Improve the Care of Terminally-Ill Oregonians. (2006). *The Oregon Death with Dignity Act. A guidebook for health care providers.* Portland, OR: Author. Archived at www.ohsu.edu/ethics

United States Renal Data System. (2005). *Annual data report.* Retrieved from www.usrds.org/adr.htm

Weight of the nation (2012, May 14). HBO Productions.

Weissert, W. G. (2003). Medicare Rx: Just a few of the reasons why it was so difficult to pass. *Public Policy & Aging Report, 13*(4), 1, 3–6.

Wolinsky, H., & Brune, T. (1994). *The serpent on the staff: The unhealthy politics of the American Medical Association.* New York, NY: Putnam.

Chapter 7
Social Determinants of Health

21st-Century Social Work Priorities

Gary Rosenberg

> What will the social work profession look like in 2025?

Introduction

Some prognosticators see the profession of social work being vibrant, growing, and robust while its formal education continues to expand to hundreds of universities across the country. Others, much more pessimistic, might restate the question by asking: Will the social work profession be viable in 2025? The emergence of new "professional disciplines," which are slowly carving away and taking over some of the social work profession's traditional responsibilities, are gaining public legitimacy by state regulatory bodies that are adding new professional licenses to these developing disciplines. Life counselors, mental health workers, marriage and family therapists, and health navigators are examples of the national growth of the new professions.

Even with the introduction of new human service disciplines and the ongoing redefining of the scope and function of the social welfare system, the social work profession will continue to grow with the future focus on four areas: continued emphasis on the individual; alignment with public health; the growth of social development as a practice arena; and the fusion by social determinants of the profession's knowledge base with a new context that combines external political, economic, moral, and existential elements.

As the 21st century unfolded, two major change efforts attempted to shift the profession's sense of self and direction. First, social work education, through the Council on Social Work Education (CSWE), radically redesigned its accreditation standards. The second effort involved a meeting, which came to be known as *Wingspread,* of 10 social work professional associations, including among others the National Association of Social Workers (NASW) and CSWE.

CSWE's Commission on Accreditation redesigned its *Educational Policy and Curriculum Standards* (EPAS) to reflect a "competency-based" curriculum, which was further refined in 2008 (Council on Social Work Education [CSWE], 2008). Curriculum moved away from an "input" emphasis to an outcome model. A program's focus was now squarely on the students, achievement of 10 core competencies, with each competency assessed through a set of specific practice behaviors. The outcome approach opened the door to new possibilities of curriculum structure and student experience, though it mandated that there be a close engagement with the practice community to help students better understand the evolving needs in agencies. For the first time since CSWE was organized in 1962, graduate programs, with their focus on advanced specialized practice, EPAS, provided a great deal of latitude in developing unique, educational models; BSW programs, on the other hand, remained constrained to the same "generalist" model. One could infer from that the 2008 EPAS wanted graduate programs to "break the cookie-cutter mold" that has long handcuffed education and craft unique, progressive programs that could be responsive to the new world described in this chapter.

The June 2007 Wingspread Conference, held in Racine, Wisconsin, brought together 10 of the largest social work membership associations in an attempt to find common ground. There was a strong feeling that the profession had become fragmented with the growing number of professional membership groups. The actual number of membership associations was unknown, though estimates were that there are as many as 55 to 60 different social work groups. Essentially, no one group spoke for the profession and, as a result, a feeling of marginalization and malaise was quickly taking hold. Many thought that NASW represented the profession, yet with the U.S. Department of Labor reporting more than 600,000 social work positions nationwide, NASW's membership totaled approximately 150,000 or 25% of all degreed practitioners; by 2012, NASW membership dropped to 145,000 while the number of positions increased to 650,500. The Wingspread participants signed an agreement that stated "We resolve to create a unified profession with one social work organization by 2012" (Unification, 2007).Very quickly, the "politics" of the various professional associations came into play and the goal of Wingspread died—none of the groups was willing to merge into a new association for fear of losing its own identity.

In 2012, the social work profession remains disjointed and fragmented. Professional insecurity continues to chain the profession to an obsolete model that is irrelevant for the 21st century. Although the profession's educational arm has tried to move ahead, the overall fear of change holds all back.

This chapter identifies four points that set a new way for social work to remain relevant in the fast-changing, global economy. Even so, one cannot help but be struck by his recognition that the "individual" will continue to be the focus of the profession. Is this pandering to the power base within the profession? The strength of licensing/regulation practice laws in every state with the heavy emphasis on the individual, for example, clinical work, certainly must be recognized. Specht and Courtney's (1995) stinging critique that the profession lost its heart and soul resonates well into the 21st century. Has the construct of social justice merely become a "dashboard ornament," a talking point for the social work profession, or does it still strongly reverberate in all arenas of the profession? This is not to say that individual or private clinical work does not reflect a social justice model, however, the profession's aggressive move into private clinical work certainly diminishes such prospects. Why, as Specht and Courtney lamented, has the social work profession essentially moved away from the poor? Why is the profession not a leader in the current immigration policy debates or aggressively pursuing health care reform?

As the profession moved into the "therapy" world, other professions began to engage in practice that was once the domain of the social workers. Nurses began to take on many tasks that were once the sole province of medical social workers; today public health services, ostensibly through the U.S. Office of the Surgeon General and the Centers for Disease Control and Prevention, have evolved without the full engagement of the social work profession; certainly the entire arena of health disparities, especially projects funded by the NIH National Institute on Minority Health and Health Disparities, have only recently gained the attention of social work education.

Although Wingspread may have died, a worldwide effort in the social work community became reality in Spring 2012 with the adoption of the *Global Agenda for Social Work and Social Development, Commitment to Action.* Drafted by the three major international social work associations—the International Federation of Social Workers (IFSW), the International Association of Schools of Social Work (IASSW), and the International Council on Social Welfare (ICSW)—and adopted by major U.S., international, and numerous professional groups worldwide, the Global Agenda was presented to major political bodies including the United Nations. The Global Agenda resurrects the profession's mission by stating,

> *We commit ourselves to supporting, influencing and enabling structures and systems that positively address the root causes of oppression and inequality. We commit ourselves wholeheartedly and urgently to work together, with people who use services and with others who share our objectives and aspirations, to create a more socially-just and fair world that we will be proud to leave to future generations*

(The Global Agenda, 2012, p. 1).

This chapter encourages the profession to stake out a new, more relevant direction in the 21st century. Rather than relying on U.S.-based social work membership associations, which seem only concerned with their self-interests and survival, social workers will be better served by taking Rosenberg's lead and engage in the Global Agenda. Doing so will ensure the profession's relevancy and, most importantly, realize the outcomes of peace and justice for all people.

This chapter describes the state of health care social work as we enter the new millennium by reviewing selected dilemmas facing the profession at the end of the 19th and 20th centuries; identifies the issues facing social work as it develops locally, nationally, and globally; and describes the challenges and dilemmas that face health social work as it strives to maintain functionality in the future. I offer four hypotheses about the future of social work that are a mixture of what I believe and hope that social work becomes by the middle of this century. Space does not allow me to fully develop the implications for both residual and institutionally focused practice, so I emphasize institutional practice opportunities as I believe that they are less well developed and are required to balance the current social work profession's practice base so it can achieve its missions.

At the end of each millennium, social workers grappled with the accomplishments, disappointments, and issues facing the profession.

Social Work at the End of the 19th Century

The original aims of social work were to link persons in a social context, address economic and social needs, and achieve social justice. As a profession, social work has been considered responsible for assisting the poor, troubled persons, and working families (Morris, 2000a).

Two significant occurrences took place at the end of the 19th century that shaped early social work in the Anglo Saxon countries: the arrival of millions of European immigrants to the United States and the era of the progressive movement. The progressive movement was a middle-class movement advocating for social and political reform against the backdrop of political and economic corruption, the poor living arrangements among immigrants, the rise of socialist ideas, and the conditions adversely affecting women and children. There was a rapid growth of voluntary nonprofit organizations funded by religious communities and leaders in the business world. These agencies allowed social work to grow as an occupation due to the need for dedicated staff. The purpose of the private institutions was to escape the politically controlled governmental social welfare programs (Austin, 2000). These agencies provided charitable relief to the need, which included material relief, moral reform, and advice and counseling. As work became more complex coordinating agencies were formed. Charity organizations were a mix of secular and religious sponsorship (Austin, 2000; Midgley, 1995; Morris, 2000b).

At the end of the 19th century, the original social workers became advocates for those in need, while considering ways to alleviate daily sufferings (Hopps, 2000). The emergence of social sciences among academia permitted new consideration of applying science to social problems (Austin, 2000).

At the end of the 19th and beginning of the 20th-century settlement house workers, family visitors, union organizers, and community workers attacked the negatives, exposed injustices, and advocated for those in need. They wrote with passion and wisdom about the social structures that needed to be changed for people to thrive in their daily lives. They believed that social problems were caused by individual malfunctions as well as by social problems affecting the individual, and that those social ills could be remedied by counseling, through social changes in the community, and by affecting social policies (Harkavy & Puckett, 1994; Hopps, 2000).

At the beginning of the 20th century, social work faced three main issues in its development: (1) Should the social worker, as a motivated, organizational employee, be working in voluntary nonprofit organizations controlled by patrons of social work or work as an independent, educated, career-oriented women guided by professional principles?; (2) Should the social worker address social problems (i.e., poverty) through the individual approach and/or through public policy initiatives advocated by social scientists?; (3) Should the auspices of social work be as part of a governmental social welfare system resembling the European model or should the concept of social work as a diverse, nongovernmental social welfare system be based on the charitable contributions by wealthy individuals? (Austin, 2000; Midgley, 1995).

Social Work in the 20th Century

The 20th century was a period of growth of new agencies, less interested in social change than the cause and effect of social problems. These agencies functioned to ameliorate an individual's crisis and rarely considered the effectiveness of their services. Health and welfare agencies sought social workers as intermediaries to advocate for their agency, interpret the available services, along with how their clients could use them. Social work's case training made us well equipped for this undertaking; social work did not have the equipment and resources to do all it had aspired to. Few of the social work jobs required those wanting to make social changes. There was less attention to the reason for social injustices and little attempt at reducing the overall problem. Half of social work's purpose was disintegrating by the 1930s. One unintended consequence of this emphasis was the slow erosion of professional specialization in group work and community organization (Austin, 2000; Morris, 2000). By the 1960s, 85% of social work students chose to concentrate on casework and only 3% chose community organization. "This reflected what the schools continued to treat as the core or base for their generic approach to the profession and very likely what students preferred for a career" (Morris, 2000). Students' interest in individual casework meant half of social work's original approach to improve harmful societal conditions had lost some of its momentum (Morris, 2000). Globally, the nation state became the primary organizing unit for providing help to people (Midgley, 1997, 2001). Health social work became largely based in the health system in hospitals, health agencies, and nongovernmental organizations. Residual-oriented practice predominated. Inequities in health services continued, with barriers to access needed health services, poverty, homelessness, and hunger affecting world populations; social disorders reaching epidemic proportions; and diseases with known cures sustaining high incidence and prevalence.

At the end of the 20th century social work faced numerous dilemmas:

- Social workers retained a belief in their mission to speak and to work for social change, but that belief was expressed in the articulation of broad objectives by, for example, the National Association of Social Workers, which lacked the technical capability and could not have generated sufficient support to realize them (Morris, 2000b, p. 31).

- Social work in educational settings reflected a concern for social justice and psychological theories more so than other social sciences. This early focus separated social work from some social sciences, particularly economic theory (Austin, 2000; Haynes, 1998).

- Research is vital to the credibility of the profession. The profession faces challenges to prove that social work interventions are beneficial. It also must provide practice-based research for practice, organizations and for policy makers (McNeill, 2006; Rosen, 2003).

Unanswered questions include:

- Can social work education keep up with the fast changing social problems and their complexities as they affect individuals and communities? (Humphries, 2004; Mohan, 2005; Noble, 2004).

- How can social work integrate global health and knowledge regarding the effects of globalization? (Findlay & McCormack, 2005; Midgley, 2001).

- How does globalization impact social justice and does it provide us with an opportunity to respond with new approaches to ameliorate social problems? (Midgley, 2004).

These are some of the issues facing us as we enter the 21st century.

- Is it possible for social work to concentrate on helping individuals clinically and also intervene and advocate for more expansive humane social welfare policies? (Briar-Lawson, 1998; Buchbinder, Eisikovits, & Karnieli-Miller, 2004).

- Can social work engage in case and class advocacy? (Abramovitz, 1998).

- What effect will globalization have on social work practice and education? (Sewpaul, 2004; Van Wormer, 2004).

- Can social work define social justice in operational terms?

- Is social justice the organizing value of social work?

- How do we respond to the economic restructuring and radical changes in welfare policy and the increasing dislocation and disadvantage for women, minority populations, and youth? youth (Noble, 2004)?

- How do we reconcile the long-standing problems among the research, education, and practice worlds?

- Can we reconcile and apply practice-based research and research-based practice? (Peake & Epstein, 2005).

Based on these questions and the unresolved issues facing the profession, here are four hypotheses about the future of social work.

Hypothesis 1. The Profession of Social Work Will Continue to Emphasize Methodological Individualism in Practice, Education, and Research

Social work has not resolved the fundamental conflicts between the remedial approach and its focus on methodological individualism and a focus on social reform and enactment of institutional provisions. Methodological individualism is drawn from epidemiologic studies of populations and may be best characterized as health and its its correlates are intrinsically tied to and best defined through individual characteristics (Blazer, 2005; Diez-Roux, 1998). Throughout social work's history and depending on the theories of social and individual problems and illnesses prevalent at the time, different aspects of individuals and their environments have been considered important in explaining problems and designing interventions to reach solutions to these problems. In health care the growing importance of chronic and infectious diseases led to the search for new causal factors, and medical and even public health research shifted to a focus on behavioral and biologic characteristics as risk factors for those diseases. Social work, with its emphasis on people and their environment, emphasized individual factors but did look at environmental factors as they affected individuals. The individuation of risk has perpetuated the idea that risk is individually determined. Lifestyle and behaviors are regarded as matters of individual choice and dissociated from the social contexts that shape and constrain them (Blazer, 2005; Haynes, 1998; Swenson, 1998).

Clinical social work health and mental health have developed sophisticated methodology and increased research evidence of its effectiveness (Proctor, 2002, 2004; Reid, Kenaley, & Colvin, 2004; Rosen, 2003). Social work research in health will, in the future, expand its focus to include group or macro-level variables and epidemiological studies that incorporate multiple levels of determination in the study of health and social work outcomes. By using these types of analyses, we can develop theoretical models that extend across levels and explain how social level and individual level variables interact in shaping health and disease. This kind of research can lead to an emphasis on social and economic factors that can focus social work toward social change as well as change focused on the individual. For example, we frequently observe an individual's level of income, but by also looking at mean neighborhood income we may be able to establish markers for neighborhood factors related to health, such as recreational facilities, school quality, road conditions, environmental conditions, and the types of available food—factors that affect everyone in the neighborhood regardless of income. Community unemployment levels likewise can affect all people in a community regardless of whether they are unemployed. To conduct such research and to provide new practice models for health social work, we develop, refine, and test theories that integrate micro- and macro-level variables and explain these relationships and interactions across levels (Blazer, 2005; Diez-Roux, 1998).

Helpful concepts include structural determination defined as "the process by which behavior of an individual (that is a person in a social group) is determined by the overall structure of the collection to which it belongs" (Bunge, 1979), and to think of "cause not as a property of agents, but one of systems in which the population phenomena of health and disease occur and to conceive populations as organized groups with relational properties rather than mere aggregates of individuals" (Loomis & Wing, 1990). This suggestion for future work does not exclude the continuation or appropriateness of testing social influences on the individuals. It is the integration of these levels that is our future task.

The practice of psychotherapy is another example of the belief in methodological individualism. In the United States we project the mood of depression into biological processes, such as a chemical imbalance, and then turn to biology to validate that mood is natural and unique to the individual. Regardless of biological vulnerability, most first episodes of major depression are closely associated with a stressful life event such as economic turndowns, job loss, victimization due to crime, trauma, and other events often out of the control of the individual. The social origins of health and disease seem to have marginal interest to those proponents of the biological origins of health and disease. Attention to social factors has been restricted to assessing individual social risk factors, such as stressful life events, or individual social outcomes of illnesses such as loss of employment or disruption of the family, making the target of intervention the individual and not the social problem or pattern. A number of researchers have raised the issues of producing knowledge for control, such as how change occurs, does change produce desired outcomes, and can beneficial change be deliberately produced. In a social context statistical analysis for social intervention is multilevel, with the use of spatial statistics and econometrics (Diez-Roux, 1998). A communities focus in the research advances scientific knowledge about how and why communities change. With a communities focus, the practice moves toward a greater understanding of health for all rather than for a single individual and provide the practicing social worker with knowledge about how to strengthen communities for human development and for social justice (Coulton, 2005; Snowden, 2005). Population thinking can inform us about factors operating at a social and community level; how social capital theory and research can illuminate prosocial norms; and how community level theory and research can inform policy. Prosocial norms combine economic theories of rational action with sociological theories of social structure and anthropological theories of interaction and exchange in social networks (Blazer, 2005; Diez-Roux, 1998; Midgley, 1995).

Social workers are located within the health and public health structures, and in nongovernment organizations, whose missions are the improvement of the human condition. It is unlikely that these structural conditions will change for the vast majority of employed workers or for the schools of social work that must meet their own admissions projections and economic demands of their universities. Health organizations are provided with economic incentives that focus on effective treatment more so than prevention, and the definitions of health are narrow and without understanding of social level variables. We will develop the knowledge about programmatic interventions for empowerment and community participation that recognize that how people live and organize their lives because of their social conditions is a target of intervention, and that theories invoking and reflecting upon the social and relational aspects of social work practice is the core knowledge base of the future (Berkman, 2004; Midgley, 1995).

Hypothesis 2. Social Work Will Align Itself With Public Health Efforts, Particularly in a Global Context

Social work and public health are concerned with health, prevention, policy formulation and advocacy, and share an ecological practice base. There are numerous existing joint degree programs and an increasing number in the planning stages. Social work and public health professionals are struggling with the inclusion of and repositioning of the importance of social determinants of health. Public health, like social work, has its theoretical foundation based largely on behavioral psychology, biomedical science, and public administration (Berkman, 2005; Potvin, Gendron, Bilodeau, & Chabot, 2005). Both professions are likely to recognize a knowledge base situated more coherently within a theoretical perspective that seeks to understand and guide the contemporary world. Social theory is likely the way that both professions will attempt to reconcile their practitioners, decision makers, and researchers (Hartman, 1990; Potvin et al., 2005; Ungar, 2002). It is this convergence of interests that a closer relationship and partnership is likely to develop between social work and public health.

Both professions have adopted a practice focus to collectively assure the conditions in which people can be healthy. The conditions are the social determinants of health including but not limited to access to affordable healthy food, potable water, safe housing, and supportive social networks. Social determinants of health broadly speaking refer to social, economic, and political resources and structures that influence health outcomes (Berkman & Kawachi, 2000).

Both professions value equity defined as the absence of avoidable and unfair differences in the determinants and manifestations of good health and longevity between the most vulnerable groups and groups that are well off. Both professions are attempting to adopt a framework for social inclusion to guide the implementation of policies and practices that reduce inequities related to income, race, gender, ethnicity, geographic location age ability and sexual orientation. The convergence of social work and public health is best understood by the following questions raised by Rosen and carried forward by Berkman (2004). Why do some individuals have hypertension? Is quite a different question from: How come some populations have much hypertension while in others it is rare? Both are targets of intervention.

Social work will gain from a public health perspective through the use of epidemiology, a focus on prevention, and a focus on populations. Public health will gain a clearly articulated social development perspective and technology, psychosocial perspective and methodology, increased understanding of individual, family, and group behaviors, and methods of change in communities. Working together in a local, national, and global level, we will be able to better identify those broad social, economic, cultural, health, and environmental conditions and look beyond biological risk factors and conduct transdisciplinary research and practice.

Hypothesis 3. A Social Development Specialty Track Will Emerge and Link Social Policies, Programs, and Economic Development

Social workers developed different practice ideologies in part due to the ever-changing social and economic environment and the rapidly changing contexts of practice. "Globalization has created new opportunities for international collaboration in the political arena where the potential of governments is to address pressing economic and social problems collectively" (Midgley, 1995). If social work is to respond to the global health problems and issues already present in today's world, it will augment its current emphasis on remedial approaches and methodological individualism with a return to its settlement house and community organization roots by adopting an institutional set of practices that link economic and social needs with integrated programs in partnerships with governments, NGOs, foundations, and communities.

Midgley and others have described how social development seeks to enhance human well-being in the context of an ongoing process of development. Social development is a process of planned social change designed to promote the well-being of the population as a whole in conjunction with a dynamic process of economic development (Midgley, 1997). Social development seeks to create formal organizations and institutional arrangements by which economic and social policies can be better integrated and by ensuring that economic development has a direct impact on the social well-being of all citizens. Reciprocally, social development encourages the formulation of social policies and programs that contribute to economic development. Investments in health care and public health, for example, can increase productivity and obviate the social and economic costs associated with debilitating diseases. Remedial social service programs can enhance and support economic development as a part of social development because they invest in human capital so important to the economic and social development of communities and countries. Social development is characterized by the following statements:

- It is a link to economic development.
- It is interdisciplinary/transdisciplinary.
- There is a defined process.
- It is progressive in nature.
- It is interventionalist.
- It is strategic.
- It is inclusive and universalistic in scope.
- Its goal is the promotion of social welfare. (Midgley, 1995)

It is beyond the scope of this paper to more fully describe the processes of social development and its social welfare roots. Its applications to our global economy and the social problems resulting from people and family disruptions, community upheavals, and preventable health problems will provide the profession with another set of methods that strive for social justice in an institutional framework. "Social development is best promoted when governments play a positive role in facilitating, coordinating and directing the efforts of diverse groups of individuals, groups and communities, and effectively utilizing the market community and state to promote social development" (Midgley, 1995).

Hypothesis 4. Social Determinants of Health Across the Life Span Will Unite the Profession's Knowledge Base With Economic and Political Factors and Moral and Existential Values

By teaching social workers developments from the social sciences, particularly those concepts, findings, and theories that inform about population patterns and variation, we can expand our knowledge base for residual and institutional practice.

Social determinants of health have their roots in social epidemiology, particularly those aspects that focus on social inequalities and their contributions to health, disease and disability (Berkman & Kawachi, 2000). To understand social determinants of health we must use data from:

- Global comparisons
- Within country differences
- Studies of individuals
- Studies from biological processes in animals and humans (Gehlert & Browne, 2006)

A number of social factors have been shown to influence the health of individuals and populations. They include:

- Socioeconomic position
- Income distribution
- Discrimination related to race, ethnicity, or gender
- Social network/social support
- Social capital and community cohesion
- Work environment
- Life transitions
- Affective psychological states (Berkman & Kawachi, 2000)

By concentrating on social inequalities, social workers will gain new knowledge on how society shapes the health of people. The characteristics of social determinants of health include a population perspective that emphasizes the social context in understanding individual behavior and operates on multiple social levels. "The enterprise of understanding the social determinants of health entails an understanding of how society operates, an appreciation of the major causes of diseases, an understanding of psychological processes and how they interact with biological mechanisms, and a readiness to learn from animal models" (Gehlert & Browne, 2006; (McLintock, Conzen, Gehlert, Masi, & Olopade, 2005).

Conclusions

The location of social work in hospitals and other health agencies, which currently limit the profession to important remedial work, will be, in the future, augmented by population focused, community-based practice and on social determinants of health and illness as a major knowledge base for the profession. The use of transdisciplinary teams of social, behavioral, and biological researchers will work to add to the knowledge base for social work practice for the future by addressing social, behavioral, and biological issues in the same analysis. Through transdisciplinary teams, we will develop a shared language with our colleagues, pool the best disciplinary theories and develop analyses that include a wide range of social, economic, psychological, and biological factors (Gehlert & Browne, 2006). Support in the United States for this approach comes from the NIH Centers for Population Health and Health Disparities Initiatives and the studies from their eight centers. One social work professor leads one center at the University of Chicago, and is interested in health disparities. She hypothesized that social isolation might affect the epigenetic regulation of breast cancer gene expression. She based her hypothesis on three sources; (1) socially isolated elders living in settings whose social ecology inhibited social interactions were more likely to have died during the 1995 heat wave than nonisolated elderly; (2) a study of 826 women waiting to receive mammograms were asked about their social situations and those who subsequently developed breast cancer had reported more isolation than those who developed fibrocystic breast disease or remained disease free; (3) social isolation was found to be associated with mammary cancer in animal models. She and her colleagues are working on the molecular pathways between social stressors and mammary tumor development while other social workers are examining community concerns, attitudes, and beliefs about breast cancer and its treatment and are conducting further research on the environmental determinants of social isolation. Efforts such as these will inform the social work practitioner, strengthen the understanding of social variables, and broaden the practice base of social work in its remedial and institutional forms (McLintock, Conzen, Gehlert, Masi, & Olopade, 2005).

There are many unsolved issues that will affect our future and the future of those we serve. Many in our world are without basic public health services. How do we reconcile local national and global priorities in health? Can schools of social work take on the tasks of educating social workers for competence in social development? When is it most useful to use evidence-based practice with its roots in logical positivism and/or practice-based research a reflective practice approach? Can social work organizations maximize the input of clients and workers as a core strategy to achieve organizational effectiveness? Can we contribute to enacting the concept of human rights by helping to restructure health systems so that health for all at a basic level can be achieved? It seems to me that we must achieve the answer to these questions in this century.

Recently the papers of Reverend Dr. Martin Luther King Jr. have become public. As King grappled with understanding social issues he wrote,

> On the one hand I must attempt to change to soul of individuals so that their societies may be changed. On the other hand I must attempt to change societies so that the individual soul will have a change. Therefore I must be concerned about unemployment, slums and economic insecurity. O am a profound advocator of the social gospel. (Jackson, 2006)

I hope that this chapter provides for discussion about the best ways for our profession to proceed into the future. As Goethe said, "Knowing is not enough; we must apply. Willing is not enough; we must do" (quoted in Berkman, 2004).

Key Terms

Future states
Public health

Social determinants
of health

Social development
Wingspread

Review Questions for Critical Thinking

1. What do you see for the future of the social work profession?

2. To what extent do you see that social development will become a major practice arena for the social work profession?

3. Does the Global Agenda have relevancy for U.S.-based social work practice? If so, how? If not, why not?

4. Is it possible for social work to concentrate on helping individuals clinically and also intervene and advocate for more expansive humane social policies and services?

5. Is social justice one of the core organizing values of social work, for example, not just a "dashboard ornament," and, if so, how can the profession define social justice in operational terms?

Online Resources

Bureau of Labor Statistics, Health Care Social Workers http://www.bls .gov/oes/current/oes211022.htm

Global Agenda for Social Work and Social Development http://ifsw.org/ get-involved/agenda-for-social-work/

History of Social Work http://historyofsocialwork.org/eng/index.php

National Institute on Minority Health and Health Disparities http:// www.nimhd.nih.gov/

Social Determinants of Health http://www.who.int/social _determinants/en/

References

Abramovitz, M. (1998). Social work and social reform: An arena of struggle. *Social Work in Health Care, 43* (6), 512–526.

Austin, D. M. (2000). Greeting the second century: A forward look from a historical perspective. In J. G. Hopps & R. Morris (Eds.), *Social work at the millennium* (pp. 18–41). New York, NY: Free Press.

Berkman, L. (2004). *The future of public health in the 21st century: The role of social determinants.* Presented at the University of Washington, School of Social Work, Spokane, WA, on February 27, 2004.

Berkman, B., Gardner, D., Zodikoff, B., & Harootyan, L. (2005). Social work in health care with older adults: Future challenges. *Families in Society, 86* (4).

Berkman, L., & Kawachi, I. (Eds.). (2000). *Social epidemiology. Oxford University Press.* NY: New York.

Blazer, D. G. (2005). *The age of melancholy: Major depression and its social origins.* New York, NY: Routledge.

Briar-Lawson, K. (1998). Capacity building for integrated family-centered practice. *Social Work in Health Care, 43* (6), 539–550.

Buchbinder, E., Eisikovits, Z., & Karnieli-Miller, O. (2004). Social workers' perceptions of the balance between the psychological and the social. *Social Service Review, 78*(4), 531–553.

Bunge, M. (1979). The Scientific Philosophy of Mario Bunge. Retrieved from http://www.ontology-2.com/pdf/bungem.pdf

Coulton, C. J. (2005). The place of community in social work practice research: Conceptual and methodological developments. *Social Work Research*, 29, 73–86.

Council on Social Work Education. (2008). Educational policy and accreditation standards. Retrieved from http://www.cswe.org/File.aspx?id = 13780

Diez-Roux, A. V. (1998). Bringing context back into epidemiology: Variables and fallacies in multilevel analysis. *American Journal of Public Health, 88*(2). 216–223.

Findlay, M., & McCormack, J. (2005). Globalization and social work: A snapshot of Australian practitioners' views. *Australian Social Work, 58*(3), 231–243.

Gehlert, S., & Browne, T. A. (2006). *Handbook of health social work.* New York, NY: Wiley.

Global Agenda for Social Work and Social Development, Commitment to Action, (2012, March). Retrieved from http://www.cswe.org/File.aspx?id = 57726

Harkavy, I., & Puckett, J. L. (1994). Lessons from Hull House for the contemporary urban university. *Social Service Review, 68*(3), 299–321.

Hartman, A. (1990). Our global village. *Social Work, 35*(4), 291–292.

Haynes, K. S. (1998). The one hundred-year debate: Social reform versus individual treatment. *Social Work in Health Care, 43*(6), 501–511.

Hopps, J. G. (2000). Social work: A contextual profession. In J. G. Hopps & R. Morris (Eds.), *Social work at the millennium* (pp. 3–4). New York, NY: Free Press.

Humphries, B. (2004). An unacceptable role for social work: Implementing immigration policy. *British Journal of Social Work, 34*, 93–107.

Jackson, D. Z. (2006, November 30). A King we never knew. *International Herald Tribune,* p. 7.

Loomis, D. and Wing, S (1990). Is Molecular Epidemiology a Germ Theory for the End of the Twentieth Century? *International Journal of Epidemiology. 19*(1): 1–3.

McClintock, Martha K., Conzen, Suzanne D., Gehlert, Sarah, Masi, C., & Olopade, O. (2005). Mammary cancer and social interactions: Identifying multiple environments that regulate gene expression throughout the life span. *Journals of Gerontology: Series B, 60B* (Special Issue), pp. 32–41.

McNeill, T. (2006, April). Evidence-based practice in an age of relativism: Toward a model for practice. *Social Work, 51*(2), 147–156.

Midgley, J. (1995). *Social development: The developmental perspective in social welfare.* London, United Kingdom: Sage.

Midgley, J. (1997). *Social welfare in global context.* Thousand Oaks, CA: Sage.

Midgley, J. (2001). Issues in international social work: Resolving critical debates in the profession. *Journal of Social Work, 1*(1), 21–35.

Midgley, J. (2004). The complexities of globalization: Challenges to social work. In N.-T. Tan & A. Rowlands (Eds.), *Social work around the world III* (pp. 13–29). Bern, Switzerland: International Federation of Social Workers.

Mohan, B. (2005). New internationalism: Social work's dilemmas, dreams and delusion. *International Social Work, 48*(3), 241–250.

Morris, R. (2000a). Introduction. In J. G. Hopps & R. Morris (Eds.), *Social work at the millennium.* New York, NY: Free Press.

Morris, R. (2000b). Social work: Century of evolution as a profession. In J. G. Hopps & R. Morris (Eds.), *Social work at the millennium* (pp. 42–72). New York, NY: Free Press.

Noble, C. (2004). Postmodern thinking: Where is it taking social work? *Journal of Social Work, 4*(3), 289–304.

Peake, K., & Epstein, I. (2005). Theoretical and practice imperatives for reflective social work organizations for mental health. In K. Peake, I. Epstein, & D. Medeiros (Eds.), *Clinical and research uses of an adolescent mental health intake questionnaire* (pp. 23–39). New York, NY: Haworth Press.

Potvin, L., & Gendron, S., Bilodeau, A., & Chabot, P. (2005). Integrating social theory into public health practice. *American Journal of Public Health, 95*(4), 591–601.

Proctor, E. K. (2002). Quality of care and social work research. *Social Work Research, 26*(4), 195–197.

Proctor, E. K. (2004). Research to inform mental health practice: Social work's contributions. *Social Work Research, 28*(4): 195–197.

Reid, W. J., Kenaley, B. D., & Colvin, J. (2004). Do some interventions work better than others? A review of comparative social work experiments. *Social Work Research, 28*(2), 71–81.

Rosen, A. (2003). Evidence-based social work practice: Challenges and promise. *Social Work Research, 27*(4), 197–208.

Sewpaul, V. (2005). Global standards: Promise and pitfalls for reinscribing social work into civil society. *International Journal of Social Welfare, 14*, 210–217.

Snowden, L. R. (2005). Racial, cultural and ethnic disparities in health and mental health: Toward theory and research at community levels. *American Journal of Community Psychology, 35*(1/2), 1–8.

Specht, H., & Courtney, M. (1995). *Unfaithful angels: How social work has abandoned its mission.* New York, NY: Free Press.

Swenson, C. R. (1998). Clinical social work's contribution to a social justice perspective. *Social Work in Health Care, 43*(6), 527–538.

Ungar, M. (2002). A deeper, more social ecological social work practice. *Social Service Review, 76*(3), 480–498.

Unification of the social work profession (2007, December 18). Retrieved from http://www.sswr.org/unification.php

Van Wormer, K. (2004). Globalization, work and social work in the USA. In N.-T. Tan & A. Rowlands (Eds.), *Social work around the World III* (pp. 48–60). Bern, Switzerland: International Federation of Social Workers.

Chapter 8
Property for People or the Property of People

Urban Housing Policy and Practice in the Developing World

Sunil Kumar

> Are the challenges to urban housing policy and practice a challenge of resources, technical know-how and institutional capacity, or are they largely one of political will?

Introduction

Possessing safe, secure, and consistent shelter is recognized as a fundamental need for all people. Yet, according to UN-Habitat in 2010, there are 827.6 million people worldwide living in slums and this number is projected to grow to 889 million people by 2020. In the United States, the National Coalition for the Homeless notes that it is impossible to capture an exact number of people who are homeless, but it is estimated that 3.5 million people experience homelessness each year. Quite clearly, lack of safe, secure, and consistent housing is a problem that crosses all geographic borders and continues to grow in sheer numbers. The United States Interagency Council on Homelessness (USICH) 2010 report, *Opening Doors, Federal Strategic Plan to Prevent and End Homelessness,* notes that "no one should be without a safe, stable place to call home" and sets as a goal to prevent and end chronic homelessness by 2014, prevent and end homelessness among veterans by 2015, and to prevent and end homelessness for families, youth, and children by 2020. As part of the 2009 American Recovery and Reinvestment Act, $1.5 billion was set aside to support the Homelessness Prevention and Rapid Re-Housing Program. Although the amount is only one small piece to the housing crisis in the United States, early research reports show positive results. Yet, the magnitude of the worldwide housing crisis is overwhelming. The issue takes on even greater significance as the worldwide "occupy" movements challenge governments to do more regarding the redistribution of resources while creating fair revenue streams. What should a government's response be to its housing situation, be it the growing number of people who live in slums or on the streets? Should this be a priority of the national government or are the best solutions found locally in a city or township? To what extent should banks and other financial institutions be engaged in securing safe, secure, and stable housing for all people? Or, should housing be left to the so-called free market economy?

This chapter on urban housing policy and practice in the developing world has three aims. First, it argues why there is an urgent need to focus on urban housing policy and practice in developing and transitional economies. The second aim is to demonstrate the fragmented nature of housing policy and practice in the developing world. In doing so, reference is made to key housing policy interventions. The third and final aim of this chapter is to provide some out-of-the-box thinking on ways in which this fragmentation can be overcome.

This chapter does not profess to provide definite answers but rather to reframe the questions that need to be asked, for as the saying goes, it is better to ask the right questions than provide answers to the wrong questions. To that end, three main questions are posed. First, and foremost, what should the starting point be in addressing the housing-policy-and-practice challenges in less developed regions. So far it has been housing itself but it will be argued that this is the wrong starting point. Urbanization, beginning with rural to urban migration, is an attempt by the poor to reduce vulnerabilities and enhance capabilities, the latter used in the manner intended by Sen (1993). But what are their prospects in such an attempt? With 48% of North Africans, 72% of Sub-Saharan Africans, 51% of Latin Americans, and 65% of Asians of all nonagricultural employment being in the so-called informal economy (self-employed, causal wage employment, and contract and piece-rate work) (International Labour Office [ILO], 2002b), with low and precarious wages devoid of even the basic forms of social security and protection — this has to be one of the key starting points. Moreover, if urbanization is now more the result of urban growth than migration, it is not surprising that urban poverty will become a considerable feature of cities.

Second, should the exclusive focus of housing policy and practice be on making all those who live in cities owner-occupiers? Although this is a laudable end, the means do not lay in a blind attempt to conferring ownership rights, especially to those who are not able to afford it. There is a sizeable body of literature on housing tenure that has convincingly argued that housing that provides mixed tenure can act as a ladder of upward mobility (Gilbert, 1991; Gilbert & Varley, 1989b; Kumar, 1996a, 1996c, 2001a, 2001b, 2002; UNCHS, 1993). This second question is not only directly linked to the first on labor market opportunities, but also has a substantial political dimension that is not helped by a large section of not-for-profits not accepting the diverse tenure argument.

The third and final question is whether the current strategies of partnerships between not-for-profit organizations and the state or partnerships between the public and the private sectors are taking the easier path of providing visible progress to the detriment of holding the state and society to account for the widespread inequality in the size of housing lots that the poor occupy, communal water and sanitation rather than services being available at the individual household level, and a voice in choosing where they live.

An Urban World—Why Fresh Thinking on Urban Housing Practice and Policy in Less Developed Regions Matters

There is a need to first identify the issues that give rise to the housing policy and practice challenges for the 21st century. Because housing is primarily about people, households, and communities, one cannot but begin with the issue of changing population distributions. The first issue of significance is the shift in the distribution of population between more and less developed regions. Of the projected world population of 9.1 billion in the year 2050, only 14% (1.2 billion) would be living in the more developed regions while the remaining 86% (7.8 billion) would live in less developed regions.[1] Thus, although this represents a 28% increase in the world's population compared to 2006, the staggering fact is that the population in less developed regions would have increased by 32% whereas the population of those living in more developed regions would have increased by only 2%.

A second significant issue is the changes in the distribution of population between rural and urban areas. In 2006, just under one half of the world's population lived in urban areas. The United Nations Population Fund (UNFPA) reported that in 2008, the majority of the world's population, 3.3 billion people, lived in cities—a first in the humankind—and will grow to 5 billion people by 2030 (UNFPA, 2007). Although the share of the urban population in more developed regions was 74% and that in less developed regions 43% in 2005, the projections are that the urban population share of the latter will be more than 50% by the year 2020. Of much greater concern is the prediction that cities of the developing world will absorb 95% of urban growth in the next two decades, and by 2030 will be home to almost 4 billion people or 80% of the world's population (UN-Habitat, 2006, p. viii).

Inextricably linked to the changes in the distribution of population and housing is an equally significant issue of poverty and inequality. Poverty is a worldwide phenomenon—for example, it is estimated that in the United States, 43.6 million people (15.1%) or one in six people were living in poverty in 2010 (Stanglin, 2011). In the United Kingdom poverty figures are based on the concept of relative poverty[2] — 11.5 million (20%) were below the relative poverty line in 2004–2005 (Poverty Site, 2007). For some developing countries, the proportion of those in absolute poverty, based on their

Table 8.1 People Living on Less Than $1.25 a Day (Millions)

Region	1981	1984	1987	1990	1993	1996	1999	2002	2005
East Asia and Pacific	1,072	947	822	873	845	622	635	507	316
China	634	425	308	375	334	212	223	180	208
Europe and Central Asia	3	2	2	2	17	20	30	10	17
Latin America and Caribbean	36	46	45	49	52	52	54	47	45
Middle East and North Africa	9	8	7	6	4	5	8	5	11
South Asia	475	460	473	462	476	461	429	437	596
Sub-Saharan Africa	164	198	219	227	242	271	294	303	388
India	420	416	428	435	444	442	447	460	456
Total	**1,482**	**1,277**	**1,171**	**1,218**	**1,208**	**1,097**	**1,096**	**1,015**	**1,373**

Table 8.2 Share of People Living on Less Than $1.25 a Day (%)

Region	1981	1984	1987	1990	1993	1996	1999	2002	2005
East Asia and Pacific	77.7	65.5	54.2	54.7	50.8	36.0	35.5	27.6	16.8
China	84.0	69.4	54.0	60.2	53.7	35.4	35.6	28.4	15.9
Europe and Central Asia	1.8	1.4	1.1	2.1	4.4	4.8	5.3	4.8	3.8
Latin America and Caribbean	12.9	15.3	13.7	11.3	10.1	10.9	10.9	10.7	8.2
Middle East and North Africa	7.9	6.1	5.7	4.3	4.1	4.1	4.2	3.6	3.6
South Asia	59.4	55.6	54.2	51.7	46.9	47.1	44.1	43.8	40.3
Sub-Saharan Africa	53.4	55.8	54.5	57.6	56.9	58.8	58.4	55.0	50.9
India	59.8	55.5	53.6	51.3	49.4	46.6	44.8	43.9	41.6
Total	**52.2**	**47.0**	**42.1**	**42.0**	**39.5**	**34.7**	**33.9**	**30.7**	**25.3**

Source: World Bank, 2009.

national poverty lines, is less than the United States or the United Kingdom (China, 4.6%, 1998; Jordan, 11.7%, 1997; and Tunisia, 7.6%, 1995). However, for the vast majority of the others, poverty is extensive. According to the World Bank's 2009 World Development Indicators for poverty, for the 96 countries that national poverty figures are available, three countries had more than 70% in poverty, 18 had between 50% and 69%, 28 had between 30% and 49%, and the remaining below 30%. Table 8.1 and 8.2 provide changes in the national proportions of the poor according to the international poverty line of $1.25/day/person, used by the World Bank.

It must be noted that the poverty figures from the World Bank are being questioned. Researchers have drawn on other data to argue that the poor are close to 2 billion as against the figure of 1 billion by the World Bank (see the discussion in Townsend, 2007).

Despite the significance of the differences in the estimation of the poor and although the majority of the poor in developing countries live in rural areas, there is evidence that the proportion of the poor is on the increase in urban areas — a phenomenon a number of commentators have termed the *urbanization of poverty*. For example, in 1999, although 64% of rural Latin

Table 8.3 **Population Below the National Poverty Line**

Country	Survey Year	Rural %	Urban %
Georgia	2003	52.7	56.2
Azerbaijan	2001	42	55
Armenia	2001	48.7	51.9
Mongolia	2002	43.4	30.3
Kenya	1997	53	49
Nigeria	1992–93	36.4	30.4
India	1999–00	30.2	24.7

Source: World Bank, 2009.

Americans were poor compared to 34% of their urban counterparts, 64% of all its poor lived in urban areas.

Table 8.3 lists some of the countries where the proportion of the rural poor is less than the proportion of the urban poor and three countries—Kenya, Nigeria, and India—where the proportion of the rural poor is only slightly more than the urban poor (between 4 and 6 percentage points).

The World Bank's World Development Report 2000–2001, *Attacking Poverty* (2000), acknowledges the work of a number of academics and researchers who have argued that neither income nor consumption measures of poverty are in themselves able to adequately capture the multidimensional nature of poverty—which encompass a range of deprivations and vulnerabilities. There is thus the need to include other dimensions such as longevity, literacy, and more recently asset deprivations: risk, vulnerability, powerlessness, and lack of voice (Baulch, 1996; Moser, 1998; Rakodi, 1995b). Concerns have also been expressed about the need to understand the differences between the causes of urban and rural poverty (Wratten, 1995). Satterthwaite (2001), for example, argues that large cities have particularly high costs of transportation, education, housing, water, sanitation, health care, and medicines and payment of various bribes and fines—resulting in the World Bank's international poverty line of $1.25 per person per day not capturing this additional spending required on nonfood essentials.

Keeping in line with this broader definition of urban poverty, UN-Habitat uses five criteria, as an operational definition of slums, to define shelter deprivation—lack of water, lack of sanitation, overcrowding, nondurable housing structures, and lack of security of tenure (UN-Habitat, 2006). Although the latter is more difficult to establish, the first four are physically verifiable indicators of shelter deprivation. Although the world's slum population has remained relatively constant at approximately 31.3% between 1990 and 2010, the actual number of people has increased from 715 million in 1990 to 827.6 million in 2010. Based on the current growth rate of the slum population, it is estimated that the world's slum population will reach 889 million by 2020 (UN-Habitat, 2009).

Planet of Slums—Why Poor Urban Housing Conditions Is Not All That Matters

Urbanization in the developing world has for at least the last half of the 20th century been characterized by a strikingly visible form of urban poverty—namely, the juxtapositioning of small residential areas of high-quality housing and services with sprawling illegal or quasi-legal[3] residential areas of very poor housing and services. The concept of slums is not new as the early experience of Europe and North America indicates—what is new is the rate at which squatter and slum formation is taking place. According to the *State of the World's Cities 2006–07,* Sub-Saharan Africa is already home to more than half of the world's slum population (195 million). It is followed by Southern Asia with 190.7 million (35%), Eastern Asia with 189.6 million (28.2%), Latin America and the Caribbean with 110.7 million (23.5%), South-Eastern Asia with 88.9 million (31%), Western Asia with 35 million (24.6%), North Africa with 11.8 million (13.3%) and Oceania with 6 million (UN-Habitat, 2009).

Slums have received renewed attention as a result of United Nations Millennium Development Goal 7 (Ensure Environmental sustainability) target 11, which is to improve the lives of at least 100 million slum dwellers by 2020 (which if met would still leave 789 million slum dwellers; but if the target is not met the forecast is that there would be 1.4 billion slum dwellers in 2020—just under a fifth of all humanity).[4] The term *planet of slums* has been used by Mike Davis, first in an article in the *New Left Review* (2004) and then in a book by the same name (Davis, 2006) to bring to the fore the challenges of this burgeoning new urban poor.

Forces behind the growth of slums vary—in the postindependence years in Africa and Asia they evolved due to rural to urban migration and weak state action, later due to natural growth and the impact of evictions and more recently due to the forces of displacement as a result of conflict particularly in Africa. In addition, the exponential growth of slums is also the result of the misplaced national (mainly evictions) and international interventions (such as the neoliberal policies of the World Bank and the structural adjustment programs of the International Monetary Fund (UN-Habitat, 2003a).

The notion of a planet of slums raises two interrelated challenges to housing policy and practice. The first challenge lies in the physical domain—housing conditions and services. On average in 2003, 6% of all urban households in developing countries lacked a finished main floor; 19% of all urban households lived in overcrowded conditions; 7.8% lacked access to safe water, and 26.5% lacked improved sanitation (UN-Habitat, 2006). It is not surprising that these conditions impose social and health costs on those that live in them. Four out of 10 slum children in some low-income countries are malnourished—a statistic comparable to rural areas of those countries; in some cities, the prevalence of diarrhea is much higher in slum than in rural children and child deaths are not so much the result of the lack of immunization as they are of inadequate living conditions; in Sub-Saharan Africa, HIV prevalence is higher in urban areas than in rural areas and is higher in slum rather than nonslum areas; and slum populations tend to be younger but die sooner than their nonslum counterparts (UN-Habitat, 2003a, p. ix).

The second interrelated challenge is one of addressing functionings and capability (Sen, 1992). Here, the notion of poverty transcends insufficient income or consumption and instead refers to whether one is able to lead a life that one values. According to Sen:

> [L]iving may be seen as consisting of a set of interrelated "functionings," consisting of beings and doings.... The relevant functionings can vary from such elementary things as being adequately nourished, being in good health, avoiding escapable morbidity and premature mortality etc.... Closely related to the notion of functions is that of the capability to function. It represents the various combinations of functionings (beings and doings) that the person can achieve. Capability is, thus, a set of vectors of functionings, reflecting the person's freedom to lead one type of life or another.
>
> (1992, pp. 39–40, italics in original)

In such a conceptualization, poverty is represented as *capability deprivation* (Sen, 1997, p. 210). In turn, capability deprivation cannot be reversed without simultaneous addressing deprivations related to livelihoods, political rights, and social protection — deprivations that seriously elude the poor. Although there is recognition that to overcome urban poverty policy and institutional reform is needed in the areas of: land, housing, and urban services; financial markets; labor markets and employment; social protection and social services (health, nutrition, education and security); and the environment (World Bank, 2007c), this is rarely the case in practice. Part of the problem may lie in the relationship being seen as a one-way street — namely that when urban policy makers and practitioners attempt to tackle poverty they acknowledge the multidimensionality of the problem. However, when it comes to housing policy and practice, only some of these dimensions are interlinked — in the main housing finance and the environment in terms of water and sanitation. Where people live and work has economic, social, and environmental costs; precarious livelihood opportunities influence living conditions; deprivations in the rights to earn a livelihood in the city increases risk; and the lack of freedoms in being able to find a solution to one's housing needs heightens vulnerabilities. Housing policy and practice needs to incorporate these capability deprivations and recognize that the means to an all-inclusive housing policy end lies in operationalizing a series of measures for the present (accounting for existing constraints and opportunities) that are amiable for improvement in the future.

The Good and the Great — International Development Organizations, Alliances, and Campaigns

The Cities Alliance and City Development[5] offer unique perspectives on proactive approaches around international development. Adopting a multidonor coalition of cities and their development partners, Cities Alliance was co-founded by UN-Habitat and the World Bank in 1999 with the view to improve,

> [T]he efficiency and impact of urban development cooperation in two key areas: making unprecedented improvements in the living conditions of the urban poor by developing citywide and nationwide slum-upgrading programs; and supporting city-based consensus-building processes by which local stakeholders define their vision for their city and establish city development strategies with clear priorities for action and investments'. Its two main programmes are Cities without Slums and the formulation of City Development Strategies.

> *(Cities Alliance, 2005)*

A recent evaluation (Universalia, 2006, p. ii) notes that although:

> The Cities Alliance has demonstrated effects on the ground, especially considering the generally modest level of resources that it can allocate to cities. Through technical assistance grants for city upgrading or strategic planning initiatives, it has also contributed to taking project experience to a nationwide or city-wide scale of action, reflected in the replication and adaptation of its initiatives and/or new or revised policy frameworks. In the cities that CA has supported, it has had some success in improving the coherence of efforts in development cooperation for urban development. The CA has been able to leverage follow-up investments in the projects that it has supported, although it will need to continuously strengthen this aspect and also help cities to pay increasing attention to domestic sources of capital where possible. The CA has contributed to the development of capacities of project stakeholders, both individuals and organizations, in areas such as strategic city planning, participatory processes, and integrated approaches to slum upgrading.

> The Cities Alliance has been less successful in two areas—advocacy and knowledge sharing—that are equally important for achieving its objectives. The CA needs to strengthen its role in generating policy coherence and increasing synergies among the different actors involved, and in influencing national or global development agendas. In a related vein, the CA has not paid sufficient attention to the process of knowledge exchange and transfer among its stakeholders (Members, clients, and other actors in urban development). The Alliance lacks an overall strategy for ensuring that its influencing and knowledge-sharing role helps it to achieve its objectives. Knowledge sharing and advocacy have been constrained by the limited time and resources that Members and the Secretariat can allocate to these areas.

> *(Universalia, 2006)*

Apart from the challenges outlined in the second paragraph above, there is a danger in focusing exclusively on a target-based approach. For example, while the banner of *Cities Without Slums* has the benefit of capturing public attention, the target of improving the lives of 100 million slum dwellers addresses a fraction of the total number of slum dwellers (close to 900 million in total by the turn of the century). In addition, there is the question of who is included in this target. Furthermore, such target setting and the emphasis on upgrading can draw attention away from other innovative solutions—such as rental housing and the involvement of nonprofits in social housing. In sum, there is the danger of providing a one-size-fits-all solution to the problem rather than recognizing the need for a "plurality" of housing provision (Keivani & Werna, 2001).

The UN-Habitat Campaigns on Good Governance and Tenure

In 2000, UN-Habitat launched two campaigns: "secure tenure" and "urban governance." The "overall development objective of the Campaign is to improve the conditions of people living and often working in slum areas and informal settlements in major urban centres of the world by promoting security of their residential tenure and a direct contribution to the realisation of the commitments of the Millennium Declaration, specifically, the goal of improving the lives of 100 million slum dwellers by the year 2020" (UN-Habitat, n.d.). The UN-Habitat website[6] speaks of some successes in India (Mumbai), the Philippines (Manila, General Santos, Davao, Iloilo) and South Africa (Durban), but these are miniscule compared to the scale of the challenge. Although the intentions of the Campaign for Secure Tenure is to be applauded, unless tenure security for the poor is nationally institutionalized with due recourse to laws protecting the right to shelter, there is little clout that the Campaign for Secure Tenure is likely to have (see, UN-Habitat, 2005, on the subject of forced evictions).

An evaluation of the Campaigns on Good Governance and secure tenure points out that:

> It is useful to note the distinction between Campaigns and Programmes. Campaigns are methods of getting the political, legal and institutional framework right, so that appropriate and effective programs may be delivered. Too often resources have been wasted on programmes which are implemented under an inappropriate framework and therefore do not deliver the expected benefits. Campaigns help to create the consensus and agreement necessary for frameworks which encourage and accommodate effective programmes. Successful Campaigns precede effective programmes.

> (Fernandes, Fuentes, & Sewell, 2005, p. 9)

Secure Title or an Entitlement to Security

It is often argued that the poor have a preference for ownership. Who would not? However, the pertinent questions to ask are: How will you pay for the costs of legal title? How would you secure housing finance solely on the basis of legal title? How would you use ownership to increase mobility? These questions are not just related to issues of affordability and finance but more importantly to the fact that the institutional framework for mortgage lending does not exist for the poor.

Tenure legalization is not a new concept, having been incorporated into slum upgrading projects in the 1980s. Proponents of secure tenure have argued that a key reason for low housing investments by the poor is the threat of eviction as a result of insecure tenure (Turner, 1972). Providing secure tenure can make a difference in reducing the threat of eviction. It might also provide security from land capture by other individuals and groups (Atuahene, 2006). Nevertheless, whether it is a necessary condition for housing investment is another matter. Some studies have shown that increasing security of tenure has a positive impact on housing investment (see, for instance, Jimenez, 1983; Struyk & Lynn, 1983) whereas others have argued that although land titles can act as an incentive for investment in housing, the "effects on credit access are modest and there is no effects on labour income" (Galiani & Schargrodsky, 2005, p. 3). Another study (Field, 2006, p. 3) notes that in urban Peru:

> [E]stimates of early program impact suggest that households with no legal claim to property spend an average of 13.4 hours per week maintaining informal tenure security, reflecting a 14% reduction in total household work hours for the average squatter family. Households are also 28% more likely to work inside of their home. Thus, the net effect of property titling is a combination of an increase in total labor force hours and a reallocation of work hours from inside the home to the outside labor market.

Two points are worth noting in relation to the Peru—first, that the high level of insecurity vis-à-vis land capture by other poor groups is specific to the context; and second, although land titling may have freed households to look for work, not much is said about the effects of this freedom on poverty.

Opponents of legalization have, however, cautioned that legalization may be neither a necessary nor sufficient condition (see, for example, Angel, Archer, Tanphiphat, & Wegelin, 1983). Others have argued that legalization can lead to the inclusion of low income settlements into the land market and lead to processes of gentrification (Burgess, 1985). To overcome these problems, it has been argued that the installation of services has more of an impact on housing investment (Strassman, 1980). This leads Varley (1987, pp. 464–65) to conclude that:

> The basic problem with the argument concerning legalization and housing improvements is that security of tenure is not a fixed, objective concept, and that it is affected by a variety of other considerations: not only the legality of tenure. Changes in residents' assessment of their security of tenure can also, therefore, be produced by other means. The most important of these is probably the installation of services, which people take as de facto indication of official acceptance of the continued existence of their settlement.

The push for a citywide land titling program only emerged from the *Housing: Enabling Markets* to work policy paper, which is explicit on the need to bring about property reforms (World Bank, 1993). Much of this thinking has been influenced by the work of the Peruvian economist Hernando de Soto (1989, 2000). In his latest book, *The Mystery of Capital: Why Capitalism Triumphs in the West and Fails Everywhere Else* (de Soto, 2000), he argues that property rights as embodied in titles are an essential mechanism for converting assets to usable wealth and estimates that if developing countries provide secure property rights to residential property, they would effectively unlock $9.3 trillion worth of what he calls "dead capital" (Buckley & Kalarickal, 2005, pp. 245–46).

De Soto's claims have received criticism from several academics and researchers (see, for instance, Bromley, 1994, 2004; Buckley & Kalarickal, 2005; Gilbert, 2002a). Some of the criticisms relate to: first, that titling is expensive not just due to institutional constraints but mainly because of the cost of adjudicating counter claims; second, that the question of an amnesty to prevent squatting becomes a way of gaining legal ownership—often this takes the form of a cutoff eligibility date for the granting of title, which then results in problems of social exclusion (Woodruff, 2001, cited in Buckley & Kalarickal, 2005); third, that the value of a title is limited if it cannot be used as collateral (Buckley & Kalarickal, 2005); and finally, that the existence of a continuum of titles means that some may value title more than others (Payne, 2002). There are two other critical issues related to land titling that have received little attention in the literature. First, the fact that land titling is not redistributive—in essence this means that those who have managed to squat on very tiny lots are only going to be eligible for the land that they currently occupy. This has the danger of maintaining the status quo in terms of the inequities in access to urban land. Second is the displacement of tenants. Given that the occupation of land by the de facto owner is illegal and that land titling would be aimed at all the residents of a given settlement, it is in the interest of the de facto landlord to maximize the amount of land received, resulting in the eviction of tenants before an official visit to verify claims.

In sum, caution needs to be exercised so as not to institutionalize the injustices in the access to land for urban housing that currently exists. Furthermore, although the UN-Habitat Campaign on Secure Tenure[7] is laudable for its aim of attempting to protect the poor from the vulnerability and risks associated with evictions, it must avoid the danger of being seen as a supporter of legalization through titling.

Civil Society, Not-for-Profits, and Others of the Same Ilk, But With a Different Perspective

The involvement of nonprofits (or nongovernmental organizations—NGOs—as they are known in the developing world) and faith-based groups in housing and human settlements is not a new phenomenon.

However, the manner in which they engage with housing and related issues has changed in certain respects.

Project by Project Interventions

Early interventions tended to be small-scale project-based ones that focused on helping the poor to build homes using appropriate technology. Cost savings were attained though the use of sweat-equity—namely contributions in the form of labor from individual households when it came to building houses and labor contributions from a given poor community for community level improvements such as water and or sanitation. These could take the form of locally based nonprofits or international faith-based nonprofits working in different regions of the world. Perhaps the most well known example of the former is the Orangi Pilot Project (OPP), in Karachi, Pakistan. Orangi is Karachi's largest *katchi abadi* (squatter settlement) and has a population of 1.2 million. The OPP was established in 1980 with the initial aim of enabling its residents to contribute financially and physically to the provision of sanitation within Orangi, based on the notion that while residents do not have the capacity to construct trunk infrastructure (the purview of governments) they could exercise their agency in building sanitation infrastructure lane by lane in their settlement. In 1988 the project was upgraded into four autonomous institutions: the OPP-RTI is responsible for sanitation; the Orangi Charitable Trust (OCT) for Family Enterprise Economic Programme; Karachi Health and Social Development Association (KHASDA); and the OPP Society, which funds housing. In Orangi, people have invested Rupees 78.79 million (about US$1.3 million) on internal development (including 405 secondary sewers) in 5,987 lanes consisting of 90,596 houses (there are 104,917 houses in Orangi). The OPP concept has been accepted by the Karachi Municipal Government and SKAA and is being applied to their development plans. Increasingly, the OPP is getting involved in policy issues and promoting macro-level solutions, based on its models, of sanitation, health, housing, and economic issues (for more details, see Urban Resource Centre, n.d.). An example of the latter is the nonprofit, Habitat for Humanity. The website notes that "Habitat for Humanity is a nonprofit, nondenominational Christian housing charity whose goal is to eliminate housing poverty and homelessness from the world, and to make decent shelter a matter of conscience and action." Habitat for Humanity states that they have built 200,000 houses all over the world, thus providing sage, decent, affordable shelter to nearly a million people. Habitat for Humanity provides households with interest-free loans for housing and requires them to contribute both in terms of sweat-equity as well as make repayments on the loans. It also uses volunteers from overseas to help (for more details, see Habitat for Humanity, 2006).

Community-Based Housing Finance

Although Buckley and Kalarickal (2005, p. 247) note "the need to develop a sustainable supply of finance to fund housing continues to be an important part of any set of policy measures to improve housing affordability," access to institutional housing finance for the poor remains largely undeveloped. For example, it has been noted that in India, "resources from the formal [public] system still constitutes a mere 16 per cent of the total investment in the housing sector because of its weak *financial base* attributed to the low household savings...furthermore...most of the finance is extended for house construction rather than for getting access to land" (Durrand-Lasserve & Adusumilli, 2001, p. 17).

The inability to use land as collateral, and not having a regular salaried job in the formal sector, excludes most of the poor and all of the poorest from institutional access to housing finance—both private and public (see, for instance, Jones & Datta, 1998; Smets, 1997). It began to emerge that the only option was to form self-help savings groups. Once again, such mechanisms for saving for emergency consumption loans is not new. Households have also actively used these mechanisms to make housing improvements both for their own use as well as for renting (Kumar, 2001b).

Nonprofits have also had a long history of providing small loans or micro-credit for income generating activities. The involvement of nonprofits in housing finance came about as a result of the realization that micro-credit provided for income generation was being invested in housing and services (Jones & Mitlin, 1998). Notwithstanding the benefits of both community-based savings and micro-credit, these mechanisms have tended to focus benefits on the individual, thereby restricting the potential for using the savings as collateral to leverage a greater volume of financial resources for housing and services.

Contemporary Activities—Federations of the Poor and Alliances

Although micro-credit and savings and credit associations of the poor provide credit to smooth consumption and production activities have a role to play, they have been limited in leveraging broader institutional support. This is partly because of a narrow focus on the immediate needs of its members, which then result in savings groups tending to operate in a fragmented manner.

A realization of the power and voice that can emanate from the coming together of poor groups to form federations and their ability to negotiate and leverage state and private sector resources though partnerships with nonprofits has begun to emerge. Federations of the poor can emerge as a result of different threats. For example, the National Slum Dwellers Federation, based in Mumbai, India was established in 1974 mainly to resist evictions. It is estimated that by 2002, it had a membership of 750,000 people in 52 cities and nine states in India. The largest membership of 250,000 households is in Mumbai (Burra, Patel, & Kerr, 2003). Although the Federation has made some important gains in negotiating evictions in Mumbai, its membership is only a fraction of all the urban slum dwellers in India.

South African Homeless People's Federation was formed in the early 1990s (Bolnick, 2001). South Africa has had a long legacy of civic struggle against the injustices of apartheid. Following the election of the first democratic government in 1994, proposals were being drawn up to channel subsidies for housing for the poor though housing developers and contractors. However, on hearing the negative experience of subsidies from the Indian Federation and the positive experience of the poor forming savings groups and receiving subsidies directly, grass-roots organizations of the South African urban poor went on to form local housing savings schemes and networked to create the South African Homeless People's Federation (Patel, Burra, & d'Cruz, 2001). A similar process has resulted in the creation of the Zimbabwean Homeless People's Federation, with exchange visits and the support of the South African Poor People's federations in Zimbabwe, Africa (Chitekwe & Mitlin, 2001).

Partnerships—Maintaining the Status Quo or Challenging the State?

The question of "partnerships with who?" is an important one as it essentially questions the role of civil society vis-à-vis state and society. As Lewis (2002) notes, there are two civil society traditions. The first is that civil society, in a social sphere, is desirable (Ferguson, 1767/1995) and secondly, in a political sense, needed to be ordered by the state to prevent self-interest and a lack of contribution to the common good (Hegel, 1821/1991). Evidence of a move from the social and political spheres to one of an organizational focus can be found for example in the work of Alexis de Tocqueville (de Tocqueville, 1835/1994) on America who "stressed volunteerism, community spirit and individual associational life as protections against the domination of society by the state, and indeed as a counterbalance which helped to keep the state accountable and effective" (Lewis, 2002, p. 571). The Alliance in Mumbai reflects a de Tocqueville approach to a great extent but with a few caveats. For instance, Appadurai (2001) notes that the Alliance in Mumbai is "apolitical," in that it enters into discussions and partnerships with whoever is in power at local or the state government levels, irrespective of ideology. This is a pragmatic approach intended to make claims on whoever is in power for the benefit of the members of the alliance. But it is this membership-based claim making that casts doubt over the extent to which it has been able to hold the state accountable to the common good of all disenfranchised people. Thus, while the sanitation program may have forced the state to extend sanitation to a vast majority of slum dwellers, the same is not the case with the housing relocation program.

The second civil society tradition, according to Lewis (2002), is the Gramscian one, which "argued that civil society is the arena, separate from the state and market, in which ideological hegemony is contested, implying that civil society contains a wide range of different organizations and ideologies which both challenge and uphold the existing order" (Lewis, 2002, p. 572). It could be argued that the alliance, while challenging the state in some ways, also helps uphold some of the existing order in that, for example, it does little to challenge the distribution of land for the poor. In contrast, an example of a nonprofit attempting to stick to its principles and not compromise is provided by the group Youth for Unity and Voluntary

Action (YUVA). A study of YUVA's attempt to forge a partnership between the municipality of Mumbai, itself, and a community group in its development to deal with landlord-tenant issues in one low-income settlement shows how partnerships can be affected by bureaucracy, politicization, and personalization. Furthermore, partnerships can also be affected by a parting of "ways of thinking" between the nonprofit and the community group (YUVA, 1999).

Transnational Alliances and Exchanges

Despite variations in the historical, geopolitical and socioeconomic trajectories of developing countries, the structural causes of injustices that the poor suffer are not that dissimilar: The poor are subject to the same vulnerabilities from eviction and suffer the same deprivations from a lack of water and sanitation across the urban developing world. One way of getting national, regional, and city governments as well as international development organizations to not only recognize their plight but more importantly to realize that the eradication of poverty and the meeting of housing and service needs can only be accomplished with the active involvement of the poor, was to increase the international profile of the poor. This has culminated in the formation of transnational alliances and the setting up of the Shack/Slum Dwellers International (SDI), which represents member federations of the urban poor and homeless groups in 11 countries in Africa (4), Asia (6), and Latin America (1) (Patel et al., 2001). The origins of this international federation stems from the work (between 1998 and 1991) of the Asian Coalition of Housing Rights (ACHR), a network of grassroots organizations and nonprofits in Asia beginning to link national groups and conduct exchange visits with the view to address issues of urban poverty, form savings and credit groups, and develop leadership among the urban poor. In 1996, a meeting of these national federations in South Africa led to the formation of SDI (Patel et al., 2001).

In Asia, although there was a clearly identified need for nonprofits, professionals and grassroots groups to "share experiences, tackle the large problem of forced evictions in the regions cities, develop opportunities for organizations of the poor and consider their place in city planning," no forum existed (Asian Coalition for Housing Rights, 2001). To fill this gap the Asian Coalition for Housing Rights (ACHR) was established in 1999 with a focus that included: acting as a pressure group and for crisis intervention in specific problems; information dissemination; providing opportunities for community organizations to facilitate sharing of experiences at the community level and for international members to deepen understanding of the major forces affecting the urban poor; facilitating experience sharing and exchange among groups, especially among the grass-roots and NGO groups; providing professional consultation for groups based on needs; coordinating with related agencies, both international and local, especially with regard to regional activities; support to empower local organizations and strengthen links among each other; support for the grassroots struggle for housing with an aim to develop the process that enables people to strengthen their own capabilities; research on key issues and innovative initiatives in the region; advocacy at international, national, and local levels; creating space for change and facilitating dialogue on local situations through by organizing activities with local groups; and support and encouragement of young professionals to get involved in community development work and deepen their understanding of the people's process (Asian Coalition for Housing Rights, 2001).

Other successes, such as when the alliance of SDI and ACHR advised the municipality of Phnom Penh to set up the Urban Community Development Fund to provide loans for housing, housing repairs and income generating activities for the poor of the city. The innovation in relation to the fund is "that it emerged from, and is embedded within, a partnership between the municipality of Phnom Penh and the communities themselves" (Patel et al., 2001).

In a globalizing world increasingly dominated by transnational capital flows associated with a delocation of old sites of production and a relocation to sites of cheap labor, it is clear that the role of the nation-state is changing or at least needs transforming. As a result, some have argued that "the contemporary world is characterised by both globalisation and localisation of politics" (Harriss, Stokke, & Törnquist, 2004). Although this discussion of the role of local politics and globalization is at the level of the nation state and other global actors, much of it applies to the localization of urban politics and the role of global alliances.

However, such experiments in "deep democracy" also face a number of challenges. Some of these lie in the approach of entering into partnerships with whoever may be in power despite the fact that they may not share the same moral goals. "Another is that the hard-won mobilization of certain groups of the urban poor may not be best invested as political capital in partnership arrangements, as opposed to confrontation or violence" (Appadurai, 2001, p. 41). Finally, the larger gamble is that "multilateral agencies, Northern funders and Southern governments can be persuaded that the poor are the best drivers of shared solutions to the problems of poverty" (Appadurai, 2001, p. 41). This leads him to conclude that "this form of a deep democracy, the vertical fulcrum of a democracy without borders, cannot be assumed to be automatic, easy or immune to setbacks. Like all serious exercises in democratic practice, it is not automatically reproductive. It has particular conditions under which it grows weak or corrupt" (Appadurai, 2001, p. 43).

Property for People or the Property of People: The Politics of Tenure

One central tendency that has dogged housing policy and practice in the urban developing world is the preoccupation with ownership. Such a preoccupation can be found in almost all the interventions explored so far.

For instance, upgrading has in the majority of cases entailed the granting of land title. Sites-and-service projects are inherently based on the notion of ownership and mortgages. As has been seen, the UN-Habitat Campaign for Secure Tenure has tended to focus on security of tenure from an ownership perspective. Land titling programs underway in urban Peru, urban Venezuela (Wilpert, 2005) and urban Cambodia, to name a few, have an explicit focus on ownership. Most recently, the relocation of some of the poor from the railway in Mumbai has also focused explicitly on ownership. So is ownership the only viable option?

The role of tenure in the life cycle of rural to urban migrants has been recognized in the literature since the late 1960s. John Turner (1968) noted that the "three basic functions of the dwelling environment are location, tenure and amenity." The basis of this observation he developed the three stage "bridge-header — consolidator — status-seeker" model of residential mobility. For the bridge-header, proximity to places of employment is a priority. As households established themselves in the city and became consolidated, they sought secure tenure with amenity being the priority of status seekers. It could be argued that the poor households in the urban south are not bridge-headers in the way Turner meant them to be. However, in terms of their poverty they are and the question is not whether they see ownership as a priority but more importantly what ownership can do for them. The question of the function of the dwelling environment was somewhat ignored as the result of the urgency of the search for an appropriate policy solution to the challenge of slums and squatter settlements, which emerged in the form of settlement upgrading and sites and services.

However, the notion that individuals and households "owned" their homes even if the ownership rights of rights were de facto rather than de jure gave rise to a focus on ownership. In the 1980s, a number of studies attempted to show that not all the poor were de facto owners but that a large majority of them were tenants (see, for example, Coulomb, 1989; Edwards, 1982). A UN-Habitat study (2003b) notes that in African cities, tenants accounted from a low of 35% in Pretoria South Africa (1996) to a high of 63% in Cairo, Egypt (1996); in Asian cities, from 28% in Pusan, Republic of Korea (1995) to 41% in Bangkok, Thailand (1998), and for Latin American and Caribbean cities from 11% in Monterrey, Mexico (2000) to 52% in Port of Spain, Trinidad (1998). In fact, homeownership has become more difficult for the lowest quintile in some Latin American countries. For example, urban homeownership declined between the early and late 1990s from: 82% to 78% in Argentina; 72% to 62% in Chile; 38% to 30% in Colombia and 73% to 65% in Peru (Fay & Wellenstein, 2005).

Gradually, the much needed focus on tenure began to emerge despite the fact that attention was on why tenants remained tenants and not become owners–namely the constraint versus choice thesis (Gilbert, Camacho, Coulomb, & Necochea, 1993; Gilbert & Varley, 1990). The body of research on tenants has grown substantially since then (Amis, 1984,

1988; Crankshaw, Gilbert, & Morriss, 2000; Gilbert, 1991, 1999; Gilbert, Camacho, Coulomb, & Necochea, 1993; Gilbert & Crankshaw, 1999; Gilbert, Mabin, McCarthy, & Watson, 1997; Gilbert & Varley, 1989a; Gilbert & Ward, 1982; Green, 1988; Kumar, 1989).

It was not until the 1990s that the tenure nexus—namely owner-ship, tenants, and landlords—was beginning to become connected. The argument of this literature is that a demand side exploration of housing in term of tenants can only useful if one has an equal understanding of the supply side represented by landlords. Much of this literature sought to describe the operation of low-income landlords in terms of their socioe-conomic characteristics and the size of their operation (Aina, 1990; Amis, 1984, 1988; Bryant, 1989; Gilbert & Varley, 1989b, 1991; Lee-Smith, 1990; Pennant, 1990). Although this body of research provided much needed evi-dence of the largely nonexploitative character of low-income landlords—in that they operated on a small scale and were often as poor or even poorer than their tenants—the research lacked a means of conceptualizing land-lordism as a phenomenon (Kumar, 1996a).

A better understanding of the reasons why low-income households become involved in the "business of renting" can be provided by a produc-tion continuum (Kumar, 1996b, 1996c). At one end of the continuum are "subsistence landlords" who are forced into letting out space even if this entails extreme overcrowding for their own household. In the middle are "petty bourgeois landlords" who may be able to survive or cope but find it difficult to make improvements in areas beyond subsistence consumption or their housing. At the end of the continuum are "petty capitalist landlords" who do not have either subsistence or consumption needs but nevertheless get involved in the business of renting to reproduce capital. Such a concep-tualization moves one away from the number of rooms to the underlying cause of why poor households become landlords. Such a framework also provides the basis for a more nuanced understanding of the complex pro-cesses social relations underpinning the development of rental housing at the city level (Kumar, 2001b).

Despite this body of research on tenants and landlords, the existence of tenure mobility—tenant to owner to landlord—creates a much better understanding of landlordism as an important part of the livelihood port-folio of the poor and support from UN-Habitat on the need to have more tenure neutral policies (UNCHS, 1989b, 1993; UN-Habitat, 2003b), there has been little movement on the rental housing policy front. Only a few coun-tries, such as South Africa, Chile, Brazil, and Colombia, have attempted to even engage with the idea of either renting or leasing as a supplementary housing policy (UN-Habitat, 2003b).

Renting is not just a question of affordability as it would be difficult to explain the high levels of renting in cities in high-income countries. Renting provides tenants with room for maneuver (Kumar, 2005).

Toward a Conclusion: The Challenge for Urban Housing Policy and Practice Lies in Asking the Right Questions

A critical examination of the urban housing policies and practices discussed thus far leads to a perspective that suggests that urban housing policy and practice has suffered three main problems: first, a one-size-fits-all solution; second, a "big-bang" approach; and third, a "fragmented" problem-solving approach. By and large these three problems stem from asking the wrong questions. It is not too late to ask the right questions and to seek a more holistic and pluralistic approach to housing policy and practice—one that aims to provide solution rooted in the realism of the lives of the urban poor and yet incorporates routes that enable poor urban households to gradually move out of shelter poverty.

The Poverty of Resources or the Resources of Poverty?[8]
Labor Markets, Urban Poverty, and Housing

With more and more people destined to live in cities and towns, it is not surprising that the locus of poverty is likely to shift to urban areas. In Latin America, although a greater proportion of the poor live in rural areas, high rates of urbanization have meant that more than half of the poor live in cities (Fay, 2005). This will be the case in urban Africa and Asia sometime in the future.

There is widespread agreement now that poverty is more than just income (see, for example, Amis & Rakodi, 1995; Satterthwaite, 1997; UNCHS, 1996) and that poverty is a multidimensional phenomenon, which encompasses a lack of income, declining access to common property resources, a reduction in state provided commodities, a lack of assets, dignity and autonomy (Baulch, 1996). Although the focus on income poverty was superseded by the basic-needs approach of the 1980, which focused on the provision of health, education, food, water, and sanitation (Stewart, 1985; Streeten & World Bank, 1981) and continues to be applied in the form of settlement upgrading, attention in the 1990s has shifted to a livelihoods approach. In a livelihoods approach, a livelihood comprises the capabilities, assets (stores, resources, claims, and access), and activities required for a means of living (Chambers & Conway, 1992). The manner in which the poor use an array of five assets or capitals—human, physical, financial, natural, and social (IFPRI, 2003; Moser, 1998; Rakodi, 1999, 2002; Rakodi & Lloyd-Jones, 2002; Wood & Salway, 2000)—to address vulnerability has led to a change in focus: namely, from one of what the poor do not have (income) to one of which how they use what they have (assets).

Labor Markets, Housing, and Income Poverty

Although the focus on a broader definition of poverty has its merits, there is also a danger in such a line of reasoning in that the questioning has shifted from the causes of poverty (the 1970s) to how poverty is managed through a combination of assets. This has a knock on effect in that less attention is being paid to addressing income poverty. Income is an important component in the livelihood of the urban poor because transactions in urban areas are highly monetized (Satterthwaite, 1997, 2001; Wratten, 1995). For example, in Latin America, labor accounts for about four fifths of the income of the urban poor (Fay, 2005). As González de la Rocha (2006, p. 85) notes:

> [P]oor urban households in Mexico face significantly different conditions today. The current situation, characterized by new forms of exclusion and the increasing precariousness of employment, is unfavourable to the operation of traditional household mechanisms of work intensification. Instead of talking about the "resources of poverty," as before, the present situation is better described by the "poverty of resources": a lack of employment opportunities in a context shaped by an exclusionary economic model.

Thus it is crucial that serious attention is paid to improving urban labor markets (Amis, 1995) and giving greater attention to the linkages between urban labor markets and housing. Rural to urban migrants have, for several decades, indicated the linkages between employment opportunities and their choice of residential location. To the contrary, housing policy and practice has, until now, paid little attention to linkages with the labor market — despite there being evidence to support it (Harris, Rosser, & Kumar, 1996; Kumar, 2001b).

Relocation, Labor Markets, and Livelihoods

It is well known that forced evictions not only destroy the housing of the poor and deprive them of physical assets that they have painfully accumulated over time but also destroy the social networks that the poor have built up to deal with vulnerabilities and crises. There is thus an argument for negotiated resettlement of the poor due to improvements in a city's infrastructure. For example, as part of the World Bank Mumbai Urban Transport Project, some 20,000 households or 60,000 people residing illegally along the railway line had to be relocated. Unlike forced evictions, this was achieved on a voluntary basis through negotiations between the municipal government and the nonprofit acting on behalf of the slum dwellers (Patel, d'Cruz, & Burra, 2002). Although Patel, d'Cruz and Burra (2002, p. 159) note that this "did not impoverish those who moved (as is generally the case when poor groups are moved to make way for infrastructure development)" and that the slum dwellers now live in secure accommodation of 20 square meters, little is said about the differential impact of the resettlement on the livelihoods of the poor — whose livelihoods were improved and whose declined. Since the poor depend on their labor, relocation can result in additional costs of time and transport to the places where they work (Urban Resource Centre Phnom Penh, 2002).

Relocation may be necessary in certain cases, for instance when settlements are located in hazardous locations. Two issues need immediate attention. First, the relationship between livelihoods and relocation has to take center stage in any discussion of resettlement. Second, there is an urgent need to distinguish and plan differently for livelihood gains that may accrue to some and losses to others. In both the Mumbai and the Cambodia examples, neither of these issues seem to have been considered.

Decent Work Deficits—Limits to Home-Based Enterprise

One of the livelihood strategies open to the poor is that of home-based enterprises or micro-enterprises. Home-based enterprises involving food preparation, small-scale manufacturing, and services are to be found in a number of poor urban settlements in Africa, Asia, and Latin America (Gough & Kellett, 2001; Kellett & Tipple, 2000; Strassmann, 1986; UNCHS, 1989). In conditions of poverty, the poor explore all means for survival, and home-based enterprises are one of them. Three points, however, are worth noting. First, that in many cases home-based enterprises are coping strategies and can provide little in the form of capital accumulation and therefore an escape from poverty. Second, it is difficult to distinguish which home-based enterprises are actually "genuine" own-account workers and which are subcontracted and are thus linked to the formal sector. The latter has major implications for wage levels and deprivations in a range of social protection benefits. Third, even in the case of genuine own-account home based enterprises, the low levels of income generation and vulnerability associated with guarantees of markets, can result in them being categorized as enterprises characteristic of what the International Labour Organisation (ILO) terms "decent work deficits."

Home-based enterprises can make an important contribution to the livelihoods of the poor and it is not being argued here that they should not be allowed. However, attention should be paid to not only the decent work deficits but also the extent to which the planning of low-income settlements can be supportive of the perusal of such enterprises.

Means or Ends: Short- Versus Long-Term Housing Outcomes

Upgrading and Land Titling: Ends or Means? Tenure and the Collective Versus Individual Provision of Water and Sanitation

Compared to sites-and-services projects, environmental upgrading of low-income settlements are continuing to be pursued, at times at a very large scale (Riley, Fiori, & Ramirez, 2001) and have included a component of community participation (see, for example, the chapters in Imparato & Ruster, 2003). As shown earlier, settlement upgrading has two main advantages. First, it does not alter the relationship between residential location and livelihoods opportunities or labor markets. Second, it helps preserve and maintain the critical social networks that the poor have built up over time.

However, upgrading also has several disadvantages. First, upgrading often does not allow the individual provision of water and sanitation given the high densities and irregular housing and land development (for an exception of the Orangi Pilot Project in Karachi, see Urban Resource Centre, n.d.). Second, it often maintains the status quo in terms of the extent of land ownership. For instance in India, the average plot in a squatter settlement is 20 square meters. Upgrading involving the provision of land titles does not attempt to explore issues of redistribution. So if all of the 60% of the population of Mumbai were to be given land titles today, this would maintain the status quo that this population only occupies 6% of Mumbai's land. Third, upgrading (influenced by the belief that all poor households in squatter settlements are de facto owners) often neglects landlord tenant relationships. Upgrading can often lead to the eviction of tenants as landlords seek to maximize their land holdings. Similar shortcomings are also part of land titling policies.

Upgrading and land titling should thus be selectively implemented in relation to the issues raised above. At the moment they are being applied as a blueprint solution to the problem of tenure insecurity. Such blueprint approaches need to be replaced with a wider canvas of approaches that are suitable to specific contexts and circumstances.

One or Several Rungs on the Housing Ladder: Ownership and Renting

Ownership may be the ultimate goal of a given society but it cannot possibly apply to all. The impoverishment experienced by a majority of urban dwellers can make ownership an economic burden. Any attempt at extending ownership has to carefully evaluate the benefits that ownership can bring. It has been shown that infrastructure investments have a greater impact on peoples perceived notions of security of tenure than a blanket program of land titling. The lack of tenure security does not preclude individuals and households from either investing in housing improvements or the renting out of rooms (Kumar, 2001b). The reality of urban development is that there will be some for whom ownership has benefits and others for whom renting is either the only option or a choice—like migrants who do not seek to remain in the city, students and employees who move to cities for short periods of time for either study or work.

The search for a tenure neutral housing policy is urgent and critical. Politicians as well as civil society organizations have to be convinced of the benefits of a housing market that provides residential opportunities for all rather than lock the poor into a "cul-de-sac" of little or no benefits from ownership.

A Friendly Critique or a Critical Fiend?[9] State and Not-for-Profit Partnerships

Nonprofits and community groups have an important role to play in housing. So far, this has primarily been in the design and implementation of housing projects and programs. Although this is an important contribution, they should also be equally involved in bringing about policy and institutional change that benefit those beyond their immediate membership. It can be said that this is partially been achieved, for example, in the Mumbai sanitation program. However, such partnerships have also involved trade-offs and it is this that needs greater scrutiny. Being involved in partnerships with the state should not preclude nonprofits from being "critical fiends."

Benefits for Some or for All? National and International Goals

In relation to the urban land titling program in Lima, Peru, one commentator notes that:

> Although I do agree with the allocation of land titles . . . I also acknowledge that this can lead to further land invasions. However, there are simple ways to circumvent a stampede. For instance, in Peru the government instituted an amnesty of sorts. The government declared that for any invasion that occurred before March 22, 1996, those who presently occupy the land receive title. For any invasion that occurred after the appointed date, occupants would be removed from the land. As long as the Peruvian government adheres to this policy and potential invaders are convinced that there will be no future amnesty, than this is a promising policy for dealing with the brooding threat of future invasions.

> (Atuahene, 2006, p. 769)

This is a clear indication of closing the door on the potential prosperity that can accrue to those seeking to migrate to cities for economic better. There are many other instances where a cutoff amnesty date is set and government declaring slum and squatter settlements as legal. This is simply not realistic especially as there is now agreement that urbanization makes an important contribution to economic growth and social development.

A similar problem arises from the UN Millennium Declaration, specifically, the goal of improving the lives of 100 million slum dwellers by the year 2020—100 million slum dwellers for now, sorry to the rest of the 900 million. Targets have their purpose in terms of attempting to ensure that governments commit themselves. However, targets have to be a means to an end and not an end in themselves.

In Conclusion: Property for People or the Property of People

The title of this chapter seeks to provoke thought among researchers, policy makers, practitioners, and politicians. It encapsulates current urban housing policy and practice in the developing world, which to a large extent has focused on "property for people." Furthermore, the emphasis has been on ownership through interventions ranging from housing finance to partnerships.

In contrast, the notion of the property of people is intended to make various housing and urban development actors cognizant of the fact that despite housing being the most visible manifestation of poverty, it is limited as a starting point for an improvement in the lives of the urban poor. In a highly monetized urban economy, income is an important instrument in negotiating pathways out of poverty. Labor is the single most important asset that the urban poor possess. However, as long as this labor is subject to "decent work deficits" its potential as a lever out of poverty will not materialize. Labor market interventions have a greater capacity to kickstart improvements in housing conditions. Thus, greater recognition should be given to the links between labor markets and housing—they should reinforce one another for mutually beneficial outcomes and not become a simple trade-off as is the case with many voluntary relocations. Water and sanitation are important contributors to the health of labor. However, housing policy and practice actors must be aware of the dangers of institutionalizing water and sanitation provision too quickly as this can set a precedent and absolve governments from ongoing responsibilities. The sheer number of the poor in cities and their varied housing needs and preferences requires a more nuanced housing policy—one that provides room for maneuver. This calls for not just a mix of ownership and renting, but also the involvement of a greater number of nonprofits in the provision of rental housing. Voice is an important component as the strategy of organizing the poor and the formation of transnational federations have demonstrated. However, there is a need to go beyond a "benefits for members only approach." Voice needs to be harnessed and made to work for the wider public good. Although there is recognition that neither the state nor the poor on their own can act in isolation to overcome the magnitude of the poverty, housing, and infrastructure needs of the poor, partnerships between them should only be viewed as a first step. Attempts must also be made to convince employers (direct and indirect) and the wealthy of the overall benefits to be gained from making a contribution to the wellbeing of their fellow citizens.

Linking the property of people to property for people requires a flexible and broad-based housing policy framework. Such a framework will enable a range of housing actors, including the poor, to be able to select the most appropriate interventions based on local needs, priorities and resources. Housing policy needs to be a tool box rather than a sledge hammer.

Key Terms

Secure tenure	*UN Millennium*	*Urbanization*
Tenure legalization	*Goals 2020*	
Transitional economies		

Review Questions for Critical Thinking

1. What is meant by "property for the people" and "property of the people"? Which do you feel is a better option for the poor and near poor?

2. Are micro-finance institutions the solution to secure housing through-out the world or do such programs depend on unique sociopolitical environments for success?

3. How is the role of "nation state" changing in the global economy, in particular as it attends to housing needs?

4. Should the poor be directly involved in finding solutions to attaining secure and permanent housing or does the complexity of the issues mandate that experts tackle this social issue?

5. To what extent will securing property rights for the poor strengthen the local, national, and global economies?

Online Resources

Asian Coalition for Housing Rights http://www.achr.net/

Global Hand, The Partnership People http://www.globalhand.org/en

Homeless International http://www.homeless-international.org/

National Slum Dwellers Federation (India) http://www.sparcindia.org/nsdf.aspx

UN-Habitat for a Better Urban Future http://www.unhabitat.org/

NOTES

1. The United Nations Population Fund defines more developed regions as "all regions of Europe plus Northern America, Australia/New Zealand and Japan" and less developed regions comprising of "all regions of Africa, Asia (excluding Japan), Latin America and the Caribbean plus Melanesia, Micronesia and Polynesia."

2. The most commonly used threshold of low income is a household income that is 60% or less of the average (median) household income in that year. The latest year for which data is available is 2004–2005. In that year, the 60% threshold was £183 (US$284) per week for a two-adult household, £100 (US$155) per week for a single adult, £268 (US$415) per week for two adults living with two children, and £186 (US$288) per week for a single adult living with two children. These sums of money are measured after income tax, council tax, and housing costs have been deducted, where housing costs include rents, mortgage interest, building insurance, and water charges. The sum of money left over is what the household has available to spend on everything else it needs, from food and heating to travel and entertainment.

3. Settlements of the poor in towns and cities are characterized by two forms of illegality. First, quasi-legal settlements—where the sale and ownership of the residential lots are legal but the conversion of use,

from agricultural to residential, is not legally sanctioned. This form of settlement is most prevalent in Latin America. The second is illegal settlements—where the occupation of either public, private, or institutional land does not have legal sanction. Both these types of settlements are called squatter settlements based on a legal classification. Slums, on the other hand, are legal places of human habitation but whose physical conditions—state of the structure, overcrowding and levels of services—are not deemed to be of the minimum standards required for human habitation. Squatter settlements are also slums by the use of this physical definition.

4. The "State of the World's Cities 2006–07" estimates that only 8 countries are on track to achieve their targets, 15 are stabilizing, 21 are at risk, and a staggering 50 countries are off track (UN-Habitat, 2006).

5. In 1996, the Cities Alliance had 20 members: Asian Development Bank, Brazil, Canada, Ethiopia, France, Germany, Italy, Japan, Metropolis, the Netherlands, Nigeria, Norway, South Africa, Sweden, United Cities and Local Governments, the United Kingdom, UN-Habitat, UNEP, the United States, and the World Bank.

6. See http://www.unhabitat.org/content.asp?typeid=19&catid=24&cid=2046

7. The overall development objective of the campaign is to improve the conditions of people living and often working in slum areas and informal settlements in major urban centers of the world by promoting security of their residential tenure and a direct contribution to the realization of the commitments of the Millennium Declaration, specifically, "improving the lives of 100 million slum dwellers by the year 2020" (UN-Habitat, n.d.).

8. The phrase "the resources of poverty" is borrowed from the title of the book *The Resources of Poverty: Women and Survival in a Mexican City!* by Mercedes González de la Rocha (González de la Rocha, 1994).

9. This is a Freudian slip but of the making of my word processor. I mean to type "critical friend" but inadvertently typed "critical fiend." My word processor did not pick up this typo. On rereading and having noticed the error, I decided to let the Freudian slip stay as this makes my argument forcefully. Apologies to my friends who have taken a critical stance again benevolent partnership—I consider them fiends (in the nicest possible sense) that seek to truly empower the poor.

References

Aina, T. A. (1990). Petty landlords and poor tenants in a low-income settlement in metropolitan Lagos, Nigeria. In P. Amis & P. Lloyd (Eds.), *Housing Africa's urban poor* (pp. 87–101). Manchester, United Kingdom: Manchester University Press.

Amis, P. (1984). Squatters or tenants—The commercialization of unauthorized housing in Nairobi. *World Development, 12*(1), 87–96.

Amis, P. (1988). Commercialised rental housing in Nairobi, Kenya. In C. V. Patton (Ed.), *Shelter: International perspectives and prospects* (pp. 235–257). Philadelphia, PA: Temple University Press.

Amis, P. (1995). Employment creation or environmental improvement: A literature review of urban poverty and policy in India. *Habitat International, 19*(4), 485–497.

Amis, P., & Rakodi, C. (1995). Urban poverty: Concepts, characteristics and policies. *Habitat International, 19*(4), 403–405.

Angel, S., Archer, R. W., Tanphiphat, S., & Wegelin, E. A. (1983). *Land for housing the poor.* Singapore: Select Books.

Appadurai, A. (2001). Deep democracy: Urban governability and the horizon of politics. *Environment and Urbanization, 13*(2), 23–43.

Asian Coalition for Housing Rights. (2001). About ACHR. Retrieved from http://www.achr.net/about_achr.htm

Atuahene, B. (2006). Land titling: A mode of privatization with the potential to deepen democracy. *St. Louis University Law Journal, 50*(3), 761–781.

Baulch, B. (1996). Editorial—The new poverty agenda: A disputed consensus. *IDS Bulletin, 27*(1), 1–10.

Bolnick, J. (2001). Utshani Buyakhuluma (The grass speaks): People's dialogue and the South African homeless people's federation (1994–6). *Environment and Urbanization, 8*(2), 153–170.

Bromley, R. (1994). Informality, De Soto style: From concept to policy. In C. A. Rakowski (Ed.), *Contrapunto: The informal sector debate in Latin America.* Albany: State University of New York Press.

Bromley, R. (2004). Power, property and poverty: Why De Soto's "mystery of capital" cannot be solved. In A. Roy & N. AlSayyad (Eds.), *Urban informality: Transnational perspectives from the Middle East, Latin America, and South Asia* (pp. 271–288). Lanham, MD: Lexington Books.

Bryant, J. J. (1989). The acceptable face of self-help housing: Subletting in Fiji squatter settlements—Exploitation or survival strategy. In D. Drakakis-Smith (Ed.), *Economic growth and urbanisation in developing areas* (pp. 171–195). London, United Kingdom: Routledge.

Buckley, R. M., & Kalarickal, J. (2005). Housing policy in developing countries: Conjectures and refutations. *World Bank Research Observer, 20*(2), 233–257.

Burgess, R. (1985). The limits of state self-help housing programmes. *Development and Change, 16*(2), 271–312.

Burra, S., Patel, S., & Kerr, T. (2003). Community-designed, built and managed toilet blocks in Indian cities. *Environment and Urbanization, 15*(2), 11–32.

Camacho, O. O., Coulomb, R., & Necochea, A. (1993). *In Search of a Home: Rental and Shared Housing in Latin America.* London: UCL Press.

Chambers, R., & Conway, G. (1992). Sustainable rural livelihoods: Practical concepts for the 21st century. Working paper number IDS discussion paper 296, Institute for Development Studies, University of Sussex, United Kingdom.

Chitekwe, B., & Mitlin, D. (2001). The urban poor under threat and in struggle: Options for urban development in Zimbabwe, 1995–2000. *Environment and Urbanization, 13*(2), 85–101.

Cities Alliance. (2005). *Charter.* Retrieved from http://www.citiesalliance.org/about-ca/charter-english.html#objectives

Coulomb, R. (1989). Rental housing and the dynamics of urban growth in Mexico City. In A. Gilbert (Ed.), *Housing and land in urban Mexico* (pp. 39–50). San Diego, CA: Centre for US-Mexican Studies, University of California.

Crankshaw, O., Gilbert, A., & Morriss, A. (2000). Backyard Soweto. *International Journal of Urban and Regional Research, 24* (4), 841–857.

Davis, M. (2006). *Planet of slums.* London, United Kingdom: Verso.

de Soto, H. (1989). *The other path: The invisible revolution in the third world.* London, United Kingdom: Tauris.

de Soto, H. (2000). *The mystery of capital : Why capitalism triumphs in the West and fails everywhere else.* New York, NY: Basic Books.

de Tocqueville, A. (1835/1994). Democracy in America. A. Ryan. London, United Kingdom: David Campbell.

Durrand-Lasserve, A., & Adusumilli, U. (2001). Issues and opportunities for the integrated provision of serviced land and credit for progressive housing: Case study Indiam—Sector 26, Vashi, Navi Mumbai. Paris, France: ACT Consultants and GRET. Retrieved from http://www.iadb.org/sds/doc/IndiaCasestudy.pdf

Edwards, M. (1982). Cities of tenants: Renting among the urban poor in Latin America. In A. Gilbert, J. E. Hardoy, & R. Ramirez (Eds.), *Urbanisation in contemporary Latin America* (pp. 129–158). London, United Kingdom: Wiley.

Fay, M. (2005). Overview. In M. Fay (Ed.), *The urban poor in Latin America.* Washington, DC: World Bank.

Fay, M., & Wellenstein, A. (2005). Keeping a roof over one's head: Improving access to safe and decent shelter. In M. Fay (Ed.), *The urban poor in Latin America* (pp. 91–124). Washington, DC: World Bank.

Ferguson, A. (1767/1995). An essay on the history of civil society. In F. Oz-Salzberger (Ed.), *Cambridge texts in the history of political thought.* New York, NY: Cambridge University Press.

Fernandes, E., Fuentes, M., & Sewell, J. (2005). An evaluation of UN-Habitat's campaigns for secure tenure and urban governance. Retrieved from http://www.unhabitat.org/downloads/docs/2200_37204_FINALREPORT%2020Feb2005%20(2).doc

Field, E. (2006). Entitled to work: Urban property rights and labor supply in Peru. New York, NY: Harvard University Press. Retrieved from http://www.economics.harvard.edu/faculty/field/papers/Field_COFOPRI.pdf

Gilbert, A. (1991). Renting and the transition to owner occupation in Latin American cities *Habitat International, 15* (1/2), 87–99.

Gilbert, A. (1999). A home is for ever? Residential mobility and homeownership in self-help settlements *Environment and Planning a, 31* (6), 1073–1091.

Gilbert, A. (2002a). On the Mystery of Capital and the Myths of Hernando de Soto *International Development Planning Review, 24* (1), 1–19.

Gilbert, A., in association with, Camacho, O. O., Coulomb, R., & Necochea, A. (1993). *In Search of a Home: Rental and Shared Housing in Latin America.* London: UCL Press.

Gilbert, A., & Crankshaw, O. (1999). Comparing South African and Latin American experience: Migration and housing mobility in Soweto *Urban Studies, 36* (13), 2375–2400.

Gilbert, A., Mabin, A., McCarthy, M. & Watson, V. (1997). Low-income rental housing: Are South African cities different? *Environment and Urbanization, 9* (1), 133–147.

Gilbert, A., & Varley, A. (1989a). From renting to self-help ownership? Residential tenure in urban Mexico since 1940. In Gilbert, A. (Ed.) Housing and Land in Urban Mexico. (pp. 13–37). San Diego: Centre for US-Mexican Studies, University of California.

Gilbert, A., & Varley, A. (1989b). The Mexican landlord: Rental housing in Guadalajara and Puebla. Institute of Latin American Studies: London.

Gilbert, A., & Varley, A. (1990). Renting a home in a third world city: Choice or constraint? *International Journal of Urban and Regional Research, 14*(1), 89–108.

Gilbert, A., & Varley, A. (1991). *Landlord and Tenant: Housing the Poor in Urban Mexico.* London: Routledge.

Gilbert, A., & Ward, P. M. (1982). Residential movement among the poor: the constraints on housing choice in Latin American cities. *Transactions of the Institute of British Geographers,* NS 7, 129–49.

Galiani, S., & Schargrodsky, E. (2005). Property rights for the poor: Effects of land titling. Buenos Aires, Argentina: Centro de Investigación en Finanzas, Documento de Trabajo 06/2005.

González de la Rocha, M. (2006). Vanishing assets: Cumulative disadvantage among the urban poor. *Annals of the American Academy, (606)*, 68–94.

González de la Rocha, M. (1994). *The resources of poverty: Women and survival in a Mexican city.* Cambridge, MA: Blackwell.

Gough, K. V., & Kellett, P. (2001). Housing consolidation and home-based income generation: Evidence from self-help settlements in two Colombian cities. *Cities, 18*(4), 235–247.

Green, G. (1988). The quest for *tranguilidad*: Paths to home ownership in Santa Cruz, Bolivia. *Bulletin of Latin American Research, 7*(1), 1–15.

Habitat for Humanity. (2006). Frequently asked questions: How habitat for humanity works. Retrieved from http://www.habitatforhumanity.org.uk/lea_faqs.htm

Harris, N., Rosser, C., & Kumar, S. (1996). Jobs for the poor: A case study in cuttack. London, United Kingdom: UCL Press.

Harriss, J., Stokke, K., & Törnquist, O. (2004). Introduction: The new local politics of democratisation. In J. Harriss, K. Stokke, & O. Törnquist (Eds.), *Politicising democracy: The new local politics and democratisation* (pp. 1–28). Basingstoke, United Kingdom: Palgrave Macmillan.

Hegel, G. W. F. (1821/1991). Elements of the philosophy of right. In A. W. Wood & H. B. Nisbet (Translator) (Eds.), *Cambridge texts in the history of political thought.* Cambridge, MA: Cambridge University Press.

IFPRI. (2003). Jessore and Tongi: Urban livelihoods in the slums. Washington, DC: International Food Policy Research Institute. Retrieved from http://www.ifpri.org/themes/mp14/profiles/jessoretongi.pdf

International Labour Office. (2002b). *Women and men in the informal economy: A statistical picture.* Geneva, Switzerland: International Labour Office.

Imparato, I., & Ruster, J. (2003). *Slum upgrading and participation: Lessons from Latin America.* Washington, DC: World Bank.

Jimenez, E. (1983). The magnitude and determinants of home improvements in self-help housing: Manila's tondo project. *Land Economics, 59*(1), 70–83.

Jones, G. A., & Datta, K. (1998). From self-help to self-finance: The changing focus of urban research and policy. In K. Datta & G. A. Jones (Eds.), *Housing and finance in developing countries* (pp. 3–25). London, United Kingdom: Routledge.

Jones, G. A., & Mitlin, D. (1998). Housing finance and non-governmental organisation in developing countries. In K. Datta & G. A. Jones (Eds.), *Housing and finance in developing countries* (pp. 26–43). London, United Kingdom: Routledge.

Keivani, R., & Werna, E. (2001). Refocusing the housing debate in developing countries from a pluralist perspective. *Habitat International, 2001/6, 25* (2), 191–208.

Kellett, P., & Tipple, A. G. (2000). The home as workplace: A study of income-generating activities within the domestic setting. *Environment and Urbanization, 12* (1), 203–213.

Kumar, S. (1989). How poorer groups find accommodation in third world cities: A guide to the literature. *Environment and Urbanisation, 1* (2), 71–85.

Kumar, S. (1996a). Landlordism in third world urban low-income settlements: A case for further research. *Urban Studies, 33* (4/5), 753–782.

Kumar, S. (1996b). *Subsistence and petty-capitalist landlords: An inquiry into the petty commodity production of rental housing in low-income settlements in Madras.* London, United Kingdom: Development Planning Unit, University College London, Unpublished PhD Dissertation.

Kumar, S. (1996c). Subsistence and petty capitalist landlords: A theoretical framework for the analysis of landlordism in third world low income settlements. *International Journal of Urban and Regional Research, 20* (2), 317–329.

Kumar, S. (2001a). Embedded tenures: Private renting and housing policy in India. *Housing Studies, 16* (4), 425–442.

Kumar, S. (2001b). *Social relations, rental housing markets and the poor in urban India.* London, United Kingdom: Department of Social Policy, London School of Economics.

Kumar, S. (2002). Round pegs and square holes: Mismatches between poverty and housing policy in urban India. In P. Townsend & D. Gordon (Eds.), *World poverty: New policies to defeat an old enemy* (pp. 271–295). London, United Kingdom: Policy Press.

Kumar, S. (2005). Room for manoeuvre: Tenure and the urban poor in India. In N. Hamdi (Ed.), *Urban futures.* London, United Kingdom: Intermediate Technology.

Lee-Smith, D. (1990). Squatter landlords in Nairobi: A case study of Korgocho. In P. Amis & P. Lloyd (Eds.), *Housing Africa's urban poor.* Manchester, United Kingdom: Manchester University Press.

Lewis, D. (2002). Civil society in African contexts: Reflections on the usefulness of a concept. *Development and Change, 33* (4), 569–586.

Moser, C. O. N. (1998). The asset vulnerability framework: Reassessing urban poverty reduction strategies. *World Development, 26* (1), 1–19.

Patel, S., Burra, S., & d'Cruz, C. (2001). Shack/slum dwellers international (SDI): Foundations to treetops. *Environment and Urbanization, 13* (2), 45–59.

Patel, S., d'Cruz, C., & Burra, S. (2002). Beyond evictions in a global city: People-managed resettlement in Mumbai. *Environment and Urbanization, 14* (1), 159–172.

Payne, G. K. (2002). *Land, rights and innovation: Improving tenure security for the urban poor.* London, United Kingdom: ITDG.

Pennant, T. (1990). The growth of small-scale renting in low-income urban housing in Malawi. In P. Amis & P. Lloyd, (Eds.), *Housing Africa's urban poor* (pp. 189–201). Manchester, United Kingdom: Manchester University Press.

Poverty Site, The. (2007). The UK site for statistics on poverty and social exclusion. The New Policy Institute. Retrieved from http://www.poverty.org.uk/01/index.shtml

Rakodi, C. (1995a). The household strategies of the urban poor: Coping with poverty and recession in Gweru, Zimbabwe. *Habitat International, 19* (4), 447–471.

Rakodi, C. (1995b). Poverty lines or household strategies: A review of conceptual issues in the study of urban poverty. *Habitat International, 19* (4), 407–426.

Rakodi, C. (1999). A capital assets framework for analysing household livelihood strategies: Implications for policy. *Development Policy Review, 17*, 315–342.

Rakodi, C. (2002). A livelihoods approach: Conceptual issues and definitions. In C. Rakodi & T. Lloyd-Jones (Eds.), *Urban livelihoods: A people centred approach to reducing urban poverty* (pp. 3–22). London, United Kingdom: Earthscan.

Rakodi, C., & Lloyd-Jones, T. (Eds.). (2002). *Urban livelihoods: A people centred approach to reducing urban poverty.* London, United Kingdom: Earthscan.

Riley, E., Fiori, J., & Ramirez, R. (2001). Favela Bairro and a new generation of housing programmes for the urban poor. *Geoforum, 32* (4), 521–531.

Rodell, M. J. (1983). Sites and services and low-income housing. In R. J. Skinner & M. J. Rodell (Eds.), *People, poverty and shelter: Problems of self-help housing in the third world* (pp. 21–52). London, United Kingdom: Methuen.

Satterthwaite, D. (1997). Urban poverty: Reconsidering its scale and nature. *IDS Bulletin, 28* (2), 9–23.

Satterthwaite, D. (2001). Rural and urban poverty: Understanding the differences. U.S Department of State. Retrieved from http://usinfo.state.gov/journals/ites/0901/ijee/satterthwaite.htm

Sen, A. (1993). Capability and well-being. In M. Nussbaum & A. Sen (Eds.), *The quality of life* (pp. 30–53). Oxford, United Kingdom: Clarendon Press.

Sen, A. (1997). *On economic Inequality.* Oxford, United Kingdom: Clarendon Press.

Sen, A. K. (1992). *Inequality reexamined.* New Delhi, India: Oxford University Press.

Smets, P. (1997). Private housing finance in India: Reaching down market. *Habitat International, 21* (1), 1–15.

Stanglin, D. (2011, September 9). Census bureau: U.S. poverty rate rises to 15.1%, highest since 1993. *USA Today: On Deadline*. Retrieved from http://content.usatoday.com/communities/ondeadline/post/2011/09/census-bureau-us-poverty-rises-to-151-highest-since-1983/1

Stewart, F. (1985). *Planning to meet basic needs.* London, United Kingdom: Macmillan.

Strassman, P. W. (1980). Housing improvements in an opportune setting: Cartenega, Colombia. *Land Economics, 56* (2), 153–168.

Strassmann, W. P. (1986). Types of neighbourhood and home-based enterprises: Evidence from Lima, Peru. *Urban Studies, 23*, 485–500.

Streeten, P. P., & World Bank (1981). First things first : Meeting basic human needs in the developing countries. New York, NY; Oxford, United Kingdom: Oxford University Press.

Struyk, R. J., & Lynn, R. (1983). Determinants of housing investment in slum areas: Tondo and other locations in metro Manila. *Land Economics, 59* (4), 444–454.

Townsend, P. (2007). *The right to social security and national development: Lessons from OECD experience for low-income countries*. Issues in Social Protection, Discussion Paper 18. Geneva, Switzerland: Social Security Department, International Labour Office.

Turner, J. (1968). Housing priorities, settlement patterns and urban development in modernising countries. *Journal of the American Institute of Planners, 34* (5), 354–363.

Turner, J. F. C. (1972). Housing as a verb. In J. F. C. Turner & R. Fitcher (Eds.), *Freedom to build.* New York, NY: Macmillan.

Turner, J. F. C. (1978). Housing in three dimensions: Terms of reference for the housing question redefined. *World Development, 6* (9/10), 1135–1145.

UNCHS. (1989). *Improving income and housing: Employment generation in low-income settlements.* Nairobi, Kenya: United Nations Centre for Human Settlements.

UNCHS. (1989b). Strategies for low-income shelter and services development: The rental housing option. Nairobi: United Nations Centre for Human Settlements (Habitat).

UNCHS. (1993). Support measures to promote rental housing for low-income groups. Nairobi, Kenya: United Nations Centre for Human Settlements (Habitat).

UNCHS. (1996). Urban poverty: A world challenge (The recife declaration, 1996). *Recife,* Brazil: UNCHS (Habitat).

United Nations Population Fund (2007). State of the world population, 2007, unleashing the potential of urban growth. Retrieved from http://www.unfpa .org/webdav/site/global/shared/documents/publications/2007/695_filename _sowp2007_eng.pdf

UN-Habitat. (2003a). The challenge of slums — Global report on human settlements 2003. Nairobi, Kenya: United Nations Human Settlements Programme (UN-Habitat).

UN-Habitat. (2003b). Rental housing: An essential option for the urban poor in developing countries. Nairobi, Kenya: United Nations Human Settlements Programme (UN-Habitat).

UN-Habitat. (2005). Forced Evictions — Towards solutions?: First report of the advisory group on forced evictions to the executive director of UN-HABITAT. Nairobi, Kenya: UN-Habitat. Retrieved from http://www.unhabitat.org/pmss/ getPage.asp?page=bookView&book=1806

UN-Habitat. (2006). *State of the world's cities 2006–07: The millennium development goals and urban sustainability: 30 years of shaping the habitat agenda.* London, United Kingdom: Earthscan.

UN-Habitat (2009). *State of the world cities 2010/2011: Bridging the urban divide.* Retrieved from http://www.unhabitat.org/documents/SOWC10/R1.pdf

UN-Habitat. (n.d.). Global campaign for secure tenure. Retrieved from http:// www.unhabitat.org/categories.asp?catid=24

Universalia. (2006). Independent evaluation of the cities alliance: Volume 1. Universalia: Retrieved from http://www.citiesalliance.org/about-ca/2006-independent-evaluation.html

Urban Resource Centre. (n.d.). The Orangi pilot project. Retrieved from http:// www.urckarachi.org/orangi.htm

Urban Resource Centre Phnom Penh. (2002). Study of relocation of urban poor communities in Phnom Penh. Phnom Penh, Cambodia: Urban Resource Centre, Phnom Penh. Retrieved from http://www.citiesalliance.org/cdsdb .nsf/Attachments/Cambodia+−+Phnom+Penh+−+Relocation+of+ Urban+Poor+Communities/$File/PP+CDS+Relocation+Study+−+Final+ Draft.doc

Varley, A. (1987). The relationship between tenure legalization and housing improvements: Evidence from Mexico City. *Development and Change, 18,* 463–481.

Wilpert, G. (2005). Venezuela's quiet housing revolution: Urban land reform. Retrieved from http://www.venezuelanalysis.com/print.php?artno=1551

Wood, G., & Salway, S. (2000). Introduction: Securing livelihoods in Dhaka slums. *Journal of International Development, 12,* 669–688.

Woodruff, C. (2001). Review of de Soto's. *The Mystery of Capital Journal of Economic Literature, 39* (4), 1215–1223.

World Bank. (1993). *Housing: Enabling markets to work.* Washington, DC: World Bank.

World Bank. (2000). *World Development Report 2000–2001: Attacking Poverty.* Oxford, United Kingdom: Oxford University Press.

World Bank. (2006). 2006—World Development Indicators: People. Retrieved from http://devdata.worldbank.org/wdi2006/contents/Section2.htm

World Bank. (2007a). Abstract of housing: Enabling markets to work (internet). Retrieved from http://www-wds.worldbank.org/external/default/main?page PK=64193027&piPK=64187937&theSitePK=523679&menuPK=64187510& searchMenuPK=64187283&siteName=WDS&entityID=000178830_981019111 94018

World Bank. (2007b). Housing and land. Washington, DC: World Bank. Retrieved from http://go.worldbank.org/OTO3F852E0

World Bank. (2007c). Urban poverty: What are the policy issues. Retrieved from http://web.worldbank.org/WBSITE/EXTERNAL/TOPICS/EXTURBANDEVEL OPMENT/EXTURBANPOVERTY/0,,contentMDK:20227683~menuPK:341331~ pagePK:148956~piPK:216618~theSitePK:341325,00.html

World Bank. (2009). 2009 world development indicators. Retrieved from http:// www-wds.worldbank.org/external/default/WDSContentServer/IW3P/IB/2010 /04/21/000333037_20100421020546/Rendered/PDF/541680WDI0200910Box34 5641B01PUBLIC1.pdf

Wratten, E. (1995). Conceptualising urban poverty. *Environment and Urbanisation, 7* (1), 11–36.

YUVA. (1999). *Our home is a slum: An exploration of a community and local government collaboration in a tenants struggle to establish legal residency.* Geneva, Switzerland: UNRISD.

Chapter 9
Child Welfare Policy

Richard J. Gelles and Carol Wilson Spigner

> The child welfare system in the United States has evolved over time and continues to evolve. Child welfare policy practice and advocacy in the social work profession has had a profound impact on policies and services affecting children and families at risk. As you read this chapter you are encouraged to consider the transition of values within the child welfare system over time, the impact change has had on outcomes for children and families and how the system should be further improved to sustain and promote healthy children and families.

Children, especially young children, are dependent on their parents, relatives, communities, and ultimately society for their survival. Children's developmental well-being may be threatened if they become orphans, if they are abandoned by parents or relatives, or if they are maltreated. The maltreatment of children has manifested itself in nearly every conceivable manner—physically, emotionally, sexually, and by forced child labor (Ten Bensel, Rheinberger, & Radbill, 1997). Historians have documented occurrences of various forms of child mistreatment since the beginning of recorded history. In some ancient cultures, children had no rights until the right to live was bestowed on them by their father. The right to live was sometimes withheld by fathers, and newborns were abandoned or left to die. Although we do not have a means to know how numerous abandonment or killing was, we do know that infanticide was widely accepted among ancient and prehistoric cultures. Newborns and infants could be put to death because they cried too much, because they were sickly or deformed, or because of some perceived imperfection. Girls, twins, and children of unmarried women were the special targets of infanticide (Robin, 1980).

Infanticide was not the only abuse inflicted by generations of parents. From prehistoric times to the present, children have been mutilated, beaten, and maltreated. Such treatment was not only condoned, but was often mandated as the most appropriate child-rearing method. Children were, and continue to be, hit with rods, canes, and switches. Boys have been castrated to produce eunuchs. Girls have been, and continue to be, subjected to genital surgery or mutilation as part of culturally approved ritual. Colonial parents were implored to "beat the devil" out of their children (Greven, 1991; Straus, 1994). Summarizing the plight of children from prehistorical times to the present, David Bakan (1971, p. 3) comments, "Child abuse thrives in the shadows of privacy and secrecy. It lives by inattention."

In many cases of orphans, abandoned children, and even maltreated children, relatives and informal community networks became involved in the caring and protection of dependent children. When kin and community were insufficient, societies developed more formal mechanisms to care for and protect children.

Concern for the rights and welfare of children has waxed and waned over the centuries, but there has always been some attempt to protect children from mistreatment. Six thousand years ago, children in Mesopotamia had a patron goddess to look after them. The Greeks and Romans had orphan homes. A variety of historical accounts mention some form of "fostering" for dependent children. Samuel Radbill (1980) reports that child protection laws were enacted as long ago as 450 BCE. Attempts were made to modify and restrict fathers' complete control over their children. Anthropologists note that virtually all societies have mores, laws, or customs that regulate sexual access to children.

The Renaissance marked a new morality regarding children. Children were seen as a dependent class in need of the protection of society. At the same time, however, the family as an institution was deemed responsible for teaching children the proper rules of behavior. Moreover, this was a period in which the power of the father increased dramatically. This dialectic—concern for children and increased demands and power of parents to control children—has been a consistent theme throughout history.

The Enlightenment of the 18th century brought children increased attention, services, and protection. The London Foundling Hospital, founded during the 18th century, not only provided medical care, but also was a center of the moral reform movement on behalf of children (Robin, 1980).

This chapter examines child welfare policy specifically in the United States, with attention to the definition of child maltreatment, development of systems for addressing abuse and neglect, and the challenges of foster care. From the founding of the nation until the present, child welfare policies have been molded by efforts at the state level that have influenced the development of policy. In this country, the states retain all powers that are not specifically reserved for the federal government. The federal powers include monetary policy, foreign policy, interstate commerce and transactions, and national taxation policy. Child protection is the responsibility of the states. Thus, there is no single, national child welfare system, nor is there one set of policies in the United States. Because states have the authority to define child abuse and neglect and to develop their own policy responses, there are in fact no fewer than 300 child welfare systems; some are state-operated, some county-based, and some are hybrid models. There are 51 sets of child welfare policies, one for each state and the

District of Columbia. Most other nations—with the exception of Australia, which has an even stronger federalist system of government—concentrate child welfare policies and programs under a single national policy. In the United States, federal policy formation has followed the development of state policies. However, today there is a federal statutory framework that shapes and is influenced by state policies through the establishment of standards and funding mechanisms.

A second feature of child welfare policy in the United States is the intersection of parental rights and children's rights. The development of parental rights and responsibilities is a derivative of English Common Law and American case law. Parental rights, though not specifically articulated in the U.S. Constitution, are embodied in precedents set by rulings of the U.S. Supreme Court and are heavily influenced by the privacy rights of citizens. Parental rights include the right to custody, control, and decision making for children. With these rights come reciprocal parental responsibilities to protect, educate, support, and care for the child. Children's rights are also developed in case law, in which the doctrines of *best interest of the child* and *parens patria* (the state as ultimate parent; Davidson, 1997) were crafted. The rights of children have been slow to develop, but have been advanced by various advocacy groups seeking to assure that children are protected from acts of omission or commission that threaten children's safety and well-being.

A Brief History of Child Welfare Policy in the United States

The early years of this country were characterized by immigration, internal migration, and the settling of new communities. During the 19th century, the United States was beginning to industrialize and build urban centers (Axinn & Stern, 2004). At the same time there were cycles of economic depression that made it difficult for families to support themselves. Child dependency prior to the 19th century was primarily the consequence of children becoming orphans. Maternal death, flu, yellow fever, or other epidemics claimed parents in young adulthood. A second form of dependency came about when parents abandoned unwanted or sickly children or when poverty, homelessness, and alcoholism led parents to desert their children in the hopes that such foundlings would be adopted and raised by individuals with more resources.

Initially, dependent children were cared for in almshouses along with the mentally ill, the cognitively limited, and those with medical conditions. Subsequently, specialized institutions were established for orphaned children (Myers, 2006). Orphanages and foundling hospitals were the primary recipients of orphaned or abandoned children into the beginning of the 20th century. Lindsey (2004) reports that in 1920 there were approximately 750,000 orphans in the United States. Orphanages, almshouses, or infirmaries (as they were called in Europe) housed children in appalling conditions. Investigations of orphanages produced exposés that portrayed children held in inhumane conditions. Even so, by the end of the 19th century there were an estimated 100,000 children housed in 1,000 orphanages (Bruno, 1957; Lindsey, 2004; Myers, 2006). These institutions were primarily funded through private philanthropy.

Well into the 19th century there was no official, law-based system of child welfare policy. The child welfare services that existed were the outcome of individual efforts or organized programs advanced by faith-based organizations or reform movements. Three significant events occurred in the mid-19th century that would provide more structure and focus to efforts to protect children.

The first movement was the product of the efforts of a Yale-educated theologian, Charles Loring Brace, who believed that there must be a better way of raising abandoned and orphaned children than in institutions. Moreover, Brace was deeply concerned about the number of children and youth (mostly immigrant children) who appeared to be wandering the streets of New York City (Lindsey, 2004). Brace founded the Children's Aid Society in 1853 and developed a system he called *placing out*. Placing out involved taking orphaned or abandoned children from New York City and sending them by train to homes in Ohio, Michigan, Illinois, and Indiana (Brace, 1859). Using a network of Presbyterian ministers to identify appropriate families, Brace placed these children with farm families. In Brace's mind, placing needy children on farms would provide them with a wholesome environment in which they could learn the core values of American culture. Between 1853 and 1890 the Children's Aid Society moved 92,000 children from the streets, orphanages, and almshouses of New York to the farms of the Midwest (Leiby, 1978). However, there was an ongoing debate into the 20th century about which kind of placement was best for children: institutions or family foster care.

An incident that occurred in New York City in 1874 provided a second opportunity to formalize child welfare policy. The case of Mary Ellen Wilson is usually considered the turning point in concern for children's welfare. In 1874, 8-year-old Mary Ellen lived in the home of Francis and Mary Connolly but was not the blood relative of either. Mary Ellen was the illegitimate daughter of Mary Connolly's first husband. A neighbor noticed the plight of Mary Ellen, who was beaten with a leather thong and allowed to go ill-clothed in bad weather. The neighbor reported the case to Etta Wheeler, a "friendly visitor" who worked for St. Luke's Methodist Mission. In the mid-1800s, child welfare was church-based rather than government-based. Wheeler turned to the police and to the New York City Department of Charities for help regarding Mary Ellen Wilson and was turned down, first by the police, who said there was no proof of a crime, and then by the charity agency, who asserted that they did not have custody of the child. The legend goes on to note that Henry Berge, founder of the Society for the Prevention of Cruelty to Animals, intervened on behalf of Mary Ellen, and the courts accepted the case because Mary Ellen was a member of the animal kingdom. In reality, the court reviewed the case because the child needed protection. The case was argued, not by Henry Berge, but by his colleague

Elbridge Gerry, a leader in the charity movement. Mary Ellen Wilson was removed from her foster home and initially placed in an orphanage. Her foster mother was imprisoned for a year, and the case received detailed press coverage for months. In December 1874, the New York Society for the Prevention of Cruelty to Children (SPCC) was founded (Nelson, 1984; Robin, 1980). The SPCC was the first organization that focused on child maltreatment in the United States. Using an "arm of the law" approach, the SPCC accepted reports of abuse and investigated and brought offending parents and caretakers to court for prosecution. Children who were rescued were released to one of the local children's aid societies for care and protection. Protective societies for children appeared and disappeared during the next 80 years.

The third development that helped to formalize child protection was the establishment of the first juvenile court in Illinois in 1899. Until this time, child protection had functioned as primarily a voluntary sector activity. In some instances, the placement of children into institutions and foster care was made by securing surrenders from parents. In other circumstances, the change in custody was informal and lacked legal oversight and protection. The legal system treated children as if they were little adults or as property of their parents. The first juvenile courts were established based on the recognition of the immaturity of children and the need to take action that would further their development. The court that had jurisdiction over dependent and delinquent children was designed to consider the child's social situation when determining what action would meet "the best interest of the child." The court was a civil court that was given the authority to assume protective guardianship, transfer custody, and sever parental rights (Williams, 1980). Eventually, all 50 states established juvenile courts, creating a legal institution that was to become the arbiter of the rights of parents and of children in cases of dependency and delinquency. This development reinforced the notion that the business of protecting children was the responsibility of the state under its *parens patria* power.

By the beginning of the 20th century, some of the key elements that would shape social policy for abused and neglected children were in place: an approach to investigation and prosecution of abuse and neglect, child placement practices that relied on both social institutions and foster family care, and the juvenile court that had the authority to intervene in the lives of families in order to protect children.

Over the next 50 years the visibility of and concern about child protection as reflected in the protective societies appeared and disappeared. The political scientist Barbara Nelson (1984) notes that by the 1950s public interest in child maltreatment was practically nonexistent in the United States (and much of the world, for that matter). Technology paved the way for the rediscovery of physical child abuse. In 1946, the radiologist John Caffey reported on six cases of children who had multiple long-bone fractures and subdural hematomas. It would take 9 more years before the medical profession would begin to accept that such injuries were the direct result of actions by children's caretakers. In 1955, P. V. Wooley and W. A. Evans not only concluded that the X-rays revealed a pattern of injuries, but that the injuries were committed willfully. Wooley and Evans went on to criticize the medical profession for its reluctance to accept the accumulating evidence that long-bone fractures that were seen on X-rays were indeed inflicted willfully.

In 1958, C. Henry Kempe and his colleagues formed the first hospital-based child protective team at Colorado General Hospital in Denver. Kempe, Silverman, Steele, Droegemueller, and Silver would publish their landmark article, "The Battered Child Syndrome," in the *Journal of the American Medical Association* in July 1962. Kempe and his multidisciplinary colleagues' article was accompanied by a strong editorial on the battered child. The article and the editorial were the beginning of the modern concern for child abuse and neglect, a concern that has grown and expanded both nationally and internationally over the past four decades.

The Initial Involvement of the Federal Government

The federal government is a recent arrival in the area of policy for the protection of dependent children, with many of the developments occurring in the second half of the 20th century. A series of antecedent events that set the stage for active involvement in child welfare policy included the 1909 White House Conference, the establishment of the Children's Bureau, and the development of the federal income maintenance program for poor children and their families. As part of the progressive era, women from the settlement movement lobbied for a federal commission on children. They had lived in urban areas with the poor and had firsthand knowledge of the impact of poverty on children. Out of their advocacy came the 1909 White House Conference on the Care of Dependent Children, which established principles to guide the care of children in the United States. Settling the debate over institutional care versus foster family care, the primacy of family foster care was established, as well as the principle that children should not be removed from their families due to poverty alone. The conference also called for the creation of a unit in the federal government to study the conditions of children (*Proceedings of the White House Conference on the Care of Dependent Children,* 1909).

The United States Children's Bureau was founded in 1912 as an agency within the Department of Labor. (The Bureau was later moved to the newly created Department of Health, Education, and Welfare, which was subsequently renamed the Department of Health and Human Services.) The Children's Bureau was founded by an act of Congress with a mandate to:

> [I]nvestigate and report on all matters pertaining to the welfare of children and child life among all classes of our people . . . especially infant mortality, birth rates, orphanages, juvenile courts, desertion, dangerous occupations, accidents, and diseases of children . . . and legislation affecting children.

(*U.S. Children's Bureau, 1912*)

Initially, the Bureau published studies that informed the public and policy makers about key issues. It also published model legislation to help advance the development of juvenile courts (U.S. Children's Bureau, 1961). An important part of their work was in the area of public education on child development issues.

The Children's Bureau has engaged in a variety of activities regarding child maltreatment and participated in the earliest national meetings on child abuse, sponsored by the Children's Division of the American Humane Association. After the publication of Kempe and colleagues' 1962 article, the Bureau convened a meeting in 1963 that drafted a model child abuse reporting law (Kempe, Silverman, Steele, Droegemueller, & Silver, 1962). By 1967, all 50 states and the District of Columbia had enacted mandatory reporting laws based on the Bureau's model. In 1974, Congress enacted the Child Abuse Prevention and Treatment Act (CAPTA) and created the National Center on Child Abuse and Neglect (Nelson, 1984). Today, the Office of Child Abuse and Neglect remains within the Children's Bureau and continues to coordinate the federal effort to prevent and treat the abuse and neglect of children in the United States. In addition to CAPTA, the Children's Bureau is currently responsible for the administration of other federal programs related to child protection, foster care, and special-needs adoption.

The third major federal initiative that would impact child welfare policy was the enactment of the Social Security Act of 1935. The Social Security Act, a cornerstone of Franklin Roosevelt's New Deal policies, established a public welfare system for poor, fatherless children and a public welfare system for the purpose of protecting and caring for homeless, dependent, and neglected children who were thought to be in danger of becoming delinquent (Waldfogel, 1998). The Social Security Act included the Aid for Dependent Children program, which succeeded "mother's pensions." As noted later in this chapter, a 1961 amendment to the Social Security Act of 1935 provided funding for children who were removed from their homes for abuse and neglect (O'Neil & Gesiriech, 2005). In 1962, the Aid for Dependent Children programs was changed to Aid to Families with Dependent Children (AFDC).

The Impact of the Child Abuse Prevention and Treatment Act of 1974

The goal of the 1974 CAPTA was to prevent abuse, disseminate information, treat children who were maltreated, and promote the development of a competent workforce. To receive funding under CAPTA, states had to enact the minimum definition of maltreatment and assure that their system for receiving and investigating reports had such provisions as a hotline number, immunity for reporters, mandatory reporting, and confidentiality. The immediate impact of the enactment of CAPTA was an exponential increase in reported cases of suspected child maltreatment. In 1967, Gil (1970) collected information regarding child abuse reporting and found

6,000 confirmed cases of child abuse in the United States. By 1976, 2 years after CAPTA was enacted, states received more than 500,000 reports of *suspected* child abuse and neglect. The number of reports doubled to 1 million by 1979, doubled again to 2 million in 1986, and reached 3 million reports in 1993. Reports of suspected child maltreatment have remained stable at about 3 million per year since 1997 (see Figure 9.1).

The number of reports is significant because it represents the actual number of reports and investigations that state and county child protective service agencies must manage. It is also worth noting that while the number of reports of suspected child maltreatment increased, so, too, did the rate of reports. In 1977, the rate of children reported as suspected victims of child abuse and neglect was approximately 10 children per 1,000 children in the United States. The rate doubled to more than 20 per 1,000 children in 1984, and doubled again to more than 40 children per 1,000 in 1996 (see Figure 9.2).

Figure 9.1

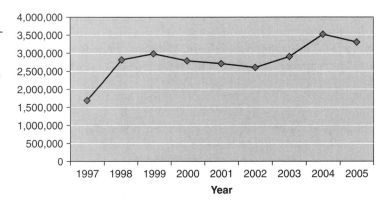

Reports of child maltreatment, 1997 to 2005. *Source*: Based on *Child Maltreatment 2005*, by the U.S. Department of Health and Human Services, Administration on Children, Youth, and Families, 2007, Washington, DC: U.S. Government Printing Office

Figure 9.2

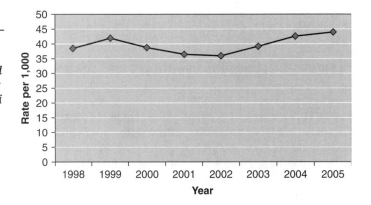

Rates of child abuse reports, 1998 to 2005. *Source*: Based on *Child Maltreatment 2005*, by the U.S. Department of Health and Human Services, Administration on Children, Youth, and Families, 2007, Washington, DC: U.S. Government Printing Office

Thus, the initial goal of CAPTA was accomplished, increasing the public identification of children who were being abused and neglected behind closed doors. The assumption behind CAPTA was that if maltreated children could be identified, state and county agencies would be able to take appropriate steps to protect the victims of abuse and neglect and hopefully help the families and caregivers who were maltreating them.

The increase in both the number of children reported and the rate of reporting was not entirely the result of CAPTA. First, CAPTA was followed up by local, and eventually national, public awareness campaigns that were designed to raise the public's (and also specified reporters') awareness of the existence of child maltreatment and the importance of reporting suspected cases. The federal model law (CAPTA) and state legislation provided immunity from prosecution for anyone making a good-faith report of suspected child maltreatment.

Second, the public awareness campaigns were accompanied in some states, and eventually in all states, with technological advances that facilitated the process through which individuals made reports. Even before CAPTA was enacted, Florida developed a public awareness campaign and instituted a toll-free telephone number so that child maltreatment reporters could make a report without incurring a toll charge. In the year after the Florida public awareness campaign and the introduction of the toll-free telephone number (1970), the annual number of reports of child abuse and neglect increased from 17 to 17,000.

A third factor that contributed to the increase in child abuse and neglect reports was the broadening of the definition of what constitutes child maltreatment.

When Kempe et al. (1962) wrote their path-breaking article about child abuse, they labeled the problem "the battered child syndrome." They defined the syndrome as a deliberate act of physical violence that produced diagnosable injuries.

The Child Abuse Prevention and Treatment Act of 1974 (Public Law 93–247) broadened the definition of maltreatment from Kempe and his colleague's more narrow definition. The definition of child maltreatment included in Public Law 93–247 (Child Abuse Prevention and Treatment Act of 1974) was: the physical or mental injury, sexual abuse, negligent treatment, or maltreatment of a child under the age of eighteen by a person who is responsible for the child's welfare under circumstances which indicate the child's welfare is harmed or threatened thereby.

Unlike Kempe et al.'s (1962) definition, this definition included categories of maltreatment for which there might not be conclusive evidence, such as neglect and emotional injury. In these areas, the standard used to define maltreatment was the "minimum community standard of care." The category was expanded with no specification of what those behaviors or the developmental consequences might be.

In 1984, the definition of child maltreatment was further broadened in the reauthorization of CAPTA (Child Abuse Amendments of 1984) by enacting the following:

> The physical or mental injury, sexual abuse or exploitation, negligent treatment, or maltreatment of a child under the age of eighteen or the age specified by the child protection law of the state in question, by a person (including an employee of a residential facility or any staff person providing out-of-home care) who is responsible for the child's welfare under circumstances which indicate that the child's health or welfare is harmed or threatened thereby, as determined in regulations prescribed by the Secretary. This refined the definition of maltreatment to cover actions taken by persons responsible for the care of the child and affirmed the role of the state in defining childhood for the purpose of protection. This change recognizes the shared responsibility of the state and federal government in the protection of children. The federal definition was changed in 1988 to indicate that the behavior had to be avoidable and nonaccidental and resulted in a narrowing of the definition by excluding accidents that were not avoidable (Child Abuse Prevention, Adoption and Family Services Act of 1988). This new clause attempted to address the issue of intent; however, it provided no clear guidance as to how to classify or categorize cases based on intent.

The most recent authorization of CAPTA, signed into law in 2003, provides more specificity in the definition of sexual abuse and further defines the Baby Doe provisions related to withholding of medically indicated treatment from infants who are seriously ill (Keeping Children and Families Safe Act of 2003, Public Law 108–36). The relevant definitions read:

> [T]he term "child abuse and neglect" means, at a minimum, any recent act or failure to act on the part of a parent or caretaker, which results in death, serious physical or emotional harm, sexual abuse or exploitation, or an act or failure to act which presents an imminent risk of serious harm;
>
> the term "sexual abuse" includes—
>
> A. the employment, use, persuasion, inducement, enticement, or coercion of any child to engage in, or assist any other person to engage in, any sexually explicit conduct or simulation of such conduct for the purpose of producing a visual depiction of such conduct; or
>
> B. the rape, and in cases of caretaker or inter-familial relationships, statutory rape, molestation, prostitution, or other form of sexual exploitation of children, or incest with children.
>
> The phrase "withholding of medically indicated treatment" refers to the failure to respond to the infant's life-threatening conditions by providing treatment (including appropriate nutrition, hydration, and medication), which, in the treating physician's reasonable medical judgment, will be most likely to be effective in ameliorating or correcting all such conditions. The phrase does not encompass the failure to provide treatment (other than appropriate nutrition, hydration, or medication) to an infant when, in the treating physician's reasonable medical judgment, the infant is chronically and irreversibly comatose; the provision of such treatment would

- *merely prolong dying;*
- *not be effective in ameliorating or correcting all of the infant's life-threatening conditions; or otherwise be futile in terms of the survival of the infant; or*
- *the provision of such treatment would be virtually futile in terms of the survival of the infant and the treatment itself under such circumstances would be inhumane. (USC Title 42 Chapter 67 Subchapter I §5106g)*

Given the broadening of the definition of child maltreatment, increased public awareness, and technological advances that made it easier to report and respond to cases of suspected child maltreatment, it is not at all surprising that the number and rates of reports have increased. It is important to note that increases in reporting do not indicate an actual increase in the occurrence of child maltreatment.

There has also been an unintended consequence of CAPTA legislation and the goal of increased reporting. By the mid-1980s, the substantiation rate for child maltreatment reports had stabilized at 40%. A founded or substantiated report of child maltreatment generally means that sufficient evidence has been found during the investigation to conclude that a child has been abused or neglected.[1] Thus, one consequence of CAPTA is that more than half of the investigations carried out by state or county child welfare agencies end with a finding that there is insufficient evidence to conclude that abuse or neglect has occurred. Not only does this mean that significant human and financial resources are invested in responding to reports that will end up providing neither protection to children nor assistance to families, but it is also the case that there is less than a 50% chance that someone who makes a report will see that report lead to anything other than an investigation. As the pediatrician Eli Newberger (1983, p. 307) put it 9 years after the enactment of CAPTA, the promise implicit in child abuse reporting laws is an empty promise for many children. Newberger believed that mandatory reporting was a false promise; the law created only intrusive investigations with few actual services offered to the families subjected to the investigations.

Foster Care Drift and the Adoption Assistance and Child Welfare Act of 1980

It is clear that CAPTA generated substantial increases in the number of children reported for child abuse and neglect. By inference, one might think that this would have also led to an increase in the number of children who were placed into out-of-home care in the United States. However, data on foster care placements (see Figure 9.3)[2] indicate that as early as 1962 there were more than 270,000 children in out-of-home care. The number peaked at 330,000 in 1971, and the next available formal estimate was 302,000 children in foster care in 1980.

Figure 9.3

Number of children in foster care 1981–2005. *Source*: **Based on Adoption and Foster Care Analysis and Reporting System, retrieved from www.acf.hhs.gov/ programs/cb/stats _research/afcars/ trends.htm**

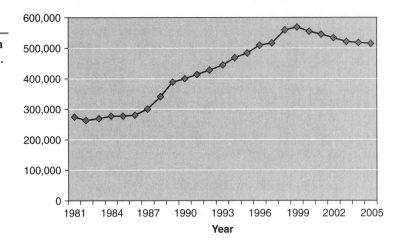

Although it appears that the actual number of children in foster care did not increase dramatically during the 1960s and early 1970s, the prevailing professional view of foster care shifted during this time. By the late 1950s, serious questions were raised about the role and function of the foster care system. Until this time, the system was focused on the removal of children from high-risk situations, and the focus of casework practice was on the placement process. Little attention was paid to what happened to children after they entered care. The landmark study *Children in Need of Parents* (Maas & Engler, 1959) documented the status of children in foster care as "orphans of the living," not belonging to their own parents or to any other set of parents. This work and other research indicated that foster care was far from temporary (Fanschel & Shinn, 1978). By the late 1970s, foster care had become a permanent status for many children who entered the child welfare system. Children placed into foster care did not reside in a single foster home; rather, they *drifted* from one placement to another, with little stability or continuity of care. The view of foster care began to shift toward that of a temporary service whose purpose was to reunite children with their families or place them in another family if necessary (Pecora, Whittaker, Maluccio, & Barth, 2000).

As a result of a 1961 amendment to the Social Security Act of 1935, children who were removed from their homes for abuse and neglect could have the costs of their placement funded from the AFDC program of the Social Security Act if they were eligible for the program had they remained at home (O'Neil & Gesiriech, 2005). The funds covered the cost of foster care but provided no funds for services to parents. The composition of the foster care population was shifting to a system that was disproportionately populated by single-parent families, children of color, and children removed from homes with incomes significantly below the poverty level (Pecora et al., 2000).

In addition to concern over "foster care drift," the paradigm of child abuse and neglect changed in the 1970s. At the time of Kempe et al.'s (1962) first publication on the battered child syndrome, the prevailing causal model was that child abuse was caused by the psychopathology of the caregivers. This model explained abuse and neglect as a function of individual psychopathy. Other models proposed that maltreatment arose out of mental illness or the use and abuse of alcohol and illicit drugs.

By the mid-1970s, the psychopathological model of child abuse and neglect was being replaced with conceptual models that placed greater emphasis on social factors such as income, education, age, marital conflict, stress, and child-produced stressors (see Gelles, 1973; Gil, 1970). Such models were more consistent with an intervention approach that envisioned foster care as a temporary placement while services and resources are directed toward caregivers to provide them means to adequately care for their children. The key assumption behind social-psychological stress models is that all caregivers want to be adequate parents, but there are structural and economic barriers that impede that desire. Children should be kept safe in temporary foster care while the barriers are addressed and removed, or at least lowered.

The Adoption Assistance and Child Welfare Act of 1980

The Adoption Assistance and Child Welfare Amendments of 1980 (AACWA) were the result of expanded recognition that children in foster care were in social and legal limbo, demonstrated permanency planning programs that documented the ability to move children in foster care back to their own families or on to adoptions, and the need to clearly shift the purpose and operation of the child welfare system.

The Adoption Assistance and Child Welfare Act of 1980 (Public Law 96–272) was designed to address the problem of foster care drift. There were *three* major components of this legislation aimed at reducing foster care drift and assuring the right of children to have permanent homes. The first major provision of the legislation was the requirement that states make "reasonable efforts to maintain a family" before they remove a child from the child's birth parents and "reasonable efforts to reunify a family" before establishing a permanency plan of adoption. The reasonable efforts requirement mandated states to provide appropriate services prior to placement and/or services that would allow for a safe reunification of a child who had been removed. The legislation, however, provided no additional funds for such services.

A second provision of the legislation was the requirement that states engage in permanency planning. In brief, permanency planning required each state to have a plan developed within 18 months of a child being placed into foster care that would assure that the child would have a permanent home, either through a safe return to birth parents or through an adoption. To facilitate permanency planning, the law established a set of procedural requirements that included development of case plans, periodic judicial reviews, and dispositional hearings at which the child's permanent plan was established.

The legislation created Title IV-E of the Social Security Act, which provided uncapped entitlement funding for foster care and adoption assistance for children who were eligible for AFDC. The foster care funding was an extension of the old AFDC provision that allowed for payment of foster care costs for poor children. In addition to permanency planning, the major policy innovation was the provision of funds to subsidize the adoption of special needs foster children. Federal funds could be used to support the cost of operating adoption and foster care programs. The funding continued to be linked to placement services—adoption and foster care—with no targeted funding for services to the families of children in need of protection. Further, states were expected to adhere to the spirit of the reasonable efforts provision and to meet the procedural and temporal requirements of the legislation in order to qualify for Title IV-E federal funds for foster care and adoption.

The Impact of the Adoption Assistance and Child Welfare Act of 1980

The available data on foster care[3] indicate that in the first few years after AACWA was enacted, there was a decline in the number of children in foster care (see Figure 9.3).

From an estimated 302,000 children in foster care the year AACWA was enacted, the number dropped to 262,000 in 1982, the lowest on record. The number of children in foster care remained under 300,000 until 1987 and then began a significant increase, reaching 400,000 in 1990.

The emphasis on permanency led to the freeing of children for adoption and the subsequent adoption of some of the children. More than 50,000 children were freed for adoption in 1982 as a result of state court action (Maza, 1983). Of the children available for adoption, 17,000 had a specific permanency plan for adoption (Maximus Inc., 1984). Of this number 14,400 children were placed for adoption in 1982 (Maximus Inc., 1984).[4]

The Indian Child Welfare Act of 1978

Between the time CAPTA was enacted and AACWA became law, a disproportionate number of Native American children were removed from their parents and placed in the foster care system. As many as 25% to 35% of Native American children in certain states were placed in the foster care system between 1974 and 1978 (Myers, 2006). Not only were the children placed in foster care, but the vast majority of the children were placed outside of their tribe with non-Indian families. In response to a multiyear study of the placement of Indian children (Fanschel, 1972), tribal advocacy challenged these practices. In a period in which Congress was actively promoting the sovereign status of tribes, the Indian Child Welfare Act of 1978 (ICWA; Public Law 95–608) was enacted (Jones, 1995). The Act established standards for child custody proceedings related to foster care, termination of parental rights, and adoption of Indian children. The standards included tribal court jurisdiction over children who reside on the reservation; the requirement of notification to the tribe of state or local proceedings involving the placement of an Indian child living off the reservation, along with tribal rights to intervene and request transfer of the proceeding to tribal court; an increased standard of proof to clear and convincing evidence; and placement preferences for the extended family or tribe (Pecora et al., 2000).

The intent of ICWA was to limit the placement of Native American children into non–Native American homes. However, ICWA had numerous ambiguities, including the definition of an "Indian child," as well as interpretation of key clauses and terms (e.g., What is "good cause"?). The Act also challenged the tribes to develop or expand their protective services and tribal court capacities.

Applicable Supreme Court Rulings

Before examining federal and state child welfare policy after 1980, it is important to also consider how case law has influenced child welfare policy in the United States. There were three major U.S. Supreme Court rulings in the 1970s and 1980s that established guiding precedents for the child welfare system. In issues of child protection and custody, the Court has been the arbiter of the relationship between parents, children, and the state.

Until the early 1970s, unmarried mothers were deemed the sole custodians of their children. For children entering foster care, the legal proceedings were focused on the relationship between the child and the birth mother. Unmarried fathers were only part of the proceeding in those instances in which their legal relationship to the child was established through cohabitation. This issue was resolved in *Stanley v. Illinois* (1972) when the Supreme Court ruled that unmarried fathers were entitled to a hearing to determine their fitness in child protection custody proceedings. This right was based on the due process clause of the 14th Amendment. This landmark decision not only gave unmarried fathers a right to be heard but also gave children access to the resources of their noncustodial, unmarried parent.

U.S. law and tradition grant parents broad discretion as to how they rear their children. In *Smith v. Organization of Foster Families for Equality and Reform* (1977), the U.S. Supreme Court held that the 14th Amendment gave parents a "constitutionally recognized liberty interest" in maintaining the custody of their children "that derives from blood relationship, state law sanction, and basic human right." This interest is not absolute, however, because of the state's power and authority to exercise *parens patria* duties to protect citizens who cannot fend for themselves. The state may attempt to limit or end parent–child contact and make children eligible for temporary or permanent placement or adoption when parents (a) abuse, neglect, or abandon their children; (b) become incapacitated in their ability to be a parent; (c) refuse or are unable to remedy serious, identified problems in caring for their children; or (d) experience an extraordinarily severe breakdown in their relationship with their children (e.g., owing to a long prison sentence). Cognizant that severing the parent–child relationship is a drastic measure, the U.S. Supreme Court held in *Santosky v. Kramer* (1982) that a court may terminate parental rights only if the state can demonstrate with clear and convincing evidence that a parent has failed in one of the aforementioned four ways. Most state statutes also contain provisions for parents to voluntarily relinquish their rights. In addition, the state has the authority to return a child to his or her parents. Ideally, this occurs once a determination is made that it would be safe to do so and that the child's parents will be able to provide appropriate care.

Family Preservation and Family Support Act

The initial impact of the Adoption Assistance and Child Welfare Act of 1980 (Public Law 96–272) was a decrease in the number of children placed into out-of-home care. By 1988, however, the foster care population in the United States had exceeded the previous high of 300,000, reaching 400,000 children (see Figure 9.3). Few policy analysts have commented on why the foster care population began to increase in the late 1980s, but the increase did parallel an increase in the national rates of violent crime (Catalano, 2006), as well as an increase in use of crack cocaine in the northern industrial cities (Blumstein, 1995). Combined with the consequences of deindustrialization and the destabilization of inner-city neighborhoods and inner-city families (Wilson, 1987), the increase in foster care was likely the result of the combined impact of crack cocaine and the deindustrialization of the national economy. In short, the increase in foster care placements was not likely the result of a policy change or policy failure but of changes in the broader environment that impact the ability of parents to adequately care for their children.

While foster care placements were increasing, national policy attention again turned to efforts to decrease the need to place children in foster care. Sensitive about the number of children in out-of-home care and the resulting cost increase, many states implemented family-centered services in the late 1980s and 1990s. Among these was intensive family preservation services, which were designed to be an alternative to the placement of children. The intensive family preservation services model began in Tacoma, Washington, with Homebuilders, a family service agency. The goal of this model is to provide time-limited intensive intervention with families at imminent risk of placement. The core goal of such programs is to maintain children safely in their homes or to facilitate a safe and lasting reunification.

The Adoption Assistance and Child Welfare Act of 1980 already required that reasonable efforts be made to preserve and reunify families. The belief that intensive family preservation service programs were effective fueled a movement to provide federal funds for such programs. As part of the 1993 Omnibus Budget Reconciliation Act of 1993, the Family Preservation and Support Program was enacted. The bill created a new provision in Title IV-B of the Social Security Act of 1935 and created a $930 million funding stream (over 5 years) to fund family preservation and support programs at the state level. This was the first funding source committed to helping parents address the problems of maltreatment. Focused both on family preservation and family support, the funding addressed diversion from foster care and prevention. The law required that a significant proportion of the funds be invested in each area.

The Multiethnic Placement Act of 1994 and the Interethnic Adoption Provisions of the Small Business Job Protection Act

The most significant event that followed Omnibus Budget Reconciliation Act was the 1993 congressional election. Campaigning under Congressman Newt Gingrich's "Contract with America," Republicans took control of both the House and the Senate in 1994. This political shift marked a more conservative approach to social welfare policy, with a focus on reducing entitlement programs and the role of the federal government. Although child welfare was not a component of the "Contract with America," the fact that Title IV-E was one of the "open-ended entitlements" in the current national welfare system would capture some attention. However, the first child welfare policy issue that was taken up by the new Republican majority was interracial adoption.

As noted earlier, between the 1950s and the 1980s the foster care population became disproportionately children of color (Pecora et al., 2000). One impact of the civil rights era was to move adoption away from the traditional practice of physical matching and infant placement and to increase the acceptance of adoption across racial lines. Prior to the successes of the civil rights movement, some southern states, including Louisiana and Texas, legally banned transracial adoption (Myers, 2006). Such laws were struck down in the 1960s. Subsequently, African-American children began to be placed transracially as Native-American children had been in earlier decades. In the early 1970s, however, concern was raised over the adoption of African-American children by White families. The National Association of Black Social Workers (NABSW) led a campaign against transracial adoption. The NABSW (1974) issued a position paper in 1972 stating that

Black children should be placed only with Black families—either in foster care or adoption.[5] They viewed the loss of children through adoption as a major assault on the African-American community. A measure of the depth of concern of the Association was reflected in the statement: "We have committed ourselves to go back to our communities and work to end this particular form of genocide" (p. 159).

The NABSW resolution found a bipartisan audience of post–civil rights conservatives who opposed transracial adoption and liberals who wanted to support the positions of newly empowered minority groups. The resolution increased the awareness of adoption agencies of the need to recruit and develop families in communities of color and led to the development of targeted efforts to extend adoption service to African Americans and other families of color.

In the aftermath of the NABSW resolution, transracial adoptions declined. In 1976, Black-White placements totaled 1,076 (Silverman, 1993). In 1987, Black-White transracial adoptions were estimated to be 1,169, and adoptions of children of other racial or ethnic groups—mainly Asian and Hispanic—were estimated to be 5,850. It is difficult to ascertain how the preference for within-race adoptions interacts with the racial preferences of adoptive parents who are willing to adopt across racial and cultural lines to produce this result.

Although a small proportion of adoptions, the decline in the number of transracial adoptions contributed to the persistent findings that children of color stayed in foster care longer and were less likely to be adopted (Barth, 1997). From a policy perspective, the fact that the foster care population continued to remain at 500,000 children per year and that children of color remained in foster care longer than White children, were consistently overrepresented in foster care, and were less likely to be adopted interacted with the election of a Republican majority to Congress in 1994. This provided the context for the success of a policy initiative directed at transracial adoption. In addition, a growing body of social science research (Simon & Alstein, 1977, 1987) found no developmental disadvantages among children who were transracially adopted.

The Multiethnic Placement Act of 1994 (MEPA; Public Law 103–382, Title V, Part E) had three major goals: (1) decrease the length of time that children wait to be adopted, (2) facilitate the recruitment and retention of foster and adoptive parents who can meet the distinctive needs of children awaiting placement, and (3) eliminate discrimination on the basis of the race, color, or national origin of the child or the prospective parent.

The statutory language of the law included two prohibitions and one affirmative obligation to state agencies and other agencies that were involved in foster care. First, state and private agencies (who received funds under Title IV-E of the Social Security Act) were prohibited from delaying or denying a child's foster care or adoptive placement on the basis of the child's or the prospective parent's race, color, or national origin. Second, agencies were prohibited from denying any individual the opportunity to become a foster or adoptive parent on the basis of race, color, or national origin. Finally, to remain eligible for funding for state child welfare programs, states were required to make diligent efforts to recruit foster and adoptive parents who reflected the racial and ethnic diversity of children in the state who needed foster and adoptive homes.

Congress revisited MEPA in 1996 to address what were perceived to be loopholes in the original law. The Interethnic Adoption Provisions of the Small Business Job Protection Act of 1996 (Public Law 104–188) repealed allowable exceptions under MEPA and replaced them with specific prohibitions against *any* actions that delayed or denied placements on the basis of race, color, or national origin. The law also protected children in placements from racial or ethnic discrimination under Title VI of the Civil Rights Act of 1964, creating a right to sue. State and private foster care agencies could be sued by children, prospective parents, or the federal government for delaying or denying placements. States that delayed or denied placements based on race, color, or national origin would also be penalized by a reduction in their federally allocated child welfare funding. Neither MEPA nor the Interethnic Provisions required transracial adoptions, nor did they prohibit same-race adoptions. What the two laws accomplished was to place the foster care and adoption system under the provisions and protections of the Civil Rights Act of 1964.

States were required to modify their statutes and policies to comply with the two laws. Two common provisions in state laws needed to be repealed. First, any provision that allowed for a specified time period to search for a parent of the same racial background as the child was found to be in violation of the law. Second, a provision that established placement priorities modeled on the Indian Child Welfare Act was also a violation and needed to be repealed or revoked. The Department of Health and Human Service's Office of Civil Rights conducted a systematic survey of state statutes and policies to identify the actions states needed to take to achieve compliance. Given that Title IV-E funding was at stake, states moved to statutory and policy compliance within a short period of time. A bigger challenge was shifting the practice of a profession that valued diversity and cultural continuity.

Reassessment of the Adoption Assistance and Child Welfare Act of 1980 and the Adoption and Safe Families Act of 1997

Since 1980, federal law has required states, as a condition of eligibility for federal child welfare funding, to make "reasonable efforts" to keep a child in his or her home or reunite the child with his or her caregivers as soon as possible and practical (Public Law 96–272, AACWA). The AACWA also required states to make timely permanency decisions for children in out-of-home care that would move the child back to his or her own family or forward to adoption. The balance between reasonable efforts and decision making for children was difficult to establish.

State and local child welfare systems worked hard to meet the goal of family preservation, even in instances when the goal was difficult or impossible to achieve due to intractable family problems and/or lack of resources to meet family needs. The majority of children removed from their homes were ultimately reunited with their parents. Unfortunately, the reunification was very often fragile, and between 20% and 40% of children reunited with their parents were returned to out-of-home placement within 18 months (Barth, Courtney, Berrick, & Albert, 1994). In some instances, family preservation is inadequate and children die — nearly half of the children killed by parents or caregivers are killed after the children come to the attention of the child welfare system (Gelles, 1996; U.S. Advisory Board on Child Abuse and Neglect, 1995). Some children are killed when they remain in their homes; others are killed after a reunification; and an even smaller number die in foster care.

The AACWA was more focused on helping families and working toward reunification than on the decision making related to adoption. As implemented, the legislation did not reduce the length of time in care or move children to adoption in the numbers needed. Prior to 1997, the median length of stay for a child in foster care was 21 months (Child Welfare League of America, 1999). Approximately 18% of children in foster care stayed longer than 5 years. They remained in foster care while child welfare workers worked toward family reunification, or they remained in foster care because a reunification was not possible and adoption was not achieved for the child. Approximately 100,000 children had a goal of adoption in 1996; only 27,761 were adopted that year (Child Welfare League of America, 1999). At the same time approximately 20,000 children "aged out" of the child welfare system each year not having secured a permanent family; that is, they reached the age of majority in their state and were no longer eligible for foster care or payment of foster parent on their behalf.

An important fact influencing the enactment of the Adoption and Safe Families Act of 1997 (ASFA) was that the number of adoptions of children from the foster care system was about 20,000, and the number of adoptions was in decline (Bevan, 1996). The main adverse consequence for children in out-of-home care was that, though they might spend years awaiting reunification, a reunification might never occur. The longer children waited, the less likely it was that they would secure permanency though adoption.

The legal mandate for child welfare was revised in 1997. First, the ASFA made the child's safety and permanency the paramount goals of the child welfare system. The mandate for reasonable efforts was modified to identify circumstances in which the reasonable efforts requirement was not required. These included "aggravated circumstances," such as when a parent committed a murder of another child, when a parent committed or aided in voluntary manslaughter of another child, when a parent committed an assault that resulted in serious injury to a child, or when a parent has had his or her parental rights involuntarily terminated for a sibling of the child. Second, shorter time lines were established for reunification efforts and permanency decisions to remove barriers to adoption and reduce the time children would stay in foster care awaiting an improbable or questionable reunification. The law required states to seek termination of parental rights in the instance of children being in out-of-home care for 15 of the previous 22 months. The exception to this timeline was if children were in the care of relatives or if there was a compelling reason for not terminating parental rights that was in the best interests of the child. Third, states were required to develop a permanency plan for children in out-of-home care within 12 months of the children being placed in care (AACWA required a permanency plan within 18 months of a child being placed in care). Permanency plans could no longer include "long-term foster care." Fourth, states were encouraged to engage in concurrent planning that considered permanency plans that would be used if a safe reunification could not be accomplished.

By making safety of the child the paramount goal of the child welfare system, the ASFA of 1997 changed family preservation from *the* goal of child welfare systems to *a* goal, albeit one of the central and primary goals. The legislation also required states to make reasonable efforts to secure a permanent family for children who could not safely return home and created incentives for states to increase adoptions. The initial impact of the Act has been an increase in yearly adoptions, from 20,000 per year to more than 52,000 in 2005. The number of terminations of parental rights has fluctuated from a high of 73,000 per year in 2000 to a low of 65,000 in 2004, and finally up to 67,000 in 2005. The median length of time children stay in foster care declined to 15.5 months in 2005, while the percentage of children remaining on foster care for 5 years or longer declined to 14%. The number of children of children in foster care dropped from 552,000 in 2000 to 514,000 in 2005 (see Figure 9.4; U.S. Department of Health and Human Services, 2007). It is not clear whether these changes are due solely to ASFA, as there were other relevant federal policy changes that occurred in the same time frame, including MEPA, the Interethnic Provisions, and federal welfare reform, that set time lines for the receipt of welfare benefits, as well as work requirements for those receiving welfare benefits.

Foster Care Independence Act of 1999

Over the past two decades, the national data for foster care documented that approximately 20,000 youth aged out of foster care without a

Figure 9.4

Trends in foster care and adoption, FY 2000–FY 2005. *Source:* Based on data submitted by states as of January 2007. Adoption and Foster Care Analysis and Reporting System data, U.S. Children's Bureau; and Administration for Children, Youth, and Families, retrieved from www.acf .hhs.gov/programs/ cb/stats_research/ afcars/trends.htm

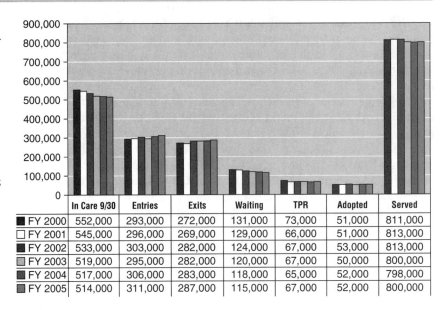

	In Care 9/30	Entries	Exits	Waiting	TPR	Adopted	Served
■ FY 2000	552,000	293,000	272,000	131,000	73,000	51,000	811,000
☐ FY 2001	545,000	296,000	269,000	129,000	66,000	51,000	813,000
■ FY 2002	533,000	303,000	282,000	124,000	67,000	53,000	813,000
▨ FY 2003	519,000	295,000	282,000	120,000	67,000	50,000	800,000
■ FY 2004	517,000	306,000	283,000	118,000	65,000	52,000	798,000
■ FY 2005	514,000	311,000	287,000	115,000	67,000	52,000	800,000

permanent family of their own (U.S. Department of Health and Human Services, 2007). The children who age out are young adults who spent a substantial part of their lives in foster care and are ill-prepared for independent living (Cook, 1991; Kerman, Wildfire, & Barth, 2002). On leaving foster care, many had not completed their education and were unable to secure or keep employment. The thousands of "graduates" of the public child welfare system experienced homelessness, depression, arrest, and early parenthood. When this issue was first addressed in 1985, Congress created the Independent Living Program (Public Law 99–272). The goal of the program was to assist foster children 16 years and older to prepare for the transition to adulthood. Funding was provided to states to create new programs to support older adolescents in care who were neither going to be adopted nor reunified with their birth families. The initial funding was solely for children eligible for IV-E. However, in 1988 all children 16 years old and older in foster care were covered.

The adolescents were made eligible to receive services for 6 months after the age of emancipation in their state (U.S. House of Representatives, Committee on Ways and Means, 2004). The federal resources were service dollars that were focused on preparation for work and the management of daily life. A few states were creative in trying to assure that adolescents aging out of foster care were supported. These states utilized other funds to create tuition waivers for college, designate a portion of entry-level public jobs for those who age out of foster care, and develop transitional housing. The major inadequacies of the initial independent living legislation was the limit on the age of children that could be served and the lack of any mechanism to meet the need for health care and housing.

In 1999, in response to continuing concerns for the adolescents in foster care who were destined to age out of the system, Congress modified the independent living program to better meet the needs of those aging out of foster care. The Foster Care Independence Act of 1999 (Public Law 106–169) extended the age of eligibility for federal funding to 21. Up to 30% of the available funds could be used to cover living costs. The law allowed youth to save up to $10,000 without losing their IV-E eligibility and created an option for states to enroll former foster children in the state medical assistance program until age 21. In a continued effort to create opportunities for former foster children, the law was again modified in 2001 to provide $50 million additional funds for education and training vouchers (Public Law 107–133).

Conclusion

The federal government has, on average, visited child welfare policy about once every 10 years. The exception was a flurry of federal legislation between 1994 and 2001. The Child Abuse Prevention and Treatment Act is renewable legislation and comes before Congress every 4 to 5 years. The child welfare–related provisions of the Social Security Act of 1935, Title IV, are not renewable, with the exception of funding for Title IV-B, Safe and Stables Families. Thus, the main funding stream and policies for child welfare do not appear on the legislative agenda on a regular basis.

States modify their statutes and administrative procedures on a regular basis. Some modifications are in response to federal mandates (e.g., ASFA); other changes are entirely locally driven. States often modify their definition of child abuse and neglect and procedures for reporting or investigating child maltreatment. Such modifications are usually made so that the state remains in compliance with the Child Abuse Prevention and Treatment Act and continues to remain eligible to receive funding under the provisions of the Act. Some state legislation constitutes significant departures from traditional child welfare policy. In the late 1990s, Florida created legislation that allowed counties to transfer the responsibilities for investigating reports of child maltreatment. Investigations in nearly every state are implemented by an agency under the umbrella of social services or children's services. Florida allowed four counties to shift the funding and responsibility for investigations to the county sheriffs.

Future Policy Issues

As states struggle to secure resources for the child welfare systems, they continue to face the ongoing fact that more than half of child abuse and neglect investigations result in no finding of abuse or neglect. In addition, funding for services for those families and children substantiated for abuse or neglect is primarily provided by local or state funding. Thus, one of the policy issues that may be addressed in the next decade is the legal definition of child maltreatment. One possible policy approach would be to reverse the expansion of the definition of abuse and neglect and create a narrower definition that could result in fewer investigations and the release of more funding for services; or states could create stricter screening procedures and reduce the number of investigations.

None of the federal legislative initiatives in the past 25 years has yielded significant improvements in achieving permanence for children in out-of-home care, assuring stable reunifications, or reducing the number of children waiting for adoption while also reducing adoption disruptions. The pendulum has swung from a concern for family reunification to a concern for child safety, but the issue of permanence remains to be appropriately and adequately addressed.

One overriding issue that impacts child welfare policy is the lack of flexibility of federal funding. The largest federal funding stream is the open-ended entitlement of Title IV-E of the Social Security Act of 1935. Title IV-E provides an open-ended federal match for the costs of children in foster care (provided the children were removed from households that would have been eligible for AFDC funding). In 2007, the funding under Title IV-E was projected to be $4.757 billion for the cost of maintaining children in foster care. Additional matching funds are provided for administration and training. Though there are billions of dollars invested in the child welfare system, those billions are directed primarily for foster care, and states have little to no flexibility as to how to use federal funds. Over the past few years, there have been proposals to make federal funding more flexible (Pew Commission on Children in Foster Care, 2004), but as yet Congress has not engaged in a serious discussion as to how to create more funding flexibility.

Children and families of color have been disproportionately represented in the foster care and child welfare system for the past 30 years. No policy to date has successfully examined or addressed that disproportionality.

Key Terms

Adoption	*Children and families*	*Family support*
Child welfare	*Family preservation*	*Foster care*

Review Questions for Critical Thinking

1. A feature of child welfare policy in the United States is the intersection of parental rights and children's rights. Discuss the development of these concepts as it applies to policy in the United States over time.

2. Discuss the child welfare movement in the United States and the three significant events that occurred that provided structure and focus to efforts to protect children.

3. Discuss the impact of the Child Abuse Prevention and Treatment Act of 1974.

4. Discuss the foster care drift and the Adoption Assistance and Child Welfare Act of 1980. What impact did this have on children and families?

5. Discuss the adoption assistance movement over time in the United States and its shift in values and focus over time.

Online Resources

Children's Defense Fund provides child welfare information on the full range of services and supports needed to promote the healthy social and emotional development and well-being of all children. www.childrensdefense.org

Child Welfare Information Gateway connects child welfare and related professionals to comprehensive information and resources to help protect children and strengthen families. We feature the latest on topics from prevention to permanency, including child abuse and neglect, foster care, and adoption. A service of the Children's Bureau, Administration for Children and Families, U.S. Department of Health and Human Services. www.childwelfare.gov/

Child Welfare League of America (CWLA) is the nation's oldest and largest organization devoted entirely to the well-being of America's vulnerable children. CWLA leads and engages its network of public and private agencies and partners to advance policies, best practices, and collaborative strategies that result in better outcomes for vulnerable children, youth, and families. www.cwla.org/

Child Welfare Policy Database provides state-by-state policy information on a range of child welfare topics. www.childwelfarepolicy.org/

The Consortium for Child Welfare (CCW) is a coalition of human service agencies established in 1980 to improve child welfare services. Our mission is to advocate for vulnerable children, youth, and families in the District of Columbia by uniting private human service providers to ensure a responsive and accountable system of care. This results in safety, family permanence, well-being and positive youth development. CCW and its members fulfill the mission by protecting children and supporting families through communication and collaboration, promoting innovation, developing resources, and advocating for the highest practice standards. www.consortiumforchildwelfare.org

International Forum for Child Welfare (IFCW) is an international non-governmental organization dedicated to the promotion of the rights and well-being of children. www.ifcw.org

National Indian Child Welfare Association (NICWA) provides publications, training, and information concerning the Indian Child Welfare Act of 1978. www.nicwa.org

NOTES

1. The terms vary from state to state, as does the standard for determining what is founded or substantiated and what evidence must be present to determine the outcome of the investigation (Myers, 2006).

2. Until 1996, the federal government did not have a formal mechanism for collecting data on children in foster care. Thus, earlier data are estimates derived from various sources and data collection methodologies.

3. There was still no official federal effort to collect data on foster care; thus, the numbers cited in the text and Figure 9.3 are from unofficial tabulations.

4. The remaining proportion of the 50,000 children whose plan was not adoption had permanency plans of long-term foster care or emancipation (reaching the age of a legal adult).

5. Conference of the National Association of Black Social Workers, Nashville, Tennessee, April 4–9, 1972.

References

Adoption and Foster Care Analysis and Reporting System. (n.d.). Retrieved from www.acf.hhs.gov/programs/cb/stats_research/afcars/trends.htm

Axinn, J., & Stern, M. J. (2004). *Social welfare: A history of the American response to need* (5th ed.). Boston, MA: Allyn & Bacon.

Bakan, D. (1971). *The slaughter of the innocents.* Boston, MA: Beacon Press.

Barth, R. P. (1997). Effects of age and race on the odds of adoption versus remaining in long-term out-of-home care. *Child Welfare, 76,* 285–308.

Barth, R. P., Courtney, M., Berrick, J. D., & Albert, V. (1994). *From child abuse to permanency planning: Child welfare services pathways and placements.* New York, NY: Aldine De Gruyter.

Bevan, C. (1996). *Foster care: Too much, too little, too early, too late: Child protection: Old problem, new paradigm.* Washington, DC: National Council for Adoption.

Blumstein, A. (1995). Youth violence, guns, and the illicit-drug industry. *Journal of Criminal Law and Criminology, 86,* 10–36.

Brace, C. L. (1859). *The best method of disposing of pauper and vagrant children.* New York, NY: Wyncoop and Hallenbeck.

Bruno, F. J. (1957). *Trends in social work, 1874–1956: A history based on the book of the national conference of social work.* New York, NY: Columbia University Press.

Catalano, S. H. (2006). *Criminal victimization, 2006.* Washington, DC: U.S. Department of Justice, Office of Justice Programs.

Child Abuse Amendments of 1984 § 42 U.S.C. § 67 (1984).

Child Abuse Prevention, Adoption and Family Services Act of 1988 §§42 U.S.C. §67 (1988).

Child Abuse Prevention and Treatment Act of 1974 § 42 U.S.C. § 67 (1974).

Child Welfare League of America. (1999). *Child abuse and neglect: A look at the states (1999 CWLA Stat Book).* Washington, DC: Author.

Cook, R. (1991). *A national evaluation of Title IV-E independent living programs for youth.* Rockville, MD: Westat.

Davidson, H. (1997). The courts and child maltreatment. In M. Helfer, R. Kempe, & R. Krugman (Eds.), *The battered child* (5th ed., pp. 482–499). Chicago, IL: University of Chicago Press.

Fanschel, D. (1972). *Far from the reservation: The transracial adoption of American Indian children.* Metuchen, NJ: Scarecrow Press.

Fanschel, D., & Shinn, E. B. (1978). *Children in foster care: A longitudinal investigation.* New York, NY: Columbia University Press.

Federal Adoption Assistance and Child Welfare Act of 1980, Public Law 96–272 (June 17, 1980).

Gelles, R. J. (1973). Child abuse as psychopathology: A sociological critique and reformulation. *American Journal of Orthopsychiatry, 43*, 611–621.

Gelles, R. J. (1996). *The book of David: How preserving families can cost children's lives.* New York, NY: Basic Books.

Gil, D. (1970). *Violence against children: Physical child abuse in the United States.* Cambridge, MA: Harvard University Press.

Greven, P. (1991). *Spare the child: The religious roots of punishment and the psychological impact of physical abuse.* New York, NY: Knopf.

Jones, B. J. (1995). Indian child welfare act: The need for a separate law. *ABA General Practice Magazine, 12,* 4. Retrieved from www.ABANET.org/genlpractice/magazine/1995/fall/indianchildwelfareact.html

Keeping Children and Families Safe Act of 2003, Public Law 108–36. § U.S.C. 42 § 63.

Kempe, C. H., Silverman, F. N., Steele, B. F., Droegemueller, W., & Silver, H. K. (1962). The battered child syndrome. *Journal of the American Medical Association, 181*, 107–112.

Kerman, B., Wildfire, J., & Barth, R. P. (2002). Outcomes for young adults who experienced foster care. *Children and Youth Services Review, 24*, 319–344.

Leiby, J. (1978). *A history of social welfare and social work in the United States.* New York, NY: Columbia University Press.

Lindsey, D. (2004). *The welfare of children* (2nd ed.). New York, NY: Oxford University Press.

Maas, H., & Engler, R. E. (1959). *Children in need of parents.* New York, NY: Columbia University Press.

Maximus Inc. (1984). *Child welfare statistical factbook 1984: Substitute care and adoption.* Washington, DC: Office of Human Development Services.

Maza, P. L. (1983). *Characteristics of children free for adoption: Child welfare research notes # 2.* Washington, DC: Children's Bureau, Administration for Children, Youth, and Families.

Myers, J. (2006). *Child protection in America: Past, present, and future.* New York, NY: Oxford University Press.

National Association of Black Social Workers. (1974). Position statement on trans-racial adoption (September 1972). In H. Dalmage (2000), *Tripping on the color line: Black-white multiracial families in a racially divided world.* New Brunswick, NJ: Rutgers University Press.

Nelson, B. J. (1984). *Making an issue of child abuse: Political agenda setting for social problems.* Chicago, IL: University Chicago Press.

Newberger, E. H. (1983). The helping hand strikes again: Unintended consequences of child abuse reporting. *Journal of Clinical Child Psychology, 12*, 307–311.

O'Neil, K., & Gesiriech, S. (2005). *A brief legislative history of the child welfare system.* Philadelphia, PA: Pew Commission on Children in Foster Care.

Pecora, P. J., Whittaker, J. K., Maluccio, A. N., & Barth, R. P. (2000). *The child welfare challenge: Policy, practice, and research.* New York, NY: Aldine De Gruyter.

Pew Commission on Children in Foster Care. (2004). *Fostering the future: Safety, permanence and well-being for children in foster care.* Philadelphia, PA: Author.

Promoting Safe and Stable Families Amendments of 2001 P.L. 107–133. (January 17, 2002).

Proceedings of the White House conference on care of dependent children. (1909). Senate Document, 60th Congress, 2nd Session, Vol. *13*, Document 721.

Radbill, S. (1980). A history of child abuse and infanticide. In R. Helfer & C. Kempe (Eds.), *The battered child* (3rd ed., pp. 3–20). Chicago, IL: University of Chicago Press.

Robin, M. (1980). Historical introduction: Sheltering arms—The roots of child. In E. Newberger (Ed.), *Child abuse* (pp. 1–41). Boston, MA: Little, Brown.

Santosky v. Kramer, 455 U.S. 745 (1982).

Silverman, A. R. (1993). Outcomes of transracial adoption. *Future of Children, 3*, 104–118.

Simon, R., & Alstein, H. (1977). *Transracial adoption.* New York, NY: Wiley.

Simon, R., & Alstein, H. (1987). *Transracial adoptees and their families: A study of identity and commitment.* New York, NY: Wiley.

Smith v. Organization of Foster Families for Equality and Reform, 431 U.S. 816 (1977).

Stanley v. Illinois, 405 U. S. 645 (1972).

Straus, M. A. (1994). *Beating the devil out of them: Corporal punishment in American families.* New York, NY: Lexington Books.

Ten Bensel, R. L., Rheinberger, M., & Radbill, S. X. (1997). Children in a world of violence: The roots of child maltreatment. In M. E. Helfer, R. S. Kempe, & R. D. Krugman (Eds.), *The battered child* (4th ed., pp. 3–28). Chicago, IL: University of Chicago Press.

U.S. Advisory Board on Child Abuse and Neglect. (1995). *A nation's shame: Fatal child abuse and neglect in the United States.* Washington, DC: U.S. Department of Health and Human Services.

U.S. Children's Bureau. (1961). *Legislative guidelines for the termination of parental rights and responsibilities and the adoption of children.* Publication No. 394. Washington, DC: Author.

U.S. Children's Bureau, § Public Law 62–116 42 U.S.C. § 191 (1912).

U.S. Department of Health and Human Services. (2007). *Adoption and foster care analysis and reporting system.* Washington, DC: Author. Retrieved from www.acf.hhs.gov/programs/cb/stats_research/afcars/trends.htm

U.S. Department of Health and Human Services, Administration on Children, Youth, and Families. (2007). *Child maltreatment 2005.* Washington, DC: U.S. Government Printing Office.

U.S. House of Representatives, Committee on Ways and Means. (2004). *2004 green book: Background material and data on the programs within the jurisdiction of the Committee on Ways and Means.* Washington, DC: Author.

Waldfogel, J. (1998). *The future of child protection: How to break the cycle of abuse and neglect.* Cambridge, MA: Harvard University Press.

Williams, C. W. (1980). Legal guardianship: A minimally used resource for dependent children. Unpublished doctoral dissertation, University of Southern California, Los Angeles.

Wilson, W. J. (1987). *The truly disadvantaged: The inner city, the underclass, and public policy.* Chicago, IL: University of Chicago Press.

Chapter 10
Public Funding of Sectarian Organizations for the Provision of HIV/AIDS Prevention and Care

Discriminatory Issues for Gay Males

Christopher W. Blackwell and
Sophia F. Dziegielewski

The Personal Responsibility and Work Opportunity Reconciliation Act (PRWORA) of 1996 greatly expanded the accessibility and feasibility of religious organizations and institutions to compete for federal and state funds to provide social services. What do you think are the advantages and disadvantages to of the PRWORA to service delivery for vulnerable groups?

Introduction

There has been significant funding increases to sectarian organizations for the prevention of the spread of the human immunodeficiency virus (HIV) and the provision of care for HIV-positive clients or those with acquired immunodeficiency syndrome (AIDS) both in the United States as well as throughout the world. The Global Fund (2012), for example, has allocated $22.9 billion in 151 different countries world-wide. Gay males continue to represent the highest risk group for infection and spread of HIV so concerns have surfaced regarding possible discrimination along with a concentration of abstinence-only treatment strategy resulting in the possibility for substandard care for HIV/AIDS clients who are gay males. This chapter explores several concerns that may evolve when religious-based organizations are responsible for care directed at this population. Some areas for concern include: the potential for negative perceptions and ideas about non-heterosexual behavior guiding the intervention efforts with a strong focus on abstinence-only prevention strategies.

Religious and Faith-Based Organizations Providing Social Services: Charitable Choice

The Personal Responsibility and Work Opportunity Reconciliation Act (PRWORA) of 1996 greatly expanded the accessibility and feasibility of religious organizations and institutions to compete for federal and state funds to provide social services. Lieberman and Cummings (2002) provided specific fiscal examples for the General Accounting Office (GAO) and found "at least 19 states have contracted with FBOs [faith-based organizations] to provide some welfare-related services" (p. 2) and certainly more have taken advantage of this provision in subsequent years. PRWORA contains a provision known as Charitable Choice, which is designed to decrease the barriers of religious organizations in their ability to compete for federal and state funding to provide social services (Bartkowski & Regis 1999; Cahill & Jones, 2002; Cnaan & Bodie, 2002; Davis, 1996; Glennon, 2000; Kennedy & Bielefeld, 2002; Knippenberg, 2003). The PRWORA provision of Charitable Choice was legislated under the Clinton Administration in 1996 and has been largely embraced and expanded by the Bush Administration (Cahill & Jones, 2002; Cnaan & Bodie, 2002; Jean, 2002; Rostow, 2003; Yang, 2001).

Charitable Choice is specifically found in Section 104 of PRWORA. Bartkowski and Regis (1999) completed an examination of the Charitable Choice policy and some of its legal terminology and concluded:

> As outlined in Section 104 of PRWORA, state governments that opt to contract with independent sector social service providers cannot legally exclude faith-based organizations from consideration simply because they are religious in nature. Consequently, the language of "choice" in this legislation is designed to underscore the importance to giving religious congregations the same opportunities that secular nonprofit agencies enjoy in competing for purchase-of-service contracts with state governments. Furthermore, Charitable Choice aims to ensure that state governments cannot censor religious expression—i.e. religious symbols or practices—among faith-based organizations that are selected to provide state-funded social services. (p. 8)

Charitable Choice allows religious organizations to compete openly for providing services, yet if organizations that are federally funded can allow their religious beliefs to guide the types of services they provide, it is possible that discriminatory practices can be either intentionally or unintentionally propagated. For example, according to the Centers for Disease Control and Prevention (CDC) 2011 report, men who have sex with men (MSM) account for nearly half of the approximately 1.2 million people living with HIV in the United States, which total 49% or an estimated 580,000 total persons data (Centers for Disease Control and Prevention [CDC], 2011). MSM represent the largest exposure category of new HIV infections and AIDS diagnoses. As many as 29,300 males were infected with HIV or were diagnosed with AIDS in 2009; 61% of these infections were in males who reported having sexual contact with other men, while 3% represented MSM and injection drug users; and the highest rate of infection was among African Americans, 44%, while Hispanics accounted for 20% of all infections (CDC, 2003). Although gay men continue to be at highest risk of infection, data also suggest infection rates among this population were increasing on an annual basis (Sternberg, 2003) more recent CDC studies report that the new estimates showed that the annual number of new HIV infections was stable overall from 2006 through 2009 (CDC, 2012). For example, HIV infections rose more than 7% from 2001 to 2002, with an overall increase of almost 18% since 1999, when the number of infections among gay and bisexual men bottomed out at 6,561 of the 40,000 total HIV infections estimated annually (Sternberg, 2003); the CDC reports that in 2006 there were an estimated 48,600 new HIV infections, 56,000 in 2007, 47,800 in 2008, and 48,100 in 2009 (CDC, 2012). The 2003 CDC report *HIV/AIDS Among Men Who Have Sex With Men* highlights this finding, thereby emphasizing the need for these males to require culturally diverse prevention and education services. This increasing prevalence, coupled with the historic disparity of HIV/AIDS infection in gay men, presents significant considerations not only in the treatment of clients diagnosed with HIV/AIDS, but also in the prevention strategies aimed at lowering infection rates among the general population. In 2005, the federal government allocated $15 billion to the prevention and treatment of HIV/AIDS (Beamish, 2006) and in the federal government's FY2012 budget the allocation increased to $21.5 billion, a 43% increase in 7 years (Henry J. Kaiser Family Foundation, 2011).

With such great funding allocations to religious organizations that are treating clients already infected, it is certain that gay men who are HIV-positive will need to access services that are provided by such religious organizations. In addition, it becomes necessary to also examine the prevention strategies employed by these organizations and the implications these strategies have on gay men.

Religiosity as a Predictor of Homophobia

Religious association is a highly studied and sensitive independent variable related to homophobia (Berkman & Zinberg, 1997; Dennis, 2002; Douglas, Kalman, & Kalman, 1985; Ellis, Kitzinger, & Wilkinson, 2002; Finlay & Walther, 2003; Herek, 1988, 2000, 2002; Herek & Capitanio, 1995; Herek & Glunt, 1993; Hoffman & Bakken, 2001; Lewis, 2003; Petersen & Donnenwerth, 1998; Plugge-Foust & Strickland, 2001; Wilson & Huff, 2001). Furthermore, social science researchers have documented the strong positive correlation between religious associations with homophobia (Berkman & Zinberg, 1997; Dennis, 2002; Ellis et al., 2002; Finlay & Walther, 2003; Herek, 1988, 2000, 2002; Herek & Capitanio, 1995; Herek & Glunt, 1993; Lewis, 2003; Petersen & Donnenwerth, 1998; Plugge-Foust & Strickland, 2001; Wilson & Huff, 2001). This linkage, however, remains multifaceted, taking into account varying denominations, religious sects, frequency of attendance at religious services, and other independent variables which help to determine overall religious association. Blackwell and Kiehl (2008), for example, failed to capture religious association as a causative factor of homophobia in nurses; and the authors concluded one potential reason for this was the vast difference between one's spiritual beliefs and their religious ones.

Lewis (2003) compared religious association and differences in overall homophobia among Caucasians and African Americans, and found that since African Americans were substantially more religious than Caucasians, the levels of homophobia also appeared higher. In addition, heterosexuals that self-identify with a fundamentalist religious denomination typically manifest higher levels of sexual prejudice than do nonreligious and members of liberal denominations (Herek, 2000; Herek & Glunt, 1993). Religious conservatism and liberalism also play a significant role, along with varying support for gay rights, where Jews were most accepting and born-again Protestants the most disapproving (Lewis, 2003).

This difference in homophobia between conservative and liberal denominations is reflected in the Attitudes Toward Lesbians and Gay men (ATLG) scale as well (Herek, 1988). Similarly, research utilizing other measurement scales of homophobia, such as the Homophobia-Scale (H-Scale), also correlated differences in homophobia among religious denominations (Finlay & Walther, 2003). On this measurement scale conservative Protestants have the highest H-scale score, followed by moderate Protestants and Catholics.

There is also a positive correlation between support of lesbian and gay human rights and conservative religious sects (Ellis et al., 2002; Petersen & Donnenwerth, 1998). Therefore, as measured by the Differential Loneliness Scale (DLS), as irrational thought process increases, so does homophobia. In addition, irrational thought processes tend to be higher among individuals who are Catholic and Protestant. This leads to greater levels of homophobia as measured by the H-Scale in these traditionally classified conservative denominations (Plugge-Foust & Strickland, 2001).

Intensity of religious feeling, frequency of religious service attendance, frequency of prayer, and importance of religion in participants' lives is also highly correlated with homophobia (Berkman & Zinberg, 1997; Herek, 2000; Lewis, 2003). Heterosexuals who rate religion as "very important" are more homophobic than those who rate religion as "somewhat/ to not at all important" (Herek, 2002). Even in disciplines such as social work, where there is great respect for diversity homophobia tends to be greater among social workers who believe that religion is an extremely important aspect of their lives (Berkman & Zinberg, 1997).

Heterosexuals who attend religious services weekly or more often have higher levels of homophobia than those who attended religious services less frequently (Herek, 2002; Herek & Capitanio, 1995). Specific religious beliefs are also associated with homophobia. Individuals who believe in an active Satan have higher levels of homophobia and have significantly greater intolerance towards gay men and lesbians than those who don't believe in an active Satan (Wilson & Huff, 2001).

For the most part, it appears that liberal Protestants and individuals not affiliated with a religion have significantly lower homophobia scores (Finlay & Walther, 2003). Those least homophobic appear to be individuals who do not self-identify themselves as Christian (Finlay & Walther, 2003).

Although there is a strong religious-associated correlation with homophobia, there does not appear to be a strong correlation between religiosity and gay/lesbian colonization (Dennis, 2002). Thus, regions of the country that have high populations of religious practitioners do not necessarily have smaller populations of gay and lesbian residents (Dennis, 2002). Because religious factors appear to have strong influences in the development of homophobia, gay, lesbian, bisexual, and transgender (GLBT) organizations such as the Human Rights Campaign (HRC) and the National Gay and Lesbian Taskforce have voiced serious concern about receiving social services through religious organizations (Blackwell & Dziegielewski, 2005).

Practices That Could Lead to Discrimination and Limited Treatment Strategy Related to Substandard Care

A comprehensive report authored by Cahill and Jones (2002) outlined multiple discriminatory and homophobic issues GLBT persons might encounter when seeking social services from faith-based organizations. Among these included proselytizing, direct discrimination and homophobic treatment, lack of access to services, and legislative loopholes which could permit substandard care by sectarian organizations to exist without proper regulatory response (Cahill & Jones, 2002).

In addition, social scientists have suggested that religious-based homophobia has been coupled with HIV/AIDS prevention efforts since the emergence of the pandemic in the United States in the early 1980s (Lugg, 1998). Lugg (1998) found in her literature review that homosexuality was explicitly and repetitiously linked with the ghastly and terminal course of the disease among religious leaders such as Jerry Falwell, Pat Robertson, and Lou Sheldon. The potential impacts of religious organizations in the treatment and prevention of HIV/AIDS to the gay male are numerous, including negative and discriminatory aspects of abstinence-only prevention programs, access to care issues, and aversion to religious service providers.

Negative and Discriminatory Aspects of Abstinence-Only Prevention Programs to Gay Men

One of the greatest concerns that could lead to discriminatory practices is the emphasis on abstinence-only prevention programs that can fail to address adult sexuality among gay males. Most professionals agree that human sexuality is a natural and normal part of adult development. Therefore, when working to limit the spread of HIV infection, abstinence, marriage, and the use of condoms are often considered the cornerstones of this type of treatment approach. So from this perspective it makes sense that religious-based HIV prevention programs are more likely to promote abstinence-only strategies and such programs have proliferated under the Bush Administration (Rose, 2005). The abstinence-only prevention programs tend to concentrate on stopping sexual intercourse from occurring (Rose, 2005) outside of the context of a loving, stable, and long-term relationship, usually defined as marriage. When using this approach as the foundation of treatment the focus on marriage as a central aspect of sexual relationships predominantly excludes gay men and lesbians, largely due to inequality in marriage policies across the United States and in various religious-based doctrines and practices. The Catholic Church's condemnation of homosexuality coupled with its ban on the use of condoms and insistence on abstinence has made it almost "impossible for the Catholic Church to work effectively to suppress the spread of HIV" (Brooks, Etzel, Hinojos, Henry, & Perez, 2005, p. 740).

Brooks et al. (2005) also suggested potential areas of discrimination with service provision by primarily African-American churches can as oftentimes black clergy may refuse to discuss sexual issues, particularly those behaviors that are associated with the transmission of the virus (anal sex, bisexuality, and homosexuality), and this lack of attention could inadvertently lead to its spread. If sexuality is limited to marriage and gay males cannot marry this sets up a situation where gay men and women are being told that their desires for human sexual contact is simply not allowed. Although some states allow some of the rights and privileges of marriage through state domestic partner policies and registries, more than 30 states define marriage strictly as being between a man and a woman (Meacham et al., 2002); as a result, gay people are marginalized within the invalidity of their relationships.

Researchers have found that the denial and ignorance of sexual relationships and activities between men who have sex with men as largely responsible for the failure of HIV prevention efforts on a global scale (Parker, Khan, & Aggleton, 1998). Researchers assessing prevention efforts in sub-Saharan Africa have discovered an almost complete absence of community-based prevention efforts specifically targeting gay males (Parker et al., 1998). This problem has also been found in many parts of South and Southeast Asia, where HIV infection rates have continued to rise, especially in China, where HIV/AIDS is an emerging epidemic (Giovanna-Merli, Hertog, Wang, & Li, 2006; Parker et al., 1998). India's outreach and prevention efforts have also been deemed largely ineffectual; secondary to a lack of concentration on efforts geared at teaching safe-sex practices among MSM (Parker et al., 1998).

Because MSM continue to represent the largest risk group for HIV infection and AIDS diagnoses (CDC, 2003), ignoring this population might actually increase their infection rates as a result of inadequate training and education regarding safe sexual practices, condom use, and avoidance of high-risk behaviors and what constitutes such behaviors. Parker et al., (1998) conclude that "conspicuous by their absence, the widespread denial of the needs of men who have sex with men in the developing world is another example of the long record of neglect that should bring shame not only to governmental agencies and donors, but to all of us who work not only for an end to the epidemic, but also for a more just and tolerant world" (p. 342).

In addition to the denial of gay sexual relationships perpetuated within abstinence-only prevention programs, abstinence-only based interventions are not supported in the literature as effective in stopping the spread of HIV infection longitudinally (Rose, 2005). Finally, religious-based interventions may be detrimental to the psychosocial well-being of HIV+ individuals. Research conducted by Jenkins (1995) found that many sero-positive individuals "feel estranged from organized religion because of doctrines that seem unsympathetic and or punitive toward HIV and those who carry the virus" (p. 132). Research suggests that behavior modification and proper training on the correct usage and distribution of condoms and the avoidance of high-risk sexual practices are much more effective and appropriate at reducing the spread of HIV and increasing safer sex, especially among gay males and subsets of gay males (Parker et al., 1998; Ross, Henry, Freeman, Caughy, & Dawson, 2004; Veerman, Tatsa, Druzin, & Weinstein, 1999).

Research has failed to demonstrate the long-term effectiveness of abstinence-only prevention programs (Rose, 2005). Coupled with this lack of evidence, abstinence-only programs tend to marginalize gay men through invalidation of their relationships largely by ignoring behaviors between MSM altogether. Data asserts the most successful interventions aimed at combating the spread of HIV are those that are culturally specific for the individual and those that address disempowering forces in people's lives (Marin, 2003). The emphasis of safer sex practices is seen as an essential component to educational interventions aimed at reducing the transmission of HIV; the most effective and reliable method to reduce HIV infection risk is through condom use (Lam, Mak, Lindsay, & Russell, 2004).

A recent increase in the sexual practice known as bare-backing (insertive anal intercourse without use of condoms) among MSM has been seen as a surfacing public health hazard (Wolitski, 2005). Six etiologies for the increase in this unsafe practice have been proposed: (1) improvements in HIV treatment; (2) more complex sexual decision making; (3) the Internet as means of meeting sexual partners; (4) substance use; (5) safer sex fatigue; and (6) changes in HIV-prevention programs (Wolitski, 2005). These etiologies are perhaps interrelated—improvements in HIV treatment could be leading to fatigue of safer sex as gay men may no longer perceive HIV as a terminal disease; and access to sexual partners who mutually use substances during sexual intercourse could be easier because of increased Internet use to find compatible sexual partners.

Ross et al. (2004) found three environmental variables predictive of safer sex practices among MSM: (1) perceived gay/bisexual men's norms toward condom use; (2) availability of HIV prevention messages; and (3) what one's religion says about gay sex. These findings have major suggestive implications for public prevention policy. Beyond these three predictors, research suggested that lack of consistent use of condoms among a subset of Latino MSM was related to adventurism and impulsivity (Carballo-Dieguez et al., 2005). These findings suggest that educational interventions that empower MSM to identify adventurous and impulsive emotions partnered with strategic methods to critically think through such situations may increase the use of condoms during intercourse. Perhaps educational interventions aimed at gay men could use case-study scenarios of such situations in teaching critical thinking and reasoning skills as research utilizing such approaches have yielded findings regarding unsafe sex practices among this population (Ross et al., 2004).

Implications of Access to Care and Aversion to Sectarian Providers Among Gay Men

If an HIV-positive gay man refuses treatment from a religious-based service provider, serious access to care issues can arise. Charitable Choice legislation contains an alternative provision that requires federal, state, or local governments to ensure that alternative secular programs be available to serve clients who object to receiving services from a religious social service provider (Cahill & Jones, 2002; Glennon, 2000). However, specifics on how this will be accomplished limit this mandate. For example, the regulations, although requiring an alternative service provider, limit choice as it does not provide funding for the nonreligious provider when a religious provider is already available.

In addition, it may be impossible to implement due to distance from such providers and time constraints of devising and organizing such alternatives when they do not already exist (Cahill & Jones, 2002; Davis, 1996). An example might be an AIDS patient living in a highly rural area who depends on a government-sponsored food pantry to provide sustenance. If the only government-contracted provider is a sectarian one, the client may refuse care because a public service provider not associated with religion is not available. Or, due to loopholes in the legislation designed to maintain the religious identity and integrity of the service provider (Cahill & Jones, 2002), the client may be subjected to homophobic and discriminatory treatment as a result of the religion's condemnation of homosexuality.

Although sectarian service providers may cause serious access to care issues, the aversion of homosexuals to religion and religious organizations, and subsequently, religious service providers, could also cause HIV-positive/AIDS clients who are gay men to not seek needed treatments, which may cause an increase in the morbidity and mortality of this population. As discussed, ever since the dawn of the HIV/AIDS crisis, some religious leaders have cited the notion that the virus was a punishment handed down from God for those who are sinners or live in "perversity" (Lugg, 1998; Stone, 1999, p. 16).

Although there is a paucity of study regarding the attitudes of gay men toward religion, it could be postulated that gay men could be less attracted to such religions as Christianity or Islam as a result of their traditional stance against same-sex relationships. The decreased likelihood of gay men to be supportive toward religion could pose a severe obstruction to the delivery of services to HIV-positive gay men, or those living with AIDS, by religious entities. Knowing that MSM continue to contribute to the majority of HIV infections and AIDS diagnoses in the United States (CDC, 2003), forcing them to receive care from religious organizations might lead to an even greater disparity in the morbidity and mortality rates endured by this client base.

Implications for Further Research and Policy Development

The exploration of the effects of religious social service providers on HIV treatment and prevention in the gay male is in its infancy. Data in this area needs to be augmented greatly to help meet public health demands and ensure optimal care delivery for those gay men who are HIV-positive or suffering with AIDS. Future critical inquiry should assess the role religion has in the life of gay men inflicted with HIV/AIDS and should also qualitatively examine the reactions of these persons who have received care from such organizations. This information can then be clearly related to the policy developed and implemented.

In addition, research needs to continue to evolve to discover the best ways to prevent the spread of HIV among MSM. Perhaps of utmost importance, however, is the need for evidence-based policies in the treatment and prevention of the infection. When sectarian organizations are expected to continue to play a pivotal role in treating and helping prevent HIV/AIDS, then policy makers must closely examine social science research about the pandemic. It is so crucial to make informed decisions about policy that evidence-based treatment strategy must be at the root of all decisions. Exploration in how to best stop infection and optimal treatment strategies for those already infected make the best use of allocated funds. Nurses, social workers, public administrators, and all those involved as stakeholders in preventing and treating HIV/AIDS in gay men must play the role of advocate to ensure social justice and equity principles in health care and social service delivery.

Funding in this area is so important but it is critical that we openly discuss the potential for discriminatory practices that could be encountered by gay men during the prevention and provision of care of HIV/AIDS by religious organizations. Increased homophobia among individuals with strong religiosity was discussed; the focus on abstinence-only prevention strategies and the neglect these programs have in addressing sexual relationships between gay men was scrutinized; and possible access of care issues associated with aversion to religious-based interventions in gay men were explored. HIV/AIDS is a very real pandemic that continues to threaten the health of the gay male population. Perhaps with future research directives and scholarly inquest, policy makers can begin an evidence-based approach that can turn the tide and clearly address issues such as disparity, discrimination, and homophobia.

Key Terms

Abstinence-only
AIDS

Gay, homophobia,
homosexual

HIV
Prevention services

Review Questions for Critical Thinking

1. Religious organizations are provided tax exemptions by the U.S. government—to what extent should such organizations be required to follow federal laws and policies? Use GBLT issues as your point of discussion reference.

2. Is HIV/AIDS a "gay" disease?

3. Should public agencies be required to provide free condoms and free needle exchange programs?

4. As of May 2012, Massachusetts, Connecticut, Iowa, Vermont, New York, and New Hampshire were the only states to allow same-sex marriage while 31 states banned same-sex marriage and legal unions. How is this a social justice issue?

5. Given the prevalence of HIV/AIDS in many parts of the world, should the United States refocus its efforts on these regions and countries, in particular Africa, which accounts for 60% of all cases worldwide?

Online Resources

The Henry K Kaiser Family Foundation http://www.kff.org

National Gay and Lesbian Task Force www.ngltf.org

National HIV/Aids Strategy http://www.aids.gov/federal-resources/ policies/national-hiv-aids-strategy/

United Nations Millennium Goals http://www.un.org/millenniumgoals/ aids.shtml

U.S. Centers for Disease Control and Prevention www.cdc.gov

References

Bartkowski, J. P., & Regis, H. A. (1999, November). *Religious organizations, anti-poverty, relief, and charitable choice: A feasibility study of the faith-based welfare reform in Mississippi.* Arlington, VA: PricewaterhouseCoopers.

Beamish, R. (2006). Religious groups get chunk of AIDS money. Retrieved from Yahoo News: http://news.yahoo.com/s/ap/20060129/ap_on_he_me/aids _prevention

Berkman, C. S., & Zinberg, G. (1997). Homophobia and heterosexism in social workers. *Social Work, 42* (4), 319–332.

Blackwell, C., & Dziegielewski, S. (2005). The privatization of social services from public to sectarian: Negative consequences for America's gays and lesbians. *Journal of Human Behavior in the Social Environment, 11* (2), 25–43.

Blackwell, C.W., & Kiehl, E.M. (2008). Homophobia in registered nurses: Impact on youth. *Journal of Gay and Lesbian Youth 5* (4), 28-48. DOI: 10/1080/ 19361650802222989.

Brooks, R., Etzel, M., Hinojos, E., Henry, C., & Perez, M. (2005). Preventing HIV among Latino and African American gay and bisexual men in a context of HIV-related stigma, discrimination, and homophobia: Perspectives of providers. *AIDS Patient Care & STDs, 19*, 737–744.

Cahill, S., & Jones, K. T. (2002). *Leaving our children behind: Welfare reform and the gay, lesbian, bisexual, and transgender community.* Washington, DC: Policy Institute of the National Gay and Lesbian Task Force.

Carballo-Dieguez, A., Dolezal, C., Leu, C., Nieves, L., Diaz, F. Decena, C., & Balan, I. (2005). A randomized controlled trial to test an HIV-prevention intervention for Latino gay and bisexual men: Lessons learned. *AIDS Care, 17* (3), 314–328.

Centers for Disease Control and Prevention. (2003). CDC HIV/AIDS fact sheet: HIV/AIDS among men who have sex with men. Retrieved from Centers for Disease Control: http://www.cdc.gov/hiv/pubs/facts/msm.htm

Centers for Disease Control and Prevention. (2011, September). HIV and aids among gay and bisexual men. Retrieved from http://www.cdc.gov/nchhstp/ newsroom/docs/fastfacts-msm-final508comp.pdf

Centers for Disease Control and Prevention. (2012, February 24). *HIV prevalence.* Retrieved from http://www.cdc.gov/hiv/topics/surveillance/incidence.htm

Cnaan, R. A., & Bodie, S. C. (2002). Charitable choice and faith-based welfare: A call for social work. *Social Work, 47* (3), 224–235.

Davis, D. H. (1996). The church-state implications of the new welfare reform law. *Journal of Church & State, 38* (4), 719–731.

Dennis, J. P. (2002). Lying with man as with woman: Rethinking the impact of religious discourse on gay community strength. *Journal of Homosexuality, 44* (1), 43–60.

Douglas, C. J., Kalman, C. M., & Kalman, T. P. (1985). Homophobia among physicians and nurses: An empirical study. *Hospital & Community Psychiatry, 36* (12), 1309–1311.

Ellis, S. J., Kitzinger, C., & Wilkinson, S. (2002). Attitudes towards lesbians and gay men and support for human rights among psychology students. *Journal of Homosexuality, 44* (1), 121–138.

Finlay, B., & Walther, C. (2003). The relation of religious affiliation, service attendance, and other factors to homophobic attitudes among university students. *Review of Religious Research, 44* (4), 370–393.

Giovanna-Merli, M., Hertog, S., Wang, B., & Li, J. (2006). Modeling the spread of HIV/AIDS in China: The role of sexual transmission. *Population Studies, 60* (1), 22–43.

Glennon, F. (2000). Blessed be the ties that bind? The challenge of charitable choice to moral obligation. *Journal of Church & State, 42* (4), 825–843.

Global Fund (2012). Retrieved from http://www.theglobalfund.org/en/

Henry J. Kaiser Family Foundation. (2011, October). U.S. federal funding for HIV/AIDS: the president's FY 2012 budget request. Retrieved from http://www .kff.org/hivaids/upload/7029–07.pdf

Herek, G. M. (1988). Heterosexuals' attitudes toward lesbians and gay men: A review of empirical research with the ATLG scale. *Journal of Sex Research, 25*, 451–477.

Herek, G. M. (2000). The psychology of sexual prejudice. *Current Directions in Psychological Science, 9*(1), 19–22.

Herek, G. M. (2002). Heterosexuals' attitudes toward bisexual men and women in the United States. *Journal of Sex Research, 29*(4), 264–274.

Herek, G. M., & Capitanio, J. P. (1995). Black heterosexuals' attitudes toward lesbians and gay men in the United States. *Journal of Sex Research, 32*(2), 95–105.

Herek, G. M., & Glunt, E. K. (1993). Interpersonal contact and heterosexuals' attitudes toward gay men: Results form a national survey. *Journal of Sex Research, 30*(3), 239–244.

Hoffman, A., & Bakken, L. (2001). Are educational and life experiences related to homophobia? *Educational Research Quarterly, 24*(4), 67–82.

Jean, L. L. (2002). Preface. In *Leaving our children behind: Welfare reform and the gay, lesbian, bisexual, and transgender community* (Sec. 1). Retrieved from the Policy Institute of the National Gay and Lesbian Task Force http://www.ngltf.org/downloads/WelfRef.pdf

Jenkins, R. (1995). Religion and HIV: Implications for research and intervention. *Journal of Social Issues, 51*(2), 131–144.

Kennedy, S. S., & Bielefeld, W. (2002). Government shekels without government shackles? The administrative challenges of charitable choice. *Public Administration Review, 62*(1), 4–11.

Knippenberg, J. M. (2003). The constitutional politics of charitable choice. *Society, 40*(2), 37–47.

Lam, A., Mak, A., Lindsay, P., & Russell, S. (2004). What really works? Exploratory study of condom negotiation strategies. *AIDS Education and Prevention, 162*(2), 160–171.

Lewis, G. B. (2003). Black-white differences in attitudes toward homosexuality and gay rights. *Public Opinion Quarterly, 67*, 89–78.

Lieberman, J. I., & Cummings, E. E. (2002). Charitable choice: Overview of research findings on implementation (GAO-02–337). Washington, DC: U.S. Government Printing Office.

Lugg, C. (1998). The religious right and public education: The paranoid politics of homophobia. *Educational Policy, 12*(3), 267–283.

Marin, B. (2003). HIV prevention in the Hispanic community, sex, culture, and empowerment. *Journal of Transcultural Nursing, 14*(3), 186–192.

Meacham, J., Scelfo, J., France, D., Underwood, A., Amfitheatrof, E., Blair, R., & Abrahms, S. (2002). Celibacy & marriage. *Newsweek, 139*(18), 28–29.

Parker, R., Khan, S., & Aggelton, P. (1998). Conspicuous by their absence? Men who have sex with men (MSM) in developing countries: Implications for HIV prevention. *Critical Public Health, 8*(4), 329–346.

Petersen, L. R., & Donnenwerth, G. V. (1998). Religion and declining support for traditional beliefs about gender roles and homosexual rights. *Sociology of Religion, 59*(4), 353–371.

Plugge-Foust, C., & Strickland, G. (2001). Homophobia, irrationality, and Christian ideology: Does a relationship exist? *Journal of Sex Education and Therapy, 25* (4), 240–244.

Rose, S. (2005). Going too far? Sin and social policy. *Social Forces, 84* (2), 1207–1232.

Ross, M., Henry, D., Freeman, A., Caghy, M., & Dawson, A. (2004). Environmental influences on safer sex in young gay men: A situational presentation approach to measuring influences on sexual health. *Archives of Social Behavior, 33* (3), 249–257.

Rostow, A. (2003, November 5). "Faith-based" discrimination suit settled. *Planet Out*. Retrieved from http://www.planetout.com/news/article.html?2003/11/05/4

Sternberg, S. (2003). HIV infection rates rising among gay, bisexual men. Retrieved from *USA Today*: http://www.usatoday.com/news/health/2003–07–28-hiv-rate_x.htm

Stone, K. (1999). Safer texts: Reading Biblical lament in the age of AIDS. *Theology & Sexuality, 10*, 16–27.

Veerman, P., Tatsa, G., Druzin, P., & Weinstein, R. (1999). HIV prevention, children's rights, and homosexual youth. *International Journal of Children's Rights, 7*, 83–89.

Wilson, K. M., & Huff, J. L. (2001). Scaling Satan. *Journal of Psychology, 135* (3), 292–300.

Wolitski, R. (2005). The emergence of barebacking among gay and bisexual men in the United States: A public health perspective. *Journal of Gay & Lesbian Psychotherapy, 9* (3/4), 9–34.

Yang, C. (2001, July 10). No deal: White House rejects Salvation Army request to protect anti-gay hiring policy. Retrieved from ABC News: http://abcnews.go.com/sections/politics/DailyNews/Bush_Salvation010710.html

Chapter 11
Social Welfare and Economics

*Redefining the Welfare State
in a Global Economy*

Howard Karger and Peter A. Kindle

> As you read this chapter consider if you believe that its central arguments have weathered the political and policy changes of the first Obama Administration. Are these changes dramatic shifts in federal programs or are these only incremental changes, which do not adequately address the qualitative shift from an industrial to a postindustrial economy?

Introduction

Since the early 1990s, domestic economic policy change has been in an almost constant state of flux, sometimes positive, sometimes negative.

- The Earned Income Tax Credit (EITC) was expanded.
- Eligibility for the additional child tax credit was enlarged.
- Unemployment benefits have been extended; payroll tax deductions for Social Security have been temporarily reduced.
- New financial regulations have been adopted.
- A new federal measure of poverty was created; the federal minimum wage was increased.
- The Consumer Financial Protection Bureau has been organized.
- Federal guarantees for student loans have been discontinued in preference for additional direct federal funding of student loans.
- Multiple federal programs have attempted to arrest the foreclosure crisis in housing.

This chapter argues that the change to a postindustrial economy, mirrored primarily in changes in labor market structures, highlights the inadequacy of the U.S. welfare state designed to serve an industrial economy.

The postindustrial labor market converted primary sector jobs with health insurance, pensions, and seniority into secondary/tertiary sector jobs that are temporary and transitional. In the postindustrial economy, the employee has not only lost access to the shared economic risk central to industrial era employee benefits, but the responsibility for labor market readiness has also shifted from employer to employee. Middle class wage stagnation, elevated income disparities, increased consumer debt, and higher poverty levels are the sad consequences.

In retrospect, the new welfare agenda presented in this chapter to cope with the postindustrial economy may not go far enough. Redistribution of income through family-friendly tax reform and corporate taxation does not address the structural inequities of the postindustrial labor market. The ceaseless and prevailing winds of globalization appear to be an insurmountable obstacle for stronger pro-labor regulations. Even minimum wage enhancements appear, without a cost-of-living adjustment, to provide only a brief respite from economic hardship.

A new welfare agenda for a postindustrial economy must focus on addressing the erosion of shared risk among the public sector, the employer, and the employee. The Patient Protection and Affordable Care Act (PPACA), if sustained after spring 2012 arguments heard in the U.S. Supreme Court, may be the first federal legislation designed for the postindustrial economy. Not only does PPACA approximate universal health care insurance coverage, it provides mechanisms to control the future escalation of health care costs that has been the bane of middle class wage increases for 30 years. Sharing the risk of retirement by strengthening the existing Social Security system, if coupled with PPACA, comes close to the portable and federally guaranteed benefits package envisioned in this chapter.

Even as we consider a new type of a welfare state, one cannot ignore that fast-changing global community. There clearly is a shifting of global power and players. The economies of many eurozone members are in a state of flux and uncertainty. The threatened economic collapse of Greece, Portugal, and Italy has dire consequences for the United States' fiscal position. Presidential European elections in 2012 saw more right-to-center administrations voted out of office and replaced by more liberal, socialist parties. No more than at any other time, the global economy is impacted by many nontraditional transinternational businesses; religious groups; and organizations, criminal groups, and terrorists organizations. Compounding this growth is the dramatic increase of the worldwide senior population who will live longer expecting more services.

As the welfare state is reconfigured, programs and services will be conceptualized through a new, distinctive set of lenses. Program eligibility will receive greater scrutiny—for example, will the retirement age increase beyond age 66 to more reflect actuary tables? Will services be selective or universal—for example, while everyone pays into Social Security retirement, should the wealthy receive a lower or no benefit while the lower wage earner will receive a higher benefit? To what extent will the government (local, state, and national) contract services to the private sector as is commonplace in the criminal justice system or with child protective services in states such as Texas and Florida?

What remains to be developed in a new welfare agenda for the postindustrial, global, technologically based economy is a strategy for labor market reform that is sustainable in light of the pressures of globalization. The broad contours of postindustrial labor market reform should include the adoption of living wage standards with cost-of-living adjustments, restructuring of higher education programs to eliminate student financial disincentives to pursue skill and credential acquisition, and public investment in work programs designed to eliminate poverty. In a postindustrial economy, *working poor* must become an oxymoron, and an opportunity to work must become a *right* rather than a possibility.

The U.S. welfare state is driven largely by economics. Specifically, social welfare services in democratic capitalist societies are fueled by tax revenues, which, in turn, depend on the performance of the larger economy. Although economics plays a major role in modern welfare states, it is not the only variable. Ideology and religion also play a significant role, especially in the U.S. welfare state, and it is reductionistic to overdetermine any one variable, including economics.

Social welfare is shaped by an amalgam of forces that exert differential influence depending on the historical period. For example, while the economic crisis of the Depression formed the basis for the New Deal welfare state, by the 1980s religion and political ideology became equally important influences in shaping welfare policy. Despite the caveat, this chapter focuses on the role of economics in social welfare policy, especially as it relates to the creation of a viable welfare state in a postindustrial global economy.

The Social Welfare State: A Legacy of the Industrial Era

Although rudimentary forms of welfare existed in the United States since Colonial times, the modern welfare state was born in the Social Security Act of 1935. When Franklin Roosevelt assumed the presidency in 1933, he faced a country divided between right- and left-wing political factions, a collapsing industrial sector replete with violent labor strikes, a banking system on the verge of collapse, and a class society at its breaking point (Cohen, 1958). FDR's response to the Depression was a massive social experiment with the objectives of relief, recovery, and reform. These New Deal programs formed the basis of the modern U.S. welfare state.

The New Deal shaped the modern welfare state in several ways. For one, federal policy was used to ameliorate some of the more egregious inequities in the labor market by enacting minimum wage laws and establishing the right of workers to strike and collectively bargain. FDR's programs also created important precedents in others areas, including the right of eligible Americans to receive public assistance. The New Deal welfare state took relief from the realm of "we will provide what we have" to an entitlement program whereby resources must be provided to those who qualify.

The New Deal shifted the responsibility from individual states providing public assistance to the federal sector providing it. Consequently, certain public assistance rules and eligibility, but not the determination of cash benefits, were standardized and applied more evenly across states. FDR's New Deal codified a policy directive that established the responsibility of federal and state governments to provide for the needs of citizens deemed worthy of receiving aid. Unfortunately, this important policy precedent was rescinded by the passage of the Personal Responsibility and Work Opportunity Act of 1996 (PRWORA) (Karger & Stoesz, 2006).

The New Deal welfare state institutionalized the responsibility of government to assist the jobless or those unable to compete in the labor market. Welfare programs, such as unemployment insurance, assisted displaced workers until they could be reabsorbed into the economy. The New Deal's social impact lasted for more than 60 years.

Despite the disdain of conservatives, the U.S. welfare state grew rapidly from the 1950s to the 1970s. In large part, this was due to the robust growth of the U.S. economy. U.S. innovation had introduced a wide range of products and services and the productivity of U.S. workers was unsurpassed globally. With this economic dominance, the United States could afford to idle a small percentage of its workforce.

Faced with an expensive war in Vietnam and a sluggish economy mired in stagflation (i.e., a combination of recession and inflation), the U.S. welfare state came under closer scrutiny in the early 1970s. This scrutiny, however, did not translate into the diminution of the welfare state. Even though President Richard Nixon dismantled the Great Society, the welfare state actually grew larger under his administration than preceding ones. Between 1965 and 1975, America's fiscal priorities were reversed. In 1965 defense expenditures comprised 42% of the federal budget while social welfare expenditures accounted for 25%. By 1975, defense expenditures comprised 25% of the budget while social welfare outlays accounted for 43%. Even in Ronald Reagan's conservative budget of 1986, with its large increases in defense spending, only 29% was defense-related compared to 41% for social welfare (DiNitto & Dye, 1987). Despite some ups and downs, the U.S. welfare state was generally in a growth mode from 1935 to the middle 1970s.

The tacit acceptance of welfare programs by Republican leaders did not reflect real support, but a recognition that Americans—despite their outward ambivalence—supported the welfare state. Republicans understood that to be elected at the national level they must appeal to working class Democrats, many of whom depended on social welfare programs such as those designed to assist in the purchase of a home (FHA and VA loans), unemployment compensation, student loans, and so forth. The challenge was how to psychologically wean these voters away from welfare, and more specifically, how to convince them that welfare programs were actually anathema to their welfare.

A powerful new force emerged in U.S. politics during the 1980s. Although fiscal conservatives had been content to snipe at the welfare state since 1935, by the 1980s they became downright serious about dismantling it. Allied with the religious right, conservatives developed the Contract with America, an agenda designed to replace government responsibility for social welfare with personal responsibility. One cornerstone of this strategy was the PRWORA, which, among other things, reversed 60 years of federal entitlement by disentitling the needy poor from receiving public assistance. To promote personal responsibility, the PRWORA mandated a tough 5-years-and-out (1 year at state discretion) lifetime cap on welfare receipt coupled with stringent welfare-to-work requirements.

The 1980s saw a shift toward commodifying what had become social utilities. Services that were formerly free or heavily subsidized, such as mental health services, suddenly became a marketplace commodity for much of the population. Other services provided by government, such as student loans or mortgages, were now a quasi- or fully privatized marketplace commodity. This change was driven by conservatives who wanted to cut taxes and one avenue was to dismantle or cut deeply into governmental welfare programs. Through a consummate sales job, a large segment of the U.S. public bought into the idea that their interests were best served by dismantling the welfare state, supporting tax cuts for the wealthy, and by purchasing more of their social needs in the private marketplace.

The Postindustrial Economy

Fiscal conservatives were correct about one thing—the welfare state was a vestige of the industrial epoch. Welfare states emerged in an industrial era marked by relatively strong labor unions and massive capital investment in domestic production. Because unions were relatively strong from the 1940s through the 1970s, universal health insurance was unnecessary for many workers whose union contracts included health plans. Many nonunionized workers were employed by large corporations that provided health insurance as a normal perk. With the notable exception of low-wage workers and the elderly (covered by the 1965 Medicare act), most full-time workers had health insurance. This is illustrated by the rise in the number of people with health care insurance, from less than 20 million in 1940 to more than 135 million by 1960 (Health Insurance Institute, 1966).

Fueled by the supposed exigencies of the global economy, by the 1990s employers had intensified their race to the economic bottom. In 2004 almost 46 million Americans, or close to 16% of the population—mainly women and children—lacked health insurance coverage. Benefit erosion declined through the early 2000s and health insurance coverage declined for all wage groups in the 2000 to 2002 period. Pension plans followed the same trajectory: By 2002 only 45.5% of the U.S. workforce had pension coverage, less than the 51% of workers in 1979 (Mishel, Bernstein, & Allegretto, 2005).

Many large employers in the 1950s also provided seniority right and some, like IBM, even promised lifelong employment. Providing lifetime employment was not altruistic per se, but based on the belief that investing in workers was a critical factor in increasing productivity. Conversely, high turnover rates hinder productivity because of the expense in replacing and retraining workers. Plus, there was an assumption that corporate loyalty and good morale was important in maintaining high levels of productivity, a concept that fell into disrepute during the latter part of the 20th century.

Employment in Postindustrial Society

The modern postindustrial economy is more dynamic and volatile than the industrial era. Modern corporations now make fewer investments in domestic manufacturing, and many prefer to outsource production to foreign producers or set up manufacturing plants abroad. As a result, the promise of lifetime employment has been rescinded by most corporations because employees are no longer viewed as having lifelong value to the company. Instead, employees are viewed as interchangeable and are just one more capital expense.

The employer is expected to train the employee in a traditional industrial setting. In a postindustrial setting the employee is expected to possess marketable skills before they are hired. Consequently, in the industrial era a high school education was sufficient to ensure that the employee had a knowledge base from which they could be trained. In a postindustrial context, the employee is expected to hit the ground running. Those who cannot—or will not—run fast enough are fired. In general, employees are fired the moment they cost more than they earn.

The industrial era welfare state was based on a full employment model with social insurance programs, such as unemployment insurance, serving as a temporary stop gap measure for frictional unemployment. However, frictional unemployment has given way to structural unemployment. Middle-age middle managers that are replaced by cheaper workers often end up structurally unemployed or forced to accept a job at a fraction of their previous wages. Those without marketable skills—or whose skills do not translate into another employment setting—can end up permanently unemployed.

If unemployment is often a consequence of inadequate or obsolete skills, then retraining becomes even more important. But in a postindustrial ownership society, workers own the problem of their obsolete or inadequate skills and are therefore expected to retrain themselves and bear the costs of that retraining. As governmental subsidies for training diminishes, for example, higher tuition costs, cuts in Pell grants and student loans, and so forth, those most in need of skill training must bear a larger share of those costs.

One major avenue for training and or retraining current and future workers has been a college degree. In general, college educated workers

Table 11.1 Median Income for People 25 and Older Year-Round, Full-time Workers, 2005 (All Races)

No HS Diploma	HS Diploma	Some College	AA Degree	Bachelor's	Master's	Professional Degree
$20,321	$26,605	$31,054	$35,009	$43,143	$52,390	$82,473

Source: U.S. Census Bureau and Bureau of Labor Statistics, Annual Demographic Survey, March Supplement, 2006. Retrieved from http://pubdb3.census.gov/macro/032006/perinc/new03_001.htm

are the only sector of the labor market where wages have been rising. On average, the median annual income for college graduates is 62% higher than for those with only a high school diploma. A college graduate with a professional degree earns 210% more than a high school graduate (see Table 11.1).

Despite the economic benefit of a college degree, the public university system is increasingly transferring more of its costs to consumers. Consequently, it is becoming more inaccessible to larger numbers of people. A general rule of thumb is that tuition rates increase at about twice the general rate of inflation. During the 17-year period from 1958 to 2001, the average annual tuition inflation rate rose between 6% and 9%, ranging from 1.2 to 2.1 times the general rate of inflation.

Higher education in Texas illustrates this national trend. In 2001 the Texas legislature deregulated tuition and fees. By 2006, tuition and fees at Texas public universities cost $4,857, a 28% increase over 2002 to 2003 after adjusting for inflation. Overall, the average cost of tuition and fees at the nation's public universities was $5,491 in 2006, a 25% inflation-adjusted increase from 2002 to 2003 (Austin, 2006). From 1989 to 2005 college tuition rose 5.94% or almost double the rate of inflation. The result of these increases is that 60% of undergraduates leave college with student loans, the average being about $20,000. Graduate and professional students borrow even more, with the average debt ranging from $27,000 to $114,000 (FinAid, 2006).

When John Maynard Keynes (1965) wrote *The General Theory of Employment, Interest and Money* in 1936, the European and U.S. economies were firmly rooted in the industrial era. This partly explains why Keynes stressed the importance of full employment. In fact, the Keynesian welfare states of Europe and the United States were largely based on programs dealing with unemployment or other labor market problems. However, in a postindustrial context the problem of unemployment is largely related to skill acquisition and the time and resources it takes to acquire the necessary skills to compete in today' global economy.

According to Michael Piore (1977), the modern U.S. economy consists of the primary and secondary labor markets. The primary labor market is composed of workers and managers who occupy stable employment positions, complete with livable wages and perks that include health insurance, retirement benefits, disability and life insurance, and paid vacations. The secondary labor market, which often consists of temporary or part-time work, is characterized by unstable employment, high-turnover rates, low pay, and a lack of benefits and other employment perks. There may also be a tertiary labor market that is similar to the secondary market, except that the jobs tend to be even more temporary (sometimes daily work), there are no benefits, the pay is lower, and workers are sometimes paid in cash and off the books. Many employees in the tertiary sector are undocumented workers.

The majority of jobs in the hospitality, light manufacturing, and retail industries are secondary or tertiary labor market jobs. These jobs are often filled by minorities, undocumented workers or immigrants, women, the disabled, older unemployed workers, and others who face job discrimination in their bid to enter the primary labor market. Workers in these positions usually earn less than a livable wage and often work two or more jobs to make ends meet.

The existence of the secondary and tertiary labor market contradicts classical economic explanations of labor and wages. Many economists view the labor market as a commodities market where rational workers seeking to maximize their economic well-being interact with rational employers seeking to maximize their profits. In theory, this supply and demand relationship determines employment and wage levels. However, this explanation fails to explain the large differences in wages and employment conditions in the current labor market. Classical economists argue that differences in wages are due to disparities in productivity based on the human capital of differing workers. However, economists such as Jared Bernstein (1995) and others have pointed out that much of this income disparity is related to institutional rather than human capital factors. In other words, it is not productivity alone that determines wages, but also racial, market, technical, organizational, and political factors. Wages may be more determined by good and bad jobs rather than good and bad workers.

Wage problems and income growth are evident when examining recent economic data. In 2005 the economy was strong, having expanded for the fourth consecutive year. Despite this, real hourly wages fell for most workers. For low- and middle-wage workers, and those with a high school degree, real wages fell by 1% to 2% in 2004. Those higher on the wage scale experienced marginal gains, although real wages were essentially unchanged even for college graduates. These stagnant wages occurred despite a strong growth in labor productivity, and were especially problematic since inflation was 2.7% in 2004 and 3.4% in 2005, which meant that workers were losing ground (Price & Bernstein, 2006). In contrast, the salaries of chief executive officers (CEOs) exploded. From 1989 to 2000 the wage of the median CEO grew 79% and their average compensation increased 342%. In 1965 CEOs earned 26 times the wage of the typical worker; by 2003 it was 185 times. U.S. CEOs earn 3 times more than their foreign counterparts (Mishel et al., 2005).

Income growth was strongly correlated to productivity throughout much of the industrial era. Between 1947 and 1973 productivity and income grew by a whopping 104%. Most family incomes benefited from the rapid increase in labor productivity and the concomitant reward of higher incomes. As the global economy matured in the mid-1970s, the relationship between productivity and income growth began to break down. Median family income grew at about one third the rate of productivity (22% versus 65%) from 1973 to 2002. According to Mishel et al. (2005), "while faster productivity growth led to a larger economic pie, growing inequality meant that the slices were divided up such that some income classes—those at the top of the income scale—claimed most of the income growth" (p. 3).

The modern postindustrial economy has ushered in almost unprecedented levels of income inequality. In the 1950s and 1960s real income growth doubled for each household in the five income brackets. This trend was reversed between 1979 and 2000, when the real income of households in the lowest fifth (the bottom 20% of earners) grew by only 6.4% compared to 70% for the top fifth income bracket. The top 1% saw their incomes rise by an astounding 184%. By 2000, the top 1% had claimed 21.7% of the nation's total income. An even starker measure of inequality is the ownership of wealth. In 2001 the wealthiest 1% of all households controlled more than 33% of the national wealth. The bottom 80% of households held only 16% (Mishel et al., 2005).

Although some economists claim that income mobility in the United States allows the poor to leapfrog to the top, the data tells a different story. Fifty-three percent of those who started out in the lowest fifth income bracket in the late 1980s were still there by the late 1990s. Another 24% had only climbed to the next fifth. In other words, 77% of those that started out poor remained there a decade later (Mishel et al., 2005).

Several factors contribute to the decline in real wages, including: a reduction in the bargaining power of workers, especially the decline of union power; the fall in the real value of the minimum wage; the growing imbalance in international trade; and the exportation of more white-collar jobs offshore. Membership in labor unions—the best security for nonprofessional workers—fell from 30.8% of nonagricultural workers in 1970 to 12.5% in 2005. Union members earn higher wages, and in 2005, full-time unionized workers had median weekly earnings of $801 compared to $622 for nonunionized workers (Bureau of Labor Statistics, 2006b). Unionized employees are also 28% more likely than their nonunion counterparts to be covered by employer-provided health insurance (their deductibles are also 18% less), and they are 24% more likely to have health insurance in their retirement (Mishel et al., 2005).

The global economy is partly responsible for the loss of 4 million manufacturing jobs from 1989 to 2002 (Karger & Stoesz, 2006). Although little hard data exists on the impact of offshoring white-collar jobs, anecdotal evidence suggests it is having a major impact on the labor force. Specifically, the threat of hiring foreign workers or moving operations offshore is being used to curtail wage growth in the technology and software industries. House Small Business Committee Chairman Don Manzullo (D-IL) summed up the threat:

> *U.S. manufacturers contract with engineers from India who send their drawings to workers in Poland who in turn ship their finished products back to America for incorporation into "American" products. Radiologists in India interpret CT scans for U.S. hospitals. Computer technicians in Ghana process New York City parking tickets ψ. The U.S. economy is growing and creating jobs, but Americans are not filling them. These jobs have been moved overseas where foreigners will work for a lot less.*

(quoted in Eskeland, 2003)

Impoverishment and Debt in the Postindustrial Era

Stagnant wages, structural employment, and income inequality has led to increasing levels of absolute and relative poverty. In 2004 the poverty rate was 12.7% (37 million people), up from 12.1% (34.5 million) in 1998. Almost 18% of children under age 18 (13 million) were poor, as were about 12% of the elderly. The poverty rate is even more striking when disaggregated by race: 24.7% of African Americans, 21.9% of Hispanics, and 8.6% of Whites were poor in 2004 (U.S. Census Bureau, 2005).

Absolute poverty thresholds tell only part of the story. About 18% of U.S. households had zero or negative net wealth in 2001. Broken down, roughly 31% of African-American households had no or negative wealth compared to 13% of White households. The median wealth for African Americans in 2001 was $10,700 or roughly 10% of the median wealth of Whites (Mishel et al., 2005).

Because of stagnant wages, high levels of consumption, and easy credit a new class of near-poor or functionally poor households has been born. These functionally poor individuals or families have incomes that are solidly middle class, but they have zero or negative disposable or discretionary income at the end of the month. This group includes homeowners who use their property like ATM machines, regularly drawing out equity to finance credit card debts or other purchases. It also includes the middle class with tarnished credit who use high interest rate credit cards or finance purchases through tricky time-deferred payments. This burgeoning sector of the middle class is economically closer to the poor than they are to the traditional middle class.

The ostensible cause of financial hardship among the functionally poor middle class is debt, something endemic to all sectors of our society. In 2006 the federal debt was $8.4 trillion, a $2.1 trillion increase over 1997. This debt is increasing by $1.75 billion a day with each citizen's share being roughly $28,000 (zFacts.com, 2012).

Consumer spending—much of it fueled by successful advertising and marketing—accounts for two thirds of the nation's $11 trillion economy and has led to Americans becoming more indebted than ever (Karger, 2005). Excluding mortgages, consumer debt almost doubled from 1994 to 2004, totaling about $19,000 a family. By 2004 Americans owed more than $9 trillion in home mortgages, car loans, credit card debt, home equity loans and other forms of credit—nearly 40% of which was accumulated in just 4 years. One fifth of the $9 trillion is in variable interest rate loans, such as credit or store cards.

Middle-income consumers are 10 times more likely than upper income families to devote 40% or more of their income to debt repayment (Uchitelle, 2004). The average household now spends 13% of its after-tax income on debt repayment, the highest percentage since 1986 (Lohr, 2004). (These figures are soft because they fail to take into account forms of predatory lending, such as payday loans, pawnshop transactions, rent-to-own and tax refund loans.) All told, household debt has increased a whopping 500% since 1957.

Consumer debt is further aggravated by low rates of personal savings. Americans saved about 10% of their disposable income in the 1980s; by 2004 it fell to a near record low of less than 1%. (Some estimates put it at −.5%.) Home equity was also the lowest in recent history due to feverish home refinancing. In 2002, homeowners initiated $97 billion in home equity loans, nearly 5 times the amount in 1993 (Karger, 2005; Murray, 2000). Although home refinancing put about $300 billion back into the economy from 2001 to 2003, consumers spent almost all of it (Paul, 2003). Not coincidentally, the foreclosure rate rose 45% from January 2005 to January 2006 (MSN Real Estate, 2006).

Credit card debt contributes to the growth of the "new poor." The average credit card balance per household is approaching $12,000, and the average U.S. family spends about $1,100 a year in credit card interest alone (Coalition for Responsible Credit Practices, 2004). Overall, credit card holders carried more than $1.7 trillion in debt in 2002, up from $1.1 trillion in 1995 (Karger, 2005). Debt is now cited as the number one problem facing newlyweds and is fast becoming a major cause of divorce (Coalition for Responsible Credit Practices, 2004).

According to Warren and Tyagi (2003), today's two-income family earns 75% more than their single-income counterpart a generation ago, but has less discretionary income after paying fixed monthly bills. Some of this is attributable to mortgage costs that have risen 70 times faster than an average father's wages (Feran, 2003). In addition, the drop in earnings of noncollege graduate males since the 1970s has forced more mothers to work full- or part time to make up the difference. This second income has not resulted in families purchasing more; instead, it is used to pay for necessities like shelter, food, clothing and transportation. Applebaum, Bernhardt, and Murnane (2003) argue that middle- and low-income families have maxed-out their earnings capacity through the employment of mothers. Having exhausted their labor reserve, these families are forced to generate additional income by ersatz means such as mortgage refinancing.

Fixed costs such as mortgage payments, child care, health insurance, and vehicles and taxes consume up to 75% of the paycheck of today's two-income family. By contrast, those costs represented about half of a middle class family income in the early 1970s. In 2002 U.S. families spent 22% less for food (including restaurant meals), 21% less for clothing, and 44% less for appliances than in 1973. Adjusted for inflation, consumer expenditures are lower than a generation ago (Warren & Tyagi, 2003).

Second incomes are used to pay for day-to-day living expenses. The result is that families are left with no reserve income for emergencies. Moreover, the anemic nature of the modern welfare state does little to ease their vulnerability to privation and bankruptcy if they face life events such as illness, death, desertion, or unemployment.

Although a second income helps pay bills, the effects are diminished by day-care costs ranging from $340 to almost $1,100 a month, clothing expenses, and the need for a second reliable car (Runzheimer International, 2004). For many families with young children, half or more of their second wage is consumed by the costs of workplace participation, and after expenses, they only see a small increase in family income. The impact of the second income is further diminished by the gender gap in male and female wages (Economic Policy Institute, 2005).

Indebtedness often leads to bankruptcy. In 2005 there were 2 million personal bankruptcies. Every 15 seconds someone in the United States goes bankrupt, a fourfold increase over 1980. About 1.5 million U.S. households filed for bankruptcy in 2003, 400% more than in 1975 (American Bankruptcy Institute, 2004). In fact, more people file for bankruptcy than graduate from college or file for divorce (Sullivan, Warren, & Westbrook, 2001). In examining bankruptcy filers, Teresa Sullivan, Elizabeth Warren, and Jay Westbrook found that they crossed all income and occupational levels and were not irresponsible spendthrifts. Instead, they had insurmountable financial problems stemming from a life crisis such as divorce, job loss, or medical problems (Sullivan, Warren, & Westbrook, 1989). The combination of stagnant and low wages, plus high debt, may lead some middle class families directly into the path of social welfare programs.

Not every economic problem can, or should, be laid at the doorstep of the global economy. However, certain trends thought necessary to successfully compete in the global economy exacerbate the general economic malaise felt by a growing number of middle class families. These trends include wage depression and stagnant incomes; the disconnect between increased productivity and wage growth; growing income and asset inequality between classes; the commodification and privatization of public utilities, such as higher education, day care, and health care; regressive tax cuts that deplete the public treasury while mainly benefiting the rich; the reduction of employee benefits; the creation of more part-time jobs without benefits; deep cuts in public services; and "starving the breast"—financially starving welfare state programs. Taken together, these trends constitute a race to the bottom by industry and government, and contribute to the growing "Indonesianization" of the U.S. workforce.

A New Welfare Agenda for the Global Economy

Conservatives argue that welfare state programs are an unaffordable luxury in a competitive global economy. They claim that New Deal welfare programs have outlived their usefulness, if they were ever useful. The demands of the global economy require fewer and more miserly social programs that divert less money from taxes, thereby freeing up more capital for investment. Conservatives argue that market solutions will tackle social problems, and at best, social welfare should be a temporary safety net for frictional unemployment.

The conservative response to the liberal welfare state has been to substitute labor policy for welfare policy (Karger, 2003, July). For example, the PRWORA was essentially a labor policy clothed in welfare terminology. Passed during a period of strong economic growth (a 2.5% growth rate in the mid-1990s) and low unemployment (4.2%), the 138 million member U.S. labor force could easily absorb 4.2 million AFDC mothers (just over 3% of the total workforce) without driving down wages or increasing unemployment. The economic giddiness of the middle 1990s reinforced the conservative belief that a job existed for anyone that wanted it.

The passage of the PRWORA represented the culmination of the long-standing conservative goal of deracinating public assistance. When the poor exhaust time-limited public assistance benefits they become a labor market rather than a welfare problem. With that change, public assistance policy was reduced to a short-term transitional step in the march toward the full labor market participation of the poor. Weak federal labor policy, an inadequate minimum wage, the absence of national health care insurance, and few workplace protections mean that former recipients now occupy secondary labor market jobs face an even shakier economic future than under AFDC (Karger & Stoesz, 2006). The future of U.S. competitiveness is not based on creating more subsistence-level secondary labor market jobs, but on increasing median income jobs with full benefits.

Contrary to the conservative perspective, the social welfare state is as necessary in a postindustrial global economy as it was in the industrial era. Perhaps even more so. To ensure global competitiveness, the nation must build and periodically rebuild its stock of human capital, thereby enhancing workforce productivity. It is also necessary to provide subsidized opportunities for workers to retrain to meet the demands of the changing labor market and the higher expectations of employers. Increased productivity is especially important since seven nations in the Organization for Economic Cooperation and Development (OECD) have already surpassed the United States in worker output. In 1950, the average per hour output of OECD countries was 41% of the U.S. average; by 2002 it was 88% (Mishel et al., 2005). The more opportunities society provides its members to enhance their human capital and workplace skills, the more productive its workforce.

Questions abound. How can progressives promote an agenda of prosperity, opportunity, and compassion that will win the hearts and minds of America's affluent, while at the same time addressing the needs of the beleaguered middle class and working poor? Which new industrial relationships will lead to greater global justice? How can policy makers ensure that a fairer portion of the rewards of the U.S. economy flows to the middle- and lower classes rather than corporate profits? These questions beg an answer in any new reformulation of the welfare state.

A new welfare agenda must raise the federal poverty threshold. The federal guidelines used to determine poverty were developed 50 years ago and are updated only for inflation. A single parent in 2006 with two children was considered poor if he or she had a yearly income of less than $16,600. The Economic Policy Institute (EPI) estimates that doubling the poverty threshold would more closely approximate the real costs of meeting a family's basic needs (quoted in Mishel et al., 2005). Because the cost of living dramatically differs in urban and rural areas, and in Midwestern versus bi-coastal regions, the poverty threshold should be calibrated on a regional or even a city level (Stoesz & Karger, 1992).

At minimum, a new welfare agenda requires: (a) the creation of family-friendly tax policies to reduce income inequality; (b) new legislation that requires everyone, including corporations, to pay their fair share; (c) stronger pro-labor laws; (d) universal national health insurance; (e) an increased minimum wage; and (f) a portable federally guaranteed non–job-specific benefits package. The remainder of this chapter discusses key components of these proposed policies.

A Welfare Agenda for the Changing Demographics of U.S. Families

A viable postindustrial welfare policy must address the rapidly changing demographics of U.S. family life. For example, about 14% of women who married in the 1940s eventually divorced. A generation later, almost 50% of those married in the late 1960s and early 1970s divorced. Because a second income is required for most families to achieve a middle class lifestyle, single mothers are inherently disadvantaged economically, which is further aggravated by the gender wage gap. The following illustrates the changing family demographic:

- In the late 1990s more than 10 million women were single parents. Twenty-seven percent of U.S. households include children with one parent; 20 million children under age 18 (28% of all children) live with a single parent; and 23% live only with their mother. One million children are added to the roster of divorced families each year. Disaggregated by race, 74% of White and 64% of Hispanic children live with two parents; 36% of African-American children live in two-parent families (*Divorce Magazine*, 2005).

- About 54% of divorced women remarry within 5 years of their divorce. Those with children live on a single income, possibly supplemented by child support.

- About 37% of families maintained by single mothers were poor in 2003, nearly 6 times the rate for married couples with children (U.S. Census Bureau, 2006).

These demographics make it important for government to establish more tax- and family-friendly support policies that allow children in single female-headed households to enjoy the same opportunities as those in dual-parent households. Although the Earned Income Tax Credit (EITC) and the Child Tax Credit (CTC) programs help single female-headed families, they are insufficient to close the income gap. For example, the maximum EITC tax credit for a very-low-income mother with two children was $4,400 in 2005. The maximum CTC credit she could claim was $2,000, bringing her *maximum* tax refund to $6,400. If the mother earned $7 an hour ($1.85 more than the minimum wage), her yearly income would be $13,440 plus the $6,400 in tax refunds, raising her total income to $19,840, or just $3,440 above the poverty line. This is far short of the $32,800 minimum suggested by EPI.

Everyone Should Pay a Fair Share

Substituting labor policy for public assistance policy has led to several problems. For one, the absence of worker-friendly labor policies rewards low-wage employers while punishing poor workers forced into low-paying dead-end jobs with little, if any, benefits. There are few consequences for low-wage employers who fail to provide their employees with a minimum number of hours, health care benefits, or other employment perks. The difference between what these employers pay and the requisite salary to support workers and their families is partly made up by publicly funded social welfare programs. In that sense, low-wage employers are parasitic because they rely on these tax and social welfare programs to bridge the gap between low wages and the real cost of living. Hence, the *real* cost of low-wage employment is paid for by taxpayers.

A hypothetical example illustrates the point. In 2012 a single person earning $7.25 an hour would have a combined yearly income of $15,080. If the wage earner had two children, that income would be $4,010 below the federal poverty line of $19,090 (see U.S. Department of Health and Human Services, 2012). The shortfall between wages and the real cost of living is made up by social programs such as EITC, CTC, and Supplemental Nutrition Program (SNAP), among others. Specifically, EITC, CTC and the SNAP alone (excluding Section 8 housing vouchers, Medicaid, or low-income energy assistance) would provide that family with a maximum yearly supplement of $13,588. Combined with benefits, the family's yearly income would to $28,668 or $9,578 above the poverty line. If federal poverty programs were abolished, the minimum wage would need to rise to nearly $14.00 per hour to compensate for the loss of governmental benefits. Americans either pay more in taxes to augment low wages (and indirectly subsidize low-wage employers) or more at the cash register. Either way there is no free lunch.

In free market capitalism, the real costs of production are theoretically incorporated into the price of goods and services. Welfare state programs usurp that requirement. For example, one of the authors recently participated in a panel discussion on increasing the minimum wage. In the final minutes of the debate, a representative from the Houston business community declared that given the EITC there was no reason to raise the minimum wage. The assumption was that EITC refunds were somehow free money, side-stepping the fact that it comes out of general revenue taxes. The money removed from the tax coffers by the EITC and CTC programs is made up by other tax-filers. Money removed from the tax base also results in less money for social programs and other human capital investments. In short, the EITC is not free money.

Although virtually everyone pays taxes, significant tax loopholes exist for corporations and the wealthy that are unavailable to the general taxpayer. Consequently, the middle class taxpayer disproportionately shoulders the tax liability created by low-wage employers. Corporate profits rise as the real costs of wages are offloaded onto the backs of moderate income taxpayers who see little tangible benefit from this tax burden. In the end, the burden of higher taxes may outweigh any savings accrued at the cash register.

Instead of spreading the real costs of low wages throughout society, tough new laws should require employers to pay their fair share, either through higher taxes, or by a higher minimum wage complemented by the mandate they provide their workers with health insurance and other employment perks. Given the high cost of administering social programs, a front-end approach requiring employers to provide higher salaries and benefits may be cheaper in the long run than trying to close the gap through social welfare programs.

The Need for New Labor Policies

Although EITC effectively supplements family income, the program does nothing for worker protections such as health, disability, and retirement benefits (Karger & Stoesz, 2006). Former beneficiaries and other low-income workers are forced to adapt to a secondary labor market that provides little except low wages. These workers have few workplace protections, and they cannot return to public assistance once they have exhausted their lifetime cap. Hence, the challenge for policy makers is to create a set of labor policies that provide worker protections and facilitate a smooth transition from public assistance to the labor force. These labor policies should protect workers from unscrupulous labor market practices, and require employers to provide benefits similar to the primary employment sector. Last, it should equalize the playing field between unions and corporations.

Health Care Reform

The need to compete in the global economy and promote durable labor force attachment requires a national health insurance plan that covers all workers irrespective of their workplace. While many middle- and upper-income workers can count on health insurance as a standard job perk, the working poor are frequently denied this benefit. This is especially true because many low-income workers are employed in part-time service sector jobs that only provide health insurance for middle- or upper-level management. Other low-income workers are employed in jobs where health insurance is provided only to the worker, and where family coverage is prohibitively expensive. About 24% of households with yearly incomes of less than $25,000 lack health insurance.

Health care coverage should be delinked from labor force participation because unless compelled by law, most low-wage employers will not provide it. Three options exist for ensuring that low-income workers receive coverage: (1) government can provide health coverage directly by expanding Medicaid to cover all adult low-income workers and their spouses, (2) government can design a new program that provides health care coverage for low-income workers, or (3) government can compel and/or subsidize private sector employers to provide insurance. The latter could be accomplished by developing federally subsidized insurance cooperatives (similar to the failed Clinton health care bill) that would permit small employers to purchase insurance at the same rates and coverage as large employers. Employers that demonstrate they are financially unable to provide coverage could receive a supplemental health insurance subsidy or voucher.

The 2010 Patient Protection and Affordable Care Act, also refered to as "Obamacare," provided numerous processions not otherwise available to millions of people. Individuals with pre-exisiting conditions, expansion of Medicaid for individuals and families, creation of state-based Health Insurance Exchanges, and establishing minimal standards for health insurance are among the numerous reforms of this act. Challenged by conservatives, the majority of the Affordable Care Act's components were upheld in a June 2012 U.S. Court case.

Even with this landmark decision, there are two essential points to consider.

First, the Affordable Care Act was "insurance reform" and did not address issues of rising medical and other health related treaments.

Second, millions of people remain uninsured. The Christian Science Monitor (Trumbull, 2010) reported that in 2019 approximately 23 million people will not have insurance.

Upgrading the Minimum Wage

The 2012 minimum wage of $7.25 an hour has been a bone of contention for decades, with sporadic increases subject to the political mood of the times. The minimum wage is important in determining overall wage structure because many employers use it as a baseline by paying $1 to $2 above it. In 2003, about 2 million hourly workers (2.9% of the workforce) earned the minimum wage (Bureau of Labor Statistics, 2003); by 2011, 73.9 million American workers age 16 and over were paid at hourly rates, representing 59.1 percent of all wage and salary workers and of these, 1.7 million earned exactly the prevailing Federal minimum wage of $7.25 per hour (Characteristics of Minimum Wage Earners, 2011).

In 2012, a bill introduced in the United States Senate proposed to increase the minimum wage to $9.80 per hour (Hall & Cooper, 2012). Such an increase would raise the wages of 28 million Americans; an additional 19.5 million workers whose wages are between the current minimum and the proposed $9.80 rate would also be impacted in a positive manner. In 2011, the leisure and hospitality industry was far and away the largest employer of minimum wage employees with 15.1% earning at or below minimum wage (Characteristics of Minimum Wage Earners, 2011).

The declining value of the minimum wage is an important issue to address in a postindustrial welfare context. In 1950 the minimum wage brought a worker to 56% of the median wage. Throughout the 1950s and 1960s, the minimum wage hovered between 44% and 56% of the average wage. By 1980 the minimum wage fell to 46.5% of the average wage; in 1988, it dropped even further to 35.7%. Overall, from 1979 to 1996 the value of the minimum wage declined 29%. Even the increase to $5.15 an hour in 1997 only raised it to 42% of the average wage, bringing a family of three to 83% of the poverty line. To have the same purchasing power as in the mid-1970s, the minimum wage increase in 1997 needed to be $6.07, or almost $1.00 higher (Center on Budget and Policy Priorities, 1997). Moreover, if inflation is calculated at 3% a year, the value of the already low $5.15 minimum wage eroded another 27% from 1997 to 2006.

The minimum wage suffers from three problems: (1) it is low in proportion to the median wage, (2) it is not automatically indexed to the cost of living or the growth in the median wage, and (3) it is not adjusted to reflect regional differences in living costs. The minimum wage does not address the real costs of living or the income needs of the working poor. Nor does it necessarily elevate a worker's mobility. Only 62% of those who earned the minimum wage from 1977 to 1997 rose above it within 1 year (Even & Macpherson, 2000).

Increasing the minimum wage would also have a significant spillover effect for the 10.5 million workers (8.7% of the workforce) who earn up to a dollar more (Rasell, Bernstein, & Boushey, 2001). This increase would raise the wages of all low-income workers by raising the benchmark for all wages. In turn, indexing the minimum wage to the median regional wage would help low-income working families earn enough to bring them above the poverty line and to compensate for gross differences in the costs of living, especially in the more expensive regions of the United States.

More than 100 communities have adopted the concept of a living wage, which is higher than the federal minimum. Typically, city or county living wage ordinances only cover a specific set of workers, usually city or county government workers or those hired by businesses receiving a government contract or subsidy (Karger & Stoesz, 2006). Correspondingly, the 100 communities that have adopted a living wage law represent only a tiny fraction of the thousands of U.S. cities and towns. Moreover, living wage campaigns will likely fail in the more conservative states that typically have the highest concentration of poverty. To ease the burden on the working poor, in July 2012, U.S. Senator Tom Harkin introduced legislation to increase minimum to $9.80 per hour (See Harkin, 2012).

Portable Benefits Packages

Two important trends exist in the global economy: (1) corporations are increasingly shedding their responsibility to provide health and retirement benefits to employees; and (2) job tenure has become volatile as lifetime employment has become almost an anachronism. As employers' needs shift, many find it cheaper and more expeditious to hire new workers rather than retrain existing employees.

The widespread reduction of benefits is obvious when one examines the share of workers covered by employer-provided health and pension plans. From 1979 to 2003, the numbers of employees covered by employer-provided health insurance plans shrunk from 69% to 56.4%. Although this drop was the steepest in the bottom two income tiers (representing a 13% drop in health care coverage), it cut across all income classes, and even the top fifth experienced an 11.7% cut. Pension plan coverage followed a similar trajectory, dropping from 50.6% of the workforce in 1979 to 47.2% in 2003. Although this cut affected all income brackets, the lowest fifth was the least affected, dropping from 18.4% of workers in 1979 to 14.3% in 2003. By 2003 less than half of middle income workers had pension plans (Mishel et al., 2005).

Benefits commonly provided in the primary labor sector, such as family health insurance, life and disability insurance, and supplemental retirement plans are rare in the secondary labor market and virtually nonexistent in the tertiary and temporary employment sectors. Encouraging steady labor force attachment requires not only higher wages, but also replicating a system of employment-based benefits similar to those currently enjoyed by most primary sector workers.

It is unlikely that job security will resurface as an important workplace issue in the near future. Equally unlikely is the hope that the majority of low-wage employers will voluntarily choose to offer benefits similar to the primary labor sector. What is likely is that the volatile nature of secondary labor market jobs will continue, and that tenure and job security in the primary labor sector will become even more unpredictable.

One solution is for the federal government to subsidize a comprehensive non–job-specific portable benefits package (Stoesz & Karger, 1992). As low- or moderate-income workers change jobs or are terminated, their benefit package would follow them. If a low-wage worker later occupies a primary sector labor market job with benefits, the portable benefits package would be discontinued and the worker given the option to cash out their contribution. A viable portable benefit package could include life, disability and health insurance; supplemental unemployment insurance; and a supplemental retirement plan. Low-income workers would be given the choice of picking specific benefits from a list of options, utilizing cost-sharing between the federal government, the employer and the employee.

Another important component of a portable benefits package would be the requirement that all employers provide unemployment insurance (UI) coverage for their workers, regardless of their full- or part-time status. Employers unable to financially shoulder added UI costs could receive governmental assistance. To maintain a social insurance feature, the modified UI benefit system would continue to incorporate eligibility and time standards, but these would be calculated on the time spent in the workforce rather than in a particular job. Like Social Security, time spent in the workforce would be portable and could be moved from job to job.

There are several ways the federal government can remedy the pension problem. One is for the government to supplement the Social Security tax paid by low-income workers, thereby bringing their taxable Social Security income up to the national average wage. That same low-income worker could then retire at age 65 with a monthly Social Security benefit of $1,127, or $13,524 a year (Social Security Administration, 2002). Alternatively, the federal government could supplement a low-wage earner's income by contributing to an Independent Retirement Account (IRA) or a Keogh fund. In either case, subsidizing a low-income worker's retirement benefits would help solidify labor force attachment and mitigate against the prospect of extreme poverty in old age and the subsequent need for public assistance.

Especially in the retail trades, corporations cut costs by relying on non–benefit-eligible part-time workers. This trend hampers the income growth, career path, and employment security of workers. Moreover, part-time workers remain at the minimum wage longer than full-time workers (Even & Macpherson, 2000). A governmentally subsidized benefits package would discourage employers from hiring part-time workers to avoid paying benefits. For instance, if all employers were required to contribute to a federally subsidized portable benefits package, there would be little incentive to hire only part-time workers. Corporations would also benefit by lowering turnover rates, resulting in less training time. Full-time workers also typically learn their jobs better than part-time workers.

Conclusion

The global economy poses powerful challenges for social workers and other welfare advocates. On the one hand, social workers can continue to mount a futile rear guard effort to defend a New Deal welfare state tethered to a quickly disappearing industrial context. On the other hand, they can propose a bold new welfare system that addresses a postindustrial global economy, which in many ways, is more obdurate than the industrial economy it is replacing. Welfare state programs are needed now more than ever given the trend toward increased income inequality, stagnant wages, unstable employment, declining union strength, a growing number of medically uninsured Americans, and the rapid growth of low-wage secondary labor market jobs. To address these problems, this chapter has outlined some specific policy initiatives relevant to the changing economic landscape of postindustrial United States.

The beginning of the the 21st century has been one of significant challenges; similarly, this is also a time of great opportunities for change. For example, some welfare advocates see corporations as opposed to social welfare. While that may have been true in the past—and in some cases still is—many corporations are beginning to reevaluate their position on social welfare. It is common among corporate America to see new policies around flex time, offering on-site child care and nursery services, extended parental leave policies, and job sharing.

Like consumers, corporations are also victimized by the avarice of the health care industry. For instance, HMOs nearly doubled their profits from 2002 to 2003, adding $10 billion to their bottom line. Top executives at the 11 largest health insurers made a combined $85 million in 2003. In 2004 the four largest health insurance companies reported $100 billion in revenues, or $273 million a day (Sirota, 2006). The sheer scope of these revenues allowed the health care industry to spend more than $300 million on lobbying in 2003, plus another $300 million in campaign contributions to politicians from 2000 to 2005 (Sirota, 2006).

Yet the American public remains ambivalent around health care and the government's efforts. For example, th American public remains unsure about its support for the so-called Obama Care. According to a 2011 Gallup Poll, 46% supported the Act, 44% opposed the act, and 10% had no opinion (Newport, 2011). In 2012, the American public seemed to remain just as unsure about the Affordable Health Care Act. A July 2012 Gallup Poll found that most of those surveyed felt that Obama Care will make things worse rather than better for taxpayers, businesses, doctors, and those who currently have health insurance (Newport, 2012).

The vigor and durability of the U.S. welfare state has surprised even its staunchest critics. At some level, most Americans know the private marketplace is too volatile and cold-hearted to entrust it with their health, welfare, and retirement. This partly explains why the Bush Administration's attempt to privatize Social Security was moribund almost from the point of inception. Although Americans want to change social welfare, they are apparently not ready to throw out the baby with the bath water. That alone opens up exciting possibilities to create a viable and robust welfare state to meet the challenges of the new global economy.

Key Terms

Global economy

Institutional and
   residual welfare

Postindustrial

Social welfare
   economics

Welfare state

Review Questions for Critical Thinking

1. To what extent has the welfare reform efforts of the Clinton Administration impacted the welfare state in 2012?

2. Should "cost-benefit" analysis be central in the evaluation of public
assistance programs or should human need be the driving factor?

3. To what extent should "state rights" overrule federal mandates regarding welfare?

4. Should all social welfare programs be designed on an institutional
model or should there be a mix of residual and institutional designed
programs?

5. To what extent, if any, are the philosophies of the New Deal and Great
Society relevant in the 21st century?

Online Resources

Center on Budget and Policy Priorities www.cbpp.org/

Discovery the Networks, A Guide to the Political Left www.discoverthe
networks.org

The Feminist Wire http://thefeministwire.com/

Progressive Policy Institute http://progressivepolicy.org/

Social Welfare Action Alliance www.socialwelfareactionalliance.org

References

American Bankruptcy Institute. (2004). Facts. Retrieved from www.abiworld.org

Applebaum, E., Bernhardt, A., & Murnane, R. (Eds.). (2003). *Low-wage America.*
New York, NY: Russell Sage Foundation.

Austin, L. (2006, April 22). Increases after tuition deregulation mirror those seen
nationwide. *Associated Press*.

Bernstein, J. (1995). *Where's the payoff?* Washington, DC: Economic Policy Institute.

Bureau of Labor Statistics. (2003). Characteristics of minimum wage workers: 2003.
Retrieved from www.bls.gov/cps/minwage2003.htm

Bureau of Labor Statistics. (2006a). Household data, annual averages. Retrieved
from www.bls.gov/cps/cpsaat45.pdf

Bureau of Labor Statistics. (2006b). Union members in 2005. Retrieved from
www.bls.gov/news.release/union2.nr0.htm

Center on Budget and Policy Priorities. (1997). Assessing the $5.15 an hour mini-
    mum wage, March. Retrieved from http://epn.org/cpbb/cbwage.html

Characteristics of Minimum Wage Earners: 2011. Washington, DC: Bureau of Labor
    Statistics. Retreived from http://www.bls.gov/cps/minwage2011.htm.

Coalition for Responsible Credit Practices. (2004). The crisis of growing consumer
    debt. Retrieved from www.responsiblecreditpractices.com/issues/growing.php

Cohen, N. (1958). *Social work in the American tradition.* New York, NY: Holt, Rine-
    hart & Winston.

DiNitto, D., & Dye, T. (1987). *Social welfare: Politics and public policy.* Englewood
    Cliffs, NJ: Prentice-Hall.

Divorce Magazine. (2005). U.S. divorce statistics. Retrieved from www.divorcemag
    .com/statistics/statsUS.shtml

Economic Policy Institute. (2005, January 5). Slowdown in male earnings leads
    to smaller gender wage gap. *Snapshots.* Retrieved from http://www.epi
    .org/publication/webfeatures_snapshots_20050105/

Eskeland, P. (2003). Chairman Manzullo: America's white-collar workers latest vic-
    tims of overseas jobs migration. *Small business committee notes* (no. 108–20)
    (June 20). Retrieved from www.wipp.org/press/200306_press/20030620_notes
    .html

Even, W., & Macpherson, D. (2000). *Rising above the minimum wage.* Washington,
    DC: Employment Policies Institute.

Feran, T. (2003, September 22). Two incomes don't add up. *Houston Chronicle,* 3E.

FinAid (2006). Student loans. Retrieved from http://www.finaid.org/loans

Hall, D., & Cooper, D. (August 14, 2012). How raising the federal minimum
    wage would help working families and give the economy a boost. Economy
    Policy Institute. Retrieved from http://www.epi.org/publication/ib341-raising-
    federal-minimum-wage/

Harkin introduces legislation to raise minimum wage (July 26, 2012). Retrieved from
    http://harkin.senate.gov/press/release.cfm?i=337354

Health Insurance Institute. (1966). *Source book of health insurance data,* 1965. New
    York, NY: Health Insurance Institute.

Karger, H. (2003, July). Ending public assistance: The transformation of US public
    assistance policy into labour policy. *Journal of Social Policy, 3*(32), 383–401.

Karger, H. (2005), *Shortchanged: Life and debt in the fringe economy.* San Francisco,
    CA: Berrett-Koehler.

Karger, H., & Stoesz, D. (2006). *American social welfare policy: A pluralist approach*
    (5th ed.). Boston, MA: Allyn & Bacon.

Keynes, J. M. (1965). *The general theory of employment, interest and money.* New
    York, NY: Harcourt.

Lohr, S. (2004, December 5). Maybe it's not all your fault. *New York Times,* p. 8.

Mishel, L., Bernstein, J., & Allegretto, S. (2005). *The state of working America
    2004/2005.* Ithaca, NY: Cornell University Press.

MSN Real Estate. (2006). Foreclosure rates across the U.S. Retrieved from http://
    realestate.msn.com/buying/Articlenewhome.aspx?cp-documentid=340866

Murray, T. (2000, November 4). Experts warn against milking home equity to extend
    debt. *Minneapolis St. Paul Star Tribune,* p. B–5.

Newport, F. (2011, March 21). One Year Later, Americans Split on Healthcare Law.
    Gallup Politics. Retrieved from http://www.gallup.com/poll/146729/One-Year-
    Later-Americans-Split-Healthcare-Law.aspx

Newport, F. (2012, July 16). Americans: Healthcare Law Helps Some, Hurts Others.
    Retrieved from http://www.gallup.com/poll/155726/Americans-Healthcare-
    Law-Helps-Hurts-Others.aspx

Paul, N. (2003, June 12). Culture of consumption. *Christian Science Monitor,* p. 18.

Piore, M. (1977). The dual labor market. In David Gordon (Ed.), *Problems in political economy.* Lexington, MA: D.C. Heath.

Price, L., & Bernstein, J. (2006, January 27). *The state of jobs and wages.* Washington, DC: Economic Policy Institute. Retrieved from www.jobwatch.org

Rasell, E., Bernstein, J., & Boushey, H. (2001). Step up, not out: The case for raising the federal minimum wage for workers in every state. *Issue Brief,* No. 149. Washington, DC: Economic Policy Institute.

Runzheimer International. (2004). Daycare costs nationwide. Retrieved from www.runzheimer.com

Sirota, D. (2006). *Hostile takeover: How big money and corruption conquered our government—And how we can take it back.* New York, NY: Crown.

Social Security Administration. (2002). Benefit examples for workers with low earnings. Retrieved from www.ssa.gov/OACT/COLA/exampleLow.html

Stoesz, D., & Karger, H. (1992). *Reconstructing the American welfare state.* Savage, MD: Rowman & Littlefield.

Sullivan, T., Warren, E., & Westbrook, J. (1989). *As we forgive our debtors.* New York, NY: Oxford University Press.

Sullivan, T., Warren E., & Westbrook, J. (2001). *The fragile middle class.* New Haven, CT: Yale University Press.

TIAA-CREF. (2001). *Making sense of Social Security: Your retirement benefits.* New York, NY: Teachers Insurance and Annuity Association—College Retirement Equities Fund. Retrieved from http://www.tiaa-cref.org/wc_libser/mss/bene fits.html

Trumbull, M. (March 23, 2010). Obama signs health care bill: Who won't be covered? *Christian Science Monitor.* Retrieved from http://www.csmonitor.com/USA/ 2010/0323/Obama-signs-health-care-bill-Who-won-t-be-covered.

Uchitelle, L. (2004, June 28). Families, deep in debt, facing pain of growing interest rates. *New York Times,* p. 15.

U.S. Census Bureau. (2005, August 30). Income stable, poverty rate increases, percentage of Americans without health insurance unchanged. *U.S. Census Bureau News.* Retrieved from www.census.gov/Press-Release/www/releases /archives/income_wealth/005647.html

U.S. Census Bureau. (2006). *American community survey.* Retrieved from www .census.gov/acs/www

U.S. Department of Health and Human Services (2012). 2012 HHS Poverty Guidelines. Retrieved from http://aspe.hhs.gov/poverty/12poverty.shtml# thresholds.

Warren, E., & Tyagi, A. (2003). *The two-income trap.* New York, NY: Basic Books.

zFacts.com (2012). *National debt clocks and savings clocks.* Retrieved from http://zfacts.com/zfacts.com/p/461.html

Author Index

Subject Index